Energ

Energy Economics in Britain

Edited by
Paul Tempest

Graham & Trotman

Graham & Trotman Ltd
Sterling House
66 Wilton Road
London SW1V 1DE
UK

ISBN: 0 86010 386 2

Typeset and printed in Great Britain.

Contents

Preface

Paul Tempest

Energy economics is, in national policy, a vital point of intersection where Government, industry, finance, research and many other interests meet. In Britain, it is not a recognised profession or academic discipline in its own right. Perhaps it is part of our national style and heritage that it never should be so compartmentalised. Indeed, energy economics is an interest which cannot easily be constrained within even national boundaries: international energy markets impinge everywhere through external demand, supply and price affecting profoundly every aspect of the economy.

THE BRITISH INSTITUTE OF ENERGY ECONOMICS

Over the last few years, an increasing need has been widely perceived for free and open discussion of the major energy and economic issues of the day. Easy communication and the joint implementation of technological progress seem, worldwide, the safest route to resolving national and international problems. Such cooperation and interchange also bring into the light national and local political myopia, bureaucratic inertia, academic dogma and the distortions of an imperfect market system.

In November 1980 the British Institute of Energy Economics was established to provide such a meeting point in London where current issues of energy and economic policy could be debated freely and exposed to external opinion. Over the previous two years an Action Committee, with Chairman and senior officials from the Department of Energy, had prepared the way by establishing a United Kingdom branch of the International Association of Energy Economists. Its initial membership of about 120 grew rapidly as soon as the branch acquired its own national identity and independence.

The pattern of BIEE meetings, seminars and conferences has been to commission the leading independent experts in their field, often professional consultants or senior members of the universities, to present position papers; and to invite each time Government and industry spokesmen to debate the issues under the chairmanship of a former head of a relevant major company, nationalised industry or Government department. Several of these meetings have generated study groups which have met regularly.

Administration has been based in Chatham House, the home of the Royal Institute of International Affairs, so that there could be effective co-ordination of the political and economic aspects of energy policy. In the research field, the BIEE has been associated with the RIIA and the Policy Studies Institute in publicizing and promoting their British Institutes Joint Energy Policy Programme.*

Close links have also been maintained with the International Association of Energy Economists which, based in Washington, provides a focal point for 15 branches in different countries and the particularly strong membership of 1500 spread over 12 branches in the United States. The quarterly periodical of the IAEE, *The Energy Journal*, has in recent years, under the editorship of Professor Helmut Frank of the University of Arizona, established a leading position in its field.

The British Institute of Energy Economics has participated in all the various international conferences of the IAEE and was in June 1980 and June 1982 host to the annual international conference of the IAEE in Churchill College, Cambridge.

The present need to co-ordinate work on energy economics in Britain prompted the BIEE to establish an archive of key papers delivered to the Institute. These are available for copying for a fee† and it is hoped to develop this service into a much more comprehensive archive of current policy papers available on energy economics.

*Details of the activities of the BIEE and IAEE are given in Annex 2 and of the BIJEPP in Annex 4.

†See Annex 3.

THIS VOLUME

The Institute has also set as an objective the publication of volumes which set out a basic framework for debate in the energy economics field and provide a vade-mecum of source material and a summary of the most relevant statistics. Two volumes with an international dimension have been published so far — *International Energy Options: An Agenda for the 1980s* (1981) and *International Energy Markets: The Changing Structure* (1983).

In the first edition of *Energy Economics in Britain* published in December 1981 in booklet form, we listed professional and university institutions active in the field, specialist journals and other organisations with an interest in energy economics. A copy of the booklet was sent to each organisation mentioned with a request for comment and amplification. The up-dated material is republished here as Annex 1. Any additions and comment will be filed in the Institute so that the material can be kept up-to-date for reference purposes and publication from time to time in the future.

This volume seeks to place a similar framework on the domestic aspects of energy economics in the United Kingdom.

First, it includes major contributions from the Department of Energy. The opening chapter covers the policy statement of the Secretary of State for Energy to the BIEE/IAEE Conference in 1982 and, for the first time, in this form and detail, the full methodology and econometrics of the Department of Energy forecasts is published (as Chapter 11).

Second, to place the official views in perspective, 17 papers have been specifically commissioned or selected from distinguished presentations to the BIEE over the past two years. Their authors come from the nationalised energy industries, the multinationals, the North Sea supply industry, the City, the universities and leading consultancies in the field. They have been selected for their positive contribution to the current debate and therefore represent many different challenges to accepted wisdom.

Third, we knew of no authoritative historical review of energy economics in Britain and are very pleased that Eric Price, the Chief Economist at the Department of Energy and new Chairman of the BIEE, has accepted our invitation to compile the last three chapters. We are also grateful to Sir William Hawthorne for the illustration, which accompanied his opening speech of welcome at the Cambridge Conference in 1982.

The following notes are intended to give a brief introduction to each part of the volume and also to give some background to the themes and issues addressed by the British Institute of Energy Economics over the past two years.

1. United Kingdom Energy Policy

A major objective of the BIEE is to provide a forum where UK Government policy and Department of Energy thinking can be discussed openly with a wide cross-section of outside interest. We are particularly happy therefore to open this volume with a major policy statement to the Institute by the Secretary of State for Energy.

In 1981 Mr Lawson's predecessor, Mr David Howell, addressed the Institute, as also in 1981 and 1982 Mr James Edwards, the United States Secretary of Energy. Other recent meetings have been devoted to Canadian, Norwegian and Australian energy policy in addition to conference sessions on official energy policy in the Communist Bloc, European Community, OPEC and the Developing World.

2. United Kingdom Energy Supply

Following very lively BIEE meetings in Chatham House under the chairmanship of Lord Robens and Lord Kearton, we asked two of the principal speakers, Professors Gerald Manners and Roger Williams, to contribute the initial two chapters of this volume on coal and nuclear energy. Over the last two years, the Institute has supported a major study of UK policy in the North Sea entitled *The Nation's Oil** by Gerry Corti, formerly of BNOC, and Frank Frazer of *The Scotsman*: we are therefore pleased to be able to include Gerry Corti's companion piece, regarding oil policy. One contribution to the 1982 Conference on gas depletion attracted press attention: this and the following paper on Electricity are by young junior economists, Niall Trimble of the British Gas Corporation and Nigel Evans of the Cavendish Laboratory, Cambridge.

3. United Kingdom Energy Demand

We include in this section extracts of two detailed papers presented at the Cambridge Conference. Conservation has been a recurrent theme of Institute meetings: two one-day seminars, the first run in conjunction with the Royal Institute of British Architects and

*Also published by Graham & Trotman, 1983.

the second with the Swedish Government were also particularly well attended.

4. Taxation and Finance

Comparative studies of taxation, licensing and depletion policy in the oil and gas industry are beginning to have a significant impact on national economic policy. By detailed comparisons, anomalies can be demonstrated and the shifts of exploration resources from one area to another, representing a multiplicity of company decisions, can be rationalised and explained. Here, Alexander Kemp and David Rose summarise their findings on UK and other taxation policy.

Similar comparative studies have been commissioned on licensing policy, but it is becoming widely apparent that to make any valid country to country comparison, one must understand the precise mix of licensing, tax and other Government involvement in each country and be able to place it in a broad economic framework.

Expectations of Government oil and gas revenue affect a wide area of Government economic policy. In this volume we have asked Homa Motamen, who runs a specialist research unit in this field in Imperial College, to summarise her own estimates of UK Government revenue to provide a reference framework for the future. The impact of North Sea oil and gas on the UK economy has been the subject of several plenary sessions of the Institute.

5. Energy Forecasting

In addition to the Department of Energy methodology, we include a description of the pioneer thinking of the Shell Group in scenario forecasting and Professor Colin Robinson's paper on Oil Price Forecasting. Three separate sessions and two panel discussions of the Cambridge Conference were devoted to this topic.

6. Oil Crisis Management

Over the last three years, the Institute has been very active in monitoring and discussing the IEA and other proposals for controlling further energy price discontinuities. The chapter by Robert Belgrave should be read in conjunction with Annex 4 which summarises the BIJEPP programme of research in this area. Since an initial meeting of the Institute in 1979 when, under the chairmanship of John Raisman, a group of City commodity brokers were invited to discuss with members the possible formation of a London futures market in oil products, a planning group has been very active in establishing and developing the London gasoil futures market which opened for business on 1st April 1981. Here Walter Greaves who has been a leading member of that team since the original BIEE/IAEE meeting recounts progress so far.

7. Interfuel Substitution

Intense interest has been manifested over the last two years in trying to establish principles and sequences in forecasting the substitution for oil of gas, coal, nuclear and other alternatives. At a practical level, it is a development, aided by major advances in computer technology, akin to the rapid evolution of refinery economics in the fifties and sixties. The current upgrading of refining capacity and whitening of the crude oil barrel make all conventional assumptions of future market shares based on historical evidence highly suspect. The marketing of gas liquids, condensates, coal-oil, slurries, methanol, gasohol, tarsands and oil shales for example all impinge on traditional oil product markets. At a theoretical level, there is a generally perceived need for a set of formulae and parameter guidelines as a basis for programming interfuel substitution scenarios. In this volume we present a seminal and highly controversial paper by Professor Robert Deam, written as the basis for debate at a lively BIEE meeting chaired by Michael Posner. Further work is planned in this area.

The optimisation of systems of UK energy supply by interconnection with Europe has also been a subject of keen current debate. Here we include a paper on a North Sea Ring Main. Since its presentation a study group on offshore electricity generation has been meeting regularly. Finally, the prospects for electricity generation using renewable energy is the subject of a separate paper.

8. The Impact of Energy on the Economy

As the final paper in this section, we have selected an important contribution by Len Brookes which begins to address what we consider to be perhaps the most fundamental issue in energy economics facing us today. The conventional wisdom on monetary economics ascribes to energy a very subsidiary role in economic growth. It is expressed, typically, in the Department of Energy paper included in Chapter 11:

> 'Although higher energy prices are likely to place severe constraints on economic activity, it is thought that the fundamental

forces generating economic growth arise, in the main, outside the energy sector, in levels of investment, productivity growth and the economic policies of the governments in the major industrialised countries.'

In the detailed historical perspective which follows, there is overwhelming evidence that new energy technology often provided, in the past, the trigger for bouts of high economic growth. I therefore close this Introduction with a rather disturbing question:

'Monetarist economics, currently widely espoused in the United States and Britain, seems, to rely, in its search for the key to growth, on the thesis that the governments of the major industrialised countries can generate spontaneously adequate investment and productivity. Is this not partly a self-delusion which misunderstands the much wider potential for progress in energy technology and which, through artificially high marginal energy pricing, produces a sharply limited outlook. By giving low priority to investment in new energy (both supply and demand sides), are we not unnecessarily and arbitrarily constraining opportunities for renewed global economic growth?'

This volume can provide no simple answer to that question. Nonetheless, in the material selected here and in its arrangement, we would hope to establish a broad framework covering the role and strategy of the energy sector in Britain. This, from the almost unique viewpoint within the OECD of temporary energy self-sufficiency, might throw some light on the current global dilemmas of energy development in general.

SECTION 1

Current Issues

PART I

The United Kingdom Energy Framework

Chapter 1

The United Kingdom Energy Framework

*Nigel Lawson**

Unlike economic policy, energy policy clearly means very different things to different countries, depending on their individual resources and circumstances.

It means one thing to Saudi Arabia: quite another to Japan. Even within Western Europe the differences are more marked than the similarities.

Norway, for example with much of her electricity generated by hydropower and huge resources of oil and gas, has little concern over the cost of energy and even less over security of supply, but has to be very wary of allowing too rapid a development of oil and gas to dominate and distort the rest of the economy.

Germany, with its massive dependence on imported energy, has to balance the strategic and economic risks of different levels of dependence on the Middle East and the Soviet Union.

For the United Kingdom with its own indigenous supplies of all the fossil fuels, and a highly developed and diversified economy, the pre-eminent objective must be to ensure that the vitally important

***Speech given to the 1982 BIEE/IAEE FourthAnnual International Conference in Churchill College, Cambridge on 28th June 1982 by Rt Hon Nigel Lawson MP Secretary of State for Energy.**

energy sector functions as efficiently and effectively as possible within the context of economic policy as a whole.

There are of course a limited number of agreed common objectives in the energy field. The Venice declaration of 1980, for example, called on all seven economic summit nations to break the link between economic growth and oil consumption through conservation and by developing alternative energy sources. Although primarily motivated by consumer concerns, this declaration was welcome to many of the oil producing countries, particularly those that take a longer view. The measures agreed at Venice have subsequently been endorsed and built up both by member states of the European Community and by the International Energy Agency. The UK has shown an impressive lead in this. Over the past two years our oil use in relation to overall economic activity has fallen by 17%.

But in general, as Secretary of State for Energy in the UK, I do *not* see the Government's task as being to try and plan the future shape of energy production and consumption. It is not even primarily to try and balance UK demand and supply for energy. Our task is rather to set a framework which will ensure that the market operates in the energy sector with a minimum of distortion and that energy is produced and consumed efficiently.

ENERGY PRICING

Energy pricing is one key to this approach, in relation to both production and consumption. If energy prices are set too high producers will be encouraged to invest in new capacity for which they may not be able to find a market. If energy prices are below economic levels then energy will be used wastefully and consumers will be encouraged to invest in inefficient energy intensive processes.

But what constitutes economic pricing of energy? Where there is a genuine market — as in oil — it is the price set by the market. Where there is no genuine market — as in electricity — prices will need to reflect costs of supply. Within this general concept there is clearly some room for flexibility, for example in response to the pressure of international competition on our industries. Hence the £250 million worth of concessions to industrial energy users, especially those with high load factors, in the last two Budgets.

Realistic pricing is a stimulus to efficiency. But its impact is muted because so much of the UK energy sector is composed of state-owned monopolies. How then can we improve the efficiency of the energy industries? The key lies in increasing the responsiveness of these industries to the forces of the market place.

We have made significant progress in this area over the past 3 years. The changes that are in prospect will further enhance the role of private enterprise and stimulate the action of market forces, thereby increasing efficiency and helping us to ensure that the supplies of fuel we need are available at the lowest practicable cost.

ENERGY EXPORT AND IMPORT POLICY

I shall return later to this subject. But there is something even more fundamental. This is to recognise, as Governments have not always done in the past, that for the most part energy is a traded good.

Primary fuels can be imported and exported. For oil, the world market is well-established, and, although international trade in gas and coal is on a much smaller scale, it is building up. There is neither need, nor particular virtue, in having domestic production equal to consumption. The key to energy policy is flexibility. We should use our ability to import or export fuels at the margin to the best advantage in the context of an ever-changing world energy scene.

In seeking to achieve this, it does not help us very much to try to guess the unguessable — namely, what UK energy consumption will be in 20, let alone 50, years' time — and then aim to produce this amount judiciously divided up between the primary fuel sources. We will do far better to concentrate our efforts on improving the efficiency with which energy is supplied and used, an objective that will remain valid and important whatever the future may bring. This means, among other things, that public sector energy investment decisions should in general be based not on a simple-minded attempt to match projected UK demand and supply but rather as in the private sector, on whether the investment is likely to offer a good return on capital. If these decisions are well based then the importing and exporting of fuels will match production to consumption on an economic basis. This does not mean that we can use imports and exports of primary fuels as a simple safety valve. We cannot turn them on or off at will. But, as international trade develops, we can expect to see our energy supply industries acquiring an additional degree of flexibility in responding to changing market conditions. And at the same time the possibility of exploiting monopoly power to raise prices will be progressively reduced.

ELECTRICITY INVESTMENT

Within this overall approach, electricity poses special problems. With the development of appropriate infrastructures coal, oil and gas can be stored, or traded, to a sufficient extent to provide market disciplines and supply flexibility. This is not true of electricity. For many of its uses there are no acceptable substitutes and, except for insignificant amounts at the margin, there is no flexibility for dealing with under- or over-supply through trade.

So the electricity supply industry, unlike the coal and oil industries, has a duty to ensure that there will be sufficient plant available to meet the top end of the range of most likely demand requirements.

But even in the case of electricity supply investment, reducing costs to help improve the efficiency of supply and hence the efficiency of the economy is at least as important as investment to meet projected demand. In this respect the electricity supply industry differs not at all from the industries involved in the supply of primary fuels. Diversification is also of particular importance for the electricity supply industry—a direct consequence of its limited ability to import. As many have found to their cost before, there are dangers in becoming too dependent on any one source of fuel.

In this context there is increasing public interest in the renewable sources of energy. The renewables undoubtedly offer considerable potential. They may well have a key role in the energy economy of the future, and the R D & D work which the Government is sponsoring is designed to evaluate this. But at their present stage of development it is unlikely that they will be able to make a sizeable and economic contribution to energy supply this century.

So nuclear power is critical both to diversification and to reducing costs. It is significant that the CEGB, in applying for permission to build a Pressurised Water Nuclear Reactor at Sizewell, has explicitly based its case on cost and flexibility grounds. The specific decision on Sizewell has yet to be taken. But the Government believes in general that if nuclear stations can be built to time and to cost they can play a significant role in helping to keep down the price of electricity in the UK, thereby helping our manufacturing industries in particular to increase their competitiveness.

This is bound to take time. But we can see by comparing the UK with France what the potential advantages are. In this country nuclear power accounts for some 13% of all electricity generated; in France the figure is about 40%. This has given important parts of French industry a substantial advantage so far as its energy costs are concerned, and the disparity is unlikely to diminish for some considerable time.

In terms of meeting demand the electricity supply industry has to look many years ahead. Power stations take upwards of 7 years to construct and have lifetimes of approximately 30 years. So the effects of decisions made now may still be apparent in 40 years' time. However unknowable the future may be, these decisions still have to be taken — and taken on the most rational basis attainable, given the electricity supply industry's need to be able to meet economically the demand that will be made of it.

ENERGY FORECASTING

Let me say a word at this point about forecasts and their more modest and modern successors, scenarios and projections. In the last 20 years — the period in which forecasting has become a major industry — we have seen some startlingly wrong predictions. For example, the Electricity Council in the 1960s and early-1970s produced forecasts for maximum demand 7 years ahead which were never less than 20% too high and in one year were about 50% out. It is only fair to add that the Electricity Council were by no means unique in this — forecasting errors are the rule rather than the exception — and that their error was in no small measure due to highly optimistic forecasts of economic growth provided by the Government of the day.

By treating energy as a traded commodity we greatly reduce the need for, and importance of, projections of UK demand and production. But for two reasons we still need to make such projections. First, for reasons I have given, the electricity industry has a special need to match capacity with likely demand and the Government which provides the finance for the industry's capital investment programmes needs to take an independent view of that likely demand. But it is only possible to form a sensible view of likely electricity demand in the context of demand for all the fuels. Second, while projections provide an unsure basis for planning they can give rise to useful questions about the coherence of policy. It is for those two reasons that my Department is now preparing a revised set of energy projections which we expect to publish in the autumn.

ENERGY EFFICIENCY

It is on the demand side of the equation that most of the errors in projections arise. The reason is a simple one. The demand side of the equation is an aggregation of decisions by millions of individual and corporate users. These range from the insulation of a domestic hot water tank to the installation of a large industrial boiler. Consumers have, since the first oil crisis of 1973/74, become increasingly aware of the need for using energy more efficiently, and conservation has become an important factor.

There is a tendency to talk of conservation as an alternative to supply. But this is misleading. Conservation is in no sense a source of energy. Rather, it is a lever on demand — a way for the consumer to cut his costs. But these decisions by consumers are often small, and always disaggregated, whereas supply investments are large and centralised. These two types of investment decision are taken by different sets of people using widely differing criteria.

The question for Government is how these two sets of decisions can best be brought together. Certainly not by central planning. It is unlikely in the extreme that we would be better off if decisions about insulating millions of homes, building power stations, operating oil refineries and distributing gas and coal were within Whitehall.

Nor should the Government seek to achieve overall and detailed control through the backdoor methods of regulations and subsidies. The Government's role is neither to induce the individual to take decisions against his better judgement, nor to waste public money in subsidising investment that is already well worthwhile. The way to bring the two sides together and to ensure that they act consistently is to give them the same information and the same realistic signals. On the demand side, the UK Government supplements the messages given by economic prices by improving the flows of information — for instance through advisory services and demonstration projects. The key here is not the amount of public money spent, but putting the message across properly. Initial results from the Extended Energy Survey Scheme (under which firms can get grants towards a survey of how to improve their use of energy, including the scope for combined heat and power) show energy savings equivalent to about £16 for every £1 invested by Government. These modest schemes can help point up the messages given by the market and can accelerate the industries' response. But above and beyond all this, the main spur must be competition, encouraging the consumer to cut his costs, and the supplier to become more responsive to the customer's needs.

This is vital. The economy is now in a fundamentally healthier position than it has been for many years. If British industry is to make the most of this it must, as an energy consumer, do all it can to increase the efficiency with which fuel is used.

THE NATIONALISED ENERGY INDUSTRIES

I said earlier that I would return to discussing the efficiency of the energy supply industries. Most of the supply industries in the UK are state-owned. In part, state-ownership came about as a means of regulating natural monopoly. But this has not always been the case; and it is time to question both the extent of the natural monopoly and, where it can be shown to exist, the most effective means of regulation. State-ownership is neither a universal necessity nor the only means of regulation.

The Oil and Gas (Enterprise) Act, which reached the Statute Book to-day, will enable us to establish Britoil, the greater part of the British National Oil Corporation, as an independent private sector oil company in its own right and will very significantly increase the competitive pressures to which the British Gas Corporation is subject. For the first time ever there will be the prospect of competition for the custom of all gas consumers taking over 25,000 therms a year. This will provide a competitive spur not only for the Gas Corporation but also for all the potential suppliers in the private sector. We shall shortly be introducing legislation to encourage the supply of electricity by the private sector.

Where we can neither privatise nor introduce real competition we have to do our best to simulate market disciplines. The external financing limits on the nationalised industries have a crucial role to play in this respect. We are now reinforcing control by setting clearer objectives for the state-owned industries, and wherever relevant, setting performance targets. For example, British Gas has been asked to reduce its costs — other than those represented by the purchase of gas — by 5% before next April.

We are also promoting external appraisals of the nationalised industries. Management consultants are being brought in for efficiency examinations of the Atomic Energy Authority and of British Gas. The Monopolies and Mergers Commission report on the CEGB is already leading to much-needed changes in the way the Board evaluates investment projects. The National Coal Board and two Area Electricity Boards are now to be given a similar examination by the MMC.

NORTH SEA POLICY

There is one major energy industry which is fully subject to the disciplines of the market. For North Sea oil, where an Eighth

Round of licensing has recently been announced, we have a genuinely free market approach. This is most unusual among the oil producing countries of the world, among whom the UK currently ranks Fifth. But in fact, it has always been the case, under successive Governments, and our removal of BNOC's special privileges has merely reinforced this important fact.

The price of North Sea oil is determined not by Government *fiat* but in response to market forces, and North Sea producers are free to produce as much oil as they wish. Even the much maligned North Sea fiscal regime is highly price-sensitive. We have made sparing use of our powers to control depletion and the rate of production, and have concentrated our regulatory intervention on minimising wasteful losses through flaring.

But we know that our supplies of oil are limited. Sooner or later we shall have to make the transition from net oil exporter to net oil importer. The obvious question is whether Government should act to defer some of the expected surplus of the next 10 years or so, to help fill the gap that may start to emerge some time in the latter half of the 1990s.

At first glance the answer may seem equally obvious; of course Government should ease the way. But behind the simple facade hides a host of complexities. Prospects for UK demand and supply, and for the world price of oil over the next 10 or 20 years, are highly uncertain. We also have to consider whether action now would have any real economic justification. We have to consider whether it would damage either our more immediate prospects of general economic recovery or our longer-term objective of maximising the economic exploitation of the North Sea over time.

We have to ask ourselves whether we are really so unenterprising as not to be able to put to good use the wealth which derives from oil, whenever it arises. That wealth is substantial. Last year UKCS oil and gas production amounted to some £10 bn, or 4% of GNP, without taking any account of the offshore supplies industry that rides on its back.

During the course of this short talk to-day I have not sought to deliver a lecture on something known as Energy policy. Rather, I have tried to explain how I see the development of our vitally important energy resources and our energy market fitting within the wider economic objectives that the Government has set itself. This approach differs from that of previous administrations. It is one that many people with an interest in energy have perhaps been slow to understand. I am grateful to you for giving me this opportunity to explore my thinking with you.

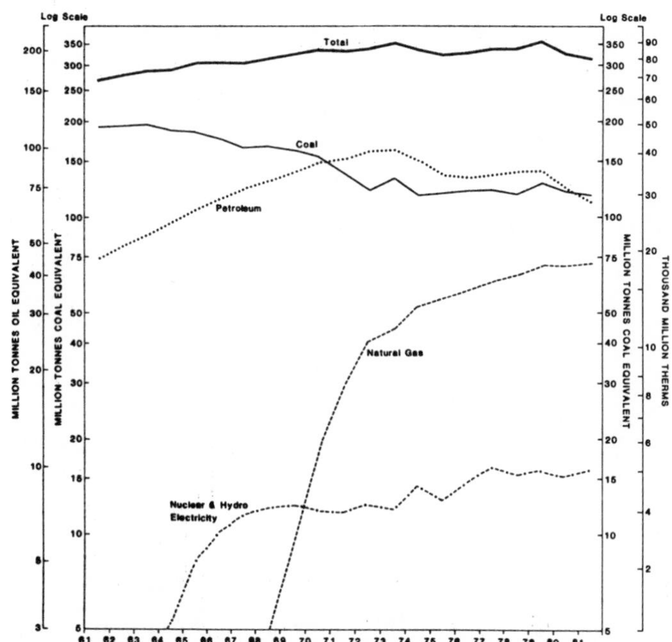

Fig. 1.1: Inland Consumption of Primary Fuels and Equivalents for Energy Use

Figure 1.1.

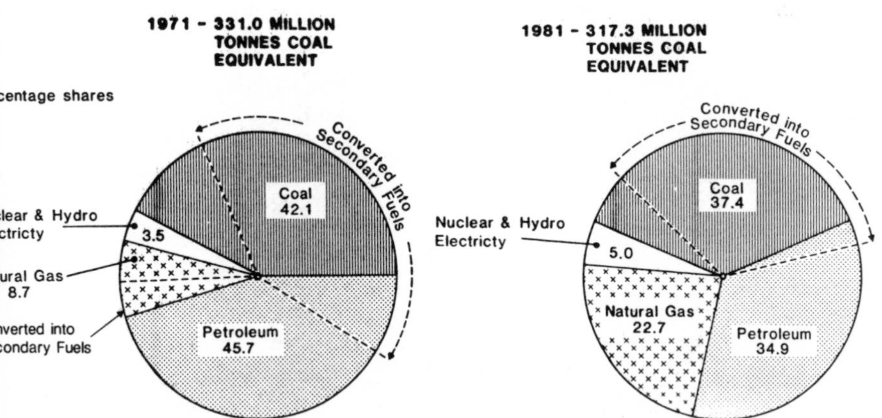

Fig. 1.2: Inland Consumption of Primary Fuels and Equivalents 1971 and 1981

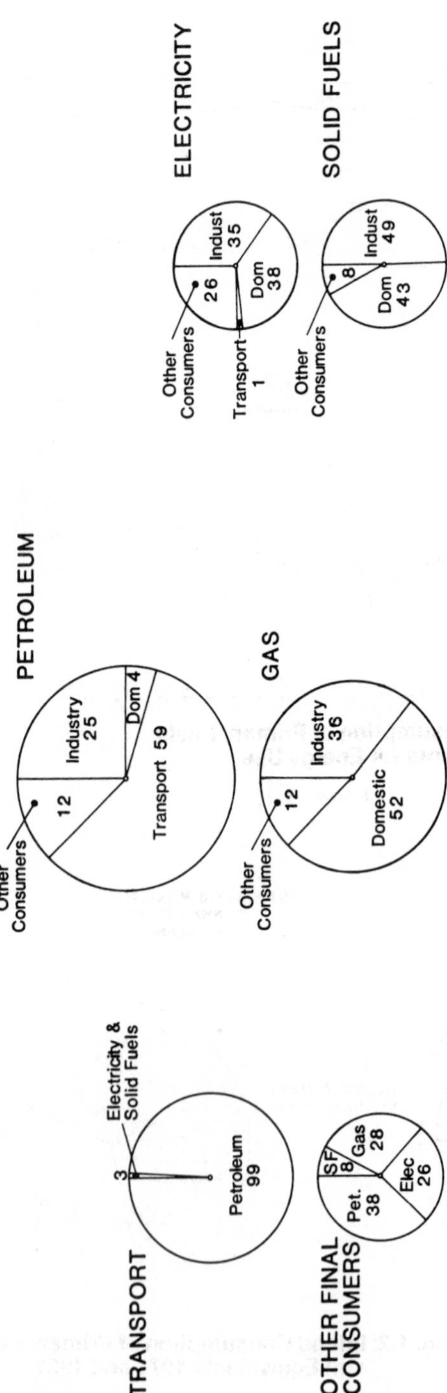

Fig. 1.3 Energy Consumption by Final Users in 1981 (heat supplied basis)

PART II

Aspects of United Kingdom Energy Supply

Chapter 2

Coal in Britain

*Gerald Manners**

The British coal industry is the sixth largest in the world. It is the leading producer of Western Europe. Employing over 210,000, it has an annual turnover of more than £4 billion and in addition generates substantial secondary economic benefits through its demands for civil engineering works, mining equipment and supplies, and transport services. The industry, however, presents its management and its owner — the British government — with many complex and persistent problems that have both economic and related socio-political dimensions. It is the purpose of this essay to introduce the reader to some of them.

In 1981 Britain produced 110 million tonnes of coal from its underground mines and further 15 million tonnes from opencast operations; additional output at private mines and from slurry gave a total production of 127 million tonnes. This was 3 million tonnes less than in the previous year and 22 million tonnes less than a decade earlier. The apparent failure of coal output to respond in some measure to the very substantial investment that had been made in the industry following the 'oil crisis' of the middle 1970s reflected only in part the very considerable difficulties involved in reversing

***Professor of Geography, University College London**

the coal industry's secular decline. It was also a measure of the industry's especially challenging market circumstances. The demand for coal in Britain in 1981 — like that for oil and for electricity — fell faster than coal production. At less than 119 million tonnes, it was 5 million tonnes lower than in the previous year. It was 20 million tonnes lower than in 1971. The changing composition of this falling coal demand will be examined later. More immediately it should be noted that these recent changes in British coal supply and demand together caused the National Coal Board both to increase the size of its stockpiles by 5 million tonnes to 22 million tonnes (creating national coal stocks, including those at power stations, of some 42 million tonnes in all) and to intensify its efforts to expand coal exports.

These developments, plus the expectation of yet further falls in the country's demand for coal, caused first the Minister responsible for the industry and then later the Chairman of the National Coal Board publicly to suggest that the country's coal production capacity should be brought more closely into line with market circumstances and the industry's medium term sales prospects. In opening the debate on the second reading of the Coal Industry Bill 1982, for example, the Under-Secretary of State for Energy, Mr John Moore, noted that 'Neither the world, nor the coal industry's own performance, has matched the expectations of 1974; and the coal industry must live in the real world . . . adjusting its plans and programmes, and adapting itself to stay competitive in a changing energy scene'. Subsequently at the Annual Conference of the National Union of Mineworkers in July 1982, the new Chairman of the National Coal Board, Mr Norman Siddall, pointing to the need to reduce the losses incurred by the industry's highest cost pits, urged that 'It cannot be right that about 12 per cent of our output should lose £250 million as it did last year'. The early closure of that capacity would bring the size of the industry down to a level more appropriate to the existing and prospective markets for British coal.

The difficulties involved in adjusting the coal industry's market and production ambitions to match changed economic and energy circumstances, however, are considerable. They derive in some measure, of course, from the inevitable and at times fundamental uncertainties that surround any forecasts about the future structure and magnitude of British coal demands, the likely size of coal imports and exports, and hence the prospective market for NCB coal. They also stem, however, from the persistent unwillingness of the National Union of Mineworkers even to contemplate — let alone endorse and cooperate fully with — such a programme. Although the miners' union has agreed to a measured programme of mine closures, substantially for reasons of seam exhaustion and geological difficulties at particular pits, they have set their face against any accelerated programme of closures, insisting that the industry must remain wedded to earlier production ambitions and, by implication, that somehow or other additional markets for coal must be found.

In this essay, the production, marketing and adjustment problems of the coal industry will be examined in turn. Stress will be laid upon the contrast between the high hopes that were held out in the middle 1970s, immediately following the 'oil crisis', for the growth and economic prosperity of the British coal industry, and the disappointments and uncertainties that surround the industry today. The options that lie before the National Coal Board, inevitably by international standards a relatively high cost producer, will be examined in the conclusion.

COAL PRODUCTION: PLANS AND ACHIEVEMENTS

In response to the transformed energy situation of the early 1970s, the National Coal Board and successive governments have for some years been committed to a substantial capital investment programme designed first to stabilise, and subsequently to increase, British coal production in both existing pits and new mines. Over £3 billion was invested in the industry between 1974 and 1982.[1] The Board's initial *Plan for Coal*[2] in 1974 proposed that production should be raised from the 130 million tonnes that had been won in 1973 to between 135 and 150 million tonnes in 1985. Two years later in 1977 the Tripartite Group,[3] representing the government and the National Union of Mineworkers as well as the Board, proposed in *Coal for the Future* a production target of 170 million tonnes for the year 2000; of this output, it was suggested that 20 million tonnes would be won by open cast methods. These objectives were firmly embraced in the Labour Government's Green Paper on *Energy Policy*[4] in 1978, although the precise routes that the National Coal Board has sought to follow in order to reach them have changed over the years.

Plan for Coal sought to reach the 1985 target of 120 million tonnes of deep mined coal, plus 15 million tonnes opencast, by means of 20 million tonnes from new mines, 63 million tonnes from existing but modernised pits, and 37 million tonnes from older and smaller pits. By 1977, however, it was clear that the process of planning, getting permission for and sinking new mines was taking much longer than had originally been estimated, and that the maximum output that the planned new mines could possibly yield by the mid-1980s would be 10 million tonnes of coal. The Board therefore supplemented its original plans for modernising and reconstructing their existing pits and raised the 1985 production target for collieries in this category from 63 to 89 million tonnes. At the same time, the Board's ambitions for its oldest and relatively high cost mines were revised downwards — from 37 to 21 million tonnes. In its evidence to the Commission on Energy and the Environment[5] in 1979, however, the Coal Board confirmed that, even without any further major investment decisions, its 1985 deep mine capacity would be 120 million tonnes and therefore 'on target' for the 1974 Plan (Table 1).

In that same document, and looking further ahead to 1990, the Board also argued that, as a result primarily of seam exhaustion, the industry's underground capacity was likely to fall at a rate of 3 million tonnes each year after 1985. With a production target of some 145 million tonnes in 1990, their ambition therefore was to plan a further 25 million tonnes of new and expanded capacity, amongst which would be the three large 'Vale of Belvoir' mines proposed for North East Leicestershire. Looking still further ahead to the year 2000, the Board saw the continuing decline of existing and older capacity to some 80 million tonnes. They took the view that a further 15 million tonnes of capacity could be added to that at existing mines, and that opencast mining could continue at a level of at least 15 million tonnes. In order to reach their year 2000 production

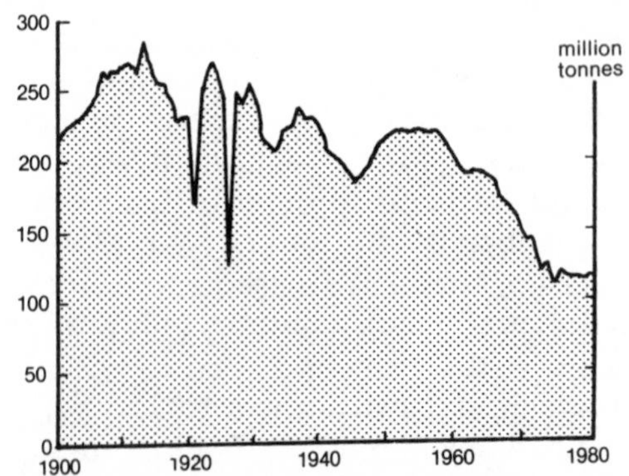

Fig. 2.1: The production of coal in Britain, 1900-80

target of 165–170 million tonnes, therefore, it was judged that new mining capacity of some 55 million tonnes would be needed during the 1990s. In the first instance, the ambitions of the Board to attain this goal were reflected in a vigorous and successful exploration programme. Together with existing geological and mining knowledge, this confirmed that the country's coal reserves were more than sufficient for such a scale of development. Indeed, for some time now, it has been the bold claim of the Board that Britain has enough reserves of coal to last at least 300 years at existing rates of production.

Given the history of the British coal industry since 1914, a period during which its output has substantially, albeit erratically, fallen (Fig. 1); and given especially the rapid contraction of the industry during the 1960s when both the number of mines and the workforce were halved and production fell from 184 to 134 million tonnes; the Board's plans of the 1970s were undoubtedly ambitious. They implied the injection of large sums of public capital into the coal industry over an extended period. They required sustained improvements in mining productivity if the National Coal Board was to become both increasingly competitive with other fuels and avoid a substantial increase in its workforce and costs. They necessitated the spread of mining activities into localities that currently have no such tradition, implying the construction of new communities — homes, schools, hospitals, shops and churches — new roads, new railways and the like, and thereby altering both the land use and the appearance of some parts of the country. The plans meant a substantial shift in the geography of the industry away from the higher cost coalfields of Scotland, Wales, Lancashire and North East England especially, and a greater concentration of mining activities in the lower cost 'central' coalfields of the Midlands and Yorkshire (Fig. 2).[6] And they were based upon the presumption that there would be a decisive reversal of the fortunes of the coal industry in the markets for energy, with British consumers turning increasingly to the National Coal Board to satisfy their energy needs. The latter reversal of market fortunes, as will be seen later, has been slow to materialise.

In the short term, however, the achievements of the coal industry have in some respects matched its plans. Output in the 1970s, temporarily reduced of course by the major strikes of 1972 and 1974, was stabilised at between 120 and 130 million tonnes each year, and new capacity was provided for a modest increase in production. Meanwhile, the number of collieries was reduced from just under 300 in 1970 to 200 in 1982, and the industry's workforce fell from 290,000 to 210,000 over the same period. Productivity did not improve at anything like the pace that was once thought possible;

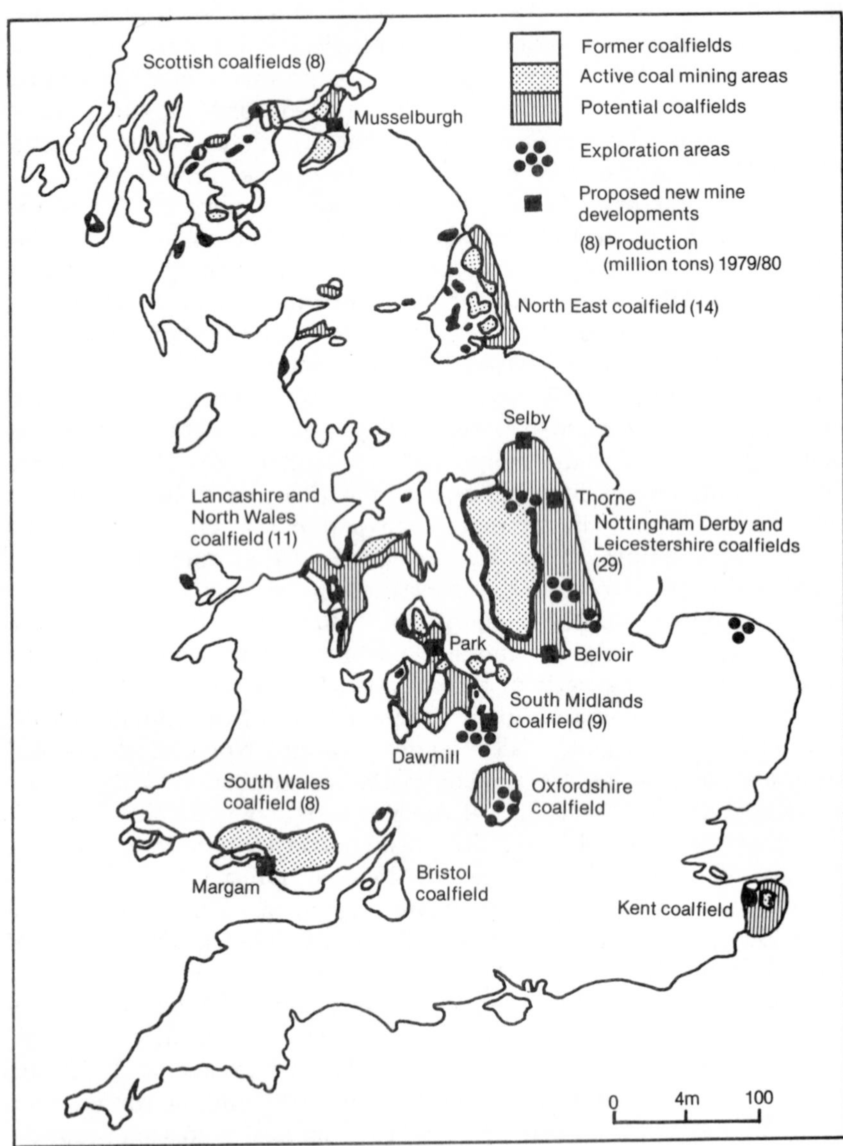

Fig. 2.2: The coalfields of Britain, 1980

but output per man-shift did advance from 2.24 tonnes in 1970 to 2.38 in 1981 and above 2.50 tonnes in 1982.[7] These advances should not go unrecognised. However, they still left the industry with a considerable variety of production facilities; some are highly productive yielding low cost and competitive coal, but others — as a result of their age and mining conditions — are exceedingly high cost by any standards.

Despite the very considerable advantage that the exceptional energy price rises of 1973/74 and 1979/80 gave to the coal industry, the finances of the National Coal Board have not improved to anything like the degree that the government and many others once thought possible. Indeed, during the last two years of increasingly difficult market conditions, they have deteriorated quite markedly. The early 1970s were years of substantial losses on all coal mining operations — for example, £120 million in 1971/72 and £130 million in 1973/74, before interest was charged on capital. Colliery losses were even greater, at £135 and £146 million, respectively, in the same two years. The middle 1970s saw a significant improvement in this situation, and by 1976/77 the Board's collieries (once again before interest charges) produced a modest profit of £19 million. Since that year, however, the finances of the industry have deteriorated once again and the Department of Energy's 1982/83 estimates, for example, have made provision for the expenditure of £762 million of public funds to support the industry.[8] (This figure in fact includes £219 million for expenditure incurred, but not paid, during the previous year.) Thus, earlier government ambitions to phase out the industry's deficit grant and other subsidies as its productivity and profitability improved have had to be set aside until such time as the Board's cost structure and finances could be radically improved. Such an improvement requires, *inter alia*, the industry's speedy adjustment to its changed market circumstances. It is to these that this essay next turns.

MARKET TRENDS AND UNCERTAINTIES

The 1973–74 oil price rise gave the coal industry a new and substantial competitive advantage in at least some markets for energy. *Plan for Coal* had asserted that 'on the basis of commercial pricing the coal industry now has the capability for the first time for many years to bear its full production costs and still compete overall with oil'.[9] Industrial users of coal paid 9% more per therm than did industrial users of oil in 1973; but a year later industrial coal prices were approximately half those of oil, and although the gap subsequently fluctuated in size, by 1982 coal prices were still about half those of oil on a heat equivalent basis. Nevertheless, British coal consumption in 1981 was some 15 million tonnes below that of 1973 — 118 million tonnes as compared with 133 million tonnes — and a growing body of observers found it difficult to see when, if at all, a market upturn might appear.

Two principal factors underlay the failure of the coal industry to reflect in its sales the substantial cost and price advantage that it inherited. The first was the fact that the overall market for energy in Britain contracted between 1973 and 1981 from 354 to 316 coal equivalent tonnes; this latter figure contrasts acutely with the 400 million tonnes which was the bottom of the range forecast by the National Coal Board in 1974 for the year 1980 when *Plan for Coal* was being devised. The second was the failure of both the Board and the government to analyse with care the very limited opportunities for substituting coal for alternative fuels in the short term and the considerable market resistance of many consumers to a renewed dependence upon coal. Both of these points can be illustrated by a cursory analysis of changes in coal demand in recent years.

The largest market for British coal is that provided by the electricity generating authorities. In 1981 they accounted for 87 million tonnes out of a total home sales of 119 million tonnes, some 73%. Purchases by the Central Electricity Generating Board and the South of Scotland Electricity Board were some 2 million tonnes lower than in 1980, but significantly higher than the 76 million tonnes sold in 1973. In the immediate wake of the oil price increase, each Board took advantage of the fact that it had a mix of coal and oil fired plants and increased the use of its coal fired facilities, thereby substantially reducing its oil burn. The consumption of oil by the two generating boards fell from more than 17 million tonnes in 1972 to 5 million tonnes in 1981, and by the latter year its use was reduced essentially to peak load generation in gas turbine and diesel sets and to the 'technical minimum' in the larger stations.

Any increase in the use of coal between 1973 and 1980, however, was checked by two developments.[10] First, the recession of 1980–82 reduced total electricity demand (from 279 Twh in 1979 to 260 Twh in 1981), thereby limiting the primary fuel requirements of the generating industry. Second, from the late 1970s, new generating plant which had been designed and ordered before the 1973 oil crisis became available to the Boards; once available, it inevitably displaced some coal fired capacity. The late commissioning of the Advanced Gas Cooled reactors and the completion of new oil-fired plant together depressed the level of coal demand. Yet further reductions appear likely into the middle 1980s since increased output from the nuclear stations, and the prospective use of natural gas liquids at the Peterhead power station in Scotland, will further displace coal-fired capacity. In the absence of a substantial growth in the overall demand for electricity, therefore, only the completion of the Drax B power station — prematurely ordered in 1978 with the objective of assisting the power plant manufacturing industry — is likely to produce a significant but still not dramatic upturn in the demand for coal by the electricity industry in the middle 1980s. By 1990, therefore, the consumption of coal by the generating boards could well be less than 80 million tonnes (Table 2).

All other markets for coal have contracted relentlessly in recent years. In 1973, coke ovens (in particular those of the steel industry) used nearly 22 million tonnes; by 1981, consumption was less than half that level. Coal use by industry in general during the same period fell from 12 to 7 million tonnes, and domestic use halved from 14 million tonnes. Of all these markets, only that of industry would appear to have the potential for some growth in the immediate future. Coal's substantial price advantage per therm over other fuels offers particular advantages to those firms needing to raise bulk steam, and the conversion of boilers to burn coal is now assisted by a government subsidy.[11] However, whilst some firms are indeed in the process of converting some of their boilers to use coal — including such large energy users as ICI, Dunlop and Courtaulds — the depth of the early 1980s recession and the simultaneous restructuring of British manufacturing industry are together likely to depress the overall demand for energy in that sector and so leave only a small net increase in the demand for coal by industry in the medium term.

Compared with a British market for 123 million tonnes of coal in 1980, therefore, the National Coal Board is unlikely to have a home market in excess of 110 million tonnes in 1990; indeed demand could be even lower. By comparison, the assumption built into the reference case of the 1978 Green Paper on *Energy Policy* was 146 million tonnes, whilst the range suggested by the Department of Energy in their *Energy Projections 1979*[12] was 124–132 million tonnes.

The prospects for the 1990s — and it is for that decade that further investments must now be planned and made by the National Coal Board — are inevitably less certain. It cannot be escaped, however, that successive forecasts made by the electricity generating authorities have indicated a declining use of coal in that decade, consequent upon their preference for the construction of more nuclear power stations. The Boards appear convinced that the balance of evidence remains in favour of adding additional nuclear power stations to their supply systems, a proposition that has met with broad government approval.[13] The construction of such stations would, of course, still leave coal as the major source of primary fuel for the generating industry for many years; but its relative and absolute importance would decline. There is no serious expectation of a significant upturn in the demand for coking coal by the steel industry or in the domestic market beyond 1990. The need for synthetic natural gas based upon coal is unlikely to occur this side of the year 2000. The market prospects for coal in the 1990s, therefore, rest very heavily upon the expansion of sales to industry in general. Yet a substantial increase of sales to this market cannot be taken for granted. The overall rate of growth of the national economy; the country's changing industrial structure; the rate at which energy conservation measures are adopted; the availability and the price of competitive sources of energy, especially natural gas; trends in the real costs of winning coal in the 1980s; the regularity with which coal supplies are interrupted; the advances which are made in new coal burning technologies such as fluidised bed combustion;[14] and the extent to which public subsidies are made available to the coal industry; all these factors — and others — will affect the overall demand for coal in Britain in the 1990s.

An earlier study by the present author put the year 2000 home market for coal within the range 112–130 million tonnes, with a mid-point of 121 million tonnes.[15] Robinson has suggested a range of 80–115 million tonnes, with a mid-point of 98 million tonnes.[16] Both of these figures are well below the 1978 reference case of the Department of Energy which was 165 million tonnes, or even their 1979 range of 128–165 million tonnes, a market prospect which has presumably continued to inform investment decisions and approvals in recent years.

All of these figures refer to the estimated size of British coal requirements at the turn of the century. But it must not automatically be presumed that the National Coal Board will satisfy all of that market. Nor must it be assumed that the British industry cannot win some market overseas. It is with the international context of British coal that the next section is concerned.

THE INTERNATIONAL CONTEXT OF THE BRITISH INDUSTRY

Throughout the late 1970s, Britain was generally a net importer of coal, although the quantities involved were relatively small. Imports reached a level of 5 million tonnes in 1975, fell away during the next few years and then peaked again 1980 when they were 7.3 million tonnes. Part of these imports were coking coal, bought on term contracts by the British Steel Corporation from Poland, the USA and Australia for reasons of both their quality and their price. In late 1979, the Corporation announced that it wished to double its imports to between 5 and 6 million tonnes, a quantity equivalent to half of its requirements. 1979 also saw the Central Electricity Generating Board looking overseas for cheaper supplies of coal. It was able to secure several term contracts at advantageous prices and, importing the coal via Rotterdam, was able to undercut the delivered prices of the National Coal Board at many power stations in southern England, even as far inland as Didcot.[17] Spokesmen for the Generating Board suggested that imports rise initially to 5 million tonnes, but subsequently they could be even higher if improved import facilities — as well as informal government permission — could be secured. The possibility of some 15 million tonnes of CEGB imports in the early 1980s entered into public discussion.[18] These were seen both as a means of keeping down the Generating Board's costs and as a more general spur to the improvement of the National Coal Board's efficiency. In the event, however, the 1981–82 contraction in the demand for coal in Britain, increasing overproduction, mounting coal stocks, and powerful political pressures upon the Government by coal mining interests led to a set of defensive reactions by the Board and the Secretary of State for Energy.

To reverse the rise in coking coal imports, domestic coking coal prices were reduced to levels comparable to most imports, and their volume was reduced to the absolute minimum required for 'best blast furnace practice'.

In the case of steam coal imports for the CEGB, the Government offered immediate compensation of nearly £19 million to the industry substantially to replace 6 months' imports with home supplies; the Generating Board's contracted purchases from Australia and elsewhere, and some of their stocks on the Continent, were in consequence sold on the open market. In a letter to the Select Committee on Energy of the House of Commons, the CEGB claimed that the compensation by no means covered their losses and to some degree served to demoralise those administrative staff who were involved in attempts to keep down the Corporation's costs and hence electricity prices. The compensation payment 'relates only to the identifiable short term costs and falls far short of the true costs, many of which will not be immediately apparent. The process of negotiating the claim required a great deal of senior management time, and the effect of the cut-back on the motivation of the staff who, having negotiated contracts for cheap coal, have now to sell it to our competitors, is potentially extremely costly'.[19]

Throughout the 1970s the export trade of the National Coal Board was quite modest in scale at about 2 million tonnes each year. The reasons for the limited scale of these overseas sales was partly an inadequacy of supplies over and above domestic requirements. More important, however, was the considerable gap between the costs of winning and transporting British coal to the near Continent and the delivered prices of Australian, Canadian, Polish, South African and United States' coals. The spot price of coal delivered to Western European ports in 1978, for example, was around £15 per tonne, whereas average NCB costs (excluding subsidies) were nearly £22 per tonne.[20] A third factor was the reluctance of European buyers to enter into supply contracts with the NCB given the political stance of the National Union of Mineworkers in the early 1970s and their experience following the strikes of 1972 and 1974.[21]

The early 1980s saw a significant change in the coal export situation, however. The excess of British coal production over domestic demands, and the rising level of the industry's stocks, prompted the Board to embark upon a major exporting effort in 1981 and 1982. Their task was assisted by a hardening of the price of delivered coal supplies in Western Europe as a result of congestion in several major exporting ports around the world, strikes in the United States and the political crisis in Poland. By aligning their prices down to Continental levels, the Board was able to secure a rising volume of spot sales. They exceeded 9 million tonnes in 1981. It was conceded that these sales, less their transport charges, brought a pithead return to the Board that was less than the average costs of production.[22] The Board argued in defence of its tactics, however, that the sales yielded a return that was greater than the industry's short term avoidable costs, that they generated a large and valuable cash income and that they avoided the costs of stocking the coal.[23] At least in the short term, they argued, the policy was commercially sound. Given the possibility that delivered coal prices to Western Europe could well soften in the medium term as Polish supplies recover and port congestion eases, it remains an open question as to how long such a marketing strategy would make sound commercial sense. Nevertheless, the Board appear to want to make substantial export sales part of their medium term marketing strategy. On more than one occasion it was noted that they were looking for new port facilities which would allow them to increase exports to 15 million tonnes each year.[24]

The longer-term relationship between the British energy market and the international coal trade is steeped in both economic and political uncertainties. The British coal industry is primarily a deep-mine industry. It is inescapable that, irrespective of geological conditions, deep-mined coal is more expensive to win than opencast or strip mined coal, which increasingly characterises the international industry.[25] In addition, in many parts of the world coal mining conditions underground are very much easier and cheaper than they are in Britain. Some comparative international costs of coal mining are indicated in Table 3. The subsidies required to maintain British coal exports are likely to rise in real terms, therefore, and the attractions of imports are unlikely to diminish. Only if it could be demonstrated with reasonable confidence that, after 5 or so years, the home demand for British coal would be likely to fall into line with domestic supplies — and if it could be assumed that generally speaking coal imports would continue to be denied to British coal users — would a continued (but still interim) coal export effort make economic sense. Yet such conditions seem unlikely to be met in the foreseeable future.

Moreover, attitudes towards the future of coal imports are by no means predetermined. It might be argued that Britain should give its coal industry complete protection from imports for an indefinite period. On the other hand, the West German approach affords an alternative and quite attractive model. There, the coal producers have negotiated a 15 year agreement with the electricity utilities which guarantees sales of 50 million tonnes; any requirements above that level, however, can be satisfied by a combination of domestic and overseas supplies, initially in the ratio of 1 to 1, but after 1987 in the ratio of 2 tonnes of imports to each additional domestic tonne. Such an arrangement affords both a minimum level of protection for the domestic coal industry — the second largest in Western Europe, but with production costs somewhat higher than the average in Britain — and an incentive to the German coal producers to strive for greater efficiency in the face of import competition.

The outcome of such a policy will depend in part, of course, upon the future price of imported coal — which is not without its uncertainties. Several factors suggest that international coal prices are likely to increase at a slower rate than the NCB's production costs. The International Energy Agency[26] have argued that the world coal industry 'due to its relatively untapped resource base, is usually characterised as a constant cost industry, and coal supply curves are generally expected to remain relatively flat in real terms over the foreseeable range of coal demands likely to persist throughout the rest of the century'. The IEA have further noted that the international coal industry is characterised by a geographical diversity of resources, by vigorous competition in international markets, by a lack of corporate concentration, by the ability of new entrants to enter the market with ease, and hence by the probability that its medium term prices are unlikely to diverge significantly from its medium term costs. In contrast, both the Department of Energy and the National Coal Board at the Vale of Belvoir Inquiry argued that international coal prices would be pulled up towards (rising) international oil prices; that the costs of winning British coal would rise more slowly than the likely rise in oil prices; and that in consequence the British industry will have an increasing price flexibility with which to compete against competitive fuels. Policy discussions and decisions about the future of coal imports cannot avoid making a judgement about the validity of these conflicting views.

CONTINUING DILEMMAS FOR THE BRITISH COAL INDUSTRY

There can be little doubt that the demand for British coal at home and overseas in the 1980s and 1990s will be significantly lower than that hitherto accepted publicly by the National Coal Board and the government. To persist with the present declared investment strategy of the coal industry, therefore, would imply — quite erroneously — that either the markets for British coal will mysteriously respond to the production ambitions of the mining industry, or the economic costs of overcapacity will be willingly carried by the community as a whole. For some time, in fact, it had been clear at least to some independent observers[27] that the earlier investment plans of the industry require adjustment in the light of realistic market prospects. Without such an adjustment, the Board's modernisation plans can only be seen as a huge and speculative investment unlikely to yield a reasonable return.

Within an adjusted set of market forecasts the National Coal Board could still, of course, continue to pursue an essentially 'high investment strategy', designed to create a highly capital intensive industry —

more automated and productive than at present, making full use of modern technology and with a declining use of labour. Such a strategy undoubtedly has a powerful economic logic whilst 'the total cost of coal from new capacity, including capital cost, . . . (is) below the wages and other operating costs of much existing capacity'.[28] Moreover, the approach would so shift the cost structure of the industry that it would be less vulnerable to relatively high wage increases, and provide a sound basis for expansion in the 1990s should the opportunity arise. A high investment strategy would, of course, impose considerable social costs upon both the industry and the community at large. It would involve the substantial reduction of colliery manpower and the early closure of many older, high cost pits in localities where alternative jobs are difficult to provide. It would also involve a radical shift in the geography of the industry towards the 'central coalfields' of the East Midlands and South Yorkshire, and away from the mining communities of Scotland, North East England and South Wales. The same strategy would also impose certain new environmental costs to the extent that some of the new mining facilities would be located in areas that previously have not experienced the impact of mining operations.

An alternative approach towards the future of the British coal industry would, of course, be to minimise new investment by taking full advantage of existing mining facilities and the present mining labour force, whilst still accepting the need to close some of the Board's older mines in the light of market circumstances and as their reserves become exhausted — the Board has pointed out that, without further investment, some 2 or more million tonnes of capacity will be lost each year. Such an approach would mean that the Coal Board could not hope for any significant improvements in its overall labour productivity; it would weaken the industry's position by comparison with overseas suppliers; and it would imply that the country would be in a relatively weak position to satisfy from indigenous supplies any growth in the demand for coal that might occur in the 1990s. However, it would mean that fewer jobs would be lost in the mining industry in the short term, and that the additional environmental costs of coal production would be relatively small.

It would be pointless to search for an 'ideal' strategy for the British coal industry in these highly generalised terms. The enormous uncertainties surrounding the future markets for energy, and the extensive multiplier effects of the industry throughout the economy, mean that the costs and benefits of alternative planned courses of action elude confident measurement. Nevertheless, choices — pitched somewhere between the two extreme routes to the coal industry's future that have been outlined above — cannot be realistically avoided. This is primarily the task of management, but it also requires a number of major decisions from government and the general collaboration of the union. It is essential, therefore, that all three parties involved in shaping the industry's future should approach this unenviable task cooperatively. There is no escaping that, quite properly, both social and political as well as economic judgements must bear upon their decisions. It is perhaps unfortunate that the structure of the industry and its workforce is such that so many centralised decisions on this matter are inevitable. There can be little doubt, however, that decisions on a new and realistic strategy for the British coal industry are long overdue.

REFERENCES

1. House of Commons, *Official Report, Parliamentary Debates*, 2 February 1982, Coal Industry Bill, Second Reading, p. 131.
2. National Coal Board, *Plan for Coal*, NCB, London, 1974.
3. Tripartite Group, *Coal for the Future*, Dept. of Energy, London, 1977.
4. Secretary of State for Energy, *Energy Policy: A Consultative Document*, Cmnd. 7101, HMSO, London, 1978.
5. National Coal Board submission to the Commission on Energy and the Environment, 1979, unpublished.
6. J. North & D. Spooner, The geography of the coal industry in the U.K. in the 1970's, *Geographical Journal*, pp. 255–72, (1979).
7. House of Commons, *Official Report, Parliamentary Debates*, 4 March 1982, Coal Industry Bill, Third Reading, p. 424.
8. House of Commons, *Supply Estimates 1982–83*, Class IV, HMSO, London, 1982.
9. National Coal Board, *Plan for Coal*, NCB, London, 1974.
10. Gerald Manners, *Coal in Britain — An Uncertain Future*, Allen & Unwin, London, 1981.
11. The Department of Industry administers a grant scheme to encourage industrialists to switch from oil-fired boilers to coal-firing.
12. Department of Energy, *Energy Projections 1979*, D En., London, 1979.
13. See Chapter II/2 of above volume.
14. G. Manners, *ibid.*, p. 74.
15. G. Manners, *ibid.*, p. 85 ff.
16. C. Robinson, Vale of Belvoir Inquiry 1979–80, proof of evidence, day 40; see also C. Robinson and E. Marshall, *What Future for British Coal?* Hobart Paper 89, IEA, London, 1981.
17. R.N. Razzell, Vale of Belvoir Inquiry 1979–80, proof of evidence and cross examination, days 32 and 33.
18. *The Times*, 27 February 1980.
19. House of Commons, *Fourth Report from the Select Committee on Energy*, Session 1981–82, HMSO, London, Appendix 4.
20. G. Manners, *ibid.*

21. N.J.D. Lucas, *Energy and the European Communities*, Europa, London, 1974.
22. House of Commons, *Second Report from the Select Committee on Energy*, Session 1981–82, HMSO, London.
23. House of Commons, *ibid.*, Appendix 4.
24. House of Commons, *ibid.*, para. 22.
25. A.T. Shand in M.T. Portillo (ed), *National Coal Conference '78*, Conservative Central Office, 1978.
26. International Energy Agency, *Steam Coal Prospects to 2000*, IEA, Paris.
27. G. Manners, The changing energy situation in Britain, *Geography* **61**, pp. 221–31, (1976); Alternative strategies for the British coal industry, *Geographical Journal* **144**, pp. 224–34, (1978).
28. Secretary of State for Energy, *Energy Policy: a Consultative Document*, Cmnd. 7101, HMSO, London, p. 27.

Chapter 3

British Nuclear Power Policies

*Roger Williams**

By the late seventies nuclear power had become both a major and a highly controversial element in British energy policy. The process by which this situation had been reached is naturally of considerable historical interest, especially for the light which it throws on the making and implementing of public policy, but it is also of great significance because of its implications for the future of nuclear energy in this country. The aim of this chapter is to identify the main issues in the development of British nuclear power to date,[1] the better to assess what may be the main issues in the years immediately ahead.

MILITARY ORIGINS

The first point to be made is that although civil and military nuclear issues have become increasingly separate in Britain, the civil development effort grew out of what was originally an exclusive military programme and, as will emerge below, the military origins

***Professor, Department of Government, University of Manchester.**

of British nuclear power have left their mark right down to the present time. In the immediate postwar period Britain concentrated on the technical and industrial steps necessary for the construction of nuclear weapons and there were as a result virtually no resources to spare for work on nuclear energy. At the same time, the passage of the McMahon Act effectively ended American assistance and forced Britain to determine her own path in nuclear development. Since the quickest route to a nuclear weapon then lay with the manufacture of the fissile material plutonium in a nuclear reactor, the most urgent question naturally became the selection of an appropriate reactor technology. Many different reactor types were in principle suitable but in fact technical and safety considerations essentially compelled the engineers to opt for an air-cooled, graphite moderated, natural uranium reactor. The consequences of this defence-oriented decision are still with us in the civil field in 1982.

At the outset there was a suggestion that the military requirement for plutonium be met in two stages, the second of which would have involved not an air-cooled reactor as in the first stage, in which the reaction heat was vented to the atmosphere and thus wasted, but one with closed-cycle cooling, so that the heat could have been used to raise steam and thus produce electricity. However, the defence needs were ruled to be too pressing to allow the extra time this would have taken, and so the opportunity of constructing a dual purpose plutonium/power reactor was foregone at this time. This decision was not as important as that which had determined the choice of the gas-graphite natural uranium reactor in the first place, but nevertheless, by putting off for several years serious pursuit of a power reactor, it meant that the eventual decision in 1955 which established the first commercial nuclear power programme in Britain was based on much less practical experience of power reactors than might by then have been available.

The technical and safety considerations which had led to the choice of the gas-graphite natural uranium reactor eased a little in the late forties, and there was also at that time some feeling that a reactor based on this concept would be less commercially attractive than one using enriched uranium as fuel. But despite this lack of confidence, there was enough enthusiasm to keep the natural uranium reactor concept alive, and indeed a dual purpose power/plutonium design had been worked out by the end of 1952. This continued to be based on the original plutonium producing reactors but instead of air cooling the reaction heat was now to be used to raise steam by means of the closed cycle circulation of carbon dioxide. A power station based on this design might well have been built shortly afterwards for the electricity authorities, who were well disposed, but the military now increased their plutonium demand and in consequence the dual purpose design was reoptimised so that plutonium would be the chief product and electricity the byproduct. In March 1953 government approval was given for a plant based on this design and there followed the building of what became known as the Calder Hall station.

It could fairly be argued that in settling upon the gas-graphite natural uranium reactor Britain had had initially no real choice, but it would also have to be acknowledged that the confirmation of this choice as represented by the building of Calder was at least a little less circumscribed, and that a switch to another reactor technology might have been made in the early fifties. In particular, by this time it was becoming clear that the United States, for whom submarine propulsion rather than a commercial power station was the next most important reactor objective after plutonium production, was going to put its main emphasis on the light water cooled and moderated reactor using slightly enriched uranium oxide fuel.

CREATION OF THE UKAEA

Up to this time nuclear development in Britain had been a departmental matter but, thanks largely to Lord Cherwell, Paymaster General, a long associate of Sir Winston Churchill and his adviser on nuclear energy, a unique new arrangement was now created. This was the establishment in 1954 of the Atomic Energy Authority, a kind of 'half-way house' between a government department and a nationalised industry. The Authority inherited on their creation the enormous prestige which had accrued to the existing atomic energy organisation as a result of the successful testing of the atomic bomb in 1952, and in their first chairman, Sir Edwin, later Lord Plowden, they had a civil servant thoroughly versed in the ways of Whitehall. Naturally enough, with these advantages, the Authority's standing continued to grow — and not only their standing, for their staff also grew, from 17,000 in 1954 to a peak of 41,000 in 1961.

The choice, and later confirmation, of the gas-graphite natural uranium reactor and the setting up of the AEA stand out as the first two of six major decisions taken in the first decade of Britain's civil nuclear development, the ramifications of which remained clearly evident more than a quarter of a century later. The next two of these decisions now followed quickly, and both owed much to the AEA's reputation and the fact that at this time there was of course no other British source of expertise on nuclear affairs — though, as will appear, the decisions themselves were respectively industrial and economic rather than strictly nuclear, and the AEA were not really well placed to advise on either, and certainly did not deserve the decisive influence they appear to have enjoyed.

The industrial decision was that nuclear power stations could best be built in Britain by encouraging the creation of all-purpose companies called consortia, each capable, by subcontracting with its parent companies, of undertaking the complete, or turnkey, construction of a nuclear station. Obviously this was not the only way of proceeding — existing strong companies in relevant fields could have been used as nuclei for new organisations, or the electricity authorities might have performed the overall contract management function themselves for instance. But the consortia approach was judged to have much to recommend it at the time, given that industry was cautious and that a rapid build up of capability was thought to be needed, and its clumsiness, and intrinsic weaknesses, revealed themselves only over time.

The economic decision referred to above, arrived at in 1955, was that in Britain nuclear power could from the start more or less compete with electricity generation in coal powered stations. It is vital to appreciate that the background against which this judgement was made consisted of a real fear, European as well as British, that the coal industry would soon be unable to meet the growing demand for energy, and that oil could offer only a temporary breathing space. The advent of nuclear energy in this context was therefore widely seen as providential. This being so, nuclear cost estimates were subjected to much less rigorous criticism than would have been the case had energy supplies been buoyant. The economic expectation entertained about nuclear power in Britain was expressed formally in a White Paper in February 1955. This set out a provisional programme for 1.5–2 GW of nuclear power, installed capacity at the time being some 20 GW. It is still not clear in detail how the economics of nuclear generation were expected to be 'about the same' as those of contemporary coal stations. What can be said is that this conclusion was reached only by making two large and, even then, dubious assumptions: first that the plutonium produced by the nuclear power stations would itself have a value of up to 50% of the cost of a unit of electricity; and second, that coal stations would present a more or less stationary economic target for nuclear power to aim at.

These two assumptions were singularly ill advised even in 1955, but worse was now to follow, in that in 1956 there occurred three almost simultaneous events which turned the unwisdom of 1955 into the folly of 1957 — and folly remains the right description notwithstanding that certain advantages have in the event been obtained from the out-turn. These events of 1956 were, in October, the opening of Calder Hall and the receipt by the electricity authorities of the first tenders for the programme of nuclear stations announced in 1955, and in November, the announcement of oil rationing as a result of the Suez crisis. Although Calder Hall was not, given its principal function of plutonium production, the world's first nuclear power station, this claim for it tended to stick and there was a very understandable euphoria at what Britain had achieved: above all and at least, Calder proved that nuclear power stations really could work. The significance of the first nuclear tenders was that they were for stations substantially larger than had been anticipated in 1955: larger stations meant fewer than the twelve envisaged in 1955 if the 1955 programme were to be adhered to, but by this time no less than five consortia had come into being and they were naturally hungry for work. The impact of the Suez crisis needs little explanation. Suez is perhaps best viewed as the necessary condition, given the continued expectation of an early coal shortage, for the decision announced in March 1957 to expand the 1955 nuclear programme to 5-6 GW by 1965, a trebling or quadrupling of what was already an ambitious programme.

This decision of 1957 was the fifth of the six referred to above as having largely shaped British nuclear development over the ensuing 25 years. The sixth decision came later in 1957 but to grasp its significance one must examine the process of reactor assessment and reassessment which occurred within the AEA in the mid fifties. In the first place, there was only one reactor type on which the first nuclear programme of 1955 could be based. This was the reactor then in process of construction at Calder Hall. It became known as Magnox after the magnesium alloy used to can its fuel, the initial plutonium production reactors having had aluminium cans unsuitable for operation at the higher temperatures desirable for power production. The Magnox can was giving trouble as late as January 1955, jeopardising the success of Calder Hall, and there was still almost no irradiation experience when the first commercial tenders were received in 1956. In view of these uncertainties about the Magnox reactor, it was understandable enough that the 1955 White Paper should tentatively suggest a move to liquid cooled reactors for the last four of the envisaged twelve station programme. However, by the time the 1957 decision to treble the 1955 programme was taken, confidence in the Magnox reactor had grown to the point where it was expected that the whole programme would be based on it, and so indeed it was, a total of nine stations eventually being constructed. From now on gas cooling became, to use Sir Christopher, later Lord, Hinton's words, 'the cardinal belief of the British reactor creed', with profound consequences. The AEA certainly considered seriously the possibilities of other reactor types, in particular the two versions of the American light water reactor (LWR) which had by this time identified themselves, the pressurised water reactor (PWR) and the boiling water reactor (BWR). But in the end they decided, especially because of the uranium enrichment costs they expected to be associated with the LWRs, that these reactors were not the most suitable type for Britain. The Authority therefore turned back to gas cooling, thus a second time confirming, in comparison with LWRs, their preference for this technology.

So it was that the AEA came forward in July 1957 with a request to build a 33 MW Advanced Gas Cooled Reactor (AGR), a reactor they were later to refer to as the Mark II version of Magnox, but one whose technical features were seen in 1957 as requiring the construction of an experimental version to pave the way for commercial stations later. The AEA's request to build the AGR, squarely their own decision, was more or less routinely approved, construction started and the reactor came into operation in 1962. The Authority did not thereafter completely close their eyes to other reactor types. In particular, in 1962 they decided that they wanted to build a 100 prototype Steam Generating Heavy Water Reactor (SGHWR), a reactor which in their judgement combined some of the best features of the American BWR and the Canadian Heavy Water Reactor (CANDU). Approval for this too was given and the SGHWR prototype came into operation in 1967. The Authority also in due course decided, with European partners, to build a High Temperature Reactor (HTR). This, like Magnox and the AGR, was gas cooled, though the gas in this case was helium rather than carbon dioxide, and the Authority later liked to consider the HTR as Mark III of their gas cooled reactor line. From 1960, when construction started, high hopes were entertained for the HTR, but the project eventually ended in 1975 for lack of support. The Authority were also committed from the early fifties to development of the fast breeder reactor (FBR), capable of being fuelled by a mixture of the plutonium produced in first generation reactors and the depleted uranium left over after enrichment. Since this reactor could also produce further plutonium, understandably it was seen as the apotheosis of reactor development. An experimental FBR came into operation in 1959 and a 250 MW prototype was approved in 1966, both at Dounreay in the North of Scotland.

In the light of these other reactor projects, it would not be true to say that the AEA had all their eggs in the gas-graphite basket, still less, though in the fifties and sixties this was often said by the AEA themselves, that their approach was narrow-front. But it is correct to conclude that through the late fifties and early sixties the AEA became increasingly committed to their AGR, to the point that if a new British reactor were to be adopted for a second nuclear programme starting in the mid sixties, then that reactor could only be the AGR. The inevitable technical development problems which the AEA encountered with the AGR, especially with its fuel canning material and the radiation behaviour of its graphite moderator at its high temperature of operation, only served to confirm to the AEA, as they were overcome, that they had made the right development choice. But, as must now be explained, because of the way in which the various nuclear power decisions had been taken, this conviction was the AEA's alone, a circumstance which by 1963 was making for serious political difficulties.

The decision in 1955 to have a programme of nuclear power stations was the Government's own, taken naturally on the advice of the AEA, but without the participation in detail of the electricity authorities. The latter accepted the proposals as reasonable despite having had little more than a month to comment on them. In part no doubt this was because they had for some years been interested in beginning to exploit the new technology, in part perhaps because they thought it best to embark gracefully on an undertaking which so clearly had the Government's full support. The electricity authorities were associated more closely with the expansion of the nuclear programme in 1957, but of the three programme sizes considered at that time would have preferred the middle one, for 4.5 GW, rather than the 6 GW programme which was chosen. Again, however, the Government were firmly resolved and again the electricity authorities carried insufficient weight to influence the decision. But circumstances and the Government's own action were now between them to redress this weakness decisively, though this was not at all what the Government had in mind when they translated Sir Christopher Hinton from the AEA to be the first chairman of the Central Electricity Generating Board, the new electricity generating authority for England and Wales created in 1957. Sir Christopher had been the principal architect of nuclear power while at the AEA, and it must have seemed very logical to move him to the CEGB, where the centre of gravity of Britain's nuclear development would in future be, so that he might repeat there the successes he had had with nuclear power while at the Authority.

One of Sir Christopher's last decisions as managing director of the Authority's industrial group was to put forward the proposal for an experimental AGR, as mentioned above, and as late as 1960 he continued, as CEGB chairman, to look to an early commercial order for this reactor. But economic circumstances in the late fifties moved sharply against nuclear power. It was not so much that the nuclear engineers failed to keep their promises. It was rather that three other major developments undermined nuclear power's position. First, there came about a new and easy availability of cheap oil, which in turn led to a coal glut and severely altered the long-held assumptions in regard to the coal industry. Second, there was the fact that substantial economies of scale began to be realised with conventional generating plant, so that nuclear power found itself chasing a moving cost target rather than the stationary one anticipated in 1955. And third, there was the unpleasant fact for nuclear power that, with growing appreciation of the difficulties occasioned by FBR development, and no alternative means of using the plutonium produced by first generation reactors, the plutonium credit given to these reactors in working out their unit generating cost had steadily to be reduced to virtually zero.

TECHNICAL DITHERING

The CEGB in these circumstances found themselves with a very uneconomic and capital intensive nuclear power programme but also, in the person of Sir Christopher Hinton, with a chairman carrying the professional authority necessary to get a reduction of that programme. Even so, it was not until June 1960 that the Government announced that they had agreed that the nuclear programme should be cut back. The target would now be 5 GW, the lower of the two figures suggested in 1957, and the programme would also be stretched out over another two years. The CEGB would ideally have liked an even larger cutback but recognised that there were limits given the need to be fair to the construction industry. As it was, this industry was now in considerable trouble, and although amalgamations reduced the number of consortia from five to three, there was still not really in the early sixties enough work for three.

Having secured some reduction in the CEGB's expenditure on nuclear power, the CEGB chairman continued in the early sixties to protest that any second nuclear power programme must not leave the CEGB as economically disadvantaged as had the first. In this connection, Sir Christopher specifically raised the possibility that the CEGB might want to look abroad for a new reactor type. In 1961/2 it was Canada and the CANDU reactor in which Sir Christopher found himself receiving offers from American reactor vendors which he felt had to be taken seriously. The AEA had technical difficulties enough at this time with the development of their AGR not to need the further complication that, even if the AGR proved technically sound, the CEGB might still wish to look elsewhere for economic reasons. Inevitably, the relationship between the Board and Authority came under considerable strain, nor was this confined to the AGR and its prospects. The CEGB also thought it wrong, for instance, for the AEA to embark upon the SGHWR, as they did at this time, without, as the Board saw it, carrying the Board with them in this new commitment.

The Government could not escape being drawn into a conflict of features which, on a strict interpretation, seemed not to be consistent bringing together the Board and the Authority might agree on the reactor to be adopted for a second programme, these hopes in the end came to nothing and the Government were left with the impossible decision, that of having to choose between the AEA and the CEGB on a technical question, whether or not to direct the CEGB to proceed to building the AGR. Faced with this dilemma the Government took in 1964 what must have seemed a shrewd decision. Instead of themselves making a political choice they asked that the Board invite competitive tenders for their next nuclear power station, the tenders to be based on either the AGR or a water moderated reactor of proven design, deciding between the resulting offers on their merits, though subject still to a final government review.

AGR VERSUS LWR

The resulting delay of a year from 1964 to 1965 came at a very uncomfortable time for Britain. Efforts were still being made in 1964 to sell the Magnox reactor abroad — there had been only two such sales, to Italy and Japan, in the late fifties — but these efforts were bound now to fail given that Britain was herself moving on from Magnox. On the other hand, there still remained a possibility that the AGR might be passed over for an LWR, and this allowed American firms to establish a permanent advantage as they sought to exploit internationally their domestic economic 'breakthrough' of 1963, its 'loss leader' character notwithstanding.

The comparative appraisal of the tenders they had received was carried out by the CEGB, with AEA assistance, early in 1965. By this time the Conservatives had been replaced by a Labour Government committed to making technology a central element of their strategy for regenerating Britain, and Sir Christopher Hinton was no longer at the CEGB. Rumours that the AGR had defeated American competition began circulating in March, but formal confirmation did not come until May and details not until July. These details were published in summaries which were translated into six languages, but they were far too sketchy and suggested too many shortcomings in the methodology of reactor comparison to impress professional opinion abroad and indeed, despite continued hopes thereafter, no AGR export sale resulted.

A great weakness of the comparative analysis of the best AGR tender and the best LWR tender as set out in the summaries was that the whole of the advantage which the AGR was shown by the figures as enjoying over this LWR was less than the advantage notionally given to the AGR on the grounds that, unlike the LWR, it could refuel while still on load. But an even more serious weakness of the 1965 comparative appraisal was that the reactors compared were paper ones — a particularly unsatisfactory consideration in the case of the AGR given that a commercial version of this reactor involved a twentyfold scaling up from the 33 MW prototype.

The 1965 reactor appraisal, then, impressed few foreign observers, and that the AEA had assisted the CEGB in conducting it only further convinced such people that matters had somehow been arranged to favour the AGR. In vain did the CEGB protest that this was not so, that there had been no political pressure put on them, and that they were convinced of the AGR's merits.

The adoption of the AGR in the face of the American competition was a surprise of one sort. The choice of the consortium to build the first AGR station was a surprise of another. Only one of the consortia in fact had tendered an AGR design judged in the appraisal to be better than the best LWR, and this consortium's design contained features which, on a strict interpretation, seemed not to be consistent with the tender specification, and which therefrom led to rumblings and complaints from the other consortia. The order for the first AGR station, to be sited at Dungeness as a second, or B, station, there already being a Magnox, A, station there, actually went to a consortium disadvantaged by the CEGB in connection with the last station of the Magnox programme. This consortium were to have built one of the two reactors of this latter station, at Wylfe, but after long negotiations the CEGB eventually gave the whole order to the other consortium involved in a move which led to some sharp criticism of the Board and of its chairman. Following this event, in 1963, the disadvantaged consortium had been very short of work and had become seriously weakened, and it was in fact a condition of the CEGB's award to it of the first AGR station that it take steps to strengthen its managerial capability. Herein lay new difficulties, but in 1965 these were still in the future.

The 1965 decision to adopt the AGR for a commercial programme confirmed the decision which the AEA had effectively taken eight years before, to move from natural to enriched uranium fuelling. This now led to the need to provide a British source of this substance, first by reopening the mothballed military enrichment facility, and later through the development of a new enrichment technique in conjunction with the Dutch and West Germans. Ironically, the level of enrichment required with LWRs having helped to turn the AEA away from these reactors in the fifties, the eventual enrichment level needed with the AGR was actually little less. This was because the AEA's original choice of fuel canning material for the experimental AGR, beryllium, precipitated too many problems and had to be abandoned in favour of stainless steel, and stainless steel unfortunately absorbs more neutrons than does beryllium and thus requires a better source of neutron supply in the first place, in other words a higher level of fuel enrichment. Another main effect of the 1965 decision for the AGR was to underline the probability that the selected reactor would be used for the whole second programme. As announced in 1964 this programme was to have been of some 5 GW but the 1965 decision encouraged an expansion to 8 GW, and despite ritual observations about preserving flexibility, the AGR was indeed used for all five stations.

COMPETITION WITH COAL

Between 1958 and 1965, as explained above, the CEGB had resisted nuclear power on the grounds that it was less economic than fossil powered stations. But in 1965, in addition to the comparative reactor appraisal, they compared the best AGR design they had been offered with a contemporary coal station, satisfying themselves that nuclear power was at last more economic than coal. Over the next five years this brought the CEGB and their new chairman, Sir Stanley Brown, supported by the AEA, into bitter conflict with the NCB and their chairman, Lord Robens. Lord Robens complained repeatedly in the late sixties that the economics of coal and nuclear power were not being compared on a fair basis, but in White Papers on Fuel Policy in 1965 and 1967, and in respect of particular decisions like that of 1968 to put an AGR station at Hartlepool on the edge of the Durham coalfield, the Labour Government, despite their affiliations with the miners, accepted the arguments for nuclear power. The Government were fully prepared to assist the coal industry in its consequent rundown, but they judged the economic arguments in favour of nuclear power to be compelling. In retrospect it is clear that this assessment was, to say the very least, premature and that the coal industry was made to suffer unnecessarily.

CONSTRUCTION DIFFICULTIES

The judgement was premature because of the difficulties which gradually emerged in the late sixties and early seventies with the AGR stations as they were in process of being built. There were problems both of technology and of management. Remarkably, the mistake of a multiplicity of designs which had added to the expense of the Magnox programme was repeated and three designs of AGR were built. In addition, scaling up from 33 to 600 MW proved no straightforward undertaking, there were component development difficulties, and several severe technical problems progressively revealed themselves. These problems would have taxed even a sound construction organisation, but it quickly emerged that the consortium given the job of building the first commercial AGR simply could not cope. A new reorganisation of the construction industry now began. This was to continue almost without a pause for more than a decade, adding to the weakness and uncertainty of the industry in the interim, and one of its first casualties was the consortium building Dungeness B itself, the work at this site having to be taken over by one of the remaining two consortia. The first stage of reorganisation having eliminated one of the consortia, as a result of the refusal to merge of the boiler making companies involved, public shareholdings were established in the other two consortia, these consortia becoming known thereafter as design and construction companies. This new arrangement in turn lasted only from 1969 to 1973, when after protracted negotiations all pretence of competition was abandoned and a three-tier arrangement was brought into being. This consisted of a National Nuclear Corporation as a holding company, a Nuclear Power Company as its operating arm, and the General Electric Company as management agency, the latter company having 50% of the shares, seven companies from the rest of industry 35% and the AEA 15%. General Electric's dominant role in this new structure was a direct result of the then Conservative Government's hope that its head, Sir Arnold Weinstock, would be able to create a strong construction organisation, but when, as explained below, the Labour Government of 1974 decided not to adopt the PWR, GEC became unhappy, their 50% holding was reduced to 30% in 1976, the AEA taking up the balance, and after further protracted discussion GEC's management role in the NNC/NPC was ended in 1980.

By the early seventies the construction difficulties with the AGR stations made the electricity authorities determined to order no more of them until those building had actually begun to generate power. There was a striking parallel here with events of a decade earlier, though then it had been uncertain nuclear economics which had made the electricity authorities unwilling to order, and here the problem was mainly technical. There was even a parallel in the setting up in the early seventies, as in the early sixties, of an official committee to try to resolve the difficulties. In this instance, however, the Government went further, also creating a Nuclear Power Advisory Board representing all the main interests.

The chairman and deputy chairman of the CEGB both changed in 1972 and this, given the serious problems with the AGR, led the CEGB to look once again, and with increasing interest, at the LWR, but whereas had they ordered an LWR in 1965, it would have been of the BWR type, now the CEGB's interest was centred on the PWR. In 1972 this new interest did not greatly matter since the CEGB were clear at that time that they did not need any more reactors immediately. However, in 1973, the Board underwent an enormous change of mind, and by the end of that year they were talking in terms of ordering nine nuclear stations in the period 1974–9 and a further nine in the period 1980–3. This was an astonishing transformation in the course of a year, especially since the Board indicated that they had revised their plans *before* the Israeli-Arab war of October 1973. The Board were no less clear about the reactor they wanted for this huge new tranche of nuclear power — the PWR. This they regarded as a 'bread and butter' reactor, and there was in their view no other such reactor. The AGR they thought even less suitable than it had been in 1972; had it not been for the AEA's preference for the AGR they might well, they said, have ordered the SGHWR in the late sixties, but that reactor as result of not having been developed commercially, was now obsolete; and the HTR, though perhaps having the greatest potential of all, continued in their view to need much more development work. Of the other possibilities, while they acknowledged that Magnox was as proved as the LWR, the Board thought it far too expensive, and CANDU they disqualified on the grounds that it had not been widely ordered internationally.

SELECTION OF THE SGHWR

Thus in 1973–4 as in 1963–4 there came about a major reactor crisis, and in 1974 as in 1964 there was a change of government. But there was a sharp difference in the way in which the 1974 crisis was resolved as compared with that of 1964. In this case the new Energy Secretary, Eric Varley, made his own political decision. His choice lay between the PWR, which the CEGB, and probably the majority of industry, wanted, and, despite the CEGB's opinion of it, the SGHWR. Chief champion of the SGHWR was the South of Scotland Electricity Board (SSEB), a tenth the size of the CEGB, and for the first time taking a line firmly independent of the latter. The AEA, naturally enough, were also willing in these circumstances — the AGR being out of the running and no other British reactor being ready — to stand up for the SGHWR, and so also in effect was the Commons Select Committee on Science and Technology, which had reported several times on nuclear power since its creation in 1966. Unsurprisingly, given that all interests, including the SSEB, were represented on it, the Nuclear Power Advisory Board were unable to reach a unanimous view. In this confused situation with positions polarised and passions roused, Mr Varley chose the SGHWR, taking the opportunity at the same time to disagree with the CEGB's demand forecasts and therefore approving only a small, 4 GW, SGHWR programme.

For a short while, as attempts began to formulate an agreed SGHWR design, calm descended. Then yet new doubts began to surface about the wisdom of the choice which had been made. As early as 1975, with recession cutting electricity demand, the CEGB began to indicate that they were not after all in urgent need of nuclear power. Confirmed in 1976, this second major about-turn by the CEGB quite understandably came in for widespread criticism. There were also arguments in 1975–6 about the SGHWR's readiness for commercial construction, and real fears that the same mistake in scaling up was about to be made with this reactor as had been committed with the AGR in 1965. Although some suspected that obstruction was taking place by those interests opposed to the SGHWR, when the Chancellor announced a year's delay in the SGHWR programme in 1976 as part of a round of public expenditure cuts, there was also fairly general relief in the industry.

In the Science Committee's investigation of the PWR before the 1974 decision, it had come out that Sir Alan Cottrell, Government chief scientist and an eminent metallurgist, had doubts about this reactor on safety grounds. In announcing the 1974 decision for the

SGHWR the Energy Secretary avoided this question but he did ask the Nuclear Installations Inspectorate (NII) to complete a general examination they already had in hand of the broad safety issues thrown up by the PWR. The NII, regulatory arm of the industry, had then been in existence for some fifteen years but only with the possibility of the PWR being introduced into Britain in 1973-4 did it begin to play a role in policy matters as against its narrower and more functional responsibility.

The chairman of the AEA suggested in 1976 to a new Energy Secretary, Mr Tony Benn, that the 1974 decision be reconsidered, and the latter, though not well pleased, in response asked for the Authority's considered opinion. The Authority therefore convened a group which in due course recommended first, that the SGHWR be stopped, and second, that it was probably best after all to adopt the PWR: the SSEB were represented on this group and still dissented. Following Sir Alan Cottrell's observations in 1974 on PWR safety an AEA study group under the Authority's deputy chairman, Dr Walter Marshall, had studied the safety questions associated with the PWR's pressure vessel, reporting favourably in 1976. Sir Alan Cottrell accepted the quality of this group's work but also continued to distinguish between the theoretical and practical requirements of PWR safety.

SUPPORT FOR THE PWR

The first two of the AGR stations at last began to generate electricity in early 1976, and although the first AGR station, Dungeness B ordered in 1965, was still then years from completion — it was eventually expected to begin generating shortly after this chapter was finished in the spring of 1982 — the AGR now began to re-enter the reckoning. Later in 1976 the Energy Secretary agreed to a suggestion from the National Nuclear Corporation that the Corporation should review the three reactors now again in contention, the PWR, the SGHWR and the AGR. The resulting survey and the NII report on the generic safety of the PWR were both published in the summer of 1977. The NII's analysis concluded that there was no fundamental safety reason why a PWR should not be ordered for use in Britain. The NNC report argued that there was no remaining case for the SGHWR, and otherwise came down in favour of the PWR on grounds of cost and export potential, but with the proviso that because this reactor was not ready for immediate ordering in Britain and the AGR was, there should in the interim be a further AGR order, this because of the construction industry's urgent need for work, and despite the fact that pursuing two reactors would inevitably divide the resources available.

The situation now developed into a new reactor crisis with Cabinet deliberations in late 1977 and early 1978. The Government's decision was eventually made known at the end of January 1978. In a very carefully worded statement the Energy Secretary then announced, as had been expected, that the SGHWR programme of 1974 was being cancelled; confirmed that the Government and electricity authorities agreed two early nuclear orders were needed and that these must necessarily be for redesigned AGRs; and, in the most controversial part of his remarks, gave guarded approval for the CEGB's desire to establish the PWR as a valid option, provided all clearances were granted, with construction of a first PWR to start not sooner than 1982. Mr Benn was later, after leaving office, and in the wake of the serious LWR accident at Harrisburg in the United States, to repeat several times that he had felt under great pressure from the PWR lobby before winning Cabinet support for his 1978 policy of double-banking. Clearly, this policy left the door open as never before to a PWR order, but without providing certainty that such an order would ultimately be forthcoming.

How Mr Benn, or another Labour Energy Secretary, would have proceeded from this position cannot be known, because in Spring 1979 Labour were defeated at a General Election and the Conservatives returned to office. The Prime Minister, Mrs Thatcher, was well known to be a supporter of nuclear power, and she and other members of the Government, including her Energy Secretary, Mr David Howell, were also known to be admirers of the major French commitment to nuclear power and the PWR. The Government confirmed shortly after coming into office the outgoing Government's two new AGR orders, but in a considered statement of December 1979 made at last a firm commitment to the PWR, saying clearly that they wished, subject to clearances and a public inquiry, the next nuclear order to be for this reactor. Construction of this they hoped could start in 1982. It would be part of a new 15 GW programme over ten years, though the reactor choice for the later stations in the programme the Government said would remain open. The Government also revealed at this time that they proposed to consolidate the three-tier nuclear construction industry into one organisation under a new chairman.

THE SIZEWELL ENQUIRY

Subsequent to this announcement there were delays both in actually placing the contracts for the two new AGR stations announced in 1978, and also in settling the date for the PWR inquiry which had been promised. In the case of the two AGR stations, falling demand and a desire to cut public expenditure led to a further review early in 1980 by the Central Policy Review Staff at the request of the Prime Minister, and even after this there were contractual difficulties due to the restructuring of the construction industry and the NNC's low capitalisation. The AGR contracts were eventually placed in the Spring of 1981. With regard to the projected PWR inquiry, it was finally announced in January 1982 that this would start a year later, in January 1983.[2] The CEGB had indicated in October 1980 that they proposed to site their first PWR reactor at Sizewell in Suffolk, where there was already a Magnox station. To speed up the elaboration of the PWR design a special task force had by this time been created under Dr Walter Marshall, successor to Sir John Hill as chairman of the AEA. At the same time as they announced the date of the Sizewell inquiry the Government also stated that the CEGB would be publishing details of their PWR proposal in April 1982, and the NII a report on the reactor's safety in June 1982. Despite the slippage which had occurred with the PWR project, by early 1982 the Government continued to maintain that, provided the result of the Sizewell inquiry were favourable, a firm PWR order could be placed within the lifetime of the 1979 Parliament.

The Government's nuclear plans were criticised in 1981 by both the Monopolies Commission in a major report on the CEGB,[3] and by the Commons Select Committee on Energy in their first report.[4] In addition, the Government were further embarrassed by the departure within a year of the man they had supported to run the reorganised NNC. The Monopolies Commission found the CEGB's investment appraisal techniques seriously defective and in effect implied that the Board were deluding themselves about the margin of economic advantage enjoyed by nuclear power. The Energy Committee in their report were concerned both about the scale of commitment implied by a 15 GW nuclear programme, and by the fact that two reactors were still being developed for this. Like several other sources over the previous twenty years, this Committee would also have liked the CANDU reactor considered seriously.

THE ANTI-NUCLEAR MOVEMENT

Such in brief have been the main contortions over more than twenty five years concerning the choice of reactor, scale of commitment to nuclear power, and structure of the nuclear industry. Since 1974 there has also been in Britain, as there had been since the early seventies elsewhere, a very visible public opposition to the further development of nuclear power and its associated facilities. This opposition manifested itself initially mainly in the United States, and since it was focussed especially on the safety and environmental characteristics of the LWR, it was not surprising that it should surface in Britain when one of these reactors was being considered in 1974. The first significant opposition group to identify itself was Friends of the Earth, itself an offshoot of an American parent, and this organisation has remained in the van of the opposition movement. In addition, many other groups have become established since 1974 to oppose nuclear power nationally or locally, and many pre-existing groups, the Council for the Protection of Rural England for instance, have also evolved critical positions on the subject. The nuclear opposition's first British target, the LWR, disappeared temporarily with the 1974 decision for the SGHWR, but in 1975 two other targets were identified, the possible construction of a first commercial demonstration fast breeder reactor (CFR) and the proposed building of a thermal oxide reprocessing plant (THORP) to reprocess spent fuel from LWR and AGR reactors of foreign as well as British origin. In 1975 it seemed that the AEA might succeed in pressing the Government to order a CFR at an early date and much effort was therefore deployed by the nuclear opposition to prevent this. Perhaps partly as a result, but really much more because of circumstance — the need to decide first on a first generation reactor, whether AGR, SGHWR or PWR, and the fall in electricity demand — the prospect of a CFR order gradually receded in the late seventies, so that at the time of writing, Spring 1982, no decision on this subject seemed possible for several years, until after in fact another major inquiry, which itself could hardly be held earlier than the mid eighties.

But if a CFR did not in the event materialise as a real target for the nuclear opposition in the mid seventies, THORP did. It was the wish of British Nuclear Fuels Limited, the fuel arm of the AEA which had been split off in 1971, to build this and to accept foreign spent fuel for reprocessing it as a matter of commercial business. In spring 1976, after a brief public debate, BNFL duly received government approval to proceed. Opposition to THORP however continued to grow, and that autumn there was also published a report by an official body, the Royal Commission on Environmental Pollution, very unorthodox in its deep and reflective observations and reservations about nuclear power. In the circumstances, and especially following the revelation that a major leak of radioactive material had occurred at Windscale, projected site for THORP, a public inquiry became virtually inevitable. This inquiry was held in the summer of 1977 and the various opposition groups exerted themselves to the limit in the long and exhaustive process of giving evidence. This made their disappointment, and bitterness, all the greater when the inspector in his report on the inquiry eventually found for the THORP proposal in a wholly uncompromising way, a recommendation in due course accepted by Government and Parliament.

The Windscale Inquiry of 1977 constituted the first climax of the opposition to nuclear power in Britain. The Sizewell Inquiry in respect of the PWR has long been expected to become the second such climax. Between, and indeed before the Windscale Inquiry, several other nuclear targets have also been the subject of attack by the nuclear opposition. Chief among these targets were the sites selected by the nuclear authorities for test borings to establish stable geological formations for the permanent disposal of nuclear waste. In this case the authorities eventually decided, in the face of vigorous local opposition, that research abroad and the possibility of storing nuclear waste on the surface for up to 50 years between them made unnecessary completion of a programme of test drilling in Britain.[5] Other nuclear targets have included the movement of spent fuel by rail, uranium mining in the Orkneys, and the sites selected for the new AGR stations announced in 1978. Issues like civil liberties, held by the nuclear opposition to be threatened by the security requirements essential to nuclear development, permitted routine discharges of radiation from nuclear facilities, and the links between civil and military nuclear development, have also all continued to attract attention.

There is, naturally, much scope for argument about the lessons to be drawn from Britain's successes and failures in the development of nuclear energy, and one must also remember that any judgement needs must be interim. It is with these provisos in mind that an attempt will be made in the remainder of this chapter to draw some tentative conclusions.

INTERNATIONAL COMPETITION

Perhaps the first point which should be made is the general one that any independent national technological development effort by Britain must expect eventually to encounter significant competition internationally. When that competition is backed by the resources and market skill of the United States, then unless the British product enjoys exceptional techno-economic advantages, it must expect to meet with great difficulties. The challenge presented by the United States, and other technologically strong countries, is not an occasion for despair but it does require a far greater international awareness, commercial shrewdness and engineering drive than was evidenced by Britain in the development of nuclear power.

DOMESTIC ORIENTATION

A second important point concerns the relationship between a particular technological product, such as a nuclear reactor, and the circumstances in which it is developed and exploited, these circumstances comprising at least original motivation, economic context, organisational arrangements, and international orientation. By contrast with the United States, Britain's civil nuclear development was domestically rather than internationally oriented, to the point almost of the parochial. The organisational arrangements in Britain — AEA/consortia/CEGB — again by contrast with the United States left far too much of the decision-making authority with a body, the AEA, which lacked commercial experience. These arrangements also encouraged duplication and dispersion of effort, and this without the offsetting advantage of creating real competition, such competition as occurred usually having been confined to details since the basic reactor technology all derived from the AEA. As to the economic context of nuclear power, although market conditions were absent in both the USA and Britain — reactor research and development and fuel costs having been subsidised in each case to a substantial extent — in the United States the utilities were ultimately free to make their own decisions on power station purchases in a way which was never true of the British electricity authorities.

INFLEXIBILITY

A third striking feature of British reactor development lay in its inflexibility. Thus, there was a first commercial *programme* in 1955, a second *programme* in 1964, and even a third *programme* in 1974. The third of these programmes, as explained above, was ultimately abandoned and other arrangements made, but in all three cases at the outset, and in the first two in the outturn also, and despite the nominal possibility of other reactor types being introduced as the programmes proceeded, the commitment was really to a single reactor type. The consortia structure was another source of inflexibility, and the reduction in their numbers from five to three in the late fifties and early sixties, then from three to two in the late sixties and early seventies, and finally to one in the rest of the seventies, were protracted and debilitating processes. In the creation of the AEA lay yet another rigidity. The problem here was first, that as well as an R & D organisation there was created in the AEA a powerful special interest, provided for by parliamentary vote but largely free of the political constraints which, at least to a degree, limit government departments. Meant to benefit from the strengths of both the nationalised industry and the government department forms of organisation, the AEA in fact perpetuated instead, from the point of view of the national interest, far too many of the weaknesses of these two types of body. A further inflexibility in the AEA derived from the inevitability that the centre of gravity of the nuclear development programme must eventually become industrial and commercial rather than scientific. When this happened, and by the middle sixties it was well on the way to coming about, other functions had to be invented for the Authority, hence the Act of 1965 allowing it to do non-nuclear research and development, and the splitting off of BNFL in 1970.

Nor were the nuclear rigidities confined to the programmatic nature of Britain's nuclear commitment and the existence of the AEA: in the CEGB too lay a formidable source of immovability. In the period between 1960 and 1965 the Board did constitute some sort of check on the Authority, though an insufficient one even then so far as determining the Authority's reactor development programme was concerned. But after 1965, when Board and Authority were in agreement, challenge of their mutually supportive positions was virtually impossible and ministers and departments were practically impotent before them. Not until the SSEB 'broke ranks' in the 1972–6 period did government have access to a significant dissenting voice, and even then the SSEB was too small in relation to the CEGB to be a decisive element or to contemplate its own independent path.

PUBLIC ACCOUNTABILITY

This matter of a check on the AEA, or more broadly, the public accountability of the nuclear development programme, is a highly significant one. It can indeed be argued that had accountability been better, then the real problems of the British nuclear industry must have come to light both sooner than they did, and also in a way more likely to lead to remedy than was the case with the process by which shortcomings did in fact emerge. In effect, and in general, Britain relies very heavily on the government of the day ensuring that public sector bodies and policies are accountable directly or indirectly to ministers, these ministers and the Government as a whole then being in turn accountable to parliament and also ultimately, via general elections, to the country as a whole. There are considerable difficulties with any arrangements for securing public accountability which one may choose to postulate, but it has to be said that the culture of central government in Britain leaves much to be desired as regards this accountability, perhaps especially in regard to the control of technological programmes. There is not scope here either to justify this opinion in depth or to draw out all its ramifications. Nor should it be claimed that good public accountability would have prevented all the nuclear difficulties Britain has experienced. But better accountability could hardly have failed to help if policies and decisions had had to be defended in detail in the fifties and sixties. As it was, Government in those decades (and also, for the most part in the seventies) refused to publish official reports, parliamentary committees mostly failed either to get to the heart of the problems or else to sustain a professional critique of policy, and there did not exist within government itself rigorous enough procedures for identifying and rectifying problems with urgency and thoroughness. The Royal Commission report of 1976 having helped considerably in general, the Windscale Inquiry in the late seventies was perhaps one step in roughly the right direction, but one step is no more a journey than one swallow a summer, and by 1977 in any case most of the basic nuclear decisions had all long been taken.

THE SAFETY RECORD

It should be said here that in one respect, safety, the British development of nuclear energy has been outstandingly successful and although inevitably there have been accidents and errors, the Windscale incident of 1957 remains after a quarter of a century the worst of these. The regulatory arrangements laid down after that accident have certainly contributed to this happy situation, and this again makes one wish that nuclear economics and commerce had been taken as seriously, and handled as carefully, as the safety issues.

As regards the impact of nuclear energy development strictly on British energy policies, the effects have been numerous and several have already been noted above. In the first place, it was not unreasonable in 1954 that a special body should be set up to conduct nuclear research and development — other countries had already by then taken or were about to take similar measures. In their report of 1976 the Royal Commission on Environmental Pollution suggested that there was a case for an *energy* research and development agency, and there can be little doubt that if such a body had been set up two decades before, then the balance of national research and development effort in the energy field would have been substantially different. But such a move would have required far more foresight than was available in 1954, and this is perhaps simply one of those many instances where it is so easy to be wise in retrospect. On the other hand, it has to be acknowledged that energy research and development in Britain, and not only in Britain, was heavily slewed towards nuclear power for more than two decades, and even in 1982 is probably not fairly balanced as between the alternatives, the past continuing to exert a major influence on the present.

Research and development apart, the unfolding of the Magnox programme saw the electricity authorities invest far more in a capital intensive reactor system in the fifties and sixties than they need have done to meet their statutory obligations. On the other hand, this was much to their advantage later when they began to reap the benefit of the low fuel costs possible with Magnox. And the advantage to them of Magnox was then further increased by the coal disputes and inflation of the seventies. The mistake of excessive capital investment, it was noted earlier in this chapter, was repeated with the AGR programme of the late sixties, and on this occasion the coal industry were left with a very real grievance. But although the AGR was afterwards to disappoint, the CEGB never wavered after 1965 in their adherence to nuclear power, though several authors have continued to question whether the economics of nuclear power really are quite as good as the CEGB has continued to believe.[6]

THE CONTEXT OF OVERALL ENERGY POLICY

The public nuclear debate and public uncertainty about the balance of advantage and risk with nuclear power are also aspects of energy policy. It remains the case that the environmental implications of nuclear power dominate the public's perceptions of the hazards associated with energy supply, though other energy facilities have also come in during recent years for more rigorous scrutiny. The nuclear debate has in fact been more muted, and more lawfully conducted, in Britain than in many other countries, and judgement suggests that unless a real nuclear disaster occurs somewhere in the world in the eighties (a real disaster that is compared with the incident at Harrisburg in the United States in 1979, which in the event and despite fears, proved only a financial catastrophe and not a nuclear one) then nuclear power will probably continue to be publicly acceptable in Britain. It is, however, unlikely that the technology can maintain as low a profile as the Government would ideally like, and there are no doubt surprises still to come. Overall, one might suggest that whereas Britain cannot hope to improve much on nuclear safety in the coming decades, there can hardly fail to be some progress in the economic and industrial management of the nuclear power build up.

NOTES

1. This chapter is based largely on my book, *The Nuclear Power Decisions* (Croom Helm, London; 1980). Since that book is very fully referenced, only specific points not covered by it are referenced below, that is, the events mainly of 1980–spring 1982.
2. Hansard 9 c 128–9 (Written Answer, 22 July, 1981); 16 c 284–90 (20 January, 1982).
3. HC 315 (1980–81).
4. HC 114 i-iv (1980–81). Debated 1 February, 1982, Hansard 17 c 21–102.
5. Cf. Hansard 971 c 215–9 (Written Answer, 24 July, 1979) and 15 c 171–2 (Written Answer, 16 December, 1981).
6. E.g., Gordon MacKerron, 'Nuclear Power and the Economic Interests of Consumers', mimeo, June 1982.

Chapter 4

North Sea Oil

G. Corti

Although there had been speculation about the existence of exploitable hydrocarbons on the Continental Shelf of N.W. Europe in the years after the Second World War it was the discovery of the Groningen Gas field in the Netherlands in 1959 which provided the impetus for enhanced exploration activity in Western Europe. This activity soon extended to the United Kingdom Continental Shelf and there were successive Rounds of Licensing for the exploration and exploitation of hydrocarbon from 1964 onwards. Both the thrust behind these earlier Rounds of Licensing and the results of them focussed heavily on gas. Discoveries commenced with the group of substantial fields found in the Southern North Sea, the BP West Sole field of the Humber being one of the earliest. It is worth looking at these early Rounds before we come on to the topics of this article, namely oil, licensing, the PAC Report of 1972/3, and developments since.

THE FIRST FOUR ROUNDS

There were four successive Rounds from 1964 to 1971/2. The numbers of Licences issued, blocks or part blocks licensed and the total area licensed, is set out in Table 1.

Table 4.1. Licensing Rounds 1–4

Round	*Year of Awards*	*No of Licences Issued*	*No of Blocks/Part Blocks Licensed*	*'000 KM² Total Area Licensed*
1.	1964	53	348	80.7
2.	1965	37	127	26.2
3.	1970	37	106	21.1
4.	1971/2	118	282	63.3

All four Rounds resembled each other in that the basic policy was one of discretionary licensing. In other words companies applied for licences but the awards were in the total discretion of the Minister of Power (or later the Secretary of State for Energy). Criteria for the award of licences were announced publicly. For instance, in the First Round in 1964 the Minister of Power announced that he would be guided by five main factors:

1. The need to encourage rapid and thorough exploration and economical exploitation of the petroleum resources.
2. The requirement that an applicant should be incorporated in the United Kingdom.
3. The extent to which British oil companies receive equitable treatment in the country of any foreign owned applicants.
4. The programme of work, ability and resources of the applicant.
5. The applicant's past contributions to the development of resources on the British Continental Shelf and in the British fuel economy generally.

In the Second Round the Minister announced that in addition he would give weight to an applicant's contribution to the UK's balance of payments and to any proposals facilitating participation by public enterprise. For the Third Round the Minister announced similar criteria in the North Sea, but for the Irish Sea introduced additionally a criterion that the applicants should provide for participation by the Gas Council or the National Coal Board. In the Fourth Round the criteria for discretionary awards reverted to a similar pattern to that for the First Round.

But there were two great differences in the Fourth Round. First, in addition to 421 Blocks to be allocated at discretion (not all of which were in the event awarded) 15 blocks were to be granted to the highest bidder, that is auctioned. Second, in the years immediately preceding the Fourth Round of Licensing first of all some condensate discoveries had been made and then successively the Montrose and Forties oil discoveries were identified. So the name of the game had changed radically from a concentration on gas to one on oil.

Not unnaturally the oil industry was extremely keen to see the Fourth Round pressed on and the awards made as quickly as possible. With the wisdom of hindsight, Government in the broadest sense in Britain was not ready for the change. In the case of gas the Gas Council, as it then was, had a monopoly of distribution and sale and an effective monopsony of purchase. (There were from time to time limited exceptions to this, for instance, the right to acquire gas as a feedstock for chemical production, but these were not significant in overall policy terms.) Now, given the position of the Gas Council, it could be used as an instrument of national policy to ensure not only that the gas was brought into the UK, i.e. that control over it was established, but also that an effective pressure over the purchase price could be exercised.

Through this mechanism it was possible to ensure that the economic rents could be taken from the companies exploiting the Licences, and that the economic rents remained in the U.K. without recourse to the taxation system. Whether the rents were used efficiently, as a large part of them lodged with the Gas Council, rather than being re-distributed, is another matter.

When it came however to the discovery of oil not only was there no mechanism for control but also it very rapidly became clear that the taxation system had no provision whatsoever to cope with the situation that had arisen.

Nonetheless, and it should be said before this unpreparedness had been widely appreciated (save by one or two commentators such as Lord Balogh), the Fourth Round of awards were made, albeit nothing like as speedily as had been originally intended. Amongst the awards the 15 auctioned blocks figured and these brought in premia of £37 million to be contrasted with the eventual some tens of thousands of pounds per block which represented the income under the discretionary system.

THE 1972/3 PUBLIC ACCOUNTS COMMITTEE

In the course of the Parliamentary Session 1971/2 the Public Accounts Committee was preparing itself for its regular examination of areas of the public administration of accounts of Acts of Parliament when it began to be borne in on its then Chairman, Mr Harold, now Lord, Lever, that there was a lot to look into on the arrangements for the exploitation of petroleum and natural gas within Great Britain and the Continental Shelf. Accordingly in the course of Sessions 1971/2 and 1972 the PAC conducted an indepth enquiry into this topic and rapidly homed in on two dimensions. The first was that unpreparedness of the tax system which has been referred to above. That on the face of it, if, as by then seemed highly probable, large quantities of oil were discovered on the UKCS major oil companies would pay no taxes (being able to offset them against losses made abroad; these losses being calculated on artificial prices for oil) was only one example of what came to light on taxation. Secondly, in examining what had happened on the auction, the Committee found that the 15 blocks having produced £37 million and been awarded there was no pause to reconsider whether to change the system of awards for the discretionary blocks nor even, as was the inherent position under a discretionary system, to drastically reign back on the number of awards actually made. When official witnesses argued the merits of the discretionary system the Chairmen of the PAC, Mr Lever, subsequently succeeded by Mr Edmund Dell, pointed out that modified auction systems, that is auction systems involving pre-conditions, were perfectly well known in business.

The upshot was a very critical report by the PAC early in 1973, whose recommendations were:

(1) The government should take action substantially to improve the effective tax yield from operations on the continental shelf; and should consider among other methods the possibility of imposing a system of quantity taxation.

(2) Before any further licences are issued all aspects of the regime for licensing, especially as regards oil, should be reviewed in the light of this Report and the conclusions in paragraph 97 in order to secure for the Exchequer and the economy a better share of the take from continental shelf operations.

The conclusions of the report are annexed to this chapter but the full flavour can only be got by reading both the evidence and the full report.

Some impression of the scale of what had been going on prior to the Fourth Round of Licensing, during that licensing round, during the hearings and report period of the PAC, and in the succeeding year or two, is given by Table 2 which gives the date of discovery of

Table 4.2. Discovered Fields and Recoverable Reserves

Date of Discovery Fields in Production	*Field*	*Recoverable Reserves – mbls*
9.69	N. Montrose	90
11.70	Forties	2030
2.71	Auk	1718
7.71	Brent	50
9.71	Argyll	50
9.72	Beryl A	500
9.72	S. Cormorant	90
1.73	Piper	660
7.73	Dunlin	300
7.73	Thistle	518
12.73	Heather	90
1.74	Ninian	1050
4.74	UK Statfjord	573
5.74	Claymore	405
12.74	Tartan	200
9.75	Murchison	318

fields in production early in 1981, the name of the field, and the then (rather than initially) estimated recoverable reserves.

Put another way the scale of the recoverable reserves for these fields alone was 1.2 billion tonnes. To give yet another dimension the Department of Energy took to publishing an annual survey of activity on the UKCS, a survey which came to be known as the Brown Book. An early edition of the Brown Book already gave estimated total recoverable reserves on the UKCS of 3000 - 4500 million tonnes.

The build up of production of offshore oil was originally forecast to reach something of the order of 100 m. tonnes a year by 1980. The actual course of development was slightly slower but impressive enough. From a standing start, the figures are:

1975	1½ m. tonnes
1976	12 m. tonnes
1977	38 m. tonnes
1978	54 m. tonnes
1979	78 m. tonnes
1980	80 m. tonnes
1981	89 m. tonnes

Early in 1982 the magic level of 100 m. tonnes a year was attained and surpassed.

The significance of scale of discoveries and of the subsequent exploitation and production may be brought out by examining a number of magnitudes. By 1981 the contribution of oil and gas production to the Gross National Product was £9.8 billion or 4% of GNP. In the fiscal year 1981/2 total North Sea oil and gas revenues were estimated at rather under £6½ billion or 9% of the total yield of taxes and duties. Direct employment in the industry and its immediate suppliers was estimated at 60,000-100,000 and this has usually been taken to be additional employment, that is jobs created. The value of orders placed by the industry was some £3 billion in 1981 of which roughly £2 billion or 67% was placed in the UK. The effect on the exchange rate was for a while quite dramatic. Against the dollar the pound eventually rose from about $1.70 in the mid-1970s to $2.40 to the pound early in 1981. It has since for a variety of reasons (interest rates in the American economy and the flabbiness of the oil price worldwide amongst them) relapsed back very rapidly to $1.70 late in 1982, but the £/$ exchange rate should not obscure the fact that the pound's movement *vis à vis* many other currencies has been one of gradually emergent relative strength.

Now a point which had remained latent in the PAC's report of 1973 was the scale of total British interests in the awards made. Nonetheless on Page 89 of the Report of Session 1972/3 there is a table which shows the total British interests awarded in successive Rounds from the First to the Fourth. The figures appear in Table 3.

Table 4.3. British Interests in Rounds 1–4.

Round		*Total British Interest*
1.		22.7%
2.		33.6%
3.		36.5%
4.	auction.	20.0)
	discretionary	34.7)
Total		34.0%
Overall		32.0%

The PAC Report had provided a watershed. As an all Party document it was bound to be influential and considering what it had to say it was written in restrained terms. Afterwards its message became popularised and, unfairly to some, the impression was given that 'it had been given away' or 'our oil has been given away'. In the event both major parties decided on major tax changes and reforms and both considered how, by various methods, to improve control over 'our oil'.

THE FIFTH, SIXTH AND SEVENTH ROUNDS

When the next Round of licensing took place in 1977 it was against a radically different taxation regime. Furthermore this relatively small Round with 44 blocks awarded comprising 8.9 thousand sq km entailed a reversion on a greatly increased scale to an experiment used in the Third Round of Licensing. Whilst the discretionary system was retained it was mandatory that BNOC (the fairly recently created British National Oil Corporation) be a 51% partner in every application and thus award. This was a fairly cumbersome method of proceeding which landed BNOC with a very heavy potential bill for exploration costs as it was to pay its way. Not surprisingly, however, it transformed the percentage of UK interest to 70.5%.

The Sixth Round of Licensing followed almost immediately in 1979 and eventually 42 blocks representing 9.3 thousand sq km were awarded. The very costly Fifth Round precedent was not followed and rather companies were invited to put forward other ideas on how they could involve BNOC. This entailed a much bigger change than was at first perceived publicly, for it represented a move towards a limited form of bidding or competition as had been advocated by the PAC. The up-shot was that in nearly two-thirds of cases BNOC was 'carried' by its private sector partners for at least a limited amount of the exploration expenditure. The burden on BNOC and the indirect call on public funds was thus eased. In this Round the percentage UK interest remained very high at 67%.

In describing the elements of contribution to BNOC's position in Round 6 the Government had made it plain that 51% control over the oil was a minimum and not a bargainable point. By this time the long drawn out saga of participation negotiations was pretty well complete and, through the mechanism of oil options at market price, British Governments had established their control over the physical oil.

Round 7 in 1980 under a Conservative Government saw BNOC no longer as the chosen instrument of Government policy, save as an exerciser of the 51% participation oil options. The Corporation had to compete as another British enterprise. The Round yielded 90 blocks covering 17.2 thousand sq km but the removal of BNOC from the position of chosen instrument was accompanied by another and significant development. Applications for blocks in the relatively well established Central and North North Sea were only to be awarded by the payment of a £5 m lump sum payment. As against this the applicants within the designated area could nominate their preferred blocks. Again this was a form of limited competition, another variant of the theme advocated by the PAC and ensuring a rapid inflow of £210 million into public funds. The percentage UK interest fell markedly to 48%.

THE EIGHTH ROUND

Now in 1982 an 8th Round of Licensing has been announced for operation in 1983. The intention is to licence up to 85 blocks of which 15 will be auctioned in the mature oil provinces of the Central North Sea. The requirement for 51% participation oil options remains. It will be very interesting to see what happens to the UK percentage interest. It will also be interesting to see how the yield on the 15 blocks awarded compares with the £5 m a block premia of the 7th Round of Licensing (provided like with like is compared on the mandatory work programmes). This will be especially so as the prospects are of a licence Round and an auction taking place against soft oil prices and with an oil industry which world wide is likely to be in a continuing cash flow squeeze.

A welcome element in the public conditions for the 8th Round is the weighing of the applicants' contribution to the employment and involvement of UK organisations in research into new concepts and in the design and demonstration of associated techniques and equipment for application on the UKCS. What this is all about is a vexed topic. Oil companies get used to modes of operation and these modes of operation include assembling suppliers of all sorts of specialised services and equipment for the operations being conducted. Not unnaturally some familiarity grows up between purchaser, that is the oil company, and the supplier. This leads to a bias towards working with known suppliers who have often shared experience. One of the conclusions from the relatively very low UK interest in the early Rounds of Licensing was that the foreign companies (and they were foreign in respect of exploration and exploitation whatever their long standing base of refining and marketing in Britain may have been) had a propensity to prefer working with foreign suppliers, that is specialists of their own nationality. Once oil was discovered it took a little while for this to be fully appreciated, but after 1972 and the IMEG report steps were taken to correct the position. As noted above in global terms these have been quite successful, but the total terms mask the fact that rather a large part of the UK share is for relatively low technology and relatively unspecialised supplies of equipment, and that in some areas the British offshore industry remains wholly devoid of expertise. The reality of human contact and preference will have to continue to be taken into account and special attention paid to the role of the British or largely British 'expro' oil companies if this very serious shortcoming is not to be corrected. For the aspiration must be that the strengthened British companies turn from their own backyard to the rest of the world (as BP and the Anglo-Dutch, Shell, have always been so engaged) they will not only take their own know-how but take the know-how of British specialist services and supply companies with them.

ACTION AND INACTION FOLLOWING THE PAC REPORT

For the scale of reserves on the UKCS is now estimated at 2100 to 4300 million tonnes of which about 450 million had been produced to date. The value of these reserves in present day oil prices is £315 billion to £675 billion. With the relative economy in the utilisation of all fuels and notably oil, which has come about primarily as the lagged effect of successive hikes in the price of oil since 1973/4 and partly of the concomitant greater consciousness of the need for active energy conservation, the prospects of these reserves running out in the short term future has much diminished. Even at the foreseen levels of production it would be quite some years before it dips down below UK consumption (short of a major upturn in world economic activity or of a reversal of the trend towards relative energy conservation). Arguments about depletion and recently discovered repletion policies have tended to take place in a rather insular perspective and forecasts based on the relatively low level of exploration activity of recent years should not be allowed to obscure the fact that discoveries continue to be made. Not all of these are presently economically exploitable, either because they are small or entail complicated structures or comprise heavyish oils, but the history of other oil provinces throughout the world suggests that the prospect of Britain rapidly running out of oil and gas is a relatively low risk.

Against this background let us revisit the PAC report and see both what has been achieved and how its concerns have stood up to the test of time. Three strands may be distinguished. These are respectively, tax, control and 'take'. The third is assumed to be a more complex factor than that simply of tax yield, and to be a function of the total wealth, with part of it accruing nationally, the taxable base and then the tax yield within it.

The tax structure has been reformed to correct the deficiencies identified by the PAC and it would be a brave man indeed who argued that there were no deficiencies in the tax system at the time. Criticism as to the use made of the economic rents once these were identified and made a matter of policy choice is another and very much broader question as mentioned above and one on which strong reservations may be entertained. It should also be noted that after the remedying of the tax inadequacies further, usually upward, changes were made in the tax system and the thrust behind these was quite different, it was a use of taxation as a weapon to raise more revenue. The tax structure as we have it now is quite unnecessarily over-complicated and very severe doubts may continue to be held about its structure at the margin where it impinges on additional exploration, the entry of newcomers into the market and the evaluation and exploitation of marginal discoveries.

On control, or rather one element of it, after a period of groping for a solution, a way through the wood was found in the form of the 51% oil options at market price. These are broadly compatible with private property rights; with treaty obligations; and are singularly unlikely to invite economic retaliation, so the concern touched on by the PAC has been recognised and in this particular element a limited solution has been found.

THE ECONOMIC IMPACT

On the 'take' or national benefit with the wisdom of hindsight a limited reservation must be entered about the PAC Report. Whilst there was and is some undoubted validity in the Committee's criticism of the failure to draw back part way through that Round when at least two opportunities arose, the Committee nonetheless appears to have underestimated the force of Officials' arguments that to press on was a very important national objective. The measure of interest that the Fourth Round of Licensing, in the wake of discovery, notably of the Forties Field, stimulated in the world oil industry, made the UKCS the 'hottest play' in the world for a while. Without that degree of activity it must be doubted if discoveries on the scale outlined above would have followed in anything like the time scale described. Although the analogy is very imperfect, a European country which has followed a diametrically opposed policy is France and much of France's hydrocarbon potential remains relatively unexplored compared to the UKCS. So that the one sided picture which emerged from the PAC Report on North Sea oil and gas does require some measure of redress. Some measure only, however, because it was not necessary as the Committee pointed out, to assume that there was a public commitment to press ahead with the Round of awards on the scale that actually took place. This was logically completely contradictory to the whole essence of discretionary licensing. Still, the perspective of time suggests a less harsh judgement.

Furthermore, and without pretending that the discovery and exploitation of oil is always an unmixed blessing, those who would prefer it never to have happened, or that it should have happened on a tiny scale, should reflect on the state of the British economy and its ability to support 3 million unemployed at better than subsistence level without the advent of North Sea oil and gas. Perhaps no allegedly economic argument of the past few years has been shallower than the cry 'leave the bloody stuff in the ground'. Since without benefit of implementation of this prescription the other elements which called forth the plea, high dollar exchange rates and high interest rates, have changed, it will be very interesting to see how its advocate progresses.

It seems desirable and necessary to carry out more empirical studies of the phenomenon of the discovery and exploitation and the politico-economic impact of our own oil and gas. Take the three strands emerging from the PAC Report and identified above. There have been a lot of studies recently of tax structure. Some of the comparative studies such as A. Kemp and D. Rose's *Inefficient Collectors of Economic Rents*, 1981, and J. Mitchell's *U.K. North Sea Taxation At a Turning Point*, 1981, are worthy of note. But as yet it could always be argued, and indeed has been by Governments, that we lack the track record for empirical studies to be wholly convincing.

GOVERNMENT OWNERSHIP, CONTROL AND MANAGEMENT

On the topic of control the author of this article, together with Mr Frank Frazer of the Scotsman, has studied in some depth the phenomenon of participation which comprises control, and publication of the results is expected early in 1983.*

The phenomenon of national ownership has been singularly little looked at. The advocates of the auction system of awarding licences, Kenneth Dam in *Oil Resources*, 1976, and Colin Robinson and John Morgan in *North Sea Oil in the Future*, 1978, have tacitly left this subject well on the sidelines, yet its importance is very far from negligible as witness the estimates of £2 billion per annum for interest, profits and dividends due abroad in 1980 and 1981 as published by the Treasury in its Economic Progress Report. The question is not 'could we and should we have developed our own oil reserves entirely ourselves?'. This is an unrealistic autarkic position. Not only would this have been inconsistent with treaty obligations and invite gross economic retaliation, but Britain's logistic base in the industry was insufficient save for an extraordinary slow or halting development. The question is rather would a substantially higher percentage of national ownership than the extraordinarily low interests of the early Rounds, have so retarded development as to have made a significantly lower contribution to GDP despite the fact that interest, profits and dividends due abroad might have been lower.

APPENDIX

Parliamentary Accounts Committee Report of 1972/3

Summary of Main Conclusions

97.—(1) We regard it as unsatisfactory that U.K. tax revenue from continental shelf operations should be pre-empted by the tax demands of administrations elsewhere in the world; and that for tax purposes capital allowances on extraneous activities, such as tanker operations elsewhere, should be used to offset profits on continental shelf operations (paragraph 62).

(2) Under the present arrangements the U.K. will not obtain either for the Exchequer or the balance of payments anything like the share of the "take" of oil operations on the continental shelf that other countries are obtaining for oil within their territories (paragraph 66).

*The Nation's Oil, Graham & Trotman, London. This chapter was written in Autumn 1982.

(3) We consider that it is unsatisfactory that the Department should not have access to licensees' costs: this is an area where equality of information between the government and the licensee would be equitable (paragraph 70).

(4) We consider that, even disregarding the taxation points referred to in sub-paragraph (1) of this paragraph, there are grounds for considering that the U.K. terms have tended to lag behind those of other countries right from the start (paragraph 71).

(5) We consider that by the time invitations were issued for the fourth round of licensing in June 1971 the fear of repercussions from O.P.E.C. countries, whatever value might have been put on this consideration in earlier rounds, needs not in any way have inhibited the Department from offering blocks on more appropriate terms (paragraph 73).

(6) The second and third rounds of licensing had been framed on the initial expectation that offshore petroleum would be in the form of natural gas, but the position was materially altered before the fourth round by the discovery of oil which would be handled and distributed by private companies and not by a nationalised industry (paragraph 75).

(7) In our view, before matters of such importance as the timing, size and terms of the fourth round were decided there should have been full interdepartmental consideration (paragraph 77).

(8) While we accept that to scale up the £37 million receipts from the tender experiment in proportion to the total number of blocks allocated in the fourth round would be misleading for the purpose of judging what additional premia might have been received if they had all been put out to tender, it is obvious that the additional receipts might have been substantial, even without extending the use of the tender system, if a different approach to the administration of the round had been adopted in the light of the tender results (paragraph 80).

(9) We are not convinced that it is impossible to combine the advantages of the discretionary system (e.g. the imposition of an obligation on the licensee to perform a satisfactory work programme) with the obtaining of premia by auction (paragraph 82).

(10) We consider that, as the object of the tender experiment was to learn lessons, it should have been conducted before and not simultaneously with a major fourth round of licensing; and we think it could have been completed during 1971 before applications were

invited for the bulk of the fourth round blocks without resulting in any significant loss of time (paragraph 83).

(11) We are surprised that, when the results of the tender competition (resulting in successful bids totalling £37 million) were known on 20th August 1971, the questions of reconsidering or withdrawing the invitation for the discretionary allocation were not discussed interdepartmentally or put to Ministers for a policy decision (paragraph 84).

(12) We consider that quite apart from the tender experiment and making due allowances for the advantages of hindsight, the Department should have considered tougher terms in the light of the improving prospects of the North Sea, the hardening of terms elsewhere and the growing realisation of the implications of the taxation regime (paragraph 86).

(13) We are concerned that so many production licences have now been granted with the result that the most promising areas of the North Sea have already been allocated on the original terms (paragraph 87).

(14) The most striking fact to emerge from our review of the four rounds of licensing is that the terms for each, apart from the limited tender experiment, have remained virtually unchanged since they were fixed in 1964, before any discoveries had been made and when the potentialities of the shelf were unknown (paragraph 88).

(15) We are concerned that the licences granted remain valid, without a break clause exercisable by the Department, for 46 years; and that there is no provision for variation or renegotiation of the financial terms, however large the finds, or for obtaining a degree of government participation (paragraph 89).

(16) We were surprised that a thorough examination of the opportunities for British industry and employment had not taken place much earlier than 1972 (when the I.M.E.G. report was commissioned) as the full opportunities of the discoveries became apparent (paragraph 95).

Chapter 5

Gas Prices and Exploration

*Niall Trimble**

INTRODUCTION

Over the last year or so there has been a great deal of comment about the prices paid for North Sea gas by the British Gas Corporation. A number of commentators have suggested that the reserve potential of the North Sea is very large but the low prices offered by British Gas have destroyed the incentive to explore. As a result, they claim that exploration has fallen to fairly low levels and the high reserve potential has not been reflected in the discoveries made. This paper examines the position on exploration and reserves to show that this view of matters can be very misleading and that exploration levels have been influenced by a range of factors, some of which may be more important than price.

*Energy Policy Department, British Gas Corporation. A version of this paper, delivered at the 1982 Cambridge Energy Conference, is being published in Gas Engineering and Management in September 1982. The paper represents the personal views of the author and is not an official British Gas view.

EXPLORATION LEVELS IN THE SOUTHERN BASIN

The problem which seems to have stimulated most of the comments on gas prices and exploration is the run-down in the number of rigs operating in the Southern Basin of the North Sea in the mid/late seventies. It is probably fair to say that gas prices have played some part in this decline but there are clearly other influences at work, which may have been more important.

(a) The pattern of licensing

Most of the blocks in the Southern North Sea were licensed in the 1st and 2nd rounds, seventeen or eighteen years ago. These are the oldest offshore licensed areas in UK waters and it is hardly surprising that the number of rigs working has dropped off in an area that is now mature in licensing terms. The timing and pattern of exploration is also influenced by the terms of the licences as well as the dates on which they were granted. In the UK all licences include a provision such that half of the blocks licensed must be relinquished after six years. In addition, companies are often awarded licences in return for a work programme which commits them to drilling a certain number of wells within four or five years. The pattern of exploration that normally emerges as a result is a fairly rapid build up of rigs within 3 to 4 years of licences being granted, followed by a steady decline, which is more or less what has happened in the Southern Basin.

(b) The geological prospects

One of the greatest determinants of exploration decisions is the geological potential of the area. In general the degree of interest tends to be related to the prospect of making large discoveries there. The Southern Basin of the North Sea is a relatively small province which has already been fairly thoroughly explored and most of the significant structures appear to have been found. Most of the prospects that remain are probably fairly small and relatively uninteresting. By the end of 1980 the average number of exploration wells drilled per block in the Southern Basin was 1.21, over 50% higher than the average for the UK North Sea as a whole, (0.79). Most of the oil companies seem to agree that one of the main reasons for the decline in interest in the Southern Basin is its relative maturity in exploration terms. In a recent hearing before a House of Lords Select Committee, a Shell spokesman commented 'I would not think that there are any new discoveries to be made in the Southern Basin, which is a fairly well explored area'.

(c) The attractions of other exploration areas

The maturity and geological interest of the Southern Basin is important in a relative rather than an absolute sense because decisions on where to explore are dependent on the relative merits of several different exploration provinces. One of the reasons why interest in the Southern North Sea declined is because the later stages of exploration of this province coincided with the early development of one of the most exciting exploration provinces in the world in the 1970s, the Northern North Sea. As exploration resources were often limited in the early/mid-seventies the corollary of an expanded effort in the Northern North Sea was a decline further south.

(d) The preference for associated gas

There are considerable reserves of gas in the Northern Basin but a large proportion of this is associated gas rather than non-associated. As it is produced along with the oil much of this gas would have to be flared and wasted unless it was purchased in the fairly near future. As a result British Gas has tended to give preference to Northern Basin associated gas in recent years and since 1975 has twice attempted to organise a gas gathering system to collect the gas for transmission to the UK. The preference for associated gas has meant that the Gas Corporation has had to give a lower priority to non-associated gas from areas such as the Southern Basin. This may mean that there has been some loss of oil company interest in the area as they could not be sure they had an immediate market for any gas discovered.

EXPLORATION AND RESERVE DISCOVERIES

One further reason why the view that British Gas pricing policies have had an adverse effect on gas supply in this country may be misleading is that the discussion has been conducted solely in terms of the influences on the level of exploration. Important though exploration levels are, they are probably not as vital at the end of the day as the reserves discovered as a result of exploration. Whatever the views on exploration levels and prices it seems fair to say that the relationship between the price of hydrocarbons and the rate at which new reserves are found is not a clearcut one. It is quite possible, especially in mature exploration areas, to have a significant increase in price without a commensurate increase in oil and gas reserves as a result. The prime example of this is the United States where the historically very high level of exploration has meant that a large proportion of the reserves has already been found and so the scope for price increases to stimulate the discovery of new reserves is rather limited. In fact the volume of reserves found per foot of well drilled in the United States has declined fairly steadily over the last 20 years or so. Table 1 shows that in these terms, drilling in the 1970s was 40% less successful than it was in the 1960s.

Table 5.1. US Exploration Success (Average yearly figures)

Period	*No of rigs working*	*Average yearly additions to Petroleum reserves (tcf) of gas equivalent)*	*Total depth of wells drilled (million feet per year)*	*Billion ft³ of gas equivalent found per million ft of wells drilled*
1959-63	1744	32.5	190.7	169.7
1964-68	1293	35.3	162.6	218.6
1969-74	1189	20.0	139.3	144.8
1975-79	1950	19.2	208.6	91.7

Conversely, it is often possible to have a substantial level of discoveries without very high gas prices. The UK is probably a reasonably good example of this as exploration has been fairly successful over the last 10 years or so.

Table 5.2. Net Additions to Gas Reserves UK (tcf)

	UK
1973	
1974	1.5
1975	3.8
1976	–2.0
1977	0.8
1978	–2.5
1979	1.5
1980	0.9

Table 2 shows that since 1973 (when the government first published the figures in the Brown Book) remaining proven and probable reserves of gas in UK have risen in most years. At the end of 1980 these reserves were 11% above the level of 1973, despite consumption of 9.3 tcf over this period. The 1981 Brown Book also shows that no less than 28 gas/condensate fields had been discovered, but not contracted by the end of 1980. British Gas has also surveyed the prospects in the North Sea and found no less than 69 new sources of gas which have already been discovered. (This includes associated gas as well as non-associated.) The total reserves involved in the 69 fields appear to be around 20 tcf, cf. total remaining reserves in contracted fields of 23 tcf.

CONCLUSIONS

The evidence presented in this paper has shown that although the number of rigs working may well have declined in one sector of the North Sea, exploration has been remarkably successful and a large number of fields are now available for development and purchase when required. Under these circumstances it seems hard to conclude that the position of British Gas in the market has had an adverse effect on exploration for gas. The paper has also shown that the discovery of new reserves of oil and gas is probably more influenced by geology than by price. This is important because it means the extent to which one can alter the supply of gas by altering the price may be rather limited.

Chapter 6

Electricity Investment Planning in the UK

*Nigel Evans**

INTRODUCTION

The Central Electricity Generating Board (CEGB), the utility responsible for electricity generation in England and Wales, has recently been severely criticised both by Government agencies[1,2] and in the academic literature[3,4] for deficiencies in its long term planning. Similar criticisms have been made of the South of Scotland Electricity Board (SSEB). In particular, attention has been focussed on the unrealistically high forecasts of electricity demand made throughout the 1970s which have resulted in high levels of plant overcapacity.

In an attempt to quantify both the extent to which CEGB planning has failed and the magnitude of additional costs which have been incurred, a simulation study of the CEGB supply system has been performed.[5] The familiar cost minimising linear programming (LP) approach was used in the study, the results indicating that the performance of the CEGB during the 1970s has, in many ways, not been as poor as some of its critics have claimed.

To understand why this may be so, it is necessary firstly to take a

* **Energy Research Group, Cavendish Laboratory, University of Cambridge.**

historical perspective of the electricity supply industry in England and Wales and then examine the present planning environment in which the CEGB must make investment decisions for the future. The paper concludes with some general comments on other factors which are likely to become increasingly important in the area of electricity investment planning in the future, particularly the problems of electricity pricing and uncertainties in future demand.

A HISTORICAL PERSPECTIVE

Up to 1965 the growth in maximum demand on the CEGB system (the quantity of interest when assessing new capacity requirements) was high, averaging over 8% per annum. To meet this rapid increase in demand a significant programme of plant construction was necessary. The net system capacity in 1954/55 was a little over 17 GW, ten years later it had doubled to just over 34 GW. Even this level of plant installation was insufficient and some capacity shortages were experienced throughout the 1960s and into the first two years of the 1970s.

During the 1960s future demand forecasts were made for six years ahead by extrapolating past growth trends. This approach appeared reasonable during a period of high demand growth; any excesses of generating capacity would be short-lived and the adverse effects on the economy as a whole of possible under-capacity of plant were considered untenable.

Such an approach to forecasting obviously took no account of important structural changes in the energy supply field that were occurring at this time. In 1965 gas started to be made from oil instead of coal with natural gas making further inroads after 1968, particularly in the domestic space heating sector. This helps to explain the low and often erratic growth of demand after 1965. In addition, electricity demand growth was strongly influenced, along with energy demand generally, by the 1973 oil price rise. During the 1974-1979 period the maximum demand met by the CEGB was increasing at a rate of only 1½% per annum while the growth in total electricity supplied was just under 1% per annum. More recent figures reveal no upturn in demand growth, the total electricity supplied by the CEGB in the year to April 1981 being, in fact, the lowest for four years.

By 1973 the CEGB was using a more sophisticated forecasting methodology which included estimates of electricity's share of total energy demand at sub-sector level under the broad sectoral classification of domestic, industrial and commercial. A key input to the models used was the future rate of growth of GDP. For a number of reasons, including over-optimistic advice from Government, the GDP growth rate was consistently overestimated throughout the 1970s.

The overall effect of the various inadequacies of the CEGB's forecasting methods was that electricity demand during the 1970s was greatly overestimated. As a result, the CEGB was faced with an overcapacity of plant.

Overcapacity

Throughout the 1970s the amount of installed capacity on the CEGB grid was well in excess of peak demand, being 46% greater in 1973. This does not, of course, mean that the CEGB had a 46% overcapacity of plant as, in any large consolidated supply system, a margin of spare capacity in excess of anticipated demand (the planning margin) must be allowed for to ensure security of supply. Within the CEGB the planning margin is currently set at a level which would result in disconnection through shortages of generating plant for three or four winter peaks in every hundred. The basis for this standard is somewhat *ad hoc* — if the planning margin was set at an optimal level the supply security would be increased to the point at which marginal supply costs of increasing reliability were equal to the expected benefits from the marginal shortage costs avoided.[6] In any event it appears that a 46% margin of generating capacity over demand is excessive and will certainly have led to increased costs. The magnitude of these additional costs is related to the marginal plant on the system.

During the late 1960s and throughout the 1970s a large amount of new plant was commissioned by the CEGB. These stations, with generating sets of 500 and 660 MW and high thermal efficiencies, assumed the role of base load operation with the result that the marginal plant on the system during the period became the small coal and oil-fired stations with low thermal efficiencies (typically between 16 and 20%). In many instances these were of some considerable age. The cost to the CEGB of maintaining such a high planning margin was therefore just the cost of maintaining these old coal and oil stations (given that all capital costs had been recovered and no fuel charges were payable as the stations were not being operated). This was considered to be worthwhile from the CEGB's viewpoint as high demand growth rates were still being forecast in the early 1970s. In addition, delays in construction programmes (particularly the AGRs), combined with lower than expected availabilities of 500 and

660 MW plant during early years of operation, pointed to possible capacity shortages.

By the late 1970s CEGB planners accepted the fact that the optimistic demand forecasts made ten years earlier would not be realised. With the availabilities of the newest stations steadily improving, a systematic policy of plant retirement was introduced. This policy has also been criticised,[7] particularly as some plant has been retired before the end of its economic lifetime. However, much of this plant retirement has taken the form of routine replacement (several of the stations removed from service during the 1970s being more than 40 years old) and a study of stations retired prematurely reveals all of them to be over 20 years old, having small generating set sizes and low thermal efficiencies. In addition, several of these stations were oil-fired. Having made errors in demand forecasting and operated with unnecessarily high planning margins, the CEGB obviously felt that retaining this old plant on the system would exacerbate their problems.

Plant mix

Closely linked to the problem of overcapacity is the question of plant mix. It is clear that the 1973 oil price rise and subsequent further increases in 1979 were not anticipated by the CEGB. In the year to April 1981, 16% of the CEGB's capacity was provided by oil-fired plant with almost 4 GW being met by just two stations (Fawley and Pembroke). With a further 5 GW of oil plant ordered between 1971 and 1973 due to come on line within the next year, it may be seen that a significant amount of the CEGB's newest and most efficient plant will be oil fired by the middle of the 1980s. The CEGB's response to the current high price of oil (which in 1980 was 50% above the price paid by the CEGB for coal)[8] has been to reduce the oil burn by resorting to single or two shift operation of the large oil-fired stations and replacing generation with coal-fired plant.

The significant flexibility in plant operations displayed by the CEGB in recent years in response to the large increase in the price of oil relative to the price of coal arises from having both coal and oil plant in the group of highest efficiency stations. As relative fuel prices change, coal and oil plant may change places in the merit order and provide a greater or lesser proportion of base load generation.

The long-term outlook for the CEGB's oil-fired plant is uncertain. If the current coal/oil price differential persists these large and efficient stations will operate with low load factors (rather than as base-load plant), the cost of which, relative to the position foreseen by the Board in the early 1970s, is likely to be considerable. The likelihood of conversion of these stations to coal-burning appears extremely remote given the high capital expenditures that would inevitably be involved and the difficulties (both political and institutional) that might be expected in securing adequate supplies of coal at low cost.

There are two ways in which these oil-fired stations may become less of a financial burden to the CEGB than they now appear. The first is if the price of oil falls relative to that of coal (as predicted by some observers[9] and as recently occurred during the period 1977–1979 and again during the early part of 1982) in such a way that generation by new oil-fired plant is preferred to generation by older coal plant of relatively low efficiency. The second will occur if a significant upturn in electricity demand occurs during the late 1980s coinciding with a low level of new plant construction. In such a situation the oil-fired stations would be necessary to maintain an adequate level of supply security.

In addition, it should be noted that the capital costs of large oil stations have generally been lower than for either coal or nuclear stations, a mitigating factor if their long-term operation as low or intermediate load plant proves to be necessary.

FUTURE PLANT CONSTRUCTION

Given this background of unrealistic demand forecasts and plant overcapacity, concern has also been expressed at current plans for future plant construction. However, some of the CEGB's critics have failed to realise the extent to which the existing mix of plant (with respect to both age and type of fuel used) influences capacity requirements to the end of the century.

The Board's estimates of likely installed nuclear capacity by the year 2000 have consistently appeared unrealistically high.[10] The most recent view adopted by the CEGB, however, takes account of Government policy regarding nuclear power (15 GW of nuclear capacity to be ordered in the UK over ten years beginning in 1982)[11] and the total installed nuclear capacity in the year 2000 in England and Wales is currently estimated to be 24 GW. Even this figure is unlikely to be achieved. Given the fact that all of the first generation Magnox stations will probably have ceased operation by the end of the century, the CEGB's year 2000 installed nuclear capacity will only be in the region of 21 GW if the whole of the 15 GW nuclear programme is constructed in England and Wales. With this programme falling behind schedule already and work on the first

UK PWR not starting before 1984 (assuming that the conclusions of what promises to be a far-reaching public inquiry are favourable), an estimate of 20 GW for the CEGB's installed nuclear capacity in the year 2000 represents a reasonable upper bound. In practice it could be significantly lower.

It is perhaps worthwhile to compare current and planned construction programmes with likely requirements. If one adds the 15 GW of nuclear plant which may be constructed in the period to the year 2000 to the capacity of all plant currently under construction, one obtains a figure for gross capacity of approximately 27 GW. By the year 2000, 26 GW gross of steam driven generating sets currently on the system (out of a total of 57 GW) would be 35 years old or over with only 1 GW being large plant of 500 MW or greater. In addition, a further 27 GW of generating sets, principally of 500 and 660 MW capacity, will be 25 years old or over by the end of the century. Current CEGB plans allow for major refurbishment of stations with large generating sets of this type, an attractive scheme from many points of view but one which will nevertheless necessitate significant capital expenditure and will inevitably result in plant outages which, for the stations concerned, will be measured in years.

It would, therefore appear from the above discussion, in which no consideration has been given to possible future growth in demand, that the CEGB may actually have problems of under-capacity by the turn of the century. In reality this may not be the case as the CEGB currently has great flexibility in its mix of generating plant and would be able to respond (albeit at high cost) to limited increases in demand in the 1990s, for example, by maintaining very old stations as peak load plant. Nevertheless, these considerations lead to conclusions which are very different from those presented elsewhere[2] and indicate that planning margins in excess of 40% will not be observed in the 1990s and during the first years of the next century, even with no growth in electricity demand. With a significant upturn in demand growth in the last decade of this century capacity shortages become a real possibility.

Given that some new plant construction will be necessary before the turn of the century, the choice of plant type has been the subject of much debate. It is now clear that nuclear power in the UK has not had the large cost advantages over coal that was originally hoped for, due to significant capital cost escalation and long delays in the current AGR programme.

For the future, the introduction of the PWR may at last justify some of the claims made for nuclear power in the past, at least as far as the economics of the system *vis-à-vis* coal plant is concerned. It would be unwise, however, to be too sanguine about the future performance of PWRs, particularly given the weak position of the UK nuclear construction industry. Lessons have obviously been learnt from past mistakes and the CEGB's insistence on adequate completion of design work before the start of construction indicates that the unacceptable long AGR construction times will not be repeated for the PWR.

On the subject of reactor choice the CEGB's forceful argument that at some stage a decision must be made and a commitment given to one system, is probably of overriding importance. A decision in favour of the PWR has much to commend it, but it is not yet possible to say whether it represents a better choice than a decision to build the costly, yet reliable, CANDU reactors or the simpler, and presumably cheaper, BWR. Even the AGR still has staunch supporters in the UK and may yet prove to be a viable system, which at least has the advantage of being like no other reactor and hence unlikely to be adversely affected by incidents at stations elsewhere in the world.

At present most of the CEGB's plans for future plant construction concentrate on nuclear stations. However, there are a number of conditions under which some construction of new coal-fired plant might appear attractive as is discussed in more detail below. A future in which both nuclear and coal stations are constructed may well represent a reasonable strategy for a large risk-averse utility, such as the CEGB, to adopt.

FURTHER CONSIDERATIONS

It is clear that past CEGB planning has been deficient in many ways. However, the results from the model which has been used to study the CEGB system and which compares actual performance with an optimal least cost path, indicate that the costs of past mistakes have not been as great as is thought in some quarters. Further, it is adverse mix of generating plant rather than plant overcapacity which most leads to unnecessarily high costs. By the late 1980s it is estimated that the price of electricity to consumers will be of the order of 9% higher than if the CEGB had responded to low demand growth and changes in the relative price of fuels, in an optimal way during the 1970s and 1980s. Obviously, any utility making plans for future capacity growth does not have the benefit of perfect foresight. For this reason it is worthwhile considering some issues which must be addressed by utilities such as the CEGB if future investment planning is to be more successful than it has been in the past.

Uncertainties in Demand

One lesson that past errors should highlight is that future demand is uncertain. As lead times for the design, approval and construction stages of large modern power stations are continuing to lengthen, the time horizon which must be considered by utility planners is increasing. This, in turn, leads to even greater uncertainties in future demand forecasts.

This uncertainty should be incorporated by the CEGB in their long-term planning. It has been shown[12] that a certain planner (i.e. one who attaches zero uncertainty to his forecasts) should operate with a planning margin of just under 20%. However, the planning margin increases rapidly and non-linearly as the uncertainty of the planner increases. The reason for this is that the costs of having plant under-capacity are much greater than the costs of having over-capacity[13] if full account is taken of the adverse effects on the economy as a whole of supply interruptions.

In addition, an uncertain planner will meet his high planning margin with plant having capital costs lower than the very high capital costs typical of modern base-load plant. For the CEGB planning under uncertainty, this would mean that nuclear stations would be built as new capacity is required but, in addition, much of the planning margin would be met by coal plant. This reinforces arguments made earlier that for new plant construction the CEGB should be considering both nuclear and coal-fired stations.

These arguments provide justification for the CEGB's present planning margin of 28% and at the same time provide some defence of their planning strategy during the 1970s. It should be pointed out, however, that CEGB forecasts have, to date, pointed to future demand being high rather than recognising the fact that demand will always be uncertain.

Pricing

When making plans for the future, a large utility should consider the pricing policies that they will adopt, or be required to adopt by some external agency (such as Government). With the advent of reliable, low-cost micro-electronic devices, the possibilities of fully interactive load control and a move to a tariff structure based on short-run marginal costs, may be explored. In such a system, electricity assumes the place of a commodity in the market place for which a spot price exists. Competition will exist with private and public cogenerators and autoproducers generating electricity along with electricity utilities. With spot pricing the instantaneous buy and buy-back price is equal and set at the short-run marginal cost of generation plus network losses and, when necessary, an 'electricity shortage premium'.[14]

This type of pricing policy appears attractive for a number of reasons. For example, the overall efficiency of fuel use will improve and there will be less need for new generating plant. In addition, there will no longer be any requirement to operate with a planning margin as supply and demand will always be balanced at the prevailing spot price.

Although a spot-pricing policy points to improved economic efficiency in the electricity sector, there are a number of disadvantages to such a policy. Firstly, it is not clear that the level of demand generated by this pricing policy will in any way be optimal for the economy as a whole. Secondly, some customers, particularly small domestic consumers, may find it difficult to respond in a sensible way to the continuously varying price. For those domestic customers who rely on radiative electric fires for space heating, for example, the only response possible to the spot price prevailing at 6 p.m. on a cold January evening in the UK, may be to freeze.

In spite of problems such as these there is likely to be some move by the CEGB and the Area Boards (responsible for sales of electricity in England and Wales) to adopt a more efficient pricing policy. Planners must be aware of such changes if future demand forecasts and capacity expansion plans are not to be seriously in error, once again.

CHP and refurbishment

As an alternative to retirement of the small and old stations on the CEGB system it has been suggested that major plant refurbishment or conversion to combined-heat-and-power (CHP) schemes should be considered. The efficiency of many of the stations retired in recent years has been extremely low and it is argued by the CEGB that the only economic option is to close these stations and construct new stations whose efficiencies are such that fuel costs can effectively be as low as one third of those at the original stations. While such arguments certainly hold for some of the very old power stations, it is also likely that, for others, major refurbishment will be economically attractive. The CEGB plans to extend substantially the life of stations with 500 and 600 MW sets by undertaking plant refurbishment but the position regarding the stations with 100 MW sets is less clear.

On the subject of CHP additional problems exist. The CEGB's brief does not at present extend beyond the requirement that electricity be produced without undue costs. For this reason a move to CHP schemes in which overall energy efficiency is improved but the efficiency with which electricity is generated falls, is not a viable option. However, if, as seems likely, the conditions under which the CEGB operate are changed to accommodate a move towards CHP, a number of older stations close to centres of population may find a new lease of life as CHP stations. Once again, the economic assessment will have to be performed carefully for each station. It does appear, however, that the current trend of building new CHP stations using diesel powered generators fails to realise much of the potential of such schemes, given the high cost of diesel fuel.

Both plant refurbishment and the possible development of CHP may influence CEGB plans for new plant construction. Even if old stations are not considered suitable for conversion to CHP, it is possible that some new capacity additions will be in the form of intermediate-sized CHP schemes. Proponents of such a strategy can point to evidence which suggests that the significant economies of scale thought to be achieved by moving to very large set sizes have not been realised in practice.[15] In any event, CEGB planners should consider the possibility that not all plant replacement will be in the form of large coal and nuclear stations — plant refurbishment and the introduction of CHP may both have a role to play.

CONCLUSIONS

In conclusion, the following general points may be made regarding past and current CEGB planning. Firstly, demand has been over-estimated in the past and high planning margins have been observed. The cost of maintaining this high overcapacity has not been as great as is thought in some quarters due to the large amount of old, inefficient plant on the system at the time. Secondly, it is obvious that the 1973 oil price rise was not foreseen by CEGB planners and the large amount of oil-fired plant which will be in operation by the mid-1980s will result in unecessarily high costs, the magnitude of which depends on future oil price levels.

Finally, it is not clear that plans for future new capacity are excessive. The CEGB is not indifferent as to whether demand is over-estimated or under-estimated (high planning margins may well be preferred to blackouts) and it is not obvious that the planning margin used by the CEGB is too high, given the uncertain nature of future demand. The choice of plant to fulfill the requirement for new capacity is not straightforward, however. There appears to be a strong case for building both nuclear and coal power stations as well as pursuing plant refurbishment and small CHP schemes where the economics appear attractive.

REFERENCES

1. Select Committee on Energy, *The Government's statement on the new nuclear power programme*, Vols I & II, HMSO, London, February 1981.
2. The Monopolies and Mergers Commission, *Central Electricity Generating Board: A report on the operation by the Board of its system for the generation and supply of electricity in bulk*, HMSO, London, May 1981.
3. Raphael Papadopoulos, 'Growth and overcapacity in the UK electricity industry', *Energy policy* 9 (No. 2), pp. 153–155 (June 1981).
4. J.W. Jeffery, 'The real cost of nuclear electricity in the UK', *Energy Policy* 10 (No. 2), pp. 76–100 (June 1982).
5. Nigel Evans, 'Electricity supply modelling: Theory and case study', Energy Discussion Paper 14, Energy Research Group, Cavendish Laboratory, Cambridge, UK, September 1981.
6. Mohan Munasinghe, *The Economics of Power System Reliability and Planning: Theory and Case Study*, Johns Hopkins University Press for the World Bank, Washington, 1979, p. 28.
7. Raphael Papadopoulos, 'Nuclear power: The enduring connection', *Energy Policy* 9 (No. 4), pp. 319–323 (December 1981).
8. UK Department of Energy, *Digest of United Kingdom Energy Statistics 1981*, HMSO, London, 1981, p. 125.
9. Peter R. Odell and Kenneth E. Rosing, *The Future of Oil*, Kogan Page, London, 1980.
10. Figures taken from the CEGB 1979–80 Development Review appear in the report by The Monopolies and Mergers Commission, *op. cit*, Ref. 2, Table 5.1.
11. Mr David Howell, the then Secretary of State for Energy, made a statement to the House of Commons on 18 December 1979 in which he outlined plans for future ordering of nuclear power stations. Mr Howell's statement, along with some reactions from the House of Commons, appears in *Atom*, (No. 28) pp. 34–37 (February 1980).
12. Nigel Lucas and Dimitrios Papaconstantinou, 'Electricity planning under uncertainty: Risks, margins and the uncertain planner', *Energy Policy* 10 (No. 2) pp. 143–152 (June 1982).
13. Dimitrios Papaconstantinou, 'Power system planning under uncertainty using probabilistic simulation', Internal Report EPU/DP/1, Energy Policy Unit, Department of Mechnical Engineering, Imperial College of Science and Technology, London, May 1980.
14. Tom Berrie, 'Interactive load control', series of six articles appearing monthly in *Electrical Review* from 11 September 1981 to 12 February 1982.

15. A.J. Abdulkarim and N.J.D. Lucas, 'Economies of scale in electricity generation in the United Kingdom', *International Journal of Energy Research* 1 (No. 3) pp. 223–231 (July–September 1977).

PART III

Aspects of United Kingdom Energy Demand

Chapter 7

Energy Conservation Policy in the Building Sector

Pat O'Sullivan and Robin Wensley***

Any effective energy policy must be based on a recognition of the elements of demand as well as supply. No easy task when supply policy traditionally involves only a very limited number of large utilities, whereas demand policy involves influencing the behaviour of a large number of uncoordinated individuals and organisations.

Now the published evidence of the Select Committee on Energy suggests that no direct market mechanism exists whereby the value of a demand decision can be directly compared with the value of a supply decision. The Government can and does invest directly in supply: whereas investment in demand reduction depends on the action of others *at best* under the influence of Government. Yet in the absence of such direct market mechanisms, any demand (conservation) policy requires not only the *establishment* of such values but also the *solutions* to the problems of getting the demand (conservation) market to respond to these values once established.

In fact the direct policy options to effect policy are limited and are incorporated in the current UK Energy Policy (and indeed the

* Professor of Architecture, University of Wales.
** London Business School.

energy policies of many other countries) namely:

> maintaining 'correct' energy prices
> providing information and incentives
> legislation to ensure minimum standards

The purpose of this chapter is to consider to what extent and indeed how the results of field measurements and consumer response measurements should be used to modify the ways in which specific demand policy actions are initiated and evaluated once the initial investment options (the major directions) have been established. Our particular expertise lies in the Building Design and Construction Industry sector which accounts for 50% of UK energy demand, and we will argue from this standpoint. We would suggests however that these arguments are representative.

Our view is that the implementation of a demand (conservation) policy within a market system should incorporate the means for:

> The recognition of and distinction between major trends and anomalies from the results of 'field' and consumer measurements.
>
> Developing measures to influence and reduce the effects of such anomalies through market intervention; as opposed to a major re-evaluation of policy that is required if it appears that major trends in the behaviour of the market have been wrongly perceived.
>
> Evaluating the effects of such measures to learn and hence improve later interventions.

ENERGY POLICY AND CONSUMER RESPONSE

To estimate the efficacy of any particular policy programme a realistic model of market response is required. To estimate demand, it is necessary to specify the form of the benefit stream. However there have often been problems in defining the nature of the actual benefits in the case of energy demand.

In the field of home insulation some of the evidence of actual behaviour — such as in loft insulation — is consistent with a simple benefit concept based on the price of energy saved. Even in this case however it is important to recognise that loft insulation often fails to result in the full 'expected' reduction in energy demand because some of the effect is taken in terms of increased room temperatures (i.e. comfort). This can, of course, be readily incorporated into a traditional model on the assumption that the effective price of the relevant good (cost per degree of room temperature) has been decreased by insulation measures. In the case of the market for double glazing, however, it has become necessary to recognise that such a simplistic model of the benefits is not adequate to explain observed behaviour. Hence it becomes apparent that, excluding substantial secondary benefits in particular cases such as noise reduction, effective room space may also be a key concern. Whilst the 'cold zone' might have seemed just the figment of a clever advertising agency it actually apparently embodies an important concept for many consumers: that double glazing means a larger living space is available during the winter months. One only needs to consider the importance that developers have always attached to overall floor space to realise that in these terms double glazing could easily prove to be a very cost effective investment compared to loft extensions which also have the added disadvantage of tampering with the roof.

Estimation of energy demand therefore raises three separate but related concerns: the correct specification of the benefit parameters; the imputed value of individual parameters on the basis of observed behaviour and the final concern with estimating such values prior to

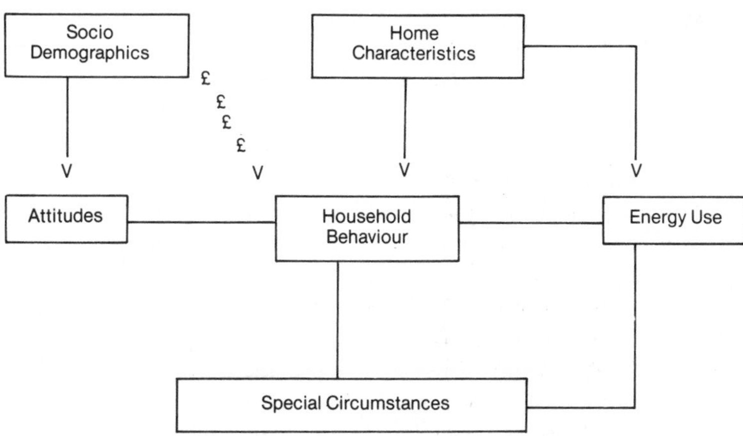

Fig. 7.1: Causal Model of Household Energy Use

actual consumer behaviour. Recently Vehallen and Raaji (1981) developed a simple causal model to explain energy use in 145 households (Fig. 1).

Energy policy in the UK has been concerned with influencing a number of these causal elements in particular home characteristics in the sense of physical building structure and household behaviour.

MODIFICATIONS TO THE PHYSICAL STRUCTURE OF BUILDINGS

Two overall issues must be considered in the case of modifications to the physical structure. First, careful consideration must be given to the extent to which any particular investment option does incorporate significant irreversibilities in terms of demand options. Second, there is a broad choice in policy terms between achieving changes by legislation as opposed to encouragement.

The impact of physical structure options on future demand choices is often not obvious. To take a current example the extensive use of wall hung gas boilers for domestic central heating has meant that future conversion to an alternative fuel will prove to be much more costly than in the case of the older free standing boilers. The reason for this problem lies not so much in the design of the boilers themselves but in the ways in which their small size and balanced flue system is exploited to install them in inaccessible places such as under kitchen sinks. Hence greater and less costly flexibility for fuel conversion at a later date depends less on the actual equipment and much more on the particular installation practice.

Legislation to achieve desired standards raises concerns both about the welfare costs of any imposition and also the likely effect on actual energy use itself. In a number of areas we have to recognise that the actual in-use performance differs significantly from the various assessments of technical potential. Verhallen and Raaji (1981) quoted evidence that some of the energy saving benefits of home insulation are reduced by higher levels of ventilation. Actual building practice in the installation of materials such as loft insulation can either reduce the effective energy savings of the measure or indeed in the other direction cause significant risks of timber rot if the insulation material is pushed into the eaves in pitched roofs (Sanders, 1981). More complex issues arise in assessing the in-use performance of energy savings measures related to lighting. Here there is evidence that even with significant levels of manual override, substantial savings can be achieved (Crisp, 1981; Crisp and Ure, 1980).

These various problems suggest that attempts to change the physical structure by legislation should explicitly consider:

the likely range of actual energy demand from individual users (in use performance) when technical standards are actually set;

the areas where in-use performance is likely to be greatest rather than technical potential;

the areas where in-use performance is robust to a wide range of possible user behaviours;

However carefully a programme of legislation is evaluated it still has significant welfare risks attached to it in that it has to be based on providing solutions to what by definition is a very variable and heterogeneous problem. In many instances this therefore suggests that a programme of encouragement to influence consumer behaviour might well prove a more attractive choice.

INFLUENCING BEHAVIOUR

Various policy measures can therefore be considered that are designed to influence individual behaviour. Some, such as specific incentives are designed to influence investment behaviour whilst others such as the original 'Save It' campaign are intended to have their principal effect on energy consumption behaviour within the given physical structure. In a number of other cases however this distinction is much less clear: for instance we can consider investments in better feedback and control systems which would then provide the facility for more cost effective patterns of consumption.

In the context of various such policy measures it has seemed reasonable to assume that a change in generalised attitudes would be a lead indicator for a change in behaviour. This would certainly appear to have been the thinking behind both the development of the original 'Save It' campaign in the UK to encourage energy conservation and also indeed the way in which the campaign itself was monitored through the attitude surveys by TNA (Phillips, Mills and Nelson 1977). In a wide range of consumer markets, however, there is evidence that changes in attitudes are not a good basis upon which to forecast changes in actual behaviour. This is not to suggest that attitudes may be unimportant but that the relationship between attitudes and behaviour is a complex iterrelated one and that in areas where attitudes seem to point in a rather different direction from behaviour, as they often do in the case of energy conservation, we should not assume that it is the attitude direction which will prove to dominate.

Various other policy measures have been designed merely to provide individuals with better and more relevant information. There is substantial evidence that individual householders, for instance, are ill informed both about energy use patterns for various activities and also the workings of even simple control systems. Work by Gaskill and Ellis, for instance has established that such additional information can have a significant effect on energy use patterns as well as, although to a less marked extent, more direct and specific feedback on actual energy consumption.

AN INTEGRATED APPROACH

The Verhallen and Raaji (1981) survey also involved the estimation of the extent to which the variability in specific variables was related to variability in others within the causal structure (Fig. 2).

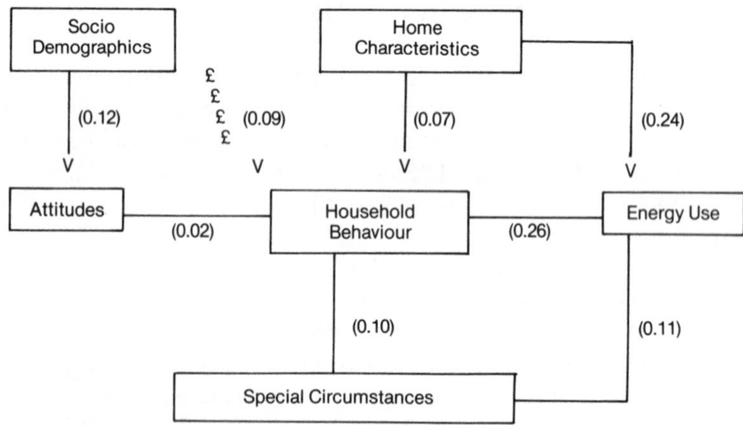

Fig. 7.2: Relationship Amongst Groups of Variables Related to Household Energy use (numbers with arrows are the proportions of the explained variance of the relevant dependent variable)

This survey clearly suggests that an understanding of actual energy use in households has to be based on knowledge of behaviour and home characteristics rather than more generalised factors such as attitudes or socio-demographics.

A further crucial question is the extent to which these two factors can be treated independently. Although the above study suggests only a limited degree of inter-relationship, other work by O'Sullivan and McGeevor (1982) implies that the inter-relationship between these two factors can be strong. For instance their study suggests that an understanding of actual energy use requires a more comprehensive knowledge of the meaning of such use patterns in both their social and physical context (McGregor, 1981). Such an approach, for instance, leads to a hypothesis that in the absence of accurate knowledge, thermostat settings will be related to the warm up time of the principal living room.

Much of the design work on low energy buildings exhibit similar problems. It is, for instance, often based on a set of performance standards which despite their apparent logic do not conform well to the crucial concerns of users. Indeed even when attempts are made to register opinions, such as in the Bedford scale of perceived room temperatures, such a measure may still not properly reflect the underlying variable of comfort level. We now have extensive evidence that many designs can fail to achieve the designed energy savings often by a wide margin.

Responses to this problem have varied. At one extreme there is the temptation to remove the people variable from the equation altogether by developing more automatic systems with limited if any opportunity for over-ride. Except in rare instances however it appears that such actions will be self-defeating: they will only encourage even more substantial by-passing of the overall system. To have a real impact we need to recognise that certain designs are likely to be very sensitive to misuse by participants whilst others will be much more robust. Indeed the problem is actually rather more fundamental: if buildings are to be designed that are actually pleasant to live and work in, then design criteria must be based on what people actually want.

INTERVENTION WITHIN A MARKET FRAMEWORK

The fact that the energy demand is complex and confusing is not in itself a justification for a wide range of policy interventions. Current UK policy is pursued within an overall market framework based on giving 'correct' price signals to both individual and corporate energy users. Although it is true that current policy also includes significant interventions in terms of both information and intervention, we would first like to consider the evidence that such actions are indeed necessary over and above an exclusive price signals' policy.

In areas where it proves extremely difficult to estimate demand an exclusive price signals' policy can be justified on two rather different bases. It can be because it provides a means whereby consistent expectations are established amongst energy users with respect to future energy prices but then each individual responds to such information in ways that they consider appropriate. On the other hand it can be argued that prices should anyway be based on supply costs and that even if consistent expectations are not established, further intervention will be difficult to justify because of the considerable uncertainties attached to its effects. How then can we judge the efficacy of a price signals' policy? We can focus our attention on the very expectations which should be directly influenced by energy prices and test whether this is indeed the case. Alternatively, we can indeed look at actual behaviour but apply caution in assessment as we discussed above. Like many product and particularly service markets there is no proper futures market and hence individual valuations cannot be adjusted by arbitrage. Hence, in terms of actual behaviour we must expect to observe a number of 'failures' in that individuals do not adopt 'economic' measures; but then lacking a trading mechanism for market valuation the concept of an 'economic' measure is itself distinctly dubious. We should be therefore more concerned about the scale and extent of such failures rather than their existence. Finally we can consider the evidence of adequate linkage between relevant expectations and action: the extent to which individuals have access to the appropriate information to respond effectively, from their own point-of-view.

Most of the criticism of energy policy in the demand sector has focussed on the second criteria: that of observed behaviour. Such problems have been extensively detailed in the evidence to the Select Committee but include the failure to incorporate obvious energy efficient measures in some commercial buildings; the fact that highly cost effective energy saving measures have not yet been adopted in various segments of the private housing market; the fact that Local Authorities have proved to be very unwilling, in certain cases, to adopt worthwhile measures and finally the very partial response of the industrial sector to energy saving options. Less work has been done directly on consumer price expectations but a recent survey of energy price expectations although highly variable did average around the desired level (Table 1).

The policy questions remain important on the basis of this information. First to what extent is such a wide range of expectations

Table 7.1. Consumer Fuel Price Expectations

	Next Year (% Increase)				Next Five Years (Compared to overall inflation)				
	−10	10–15	16–20	20+	−½	½–1	1	1–2	2
Oil	9	31	17	8	1	5	24	28	8
Gas	12	41	16	7	1	6	28	28	7
Electric	12	42	17	7	1	7	28	29	7
Coal	15	38	10	4	2	5	34	22	6

itself acceptable? Second there is clear evidence of a very limited degree of discrimination between various fuels. In the context of inter fuel comparisons it is clear that a price signals' policy on its own will take a considerable time to influence expectations in a consistent manner.

Third, there still appears to be only a very limited understanding about the means to respond to such energy price expectations anyway. From an overall view the net effect of price signals in such circumstances can be a feeling of impotence and intense annoyance. To quote a recent survey of consumers by Sadler and Spencer (1982):

> 'The current situation has engendered a deep distrust of government policy on energy (frequent price rises) and to cynicism about the fuel boards ever being willing to promote energy saving "at the expense of profits".'

It is therefore clear that however elegant a policy solution which relies solely on energy price signals, it will not avoid substantial economic and political costs. This is not, of course, to suggest that such an approach should be in any sense abandoned but more that it needs to continue to be supplemented as it has in the past, by additional measures in the form of information, incentives and legislation. We would further suggest that such measures must be seen as part of a coherent policy process that ensures that additional measures are only introduced when there is reasonable evidence that they will have an impact on the identified problem.

A COHERENT ENERGY DEMAND POLICY

A coherent energy demand policy implies two basic considerations:

> The intention of any particular measure must be considered within the overall market framework.
>
> Each measure must be a response to the recognition of a specific problem; based on a clear link between the policy action and the influence on end use behaviour; and subject to later evaluation as to its effectiveness.

The overall market framework means that specific problems must be seen in the context of both individual expectations and valuations. As we discussed above it is not sufficient to justify action on the basis of a range of individual responses but on evidence of excesses. Such excesses can clearly result from imperfections in the economic system: in particular income tax, risk, separation of costs and benefits and time horizon.

Income tax effects have a significant effect in distorting the economic logic of the market particularly in the area of household expenditure. It is widely recognised that the private householder has little if any opportunity to earn a real rate of return on his or her investments unless they are willing to accept a very significant level of financial risk. This compares with the private capital market where real rates of return tend to vary from around nil in the case of government securities to around 10% in the case of high risk equities. Hence the Treasury Test Discount Rate (TDR) of 5% in real terms relates to the medium level risk returns in the private sector without any consideration of income tax effects. The householder, however, also has to establish whether the benefits are also subject to such taxes as are most direct investment options. Hence investments where the benefits are actually in the form of reduced expenditure are particularly attractive because such benefits are not taxable. In such areas it is therefore quite likely that the use of the TDR criteria to assess policy options whilst perfectly legitimate in its own terms will not reflect the criteria that will be applied by the market.

It is also important to recognise that the issue of risk also arises in determination of the appropriate discount rate. Whilst the TDR is based on the opportunity cost of medium risk capital in the private sector, it is clearly not the appropriate one to use if the actual risks in any particular instance are either significantly above or below this medium level. In the area of individual energy conservations investments this raises two particular issues both derived from the concept of each person as a holder of a portfolio of assets. First the risk to be considered is only the systematic risk, that is the proportion of the variance which is correlated with the variance of the portfolio as a whole. Although detailed empirical work needs to be done in this area it would seem as if, *a priori*, energy saving investments are likely to be reasonably attractive in that for those who already have a portfolio of financial investments little of the particular risks attached to such an investment will actually be systematic with the rest of the portfolio. Second, however, it is clear that there are substantial risk disadvantages to those who possess non-tradeable assets (in particular only their future earning potential) which has an impact in various areas. It has been recognised that the result of consumers rather than the taxpayers bearing the risks in energy supply investment can be substantial welfare costs to such groups who tend to be disadvantaged in broader terms already (Evans, Franks and Hodges 1981); such groups are also likely to fail to undertake various investments in the area of energy conservation purely because of the absolute size of the investment compared with their available resources.

A different economic problem is to be observed in the commercial sector where the costs and benefits of any particular investment are organisationally very distinct: costs for instance may fall directly on the maintenance budget whilst any resultant savings will tend to appear under the broad category of factory overhead. In the case of commercial properties such as offices the problem can be much more acute because separate and totally independent organisations are involved. Laing, for instance, in evidence to the Select Committee commented on situations in which it is the developer or head landlord who bears the costs of energy conservation measures while the individual leasees actually reap the benefits.

A final imperfection in the market mechanism arises in the extent to which the real value of energy related investments is actually reflected in the market value of the asset which incorporates them. There is, for instance, substantial evidence that private house prices are only significantly determined by a limited number of factors: size, location, and number of rooms. Other elements, and in particular energy conservation investments are very much second order and are therefore extremely unlikely to have any significant effect on the market value of the property. For this reason a crucial element in the decision of the individual householder is the appropriate time horizon which is unlikely to exceed expectations about his future mobility. Given the fact that the mean length of stay is around 7 years with an investment lifetime of at least 20 years it is unlikely that there will be a significant level of underinvestment, particularly if the real discount rates to be applied are relatively low.

None of these imperfections should be seen to justify intervention in its own right: they merely suggest that we can expect to encounter specific problems in end use response however consistent the price signals policy. *A Fortiori*, this will be even more true in the case in which political constraints mean that there are limitations to the extent to which a long term pricing policy can be pursued indifferently to shorter term considerations.

Intervention needs therefore still to be based on recognition of specific and significant problems in market behaviour. Clearly one key issue in energy demand policy is the means by which this recognition is triggered. A continuous programme of monitoring end use behaviour must be at least one of the ways in which problems can be identified. At the same time it is also possible to consider the specific economic issues raised above as a means of identifying the structural conditions under which problems are likely to arise. This combination of structural and behavioural conditions as the trigger to energy policy intervention has close analogies to other policy areas such as regulation.

Having recognised a particular problem, it is important that the actual action proposed is justified in terms of its likely effect on end use behaviour. This may actually mean that the detailed nature of the problem must be investigated before action can be proposed. Such an investigation may need to consider not only the potential causes of the problem but also the evidence of the efficacy of various policy interventions in the case of previous analogous problems. In this context it is important to recognise that we now have a significant body of information about the impact of various energy conservation measures particularly in the US (McDougall, Claxon, Ritchie and Anderson, 1981).

Finally this process of learning and improvement needs to be continued with any new policy intervention: a continual process of evaluation is required. This has happened previously in certain areas, in particular the monitoring of the 'Save It' campaign. Unfortunately this extensive monitoring has only been publicly reported to a limited extent and on the available evidence it also failed to relate much of the attitude monitor data to actual behaviour. This is a crucial problem in programme evaluation in the conservation field since to quote Ritchie, McDougall and Claxton (1981):

> 'Consumers have expressed strong conservation views (opinion research) and have claimed to have done a wide range of conservation actions (self-reported behaviours). Even a cursory analysis of aggregate energy consumption indicates that these statements must reflect considerable exaggerations.'

On the other hand we would not wish to suggest that the process of evaluation of specific initiatives is easy. In general terms there is also considerable evidence that programme evaluation must be treated with considerable caution, particularly if it is to be viewed as objective (Pressman and Wildavsky, 1973). In a related manner it is often difficult to define an adequate measure of the specific output of an individual initiative. There is also a very significant problem in the nature of the risks involved. It is likely that most specific initiatives within a market framework will be undertaken in areas where outcomes and reponses are not easy to predict. In this sense therefore most specific interventions are risky in that there can be little certainty that they will result in the desired behaviour. In some instances this risk is masked as in the case of much legislation about building standards in which the risk becomes not that the standards are not followed but that they do not actually have the desired effect on energy use. In other cases, such as informational or financial initiatives the 'failures' will be more obvious and direct. From an evaluative perspective, however, there is little *a priori* reason to classify a specific intervention as ill judged merely because it failed. Indeed an overall programme which resulted in few if any such failures would suggest a series of not only safe but probably unnecessary initiatives. On the other hand if a longer term programme of interventions exhibits a high failure rate then this might suggest that information about demand has not been adequate to justify the level of intervention.

REQUIREMENTS FOR ENERGY DEMAND POLICY

We have argued in this paper that a focus on actual energy use behaviour suggests that an Energy Demand Policy based solely on price signals will prove to be not only ineffective but also probably politically damaging because of consumer frustrations. This is not to suggest that fuel prices should not reflect the economic cost of relevant resources but that other issues need also to be considered. For instance, even within the area of price signals themselves there are serious problems since household consumers are actually provided with very limited information about future pricing. Hence we observe the continued popularity of gas space heating and at the same time suspicions about the restricted electricity tariff based on the earlier proposal in the early seventies that it should be discarded.

Policy, therefore, will continue to require additional elements to assist in the balancing of short and long term interests and ensure that useful information is provided. Other specific problems will need to be tackled as part of a coherent policy in areas such as legislation. Policy will also need to encourage a programme of initiatives based on a process of recognition, influence and evaluation. Such a programme will inevitably be fragmented but will maintain a coherent focus on identified problems and end use behaviour. We would suggest that in the UK there are a number of specific areas which would justify early attention. These include the possible area of fuel targets in the case of gas space heating where evidence suggests that there will be very significant misallocations if policy relies solely on prices. In this context it is worthy of note that a 1981 study by Ritchie, Claxton and McDougall suggested there was even a consumer preference for energy rationing over major price increases. It is also evident from the evidence to the Select Committee that there is wide confusion in Government, Industry and amongst householders as to the appropriate means to evaluate investments in energy conservation. Rather than encourage an arcane debate amongst economists, the important concern is that useful and understandable advice is provided so that the approaches being used are at least reasonably correct.

Finally, we would suggest that Research, Development and Demonstration should also be considered in this framework. It is likely that certain promising conservation options may not get off the ground without either sponsorship at the R & D stage or encouragement at the dissemination stage. In an economic sense, R & D should be concerned with investment in developing options when the actual forms of use remain unclear: it is indeed the very optional nature of the investment which tends to move the opportunity out of the private sector and into the public. If the R & D effort related clearly to one specific type of activity we could reasonably expect it to be undertaken by those firms operating in the area. In terms of the criteria for such investments, we should value highly those options which have a very wide variability of potential outcomes and therefore also expect a considerable failure rate in our R & D programme. Hence as R & D progresses on any particular option we must expect to learn more about them and inevitably a number will become clearly non-viable. Simultaneously, however, we should be conducting a search of new options to ensure that our R & D portfolio does not stagnate.

The issues in the area of demonstration are clearly different: we are concerned with speeding up the adoption process for a particular item as well as making a final evaluation of its effectiveness. The criteria to be applied therefore relate both to evidence that the particular programme is a cost effective means of speeding the process of technology transfer (Phillipson 1978) and also the evidence that from a technical point of view in use effectiveness will really be tested.

The most important single concern is that effective interventions within the framework discussed above are actually taken. Much information is already available to identify important anomalies but it needs to be integrated to justify a coherent programme. An important issue in any such programme is the need to ensure that related actions are taken by various government departments including Energy, Environment and Industry.

Chapter 8

Interactive Load Control and Energy Management

*T.W. Berrie, B.D. Mallalieu and K.R.D. Mylon**

MICRO ELECTRONICS IN THE SERVICE OF ENERGY ECONOMICS

'A small step for man, but a big step for mankind' — could apply not only to men on the moon but also to micro-processors in the world of interactive load control and energy management.

Energy Management Systems are those devices which seek to minimise energy usage and maximise plant usage such that maximum productivity ensues. Though such systems can be human or mechanised, we are considering the latter type in this paper.

Starting from simple, electro-magnetic devices e.g. time switches and relays, etc., energy management equipment quickly utilised the computing facilities which became widely available only a few years ago and initially sophisticated, large, centrally-based systems were developed to monitor and control extensive buildings, campuses or industrial plant, where all loads can be wired back to the main equipment. With the rapid development of micro-electronics these were followed by smaller, microprocessor-based, distributed, intelligent, stand-alone outstations interconnected with centralised super-

* **Ewbank and Partners Limited and Ewbank Energy Management**

visory mini or micro computers. The outstations can communicate, when necessary, with the remote central supervisory equipment, which can interrogate the local outstation when data is required or can initiate energy management commands. Outstations can be situated some considerable distance from the central supervisory station and from each other, and make use of direct tie-line or auto dial-up PTT links using modems or use the electricity distribution system (PLC) for communication. This development introduced the potential for an extensive distributed network of intelligent, stand-alone systems interconnected via hierarchical, communication facilities used intermittently. These, in turn, gave birth to 'two-way' interactive control, whereby not only can the outstations be programmed locally by the operator to monitor and control independently their own local operations, but they can also react to the overall power system and consumer load demand changes. They can, therefore, interact with each other to maintain system balance.

Professor Tabors of MIT has coined a term from biology to describe this type of system, which he calls 'Homeostatic control' — the original meaning being 'to maintain internal balance' and used here to mean both physical and economic dynamic balance. Homeostatic producer/consumer control, like that just described, seeks to manage energy (or services) consumption over a distributed, intelligent network by the means of incentives, voluntary restrictions and temporary disconnections.

As we shall see, interactive load control is the next logical step to take in energy pricing following the spread throughout the world of tariffs based on marginal costs.

This type of control provided the facilities for communication of price and tariff incentives to persuade producers and consumers to purchase, sell or sometimes shed supplies at times beneficial to the parties involved, which as we shall see later is the basis for spot pricing. The 'spot' local price of the electrical energy or service can be related to the effect on the producers/suppliers costs of meeting the current national demand and be communicated to the consumers. These spot prices can be adjusted at regular intervals and moved up or down to match the system marginal, variable production cost at any point in time. Customers can thus have considerably more scope for reducing their bill by 'playing the electricity stock market', even compared to what they have already had under existing energy management schemes. Furthermore, the load management facilities available encourage, for example, the main electricity producer to optimise his own plant and fuel sources (including renewables) at different diurnal/seasonal periods, as well as to encourage private electricity producers (e.g. industry) to generate at peak periods in return for prices commensurate with the system marginal variable cost of production. This option can minimise the national total of new plant capital investment and utilise the nation's resource of standby, private generation capacity. Such facilities will flatten the diurnal load demand curve, increase energy conservation and improve the nation's cash-flow.

In this paper we confine most of attention to energy in the form of electricity, in that it is with electrical energy that most progress has been made with both interactive load control and energy management systems.

Electricity pricing was traditionally based[1] on **average costs**; the tariff level was determined from annual financial targets using historic costs from the utility's accounting books; the tariff structure ensures that each consumer paid his 'share' of the cost of supply in capacity costs and fuel burn. Average cost pricing gives 'signals' based only upon the present and the past; any future monies needed are ignored.

In recent years, **marginal cost** pricing has been introduced mainly to overcome this defect and it is now the declared policy of most power utilities in the world.

In marginal cost pricing past or 'sunk' costs are of no significance; only uncommitted capital and running costs provide the correct 'signal' to the consumers making additional demands.

Marginal cost pricing was the first step towards uniting electricity producers and consumers in a joint optimisation of their objective functions, which unity comes to a completion in **spot pricing.** Marginal cost tariffs are still based, to some extent, on the past development plans made some years before the tariffs are actually used, i.e. they are 'prescribed' tariffs. Spot pricing is in no way prescribed.

Marginal capacity related (per kW) charges are determined mainly from the capital costs of installing new plant or delaying the scrapping of old plant to meet an increase in demand of kW at time of system peak. The new generating plant is costed as either the 'mix' of the most recent type by fuel and size or as the 'predominant plant type and size' being currently installed.

In a marginal cost pricing system, because only consumers increasing system peak demand normally lead to additional generation, no capital charges are levied on additional demands appearing 'off-peak'. This was not necessarily the case under average cost pricing when some averaging out of historic costs amongst all consumers was often done.

Marginal energy related charges include mainly fuel, plus operating and maintenance costs of the system to meet an incremental kWH at any particular time and system location.

Marginal consumer related charges are for connections, metering and billing. These are small and are usually determined by trending past costs and extrapolating.

However, there are difficulties with marginal cost tariffs. For example, marginal fuel costs at times near system peak are often many times those off-peak. In practice, it is impolitic to reflect the full difference in tariffs. Also, marginal cost tariffs do not guarantee that the utility's financial targets will be met. Marginal cost tariffs do not guarantee that the utility's financial targets will be met. Marginal cost tariffs can be costly to administer and, to be applied satisfactorily, need to have some consumer response on the latter's reaction to them. They are most suited to large consumers in developed countries. In developing countries and for small consumers, the capacity charges are usually incorporated into the energy charges to simplify the tariff.

Increases in fossil fuel costs are often allowed for in electricity tariffs by a 'fuel cost adjustment' clause which automatically adjusts the tariff upwards with each increase in fossil fuel cost. This helps to make such tariffs less 'prescribed' from past planning exercises.

LOAD MANAGEMENT

The first load management[2] schemes of electrical energy were a direct consequence of using marginal cost tariffs because, under these, if consumers will reduce their load at times of system peak demand, this saves the power utility incremental capacity costs plus heavy running costs, which savings can then be passed on to such consumers.

Most people regard electricity as a 'premium' fuel, i.e. a fuel of a most refined grade compared for example with oil or coal. Conserving and optimising energy thus applies especially to electricity. There are many other reasons for conserving electrical energy, except at prodigious cost. Also, in order to produce and use electricity more efficiently overall, it is important to improve the load factor of the power system so as to minimise total (capital and running) electricity production costs. An improved system load factor results in more efficient use of existing plant, and reduces the need for new plant, thus resulting in lower costs to the power utility, which can then be passed on via tariffs to consumers, and especially those who participated in the load management schemes.

Load management considered with respect to peak and off-peak electricity usage[3] has been part of pricing policy of utilities for some time. Before marginal cost pricing was widely used, there were several approximate ways of discouraging the use of electricity at times of peak.

Over the last 25 years, special peak and off-peak tariffs have been greatly developed. The earliest examples were in France and the UK. Table 1 shows their broad development in the UK. Changes in the general relative tariff level are due mainly to fuel cost changes

Figures 1 and 2 illustrate how the system demand against time curve has levelled out over the year in England and Wales, indicating continuous success in load management.

Only large loads warrant the expense of complicated metering and the complex explanatory leaflets which go with special peak-load tariffs; in these cases, load management by pricing is well worthwhile. Just as we saw above, off-peak load control by pricing filled in the troughs in the demand against time curve, whilst peak-load control by pricing is designed to flatten the peaks. Table 1 gives an illustration of peak load tariffs used for this purpose.

Consumers can thus be persuaded by pricing to instigate load management on their own behalf. However, load management can also be affected by direct physical control.[4] Such physical control has existed for just as long as peak/off-peak pricing incentives in the shape of the 'current limiter'; relatively simple devices to automatically disconnect all or part of a consumer's network when the consumer's demand reaches a prescribed cut-off point. The higher the

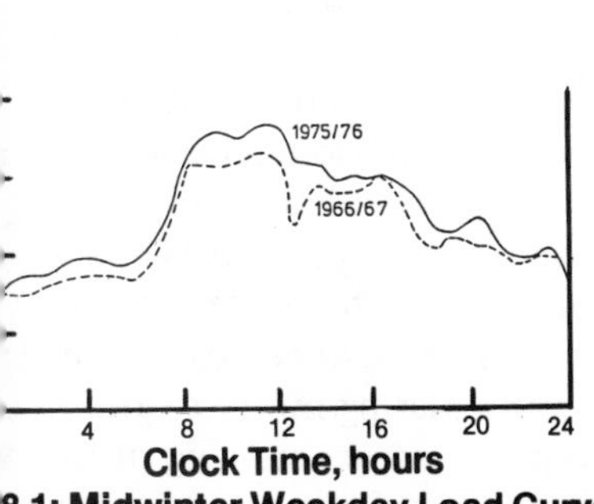

8.1: Midwinter Weekday Load Curves.
Industrial Load (at 0°C) Met at 1600 hours

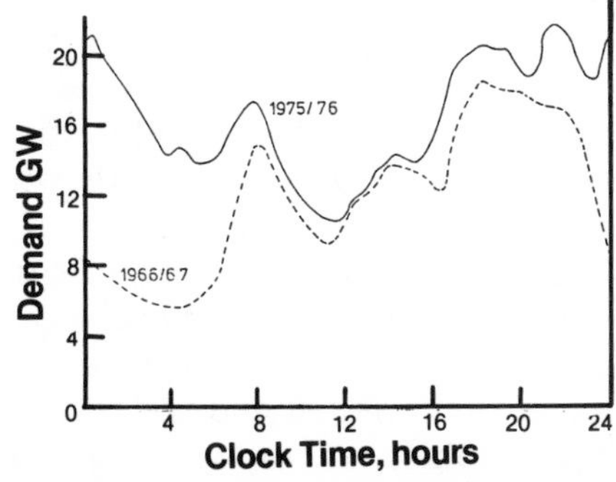

Fig. 8.2: Midwinter Weekday Load Curves.
Total Domestic Load (at°C) Met at 1200 hours

cut-off point, the higher the price which the consumer must pay for supply. There are now more sophisticated devices for fulfilling the same function:

(i) Time control devices which automatically switch loads off and on at the consumer's premises.
(ii) Manual control devices which switch loads off and on manually at the consumer's premises.
(iii) Centralised control devices which are sometimes capable of predictions using a computer.

INTERACTIVE LOAD MANAGEMENT

As stated initially in this paper, interactive load control is the next logical step to take in seeking to manage loads by energy pricing. By communicating varying spot prices to the consumer, he can be encouraged to load manage up or down and thereby benefit the energy supplier. Further encouragement can be given through a different optional tariff.

Under interactive load control at least three separate tariff options can be made available to consumers, e.g.

(i) A continuous electricity supply charged at a high-rate.
(ii) A programmed interruptible (off-peak) rate, and
(iii) Non-programmed interruptible (day and night) rate(s).

Consumers can have the facility of being able to program their loads to a selected tariff and the flexibility to vary them at will. Typically, electrical space storage heating or cooling would be allocated to the off-peak tariff; with water heating, freezers, fridges and air conditioners selected to the non-programmed interruptible tariff.

Electricity meter reading and possibly other services could normally be conducted remotely from the utility distribution HQ over the communications network with the eventual discontinuation of conventional manual methods, if this is considered to be economic. This facility will considerably speed up accounting procedures enabling virtually instant rendering of consumer billing, together with an elimination, by home display facility, of mailed invoices to consumers. However, should utilities wish to retain existing meter-reading, whilst taking advantage of the greater security of accounting available (e.g. elimination of corrupted figures), possibilities exist for sealed, portable recorders for meter readers to use. These devices would plug into the consumer's equipment memory, and could subsequently be read at the HQ computer. If required, a simply print out bill record could be handed to the consumer by the meter-reader.

Interactive control systems enable financial and accounting innovations to be introduced. Credit facilities can be offered to the consumer (possibly with incentive to maintain his electricity credit account healthy) by pre-payment from home, via bank direct-debit transfer. To assist this, an agreed credit limit can be programmed in which will initiate a warning to the electricity consumer and subsequently restrict the power supply to a predetermined level until credit is restored. Continuous display of current accounts for electrical energy and other services can be made available. Account closure and commencement due to change of tenancy or business can be very rapid, thereby avoiding previously experienced delays. Similarly, rapid revision of tariffs can be undertaken on a large scale and synchronised for all consumers.

Customers can also be offered expenditure control facilities by maximum demand limitation. This will give additional assistance to the utility in time of system peak demand to limit generation. The consumer would be able to nominate and program in a maximum kW (or kVA) demand which would initiate a warning and subsequent supply disconnection if the limit is exceeded, and until such time as load is reduced.

LOAD CONTROL, PROTECTION AND PLANNING

Individual, programmable, 'priority interrupt' consumer add-on devices can be incorporated to enable the shedding of appliances in a particular order consecutively by the control unit to reduce maximum demand. Restoration of supplies can be in reverse order. Such devices can also prevent non-interruptible loads (e.g. kidney machines) being disconnected. Such loads can be left connected and utilities register these customers on their records at the control centre.

Radio-frequency, broadcast 'teleswitch' signals can be received by some consumer units for the purpose of load management by disconnection of non-programmed, interruptible tariff circuits or initiation of maximum demand control. They can also be used to give daily reset signals to the real time clock within the consumer's equipment. Other systems use mains carried signalling to initiate load management. Such load shedding facilities should enable utilities to reduce supply cuts to a minimum. Many industrial and commercial organisations have already installed energy management systems to improve their profitability by better use of energy. The power utility's consumer interactive control units will have to interface with the consumer's own existing energy management systems. It is assumed that the utility will wish to leave to the consumer's management system, the decisions as to which items of plant can be shed at any particular time, when this function is already written into the existing software. However, the utility's interactive control units could have optional add-on consumer energy management programs at a fraction of the cost of existing energy management equipment packages and might then be particularly relevant to smaller industrial/commercial installations with simpler internal requirements.

Increased safety aspects can be provided to consumers by the protection systems incorporated in the devices. Earth leakage sensing protects consumers against faulty appliances (e.g. fraying earthy kettle leads, etc.). High and low voltage alarms could protect consumers' sensitive equipment. A 'supply failure' alarm could instantly be recorded in the utility's control centre and initiate rapid restoration of supply.

In addition, low frequency sensing can automatically disconnect the consumer, thereby avoiding massive, cascade system supplies failure, such as occurred some years ago in New York and London.

System monitoring from the utility control centre could also include alarms to indicate a consumer tampering with the device or attempting to by-pass the metering registers, thereby drastically reducing loss-of-receipts from illegal connections.

The individual interrogation facility from the control centre to measure consumers loads at any time would enable system planning requirements to be assessed and future forecasts to be more accurately predicted and subsequently monitored.

Although, the greatest developments have been within the electricity sector, similar facilities will be available for the measurement of other services, e.g. gas, water, telephones. In addition, measurements of oil tank levels, hot water tank temperatures or other instrumentation could easily be transmitted to the control centre over the network.

COMMUNICATIONS LINKS

For a system to qualify as Interactive, there must be some form of twoway communications with the supply utility. The choice will be governed not merely by economics but also the security of existing facilities. Three main types of technology are being utilised by the different companies developing systems, both here in the UK and in America.

Connection over telephone lines (PTT), which may be conventional cable or progressively optical fibre, seems to offer the most reliable two-way communication system. Since telephone lines can be used during times when they would otherwise be idle, it is clearly possible that an economic tariff for their use may be negotiated initially with the telephone company. However, once a system using this approach has been installed, there could be some cause for concern over the extent of future increased charges for line time. The systems works by detecting when the customer's telephone is out of use and if the line is not free when required, or communication is interrupted by someone making a telephone call, then the system will store the information and try again later. Although not offering guaranteed instant connection, this does provide a reliable method of intermittent communication. Consumers who have no telephone can still be serviced, since connection to any nearby telephone line will suffice.

Power line carried (PLC) or mainsborne, where signals are superimposed onto the power distribution system, can permit two-way communication. Smallscale tests carried out in the USA have revealed many potential pitfalls to be overcome before such systems as employed there can be considered satisfactory for large-scale use. Thorn-EMI claim to have avoided such problems by using a 'spread spectrum technique'.

Radio has been shown to have good potential for two-way communication in the USA, whilst in the UK a one-way radio signalling facility has been developed and tested. The cost of two-way radio and the availability of frequencies are the main problems with this approach, both of which can be largely overcome by use merely of a simpler one-way system for load management associated with a PTT link. However, the need for immediate transmission of load shedding instructions can be met by one-way radio signal. Tests have been conducted in the UK by East Midlands Electricity Board with a one-way load management system which uses coded 'teleswitch' signals on long-wave, BBC Radio 4 transmitted from Droitwich and Scotland, which can cover the whole country. Consumers receivers pick up the signals and controllers disconnect loads. Further trials are also due this summer and there are plans to develop this system into two-way, probably using telephone links.

In general, higher data transmission rates will be used with the higher quality communications links, e.g. direct-wired telephone lines.

DATA CONCENTRATION

While an individual consumer's telephone line will commonly exhibit a high proportion of idle time, this will not apply to main connections between exchanges. Furthermore, with so many consumers and the potentially enormous traffic in both directions between them and the supervisory station, it is clear that a hierarchial system is necessary to concentrate the communication messages in each direction. The upper level of such a hierarchical system would in turn be linked to other regions in a national scheme. Accordingly, a data concentrator would be placed in each local telephone exchange or local electricity substation, communicating directly to the nearest district office of the power supply company, probably over leased lines or the distribution network. This district office would in turn be connected to the regional control centre and financial accounting points. Load management and overall supervision would be covered 24 hours per day from this control centre by price signals, initiation of emergency load shedding, monitoring and accounting.

CURRENT INTERNATIONAL DEVELOPMENTS

Although many USA companies have been marketing energy management systems for some years, we understand that there are only about six currently developing two-way interactive control systems. These developments are apparently not as advanced as the UK designs. Some hardware manufacturers can offer equipment to interrogate consumers' terminals and meter remotely.

One-way utility load management trials have been conducted in the States for some time by switching loads on/off and load cycling. These have been over mainsborne and telephone links with air-conditioning being more successful. In the case of both loads, customers can store either coolth or heat to carry them over and may merely time-shift peak demand. Other tests for demand management were conducted over the radio with prior warning or disconnection. Trials have also taken place in the USA with different kinds of two-way communication links and were reported on last year as favouring telephone carrier rather than mainsborne or radio, though the latter methods have their individual advantages. No full-scale interactive load control trials are yet believed to have taken place in the USA, though partial tests have been conducted in San Diego and Illinois. Attempts are being made to initiate full-scale tests in California.

Meanwhile the interest in interactive load control with spot pricing grows in electricity authorities on both sides of the Atlantic (including Europe) and even developing countries, who see it as potential solution to serious shortages of plant capacity/availability or loss of receipts due to meter-reading corruption. There seems little doubt that the commercial sales will be very considerable when the systems have been successfully debugged and operated, and utility/consumer acceptance obtained.

SPOT PRICING

Let us now return to the topic of electricity pricing.

Marginal cost tariffs are based upon a prescribed load forecast, planned to be met by a least-cost development programme. These have had only mixed success in achieving either optimal load forecasts or optimal development; there are too many variables to be estimated accurately, e.g. the weather, consumer's demands, fuel costs, and plant availability.

As mentioned previously, recent events in the micro-processor and communications sectors make it now possible to set prices virtually at the instant in time that the electricity is consumed, rather than in the above predetermined way. These new 'spot' prices are based on the actual demand and plant conditions at the time the price is set.[5] Spot prices can be updated as often as every five minutes and even continuously, to give rapid response to system emergencies. Alternatively, they can merely be updated diurnally for a coarser, 'climatic' control.

On this basis, on a warm winter day, a spot price is lower than on a cold winter day; a circumstance not admissable under normal prescribed pricing and load management rules. The consumer and producer share alike in any good or bad fortune in the power system occurring at the instant in time of the consumption of the load, e.g. fuel being cheaper than normal, the weather being better than normal. Again, if the producer has more plant than normal, the spot price will be lower; the reverse will be true for having less plant that normal. The wastage caused by the spilling of water over dams and blackouts should both be avoided by spot pricing. Again, autoproducers will always receive a buy-back price equal to the spot price, i.e. generally much higher than buy-back prices at present.

Large consumers who make up a substantial part of demand covered by load management schemes are obvious choices for spot pricing because they will be more likely to pay for new measuring apparatus and to understand the 'message' in a spot price.

However, experiments are also proceeding using spot pricing with residential consumers, e.g. in the UK.[6]

Spot pricing thus attempts to set a price at the instant of demand. Tariffs with some form of spot pricing are not new,[7] e.g. spot pricing offered as a 'surcharge' during periods of likely plant shortages, as in Britain in the 'peak-load warnings surcharge' system for many hundreds of consumers.[8] Illinois Powder and Light Company offers spot pricing as an alternative to disconnection when plant is short[9] and may have some form of supported spot pricing for electricity demand/supply control.[10]

Spot pricing in electricity supply establishes, for the first time, a true 'market place' which enables consumers and producers to adjust supply/demand and price all simultaneously. It is workable whether a utility is publicly or privately owned, centrally or locally owned/controlled. Autogenerators and cogenerators are equal partners with mains generation and any concepts of 'firm' or 'unfirm' supplies, e.g. from renewables, are irrelevant. Electricity from any source whatever has a value/price at every instant it is available in accordance with supply/demand conditions at the time. Spot pricing also copes with electricity being a monopoly supply.

In this paper only the principles behind spot pricing can be illustrated; both the philosophy behind it and its application are in their infancy.

Some assumptions are made to keep the case simple and are as follows:

(i) All main generators are operated by some centrally controlled utility, authority or mechanism.

(ii) All capital costs and the cost of transmission and distribution losses are ignored.

(iii) Demand is never greater at any instant than total generation capacity.

(iv) The level of capital investment is chosen only once and at the start of the exercise, after which the number, type and size of the generating units remain constant.[11]

(v) Time series characteristics have second-order effects on electricity demand and operating costs; this is an assumption already used extensively in planning.

(vi) Generation start-up, shut-down and increase/decrease rates are costless and are not constrained from one period to the next.

(vii) Only current consumption determines the output function of a consumer, not past consumption.

(viii) Processes like storage are not considered except in some very obvious ways.[12]

(ix) Spot demands in each time period are independent.

(x) System running costs in each time period are independent.

The appropriate economic criterion to use for optimum decision making with spot pricing is global welfare optimisation. This means maximising the difference between the total value *per se* of electricity consumption generation, subject to electricity being available. The spot price derived at any time from such a welfare optimisation is both a 'buy' price for a net producer at that time, and a 'buy-back' price for a net producer at that time, i.e. production and consumption are treated symmetrically.

A SIMPLE GRAPHICAL SOLUTION

The solution to this simple case is shown by graphical means in Fig. 3, which plots the system marginal variable generation cost, i.e. the system lambda, against generating plant capacity (G) for a fixed (i) total capacity of plant and (ii) plant mix. The curve is either level or upward-sloping because generating units are always loaded in order of increasing variable marginal cost. The system marginal cost becomes infinite at or near the point G_{max} the vertical line in Fig. 3.

The cumulative generation cost T(G) is the area under the curve up to the value of G, representing the amount of committed generating plant at that instant. Thus $T(G_{max})$ is the total shaded area under the curve. This is the picture from the supply side.

Figure 4 shows an analogous picture from the demand side, i.e. a demand curve. The consumer sets his demand level where his own marginal value of productive output per unit equals the price i.e. at demand level D′ for price level p′ on Fig. 4. The shaded area is then the value of the consumer's production.

Optimal spot prices are obtained from superimposing Figs 3 and 4 in Fig. 5. With prices set at p′ on Fig. 4 shows that demand will be at D′. The shaded area in Fig. 5 is the net value of the short-run welfare function, i.e.

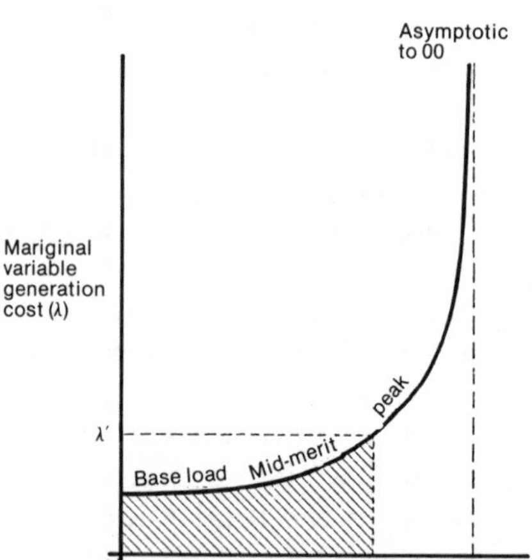

Fig. 8.3: Variable Generation Costs for Fixed Plant Capacity and Plant Availability

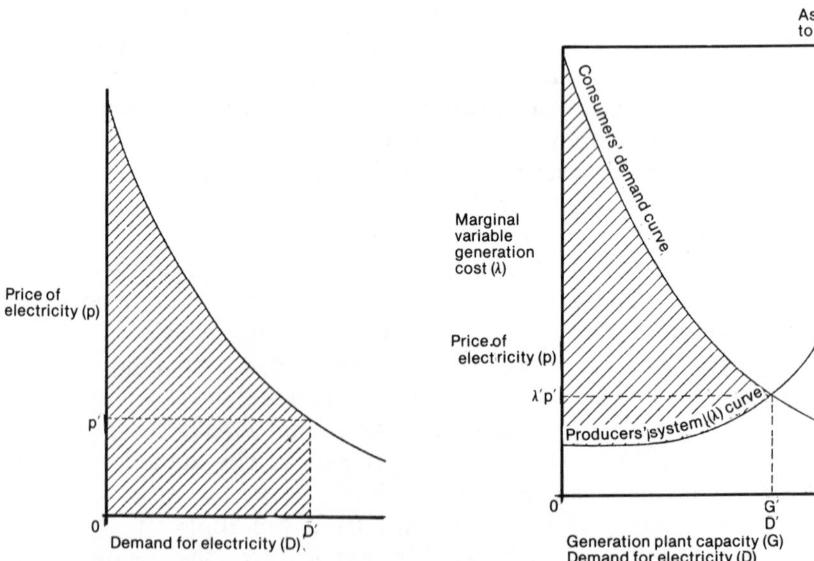

Fig. 8.4: Demand and Consumer Production Worth for Prescribed Demand

Fig. 8.5: Short-Run Welfare Value

(i) below the demand curve D, on the demand side; but
(ii) above the marginal-cost curve, on the supply side.

The shaded area gives:

> the value of the consumer's output production per unit of electricity at the margin, less the value of the producer's cost per unit of electricity at the margin.

Figure 5 shows spot pricing under normal conditions when there is at least adequate capacity to meet demand. The spot price p′ then exactly equals the short-run marginal variable cost of production λ′, i.e. at point p′ for demand D′. Figure 6 shows the mechanism for determining the spot price when all available capacity, including those of autoproducers, is fully used up. This time p′ must be set, in accordance with the previous assumptions, so that demand never increases beyond G_{max}, i.e. there is a 'premium' component in the spot price, extra to the short-run marginal variable cost of production to ensure that demand is always cut back to equal supply, i.e. in the absence of this premium load shedding would take place,

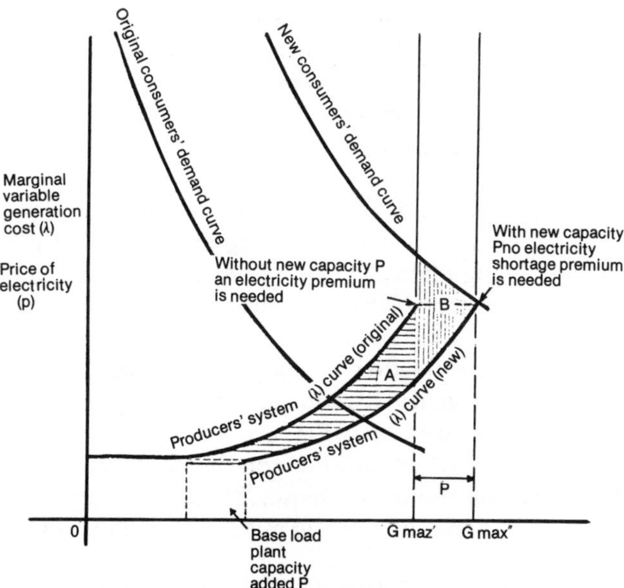

Fig. 8.6: Spot Pricing Under Normal Conditions

which is unallowable under our earlier assumptions. In practice unexpected lower availability of generating plant has the same effect as higher than expected demands. The higher the demand than expected or the lower the plant availability than expected, the larger will be the shortage 'premium' in spot price, over and above the short run marginal variable cost of production.

SPOT PRICING AND INVESTMENT

The normal investment rules of prescribed tariffs must be altered to accommodate spot pricing. To do this the earlier assumption is relaxed that spot prices are derived from a once-and-for-all quantity and mix of generating plant, with the actual realised values for demand and plant availability as random variables. The quantity and mix of generating plant to maximise total economic welfare is selected as before, but this time capital costs are taken into account. One generating plant item P is added onto the system and its effect is shown in Fig. 6. The value of the added generating plant P depends upon (i) the difference between the expected demand and the actual demand, and (ii) the actual availability of the additional plant. When not available, the additional generating plant contributes nothing to the spot price; when the plant is available the spot prices will be affected, as shown in Fig. 6. The shaded area is a graphical illustration of how the additional generating plant contributes to both the short-run welfare and the spot price. By adding the generating plant, the 'premium' to keep demand within available generating capacity limits is reduced; no premium at all may be needed after the addition, as shown in Fig. 6.

There will be a reduction in the total system fuel costs due to the introduction of the additional generating plant P if that plant is more efficient than existing plant. Thus building additional plant P has two components from which the investment rule can be deduced:

(1) The 'premium' needed to keep demand within available total generation capacity is reduced whenever plant P is available. This is shaded area B on Fig. 6.

(2) The fuel cost of generation for the spot price demand D′ in Fig. 6 will be reduced whenever plant P is operating and it is not the last generator in the merit-order. This is area A.

The total economic value of adding plant P is the summated value of these two components over the life of plant P. To examine what is the investment criterion under spot pricing, it is necessary to determine the total contribution to short-run welfare of adding an increment of plant P, as measured by the shaded areas in Fig. 6, over all possible values of demand and plant availability. This total contribution to short-run welfare is then compared with the increased capital cost of plant P. If the total contribution to short-run welfare is greater than the increased capital cost then plant P should be invested in.

LOOKING AHEAD

As stated earlier, commercially available two-way domestic equipment from the UK is planned to be on the market by the beginning of next year, to be followed by industrial/commercial units. Equipment from the USA will be available later.

However, commercial availability of hardware is one thing but individual utility economic viability and public acceptance is quite another matter and it may be some years before extensive introduction occurs worldwide. Economic pressures brought about by rising energy prices, ageing plant and the need to conserve energy may force the pace of introduction on hitherto unenthusiastic utilities and consumers. There is no doubt in our view that this is one of the most promising design concepts to revolutionise the world of energy tariffs and energy management for some years.

Spot pricing is likely to change the institutional arrangements in th electricity supply industry. First of all, spot pricing flourishes best under competition of generating plant. This makes autoproducers, cogenerators and power utilities of equal status in the electricity production process, a condition very different from today. Again spot pricing is likely to flourish best when (i) the spot price is set by a government regulated authority or authorities, private or publicly owned, who own and operate the transmission/distribution networks, (ii) private or publicly owned generators, autogenerators and cogenerators compete for supplying electricity to private or publicly owned wholesale or retail electricity loads.

Increases in size of electronic memory chips and in the capability of microprocessors, coupled with continuing decreases in price for a given performance or capacity will offer further technical support for the concept of spot-pricing, but a distinct potential reduction in the consumer's bill need to be demonstrated before widespread public acceptance of the system is likely.

Equipment and network developments will continue to proceed

apace as communications methods are advanced and transmission rates speeded up, enabling data to be processed more quickly and corrective action despatched sooner. Regional electricity distribution authority communications networks will probably be linked hierarchically on common highways to the national generation centres to optimise the use of primary energy sources and conservation. International power links will necessitate schemes being extended across national frontiers to further the cause of energy management. Problems that could occur are more likely to be concerned with social aspects and the sheer size of project management.

REFERENCES

1. Turvey, R. and Anderson, D. *Electricity Economics.* Published for the World Bank by the Johns Hopkins University Press, Baltimore 1977; Cicchetti, C.J., Gillen, W.J. and Smolensky, P. *The Marginal Cost and Pricing of Electricity*, Ballinger Pub. Co. Cambridge, Mass. 1977; Munasinghe, M. *Marginal Cost Based Tariff Calculations in Developing Countries*, EWT Dept. Report, World Bank, Washington DC 1979; Electric Power Pricing Policy, *World Bank Staff Working Paper* No. 340. 1980; Baumo, W.J. and Bradford, D.J. 'Optimal Departures from Marginal Cost Pricing', *American Economic Review*, pp. 265-283 (June 1970); and Feldstein, M.S. 'Distributional Equity and the Optimal Structure of Public Prices', American Economic Review, pp. 32-36 (1973). Also a good survey of the literature on time-of-day, etc. pricing and load management on power systems is given in: Morgan, M.G. and Talakdar, S.N. 'Electric Power Load Management: Some Technical, Economic, Regulatory and Social Issues'. *Proceeding of the IEEE* **67** (No. 2) pp. 241-313 (February 1979). Other useful papers are given in references (2), (3) and (4).
2. Acton, J.P., Gelbard, E.H., Hosek, J.R. and McKay, D.J. *British Industrial Response to the Peak Load Pricing of Electricity*, RAND report R-2508-DOW/DWP, Santa Monica, California, February 1980.
3. Manichaikul, Y. and Schweppe, F.C. 'Physical/Economic Analysis of Industrial Demand'. *IEEE Transactions on Power Apparatus and Systems*, **PAS-99** (No. 2) pp. 582-588 (March/April 1980).
4. MIT Energy Laboratory: New Electric Utility Management and Control Systems: *Proceedings of Conference*, MIT Center for Energy Policy Research and Electric Power Systems Engineering Laboratory, Report EL 79-024, June 1979.
5. Bohn, R.E., Caramanis, M.C. Schweppe, F.C. 'Optimal Spot Pricing of Electricity: Theory'. *MIT Energy Laboratory Working Paper*, MIT - EL 81 - 008WP, March 1981. Also 'New Electric Utility Management and Control Systems'; Proceedings of Conference held in Roxborough, Massachusetts, May 30 — June 1, 1979, by the Homeostatic Control Study Group, *MIT Energy Technical Report* No. MIT - EL - 79 - 024.

6. Trials for Seeboard's Interactive Control, *Electrical Review*, (26 June 1981).
7. Camm, F. *Industrial Use of Cogeneration Under Marginal Cost Electricity Pricing in Sweden*, RAND Report WD - 827 - EPRI, 1980; also Born, R., 'Industrial Response to Spot Electricity Prices: Some Empirical Evidence', *MIT Energy Laboratory Working Paper* MIT - EL - 080 - 016WO, February 1980; Gorzelnik, E.F. 'T - O - U Rates Cut Peak 3.5%; kWh by 1.3%. *Electrical World*, pp. 138-139 (15 September 1979).
8. Mitchell, A., Manning, W.G. and Acton, J.P. *Peak Load Pricing: European Lessons for US Energy Policy*, Ballinger Publishing Co., Ca,bridge, 1978.
9. ICF, Inc. 'Interruptible Electric Service for Industrial and Large Power Customers', Washington, D.C. Unpublished May 1980.
10. Schweppe, F.C. 'Power Systems 2000'. *IEEE Spectrum*, (July 1978); also Schweppe, F.C., Tabors, R.D., Kirtley, J.L. *et al.* 'Homeostatic utility Control'. *IEEE Transactions on Power Apparatus and Systems*, PAS - 99 (No. 3) (May/June 1980); Kepner, J. and Reignbergs, M. 'Pricing Policies for Reliability and Investment in Electricity Supply as an Alternative to Traditional Reserve Margins and Shortage Cost Estimations'. Unpublished MS. 1980.
11. Baleriaux, E.J., and de Guertechin, L.E. 'Simulation de l'exploitation d'un parc de machines thermiques de production d'electricite couples a des stations de pumage'. *Revue E, (edition SRBE)* 5, (No. 7), (1967).
12. Finer, S. 'Electric Power System Production Costing and Reliability Analysys Including Hydroelectric, Storage and Time Dependent Power Plants'. *MIT Energy Laboratory Technical Report* No. MIT - EL 006, February 1979.

PART IV

Taxation and Finance

Chapter 9

The Effects of Taxation of Petroleum Exploitation: A Comparative Study

*Alexander G. Kemp and David Rose**

Over the last decade Governments have given increasing attention to the taxation of petroleum production. The large increases in crude oil prices in 1973-74 and later in 1979-80 clearly focussed their attention on the large profits that could be made from this activity. Levels of taxation of this activity have now reached extremely high levels. In several countries oil companies have complained that the burden has become excessive and is impairing oilfield developments. The economic rents emanating from oil extraction are widely regarded as a suitable base for taxation but there is a danger that overzealous Governments will impose burdens which exceed the economic rents and thus cause disincentives and distortions. The dangers of this occurring are increased under most conventional systems of taxation which are not well-designed to extract economic rents to the state. Under conventional systems of taxation when marginal rates reach very high levels the dangers of distortion and anomalies are also increased.

In this paper the systems of taxation on oil exploitation applied under fifteen fiscal jurisdictions are examined from the viewpoint of

*University of Aberdeen. The full text of this paper with detailed methodology and results is available in the BIEE Archive.

their efficacy as collectors of economic rents. The main distortions emanating from overzealous taxation are then highlighted. The systems analysed are those in the United Kingdom and Norway, Australia, Indonesia, Nigeria, Egypt, Malaysia, Papua New Guinea, Alaska (two systems), US Outer Continental Shelf (US, OCS) (four systems) and Texas.

A BRIEF DESCRIPTION OF THE SYSTEMS

The fiscal regimes applied to oil exploitation generally incorporate special features and are often of remarkable complexity. The systems analysed here are those applicable to the exploitation of new oil fields. The terms are often more favourable than those applied to 'old' oil. In addition crude oil price regulations sometimes differ between 'old' and 'new' oil with higher prices being allowed for 'new' oil. Again the procedure has been to employ 'new' oil prices in the analysis. For most countries a world price of \$33.8 has been chosen for 1982. In Texas the price adopted is \$30 for 1982 and still lower levels have been used for Alaska. In some countries there is a domestic market obligation imposed on licensees or contractors to supply oil to the domestic market at very low prices. This also has been fully taken into account in the analysis. Such regulations apply to Nigeria and Indonesia. In Norway and Nigeria there is obligatory participation with the national oil companies on a carried interest basis. This has also been taken into account in the analysis. Withholding taxes are generally not included in the analysis.

The system in the UK for new fields consists of a royalty at 12½%, corporation tax at 52% and the special Petroleum Revenue Tax (PRT) at 75% incorporating the new Advance Petroleum Revenue Tax (APRT) at 20%. For corporation tax, capital allowances are available on 100% first year basis for the main items of investment expenditure. Royalties and PRT (but not APRT) are deductible. There is a ring fence round oil exploration and production activities in the UK and its Continental Shelf for purposes of this tax. The PRT is levied on a field-by-field basis. For this tax, capital allowances of 135% of field investment are allowed as a deduction on 100% first year basis up to the period of payback. Interest is not deductible. There is also an oil allowance equal to the value of 5 million tonnes with no more than ½ million tonnes being allowed in any one year. There is also a safeguard provision which in the total period up to 1.5 times the payback period reduces the annual PRT to zero when gross profits are less than 30% of accumulated field investment and puts a ceiling on PRT equal to 80% of the excess of gross profits over 30% of field investment. The new APRT is levied at a rate of 20% on gross revenues with an annual allowance of 1 million tonnes. No field will be liable for APRT for more than five years. The APRT is creditable against 'normal' PRT. If a field is so unprofitable that APRT has not been set off against 'normal' PRT within five years the amount not set off is then repaid. The APRT is also allowed as a deduction in computing payback for PRT purposes. The 'normal' marginal rate of tax is 89.5% and 93.5% if the field is in the safeguard.

In Norway, there is a sliding scale royalty ranging from 8% to 16% according to production rates. The higher rates apply to all output not just the increments. Income tax payable is a combination of national income tax at the rate of 27.8% and Municipal Tax at 23%. Depreciation for capital expenditure is allowed on a six-year straight line basis, but the allowances can only be utilised when production from the field to which they relate commences. Royalties are deductible. There is a Special Tax on oil production at the rate of 35%. Depreciation on the same basis as that for income tax is allowed. A further special allowance equal to the value of 6⅔% of capital expenditure over the previous 15 years is also available. Divided payments are deductible for the national Income Tax and in the analysis here the assumption of maximum dividend has been made as it is clearly advantageous to an investor. Special Tax is not deductible for income tax. A capital tax equal to the value of 0.7% of the value of net capital is also payable. It is not deductible for Income or Special Tax. Participation by Statoil is on a sliding scale basis related to the peak production from a field.

In Australia, royalties are at 10% of wellhead values in most states. Income Tax is at 46%. Capital allowances are based on the residual capital expenditure notion and a 20% declining balance method of determining the actual allowance. The system is more favourable than that applicable to industry generally. A 20% investment allowance is also available.

In Indonesia, production-sharing contracts are employed for oil exploitation with the oil companies becoming contractors. Signature bonuses of £1 million are common and production bonuses of £2 million when output reaches 50,000 b/d, and an additional payment when 100,000 b/d is reached. For purposes of cost recovery, intangible drilling and development costs are charged against income from a working area as soon as income becomes available. Tangible capital costs are depreciated over one half of the field life on a double-declining balance basis. A 20% investment allowance is allowed on tangible development costs and is deducted from gross production before production-sharing. The split of production after cost recovery and the investment credit is 65.9091% in favour of the state. Corporation tax is payable by contractors at the rate of 86%. Depreciation is on the same basis as that for cost recovery. There is also a tax on interest and dividends at the rate of 20% of profits after deducting corporation tax. There is a domestic market obligation at very low prices.

In Nigeria there is a system of posted prices. Royalties are based on this price, the rates being 20% for onshore production and 16 2/3% and 18½% for offshore depending on water depths. The Petroleum Profits Tax is at 85% and is based on the posted price minus notional costs (which were set at £1.50 per barrel in 1979 when the legislation was enacted) and a notional margin which was set at $0.80 per barrel. Royalties are deductible. Intangible drilling costs may be expensed and tangible development costs are depreciated over five years on a straight line basis. An investment tax credit is available at a rate of 5% of tangible capital expenditure for onshore activity, and 10% - 20% for offshore depending on water depths. There is a domestic market obligation and participation by the Nigerian National Petroleum Corporation at 60% on a carried interest basis.

In the US OCS there are several leasing systems available to the authorities. In the present study four have been considered. One has a fixed royalty of 12½% with cash bonus. The second has a sliding scale royalty according to the following formula:

$$R_j = b[1n(V_j/s)]$$

where R_j = royalty due on unadjusted value of oil produced in quarter j

b = 10

1n = natural logarithm

V_j = value of production in quarter j, adjusted for inflation, in millions of dollars

s = 2.5

There are lower and upper limits to the rates of 12½% and 65%. On new fields offshore Alaska there is exemption from the Windfall Profits Tax but in other areas it is payable. This tax is essentially a temporary excise duty payable on the difference between an adjusted base price and the world price. An adjustment is made for prodution taxes payable to state Governments. The rates of tax applicable to Tier Three or newly discovered oil were reduced in the 1981 Economic Recovery Tax Act. Offshore operators are subject to the Federal Income Tax. The general rate is 46% with lower rates for small profits. There is a 10% investment tax credit. Intangible drilling and development costs may be expensed for this tax. Since the 1981 Economic Recovery Tax Act depreciation of tangible equipment is allowed over five years. There is a cost depletion allowance for least acquisition costs. Percentage depletion is still available to non-integrated producers. (It is not included in the analysis below.) Royalties, production taxes and the Windfall Profits Tax are deductible.

In Alaska, the Federal Income Tax is levied (and Windfall Profits Tax on 'old' fields). In addition the state Government levies taxes of its own. It has employed several royalty systems in recent years. Rates of 12½% and the sliding-scale system outlined above are analysed here. There is also a production tax based on percentage-of-value with an Economic Limit Factor incorporated. On new fields, the rate is now 12½% for the first 5 years and 15% thereafter. There is also a small Conservation tax levied again based on production and a small property tax. Finally there is an income tax at the general rate of 9.4%.

In Malaysia, the system consists of a royalty at 10% plus a production-sharing system and taxes. For cost recovery, all costs are recoverable up to a maximum of 20% of gross revenues in any year. Profit oil is split 70% - 30% in Government's favour. Contractors pay income tax at 45% on their earnings. Costs as recovered for cost recovery purposes are deducted as are production bonus payments, royalty, the Export Tax and the Excess Proceeds Tax. The Export Tax rate is 25% and is applied to the contractor's exports of production share oil. The Excess Proceeds Tax is at the rate of 70% of the difference between a base price and the export price. It does not apply to new fields.

In Papua New Guinea there is a 1¼% royalty. There is a corporate income tax at a rate of 50% with capital expenditure being written off over a maximum of ten years. There is also a resource rent tax or Additional Profits Tax (APT). When a threshold rate of return on accumulated net cash flow of six percentage points above the inflation rate is achieved an APT at the rate of 22.5% of net cash flow after income tax is levied. There is an effective additional tier of APT with a threshold rate of return of 27% in money-of-the-day terms and a rate of tax of 50%. It is in effect levied on net cash flows after income tax and the first tier of APT.

In Egypt there is a production-sharing scheme with production bonuses but no orthodox taxes. There is a limit of 30% of production set for cost recovery in any one year. Capital costs are depreciated over eight years on a straight line basis for this purpose. Any unutilised cost recovery oil has to be handed back to the Government. The split of profit oil varies from contract to contract. The example chosen here relates to a recent contract which is tougher than the terms of earlier agreements. The Government obtains 80% of the first 90,000 b/d of profit oil, 83% of the profit oil in the range 90,000 b/d - 140,000 b/d and 85% of production above 140,000 b/d.

METHODOLOGY

(a) Basis for Hypothetical Fields Employed in Analysis

The analysis of the impact of the various tax systems has been conducted on a set of hypothetical fields. These have been designed to reflect the wide range of operating circumstances likely to be found in the different countries. Differences in field operating conditions are particularly characterised by variations in (1) the size of recoverable reserves in a field and (2) costs per barrel. The analysis has been conducted on fields with recoverable reserves of (a) 800 million barrels (high volume), (b) 280 million barrels (medium volume) and (c) 100 million barrels (low volume).

With regard to the shape of the production profiles for the three fields it has been assumed that peak production is around 10% of recoverable reserves. This level is attained after one year of production and is maintained for 4 years. Thereafter the decline rate is around 10% per year. These assumptions are conventional in the oil industry.

So far as cost conditions are concerned the procedure adopted has been to construct a range of model fields again in accordance with conventions employed in the international oil industry. Regarding capital costs the assumptions are as follows:

1. Low Cost = $3,000 per peak daily barrel recovered,
2. Medium Cost = $12,000 per peak daily barrel recovered,
3. High Cost = $25,000 per peak daily barrel recovered.

These capital cost figures cover a very wide range of possibilities. The Low Cost possibility would reflect conditions onshore or in very shallow water. The High Cost figure is appropriate for conditions in very deep water and adverse weather conditions. (By way of comparison it may be compared with a figure of $20,000 or so for new fields in the North Sea.)

The phasing of capital expenditure over time that has been assumed is as follows:

Time Period (Year)	*%of Total Capital Expenditure (Real Terms)*
1	10
2	25
3	30
4	25
5	10

In the model fields, capital expenditure starts in 1983. Operating costs have been set at 5% of total field capital expenditure. Where utilised in the analysis, exploration costs have been set at $50 million with $5 million in 1981, $25 million in 1982, and $20 million in 1983 (all at 1981 prices).

It was decided that four model fields could exhibit the wide range of possible operating circumstances. Following the terminology adopted above these are (1) Low Cost/High Volume, (2) Medium Cost/Medium Volume, (3) High Cost/Medium Volume and (4) High Cost/Low Volume.

(b) Financial model

The analysis has been conducted with the aid of a conventional discounted cash flow model. The financial calculations are firstly done in money-of-the-day terms and then in real terms (i.e. at 1981 prices). They show the basic financial position from both Government and oil company perspectives. Thus the different taxes are calculated in both money-of-the-day and real (1981) terms. Post-tax net cash flows, net present values at 10% and 15% and internal rates of return are calculated. The tax take is shown on a field lifetime basis by total taxes as a proportion of resources generated. Resources generated are total revenues minus all capital and operating costs.

To calculate future costs and revenues, assumptions have to be made about future oil prices, cost inflation rates and general inflation rates. For the base case in this report the average price of oil has been taken to be $33.8 per barrel for 1982. It is escalated at 9% per year in money-of-the-day terms. This is the same rate used to escalate capital and operating costs and general inflation which means that the central assumption is a constant real oil price. In the USA, crude oil prices are rather lower. For Texas the 1982 price used is $30 per barrel. For Alaska and the Alaskan OCS the price employed is $27 at the wellhead for 1982.

CONCLUSIONS

The results indicate great variations in the levels of tax burdens as well as in their structures. Some systems are progressive, others proportional and others regressive across fields of differing profitability. In money-of-the-day terms, the Australian system is the most lenient and is broadly proportional. The Texas system is also comparatively lenient and proportional. The US OCS, Indonesian, Egyptian and Nigerian systems are all broadly proportional at increasing levels of severity. The Alaskan systems and the Malaysian one are regressive. The British and Papua New Guinea systems are generally progressive as is the Norwegian one to a much less extent.

In real, present value terms, tax takes are at much higher levels on the less profitable fields than they are in money-of-the-day terms. On the more profitable fields, takes are frequently (but not always) at higher levels as well. The structure becomes regressive across fields of varying profitability under virtually all systems. It becomes extremely regressive in regimes which contain a large element of production-based taxes in their fiscal structures and the level of take frequently exceeds 100% on the less profitable fields. It is argued that in the absence of taxes the economic rents emanating from oil exploitation can be measured by the real, net present values from the fields at the rate of discount employed by the investors. The share of the economic rents taken by Government can be measured by the real, present value of the tax bill. This measure is considered appropriate as investment decisions are made on a present value basis.

The Australian system remains the most lenient on a real, present value basis but it now becomes regressive. Texas is next in leniency and follows the same pattern and is rather more severe on the high cost fields. The US OCS with 12½% royalty is on average the next most lenient but the take reaches 92% on a field of low profitability. Papua New Guinea has a slightly regressive system in real, present value terms but treats marginal fields better than Texas. The UK has a system which is arguably nearly proportional but best described as mildly regressive. The Indonesian system is regressive with the shares of economic rents accruing to the state exceeding 100% on the two poorer fields. The Norwegian system is regressive with the take (including participation) approaching 130% on a high cost field. The Alaska system with 12½% royalty is actually very lenient on the two more profitable fields but very harsh on the high cost ones reflecting the weight of the regressive production based taxes. The US OCS system with sliding-scale royalty imposes a moderate burden on the two more profitable fields but a take of around 135% of the economic rents on the two poorer fields. The Egyptian system produces a take of around 95% on the two most profitable fields but burdens of 123% and 135% of economic rents on the less profitable ones. The Alaska sliding-scale royalty system leads to burdens of 80% - 90% on the two best fields but takes of well over 150% on the two less profitable ones. The Nigerian system is very harsh on all fields and produces takes of 130% - 140% of the economic rents on the poorer fields. The Malaysian system is the harshest of all, is highly regressive and has takes exceeding 155% of economic rents on poor fields.

The above findings were on the basis of constant real oil prices. When the interaction of the fiscal systems with oil price variations is taken into account it is found that when oil prices rise the systems generally become less regressive across fields, especially in real, present value terms: the percentage take on high cost fields tends to fall sharply while as a generalisation the take on the most profitable fields shows little change. This move towards less regressive systems is particularly pronounced in real, discounted terms and is especially noticeable under regimes with significant production-based taxes which become relatively less important when oil prices rise. On the other hand when oil prices fall the tax systems generally become more regressive especially in real, discounted terms. This reflects the increased weight of the regressive production-based taxes. The UK and Papua New Guinea systems resist this trend to a certain extent especially in money-of-the-day terms. When capital cost escalation takes place, tax takes tend to increase in real, discounted terms and the systems become more regressive. Again it is the UK and Papua New Guinea systems which show some resistance to this trend.

The implications of these findings are that the fiscal systems are unsympathetic to the needs of risk-averse investors: the real tax burdens increase when operating circumstances become worse. It is all the more unfortunate that this finding operates most strongly on the least profitable fields. The root of the fiscal trouble is the use of taxes based on production which are not very responsive to deteriorations in operating conditions.

The effect of the tax systems discussed above is to produce a wide range in post-tax returns across the four fields in the different countries. The investment climate is found to be most congenial in

Australia and Texas where all fields are clearly acceptable. The next most attractive fiscal environments are the US OCS when royalty is 12½%, Papua New Guinea and the UK. The attractiveness of an environment does of course depend on cost factors as well and the UK North Sea is dominated by very high cost conditions. After that the Indonesian and Norwegian systems offer reasonable returns on low cost fields but unattractive returns on high cost situations. The two poorest fields would be unacceptable under these regimes. The Alaksan system with 12½% royalty and the US OCS system with sliding-scale royalty also offer attractive returns on low cost fields but unacceptable low ones on high cost ones. Under the Egyptian and Alaskan system with sliding-scale royalty the low cost fields are acceptable but not the high cost ones. The Nigerian system leaves the two best fields moderately attractive and the two high cost ones unacceptable. The Malaysian system leaves only the most profitable field acceptable.

The tax systems were examined from the viewpoint of an explorationist facing a set of possible outcomes, all of which were sufficiently encouraging on a pre-tax basis to encourage a given exploration programme. On a post-tax basis the position was found to be very different. On the most favourable prospect (a 1 in 2 chance of a find) exploration would be encouraged under 10 of the fiscal systems with Australia and Texas offering the most encouragement. Under the Malaysian, Nigerian, Egyptian, Alaska (sliding-scale royalty), and Norwegian systems exploration is discouraged. When the chances of suceess were 1 in 5 the US OCS with sliding-scale royalty also was discouraging. When chances were 1 in 10 only the Australian, Texas and US OCS with 12½% royalty systems offered adequate encouragement. When the chances of success were 1 in 20 none of the systems offered adequate encouragement. The results are heavily dependent on the assumptions made about the probabilities attached to the discovery of different types of fields.

The role of the fiscal systems in determining the riskiness of the various projects was examined by simple statistical analysis. Riskiness was defined as the spread in outcomes of the expected post-tax real net cash flows from five possible results of an exploration effort. The coefficient of variation was found to vary greatly across the various systems. The UK system produced the lowest risk (as defined) closely followed by Norway and Papua New Guinea. Systems with large non-profit related elements in their tax system such as Malaysia and Alaska with sliding-scale royalty were found to cause much more risks to investors. It was interesting to find that the country with the most severe tax system — Malaysia — caused the greatest risks to investors.

Chapter 10

Estimation of UK Government Revenues from Oil

*Homa Motamen**

Forecasting the magnitude of future government income from North Sea oil is an undertaking which can be best described, with considerable understatement, as being fraught with difficulties. There are so many variables to take into account and changes in any of them may dramatically affect both the level and the timing of the tax revenue flows. More specifically, even if all potential sources of oil from the North Sea could be identified and the reserves recoverable therefrom ascertained with certainty, accurate prediction would still require a detailed knowledge of the following:

1. *Government policy towards the depletion of North Sea oil reserves.*
   The government can influence the rate of depletion through its powers to grant licences for exploration and then approval for the development of established reservoirs.
2. *Capital and operating expenditure costs.*
   For each field for which development approval has been granted,

***Imperial College, London University. The full text of this paper with a detailed description of the UK oil taxation system, methodology, 10 tables of results and 3 graphs is available from the author.**

time profiles are needed for production rates and the associated capital and operating expenditure costs.

3. *The ownership of each field.*
   Corporation Tax, unlike the other three oil taxes (namely, royalties, supplementary petroleum duty and petroleum revenue tax), is payable on a corporate basis. Actual payments of corporation tax on a particular field thus depend on the activities of the participating companies elsewhere in the North Sea.
4. *Equity financing and interest payment.*
   The level of equity attributable to each field and the interest paid on any loans raised.
5. *Price of oil.*
   The dollar price of oil for each of the various grades of oil produced.
6. *Inflation rate.*
   The likely future rate of inflation of both capital and operating costs.
7. *Exchange rate.*
   The dollar/sterling exchange rate.
8. *Taxes on North Sea.*
   Details of the North Sea oil taxation system and its likely future changes.

Much of this information cannot be forecast with any degree of certainty. The full extent of North Sea oil reserves is not known. Both production from reservoirs already discovered, and further exploration and exploitation of other sources, depend on many factors not the least of which will be the future course of the price of oil. The latter is of course notorious for its uneven course over time and it would be folly to place too much reliance on any one particular forecast. Similarly, inflation and exchange rate movements are also difficult, if not impossible, to predict accurately. The pattern of ownership and the financial arrangements will vary between specific cases. Production rates, capital and operating costs are subject to the vagaries of many an unpredictable influence — for example, the weather. And last but not least, there is the overriding question of government policy towards the tax regime and the size of the take. This has been the subject of much alteration over the past years and it is not unlikely that further changes will be forthcoming in the future.

This has been by no means an exhaustive list of the uncertainties surrounding the North Sea oil industry but it does illustrate the difficulty of trying to provide reasonably sensible estimates of government income. There is a wide range of possible scenarios for each of the many variables within the system (e.g. high inflation rate, low inflation rate) and this built-in imprecision should be both allowed for in the analysis and also borne in mind when the numerical results are interpreted.

As an initial simplification, it has been decided to limit analysis to those twenty four fields for which development approval had been granted by the end of 1981. These fields are, in alphabetical order, Argyll, Auk, Beatrice, Beryl, Brae, Brent, Buchan, Claymore, Cormorant,[1] Dunlin, Forties, Fulmar, Heather, Hutton, Hutton North West, Magnus, Maureen, Montrose, Murchison UK, Ninian, Piper, Statfjord UK, Tartan and Thistle. Between them these fields were expected to yield 11,949 million barrels[2] of oil. All were licensed under the first four rounds. Hence, their effective royalty rates are less than 12½% of sales value. This limitation on the fields to be considered means that the revenue estimates provided should only be regarded as predictions of actual government income for the years up to, possibly, 1987. Thereafter, other fields, for which development approval has not yet been granted, may well be in production and thus contributing to the government coffers.

Computer simulations were undertaken for the chosen twenty four fields for the years 1976–2000 under a number of different scenarios in order to examine how sensitive the results were to alternative assumptions on oil price, inflation rate, exchange rate, depletion rate etc. But first a 'base' case was considered where the following assumptions were made:

(i) Each field was treated as if it were privately owned. This of course neglects the role of the British National Oil Corporation/Britoil as a nationalised industry. Nevertheless, this is a reasonable simplification if one considers that the state-owned company was given powers under the Petroleum and Submarine Pipelines Act (1975), and under the Oil and Gas Enterprise Act (1982) to operate as a commercial concern.

(ii) Corporation tax liabilities were calculated on a field-by-field rather than on a corporate basis because of the lack of information relating to the capital expenditure plans of individual companies. Such a procedure will, however, predict earlier payment of corporation tax than is likely to be the case in practice. This should be taken into account when analysing the estimates of the absolute levels of government revenues. However, relative levels — on different assumptions about the price of oil, for instance — should be little affected and, as such, changes are the main focus of analysis in this paper. The adopted procedure should not lead to much distortion of the results.

(iii) A general level of gearing of 25%[3] has been assumed and interest on loans has been charged at a rate equal to the assumed rate of inflation — i.e. a real rate of interest of zero per cent.

(iv) The general rate of inflation is based on the UK wholesale price index for the period 1972–1981. An annual rate of 10% has been postulated for 1982 — thereafter a rate of 8% has been assumed.

(v) The price of oil from all fields has been assumed to be the same as that for Forties marker crude. This will slightly overestimate revenues from fields with a lower quality crude (e.g. Claymore, Heather, Ninian, Piper, Tartan) but will also underestimate revenues from fields with a lower quality crude (e.g. Beryl, Montrose). The underestimated values are likely to partially offset the overestimated values and therefore, the overall distortion due to this pricing system is likely to be negligible. Actual oil prices are used for the years 1975–March 1982. Thereafter the price is taken to remain constant until the end of 1982 and the real sterling price of oil to rise subsequently at 6% per annum.

(vi) The dollar/sterling exchange rate is based on actual values for the period 1972–1981. It is forecast to have an average level of $1.85 = £1 for the first six months of 1982 and $1.90 = £1 for the last six months, at which rate it is then assumed to remain.

(vii) Oil production from the British sector of the North Sea is forecast at about 2.1 million barrels per day in 1982, rising to a peak of 2.5 million barrels per day in 1985, falling slowly thereafter to the turn of the century.

(viii) Percentage government take is calculated as the nominal sum of royalties, supplementary petroleum duty, petroleum revenue tax and corporation tax payments as a proportion of net revenues (total revenues less capital and operating costs) over the entire life of the fields considered.

(ix) Calculations were performed in nominal sterling values for six-month chargeable periods ending on the last days of June and December each year. Figures relate to payments rather than accrued liabilities and are attributed to calendar years (in preference to the normal practice of fiscal years) to maintain consistency with the analysis in the rest of the book.

Table 10.1. Total Government Tax Take[a] from North Sea Oil, 1976–2000 ('Base' Case – Current Prices)

Year	Royalties (£ million)	Supplementary Petroleum Duty (£ million)	Petroleum Revenue Tax (£ million)	Corporation Tax (£ million)	Total Government Take (£ million)
1976	24	0	0	0	24
1977	165	0	0	9	174
1978	278	0	182	316	775
1979	419	0	701	629	1,749
1980	825	0	1,938	831	3,594
1981	1,100	1,497	2,407	997	6,001
1982	1,392	2,244	1,493	1,116	6,244
1983	1,447	365	3,205	1,744	6,761
1984	1,775	0	4,386	2,756	8,916
1985	2,112	0	5,755	3,343	11,210
1986	2,360	0	7,173	3,747	13,279
1987	2,453	0	7,827	4,109	14,388
1988	2,426	0	8,994	4,634	16,054
1989	2,358	0	8,141	3,908	14,406
1990	2,312	0	7,949	4,117	14,376
1991	2,268	0	8,502	3,989	14,758
1992	2,210	0	8,379	3,391	13,981
1993	2,188	0	9,005	3,208	14,402
1994	2,182	0	9,039	2,794	14,015
1995	2,149	0	9,212	2,616	13,977
1996	2,135	0	9,352	2,256	13,742
1997	2,146	0	9,589	2,102	13,837
1998	2,037	0	9,143	1,927	13,107
1999	1,893	0	8,828	1,563	12,283
2000	1,844	0	8,567	1,541	11,951

[a]Tax take applies to proven reserves (as it stood in 1982) – see text for details.

The calculations were carried out on a field-by-field basis but only aggregate estimates of government receipts are given here. Table 1 and Table 2 give 'base' case projections in current prices and constant 1975 prices respectively. As can be seen from the former table, actual tax revenues should peak towards the end of the 1980s and fall off very slowly thereafter. By far the largest component of the total take is the income provided by petroleum revenue tax which accounts for some 59% over the whole period — a proportion which rises to over 70% of the annual take during the later years of the century. This is unsurprising since Petroleum Revenue Tax (PRT) is essentially a tax on profits and, after the mid-1980s, most of the

Table 10.2. Total Government Tax Take[a] from North Sea Oil, 1976–2000 ('Base' Case – Constant 1975 Prices)

Year	Royalties (£ million)	Supplementary Petroleum Duty (£ million)	Petroleum Revenue Tax (£ million)	Corporation Tax (£ million)	Total Government Take (£ million)
1976	20	0	0	0	20
1977	116	0	0	6	122
1978	182	0	116	202	500
1979	242	0	402	351	995
1980	411	0	964	406	1,781
1981	496	661	1,089	440	2,685
1982	571	921	614	448	2,554
1983	547	141	1,210	648	2,546
1984	622	0	1,539	948	3,108
1985	685	0	1,864	1,064	3,614
1986	709	0	2,158	1,105	3,972
1987	683	0	2,181	1,122	3,986
1988	626	0	2,325	1,171	4,122
1989	563	0	1,949	915	3,427
1990	511	0	1,760	892	3,163
1991	464	0	1,744	800	3,009
1992	419	0	1,592	630	2,641
1993	384	0	1,582	552	2,518
1994	355	0	1,472	445	2,271
1995	324	0	1,389	386	2,098
1996	297	0	1,304	308	1,910
1997	277	0	1,238	266	1,781
1998	244	0	1,095	226	1,564
1999	209	0	978	169	1,357
2000	189	0	879	155	1,222

[a]Tax take applies to proven reserves (as it stood in 1982) – see text for details.

fields under consideration will be well established and thus generating substantial net income flows. In contrast, payments of royalties and supplementary petroleum duty (until its abolition), which are both taxes levied on revenues, are more correlated to the production profile. Percentage government take is 82%.

Such nominal figures, although they correspond to forecasts of actual payments to the Exchequer, do nevertheless conceal the real flow of resources. Table 2 presents the same information as Table 1, but in constant 1975 prices. This shows that, in real terms, tax revenues should actually peak in 1988 and then decline quite quickly as more and more fields are depleted. The effect is demonstrated

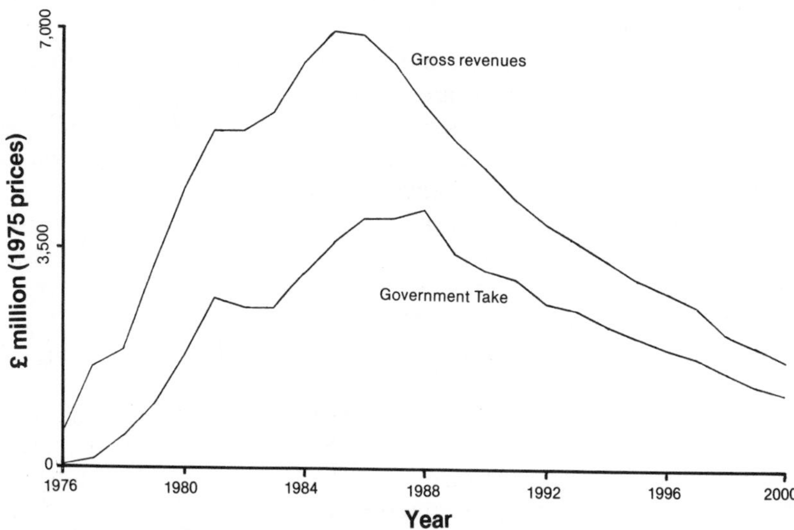

).1: Graph of Gross Revenues and Government Tax Take from North Sea Oil, 1976-2000 (Constant 1975 prices corresponding with Table 004)

strikingly in Fig. 1. Total tax take over the twenty five year period is £56,965 million in 1975 prices, which corresponds to about 57% of gross revenues.

Such are the results of the 'base' case. Five sets of simulations were then carried out to examine the sensitivity of these estimates to changes in the following parameters: the real price of oil, the rate of UK inflation, the dollar/sterling exchange rate, the rate of oil depletion, and capital and operating expenditure.[4]

The effect of varying the real price of oil is unsurprising. The higher the rate of increase assumed, the higher are both the annual flows and the overall tax take. If the real sterling price of oil is taken to remain constant from the end of 1982 onwards, the overall tax take amounts to £37,192 million; a drop of 35% compared with the 'base' case of a 6% increase. A 3% rate of increase yields a total take of £45,510 million (20% down on the 'base' case) whereas an 8% rate of increase leads to 17% more in government revenues.

The objective in simulating for different rates of UK inflation was to examine the extent to which capital allowances might be devalued and tax revenues thereby affected. Hence, it was decided that the nominal price of oil should be increased concomitantly with the postulated rate of inflation so that the real sterling rate of increase was maintained at 6% per annum — the straight 'inflation' effect would thus not be obscured by an oil price effect of the type investigated above. Two different scenarios were examined — one where the rate of inflation is forecast to be 4% and one where it is assumed to be 12%. It appears that the time profiles of tax revenues (when deflated to constant prices) are little affected and consequently overall tax takes are also very similar. A higher rate of inflation does lead to a lower tax take but the effect is small and, perhaps surprisingly, the annual figures do not always reflect the overall conclusion. In 1985, for example, the tax take is higher, the higher is the rate of inflation which has been assumed. In general, however, the positive (negative) effects which higher (lower) inflation rates respectively have on nominal gross revenues offset — almost exactly — the negative (positive) effects which they have on the real value of capital allowances.

Different exchange rate assumptions were then examined. The *a priori* expectation is that, since the price of oil is set in dollars, the assumption of a higher exchange rate should yield a lower value of gross revenues and hence government tax take, and vice versa. This is shown to be the case. Constant exchange rate assumptions of $1.8, $1.85, $1.95 and $2.0 = £1 were all simulated and these resulted in increases of 6.4% and 3.1%, and decreases of 3.0% and 5.8% respectively in the overall tax take as compared to the 'base' case. The same pattern was also repeated consistently by the annual figures. Moreover, even if the assumption of constancy was relaxed in favour of either an appreciating or a depreciating exchange rate, similar results were still forthcoming.

The effect on tax revenues of lower levels of oil depletion is again fairly easy to predict. As expected, lower production results in lower revenues and lower government take. In fact reduction of 5% below the base case resulted in a 6.1% drop in revenues to £53,472 million and a 10% reduction yielded a 12.5% fall to £49,858 million. The slightly greater than proportionate fall is due to the fact that petroleum revenue tax is subject to an exempt allowance which is relatively more significant at lower production levels. In addition an extra simulation was performed where the aggregate production level was assumed to be about 4.5% higher than in the 'base' case. This corresponded to oil extraction of 11.949 million barrels[5] within the period 1976–2000. Total government take becomes £60,803 million as compared to the £56,965 million for the 'base' case.

In contrast, higher capital and operating costs seem to have little effect on the overall size of the government revenues. Even in the case of a 10% increase above expected values, the overall tax take only falls by just over 2% to £55,608 million. The oil companies appear to shoulder most of the burden.

The above simulations have all been cases where individual assumptions made in the 'base' case have been varied and the effect on government revenue studied. There are, of course, many composite variations which could have been tried but the adopted approach was chosen in order to present results which were as clear and easy to interpret as possible. It is, nevertheless, useful to consider in addition a 'pessimistic' case to see how a combination of the individual effects might reinforce one another. One final simulation was thus undertaken where the following changes were made with respect to the 'base' case.

(i) the real sterling price of oil does not increase after 1982
(ii) the annual rate of oil depletion is 10% lower than expected after 1981
(iii) annual rates of both capital and operating expenditure are 10% higher than expected after 1981
(iv) the assumptions regarding the rate of inflation and the exchange rate were unchanged.

This scenario is not, of course, as pessimistic a set of assumptions as could have been made. But it will suffice to illustrate the point at issue. The overall tax take has fallen dramatically to £31,637 million, a drop of 45% compared to the 'base' case. Petroleum revenue tax, whose share of the total take was some 57% in the 'base' case, now accounts for less than 48% reflecting the decline in the level of profits.

REFERENCES

1. It is now believed that the Cormorant field, instead of consisting of two distinct reservoirs — South Cormorant and North Cormorant — is in fact contiguous and should, therefore, be treated as a single field for taxation purposes.
2. The figure of 11,949 million barrels refers to an estimate — current during mid-1981 — of ultimate recoverable reserves from the aforementioned fields. Estimates of recoverable reserves and depletion rates for individual fields are, however, regularly subject to considerable revision and for the purposes of these calculations, more recent forecasts have been used. These predict both a lower level of recoverable reserves and also depletion from some fields continuing into the twenty first century. Hence, the level of oil production expected during the period 1976 - 2000 is forecast here at only 11,431 million barrels.

3. 'Gearing' denotes the proportion of funds which are externally financed.
4. For an analysis of the effect of different tax regimes — up to and including that incorporating the changes announced in the course of the 1980 Budget — see the article by Homa Motamen and Roger Strange, 'Oil Revenue Outlook for Britain in the Medium Term', *Energy Policy* 9 (No. 1), 14–19 (March 1981).
5. 11,949 million barrels corresponds to an estimate of oil reserves made during mid 1981 of proven recoverable reserves from the North Sea. See Ref. 2 above.

SECTION 2

Forecasting, Contingency Planning, Theory and Macro-Economics

PART V

Energy Forecasting

Chapter 11

Methods for Projecting UK Energy Demands Used in the Department of Energy

*K.J. Wigley and K. Vernon**

The first part of the paper describes the approach used for preparing energy projections in the Department of Energy. A brief outline of the overall model is provided and the variations in main assumptions employed to produce alternative projections are indicated. The second part of the paper provides greater detail on the energy demand models developed for the domestic and industrial sectors (excluding iron and steel). Discussion is provided on estimation, stability of coefficients, goodness of fit, price and activity responses and dynamic properties. Some alternative and possible future developments on demand modelling are indicated.

INTRODUCTION

1. The aim of this paper is to describe energy demand models for the 'domestic' and 'other industry'† sectors of the United Kingdom economy and to set them within the framework of energy projection modelling in the Department of Energy. Approaches to

***Department of Energy**

†Excluding iron and steel and energy industries.

energy policy analysis within the Department have been discussed by the Secretary of State for energy in an earlier Chapter.

2. Section 2 of the paper outlines the main model calculation used for preparing energy projections and the principal variations in assumptions which indicate the range of uncertainty to be considered.

3. Section 3 sets out the model structures for energy demands in the two sectors. Section 4 provides the estimated coefficients in each case and illustrates the goodness of fit. The properties of the fitted demand models are considered in Sedtion 5, including price and economic activity, responses, dynamic properties and, for the industrial sector, the stability of coefficients in the pre-1973 period and a later period including the post-1973 data. A final section discusses alternative approaches and possible future work.

4. A set of energy projections using these techniques was published by the Department at end–1982, accompanied by a technical specification of the methods used. A description of the methods used in previous projection exercises is available in Energy Paper Number 29.[1] The most recent set of Energy Projections were published by the Department in 1979.[2]

2. ENERGY PROJECTION METHODS

5. In concept the energy projection calculation provides balances of demands and supplies of each fuel in each of a number of future years. In practice this calculation is made for electricity only, as trade at the margin will balance supplies and demands for tradeable energy forms.

6. Figure 1 illustrates the main outline of the calculation. In a given year fuel demands in each sector of the economy are determined principally by UK fuel prices and levels of economic activity. These demands, together with the pattern of trade, provide the structures of fuel production which give rise to costs of production for each fuel. UK fuel prices are influenced partly by production costs at home and partly by world fuel prices. For tradeable fuels, for example, oil or coal, domestic prices are likely to be influenced strongly by world price levels. In such cases domestic production costs together with either taxes or grants affect the level of domestic production.

Energy Demand

7. The pattern of fuel demands in the main energy consuming

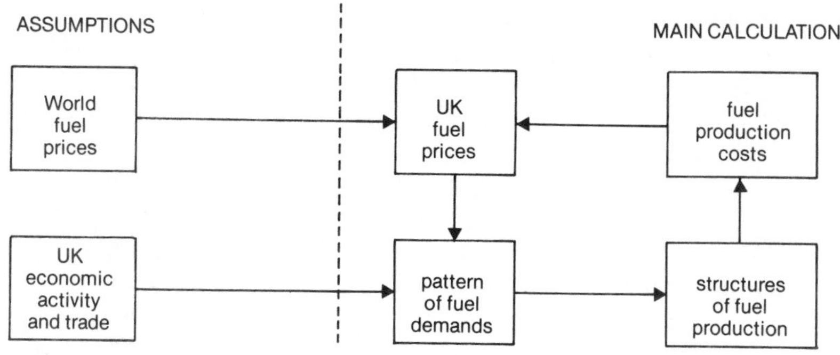

Fig. 11.1: Method for the Preparation of Energy Projections

sectors have been analysed over the period 1954–1979 and relationships established which relate the demands by each sector for each main fuel to levels of economic activity for the sector and both current and past fuel prices. Variations in annual temperature have been allowed for in this work.

8. Energy demands in transport are treated separately for road, rail, air and ships' bunkers. Demand for road transport is based on the Department of Transport models used to prepare National Road Traffic Forecasts as described in 3. These forecasts are based on assumptions for GDP growth and fuel prices and provide estimates of vehicle kilometres per annum separately for cars, public service vehicles, light vans and heavy freight vehicles. Assumptions made on saturation levels for vehicle ownership, fuel efficiency and on fuel mix provide estimates of fuel use in road transport.

9. Advice is taken from the Department of Transport on future rail electrification, growth in rail freight activity and improvements in fuel efficiency.

9. For air transport fuel projections are based on advice from the Department of Trade on forecasts of passenger traffic which are combined with estimates of average journey lengths and efficiency in fuel use.

Energy Supply

11. Detailed calculations are made for the electricity supply industry in England and Wales which chooses the operation and investment plans for different generating plant types in order to minimise the present value of the future capital and operating costs of the generating system required to meet the estimated electricity demands arising

from the demand calculation. The costs of producing electricity from marginal operating plant are used to prepare electricity prices for each consuming sector.

12. The prices of coal and petroleum products in the UK are related in the projections to assumed future paths for coal and crude oil prices in international trade. The price of gas landed in Britain is assumed to move broadly in line with assumed future gas prices in European markets and that these will be related to prices of competing oil products.

13. Alternative projections of energy demand and of the supply patterns for electricity (for which international trade is insufficient to determine UK prices) are prepared on the basis of these prices and the economic assumptions.

14. Individual investment possibilities for coal, oil and gas industries in the UK are assessed, as they arise, on the basis of the energy projections and circumstances available at the time the assessments are made.

15. For new forms of energy supply, such as biofuels, geothermal, solar, tidal, wind, etc. estimates are made of the date at which the new energy forms first become economic, of the potential level of competitive supply at the assumed future prices of other fuels and the likely rate of penetration of the new energy forms. Judgement is required in assessing each of these factors. Esimates are also made of the likely customers of these energy forms and of the conventional fuels displaced. The contributions of the new fuels are not necessarily additive, especially for those used in electricity generation, as the adoption of one form such as tidal reduces the potential of other renewables e.g. wind power.

The Calculation

16. The calculation outlined in Fig. 1 is made for each of a number of spanshot years in the future. These calculations are linked through time both by the lagged effect of prices on fuel demands, and the cost minimisation calculations for electricity supply.

17. The results of this form of calculation provide details of fuel consumption by each consuming sector and the pattern of domestic fuel production and of imports. Alternative projections are prepared by varying the many assumptions underlying the calculations.

Energy Conservation

18. The method used for calculating energy demand has two impor-

tant features. If fuel prices rise at the same rate as general price inflation (i.e. constant real fuel prices) then total demand for energy tends to rise less quickly than economic activity (GDP). In the industrial sector this non-price effect arises mainly as a result of technical change. The second feature involves additional energy saving as fuel prices rise faster than general inflation. In this case other inputs (such as capital for additional insulation or improved boiler controls) are substituted for energy as fuel prices rise relative to other goods. In addition consumers tend to use relatively less energy, to use it more efficiently and to undertake more energy conservation measures, the faster energy prices rise in real terms. In this way the 'price' and 'non-price' components of increasing efficciency in energy use are incorporated into the projections through the coefficient values in the demand equations.

Uncertainty and Assumptions

19. Clearly it is impossible to forecast the future with any degree of confidence. Major uncertainties arise from the exogenous assumptions employed for world economic activity, world energy prices and the growth and future structure of the British economy.

20. These assumptions are not independent. For given views on world energy supplies, a faster long-term rate of growth in the world economy will put more pressure on energy supplies and lead to higher energy prices. In addition, the importance of international trade to Britain implies that faster world economic growth will, as in the past, also lead to a higher rate of economic growth in this country.

21. Although higher energy prices are likely to place severe constraints on economic activity it is thought that the fundamental forces generating economic growth arise, in the main, outside the energy sector, in levels of investment, productivity growth and the economic policies of the governments in the major industrialised countries. This is compatible with the view that over a long period world markets adjust by the recycling of financial surpluses, and by energy conservation, inter-fuel substitution and the discovery and exploitation of new energy supplies.

22. For each GDP growth path, alternative combinations of more and less energy intensive industries within manufacturing, and of manufacturing and service sectors, can lead to significantly different energy demands. An analysis has been made of the performance of the major energy using industries over past periods of faster and slower general economic growth. The results of this analysis provide for each GDP growth path, both a high and a low assumption for the

growth rates of those industries, with the less energy intensive industrial and service sectors making up the assumed future levels of GDP.

23. By using different combinations of these assumptions alternative projection cases, or scenarios, may be constructed which attempt to span the range of future uncertainty. The robustness of alternative policy options may then be tested against alternative future outcomes rather than choosing an optimal policy for a single, best forecast.

24. Other uncertainties in the projections can arise through the specification and parameters used in the projection model. The extent of the possibilities here are wide and attention has been concentrated on some key cost elements in the electricity model.

3. ENERGY DEMAND MODELS: STRUCTURE

25. The approach to demand modelling described in this paper involves estimating statistical relationships between past data on the consumption levels of each of the main fuel types: solid fuel, petroleum products, gas and electricity, and the main explanatory variables of economic activity in each sector such as industrial output or real income, energy prices and a measure of temperature.

26. This has been referred to as a 'top-down' approach. Alternative 'bottom-up' approaches, which use detailed information on end-use technologies, stocks of energy-using assets and energy conservation measures are used, where reliable figures exist, as cross checks on the statistical results. These methods are mentioned briefly at the end of the paper. They raise problems for projecting future energy demands because of their requirement for detailed assumptions on future technological developments. Such analyses, where practicable however, provide invaluable insights into the possible implications of projections using statistical methods.

27. The structure of the statistical models employed are described in detail in the Appendix. The form of model for total energy demand in other industry and for domestic space and water heating is as follows. A single equation is used to obtain an estimate for total useful energy (i.e. after taking account of efficiency in use) which is then subdivided into shares for the individual fuels using current and lagged relative fuel prices as explanatory variables. For domestic space and water heating, three equations are estimated to derive the shares of the four main fuels. For other industry, the demand for electricity is treated separately.

28. The two main fuels, gas and electricity, used for domestic cooking are calculated from one equation for total useful energy for cooking and a second equation providing a split of this estimate between the two fuels. A further equation is used to derive electricity use for other household appliances.

29. The main objective in choosing the final specification of these models has been to obtain reliable estimates of the long-run responses of fuel demands to economic growth and to energy price movements in real terms. To this end some account has been taken of short-run responses in the models, using lagged values of suitable variables in the equations.

30. The energy demand models for both sectors represents small segments of much larger equation systems which have not been investigated. For other industry, this larger system is the production function and investment equation system which relates industrial output to all factor inputs, as for example in Ref. 4; for the domestic sector the larger system embraces the savings-expenditure relation and the expenditure system over all commodities (see, for example, Ref. 5). In both cases model specification and the definition of variables can be important, particularly aggregation over industries with different energy using characteristics, households at different income levels, and so on. The practical solutions to these problems are usually dictated, unfortunately, by lack of adequate data. In the models specified in this paper use of the degrees of freedom available in the data has been applied more to dynamic responses, particularly to changes in energy prices, than to the wider system of relationships which are usually expressed in static terms.

31. A number of other limitations apply to the models. Supply constraints on the individual fuels have been ignored for lack of adequate data. These may have affected gas demands during the late 1970s. Capital and other user costs associated with energy consumption act along with energy prices in affecting fuel use and substitution. Apart from domestic cooking, these other costs have been omitted, also for lack of data. Energy price ratios have been used rather than price differences as explanatory variables in fuel substitution. Whilst price differences may be an appealing factor in determining fuel choice for a given end use, say for boiler fuelling, they are not so obviously the best choice for substitution across a wide range of end uses as reflected in production theory. As a further comment, the rate of fuel substitution in the models is assumed to be unaffected by economic growth or investment rates. This is an important issue to be taken up in later development work.

4. ENERGY DEMAND MODELS: GOODNESS OF FIT

32. The data used for estimating the models is described in the Appendix. Estimated values of the parameters are provided for each equation together with statistical measures of goodness of fit. The presence of lagged dependent variables in the equations leads to a downwards bias in the estimated error ranges for parameter values and renders the standard interpretation of the Durbin Watson statistic inappropriate. Some minor serial correlation remains in the residual errors in the estimated equation.

33. Despite these difficulties, the estimated models possess a number of important properties described in the next section of the paper. In addition to the statistical measures of goodness of fit, Figs 4 and 5 illustrate the results of a simulation of the models over the data period. Whereas the estimation procedure minimises the sums of squares of residual errors in the one-year-ahead forecasts over the data period using actual values of lagged variables, the simulation exercise builds up the values of lagged energy demands as it calculates forward using actual values of energy prices, industrial output, real income and temperature. The solid lines provide the actual values and the crosses the simulated values of fuel demands. The two models capture the principal features of the data period and, along with the long-run properties of the models described in the next section, provide confidence in their use in preparing long-term energy projections.

5. ENERGY DEMAND MODELS: CHARACTERISTICS

Price, Output and Income Elasticities

34. For other industry the output elasticity for total useful energy demand is0.622, i.e. a 10% increase in the energy weighted output series used in the model leads to a 6.22% increase in total useful energy demand. This effect occurs in the same year. As explained in the Appendix, the effect of a price change works through to energy demand over a period of time. The short-run (same year) price elasticity of total useful energy demand is -0.0854 and the long run price elasticity is -0.224. These estimates may be compared with those summarised in Ref. 6. The output elasticities quoted in this paper are generally smaller than those obtained by other investigators.

Table 11.1. Estimates of Long-Run Own and Cross Price Elasticities of Substitution for other Industry.

		% change in price		
		Oil	*Gas*	*Coal and Other Solid Fuel*
Oil	% change in demand	−1.62	0.01	1.61
Gas		0.37	−1.34	0.97
Coal and other solid fuel		2.84	1.76	−4.6

However, care is needed in comparing the precise specification of the energy demand, output and price variables employed in defining and estimating elasticities for comparative purposes.

35. For the fuel allocation system in other industry the calculation of own and cross price elasticities of substitution (i.e. with total useful energy fixed) is complex. These have been calculated for 1980 and are set out in Table 1.

In Table 1 a 1% increase in the price of gas alone is estimated to lead, over a number of years, to a 1.34% drop in demand for gas (the own-price elasticity for gas) and a 1.76% increase in the demand for coal and other solid fuel (a cross-price elasticity). These elasticities are not constant but vary with the shares of each fuel in total useful energy demand. The high own-price elasticity for coal and other solid fuel is a consequence, in the model, of its low share of total useful energy demand in other industry; the value falls towards −2 as this share rises. These estimated long-run elasticities have the correct signs and their magnitudes are not unreasonable.

Table 11.2. Estimates of Long-Run Own and Cross Price Elasticities of Substitution in Domestic Space and Water Heating

		% change in price			
		Coal and Solid Fuel	*Oil*	*Gas*	*Electricity*
Coal and Solid Fuel		−2.96	0.07	2.72	0.16
Oil	% change in	0.09	−2.97	2.72	0.16
Gas	demand	0.09	0.07	−0.32	0.16
Electricity		0.09	0.07	2.72	−2.88

36. In the model for domestic space and water heating both income and price changes affect total useful energy demand with a lag. The short and long-run income elasticities are 0.53 and 0.89 respectively. The short and long-run price elasticities are —0.25 and —0.43. Comparative results may be found in Ref. 6.

37. Estimates of 1980 values of own and cross price elasticities of substitution in domestic space and water heating are provided in Table 2.

The form of this table is dictated by the additional constraints imposed on the equation system to obtain a reasonable estimated model. There are thus important judgements included in the model choice and specification. The low own-price elasticity for gas and the high cross-price elasticities in the gas column result from the high equilibrium share of gas in this sector implied by the model at the 1980 price levels. These elasticity values would adjust towards the values for the other fuels at lower gas shares in total useful energy for this purpose.

Dynamic Properties

38. The dynamic properties of the models are discussed in the Appendix. The adjustment of the models from the implied dis-

Table 11.3. Stability in Estimated Coefficients in Equation for total useful Energy for the other Industry Sector.

	1955–1979		*1955–1973*		*1961–1979*	
Estimated lag						
Constant	2.32	(6.3)	−1.8	(2.6)	5.1	(8.0)
YE	0.622	(8.5)	0.47	(4.7)	0.63	(8.2)
T	−0.0871	(3.3)	−0.076	(2.2)	−0.063	(1.8)
RPE	−0.0854	(3.1)	−0.071	(0.6)	−0.12	(4.6)
Lagged YE	0.619	(12.4)	1.24	(11.3)	0.18	(1.8)
$\bar{R}^2$	0.987		0.972		0.981	
Exogenous lag						
Constant	2.32	(26)	2.1	(25)	2.3	(19)
YE	0.622	(18)	0.58	(21)	0.64	(11)
T	−0.0871	(3.4)	−0.067	(3.3)	−0.087	(2.5)
RPE	−0.0854	(3.2)	−0.22	(4.7)	−0.075	(2.6)
$\bar{R}^2$	0.932		0.970		0.859	
Fixed lag	0.619		0.619		0.619	

equilibrium position of 1980 to an equilibrium position at 1980 prices, output and income levels are provided in Figures 6 and 7. In both cases some residual effects still remain after a ten year period.

39. It should be clear that the measure of disequilibrium in 1980 and the dynamic properties illustrated in Figures 6 and 7 result from the specification of the model and the estimated equation coefficients. The Koyck lag structure imposed on the model is simple in form in the light of the limited data available. Although the main objective has been to capture the long-run price and income responses in these models, further data over the coming years may provide improved estimates of more complex lag structures and assist in providing more reliable estimates of long-run properties.

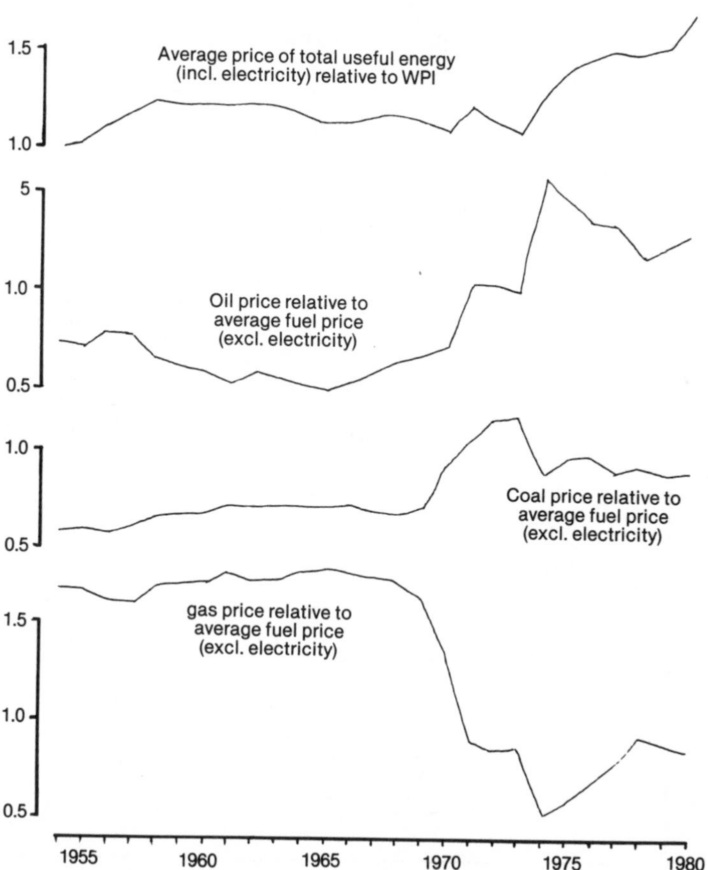

Fig. 11.2: Other Industry Sector Relative Fuel Prices (useful heat terms)

Stability and Coefficient Values

40. The suggestion is frequently made that reactions to the oil price rise in 1973 and subsequent events have caused a breakdown in the relationship between energy demand and economic growth. As far as the relative movements of Primary Energy Demand and Gross Domestic Product are concerned, this appears to be the case in many countries including the United Kingdom. However, it is arguable that this relative movement results mainly from the changing economic

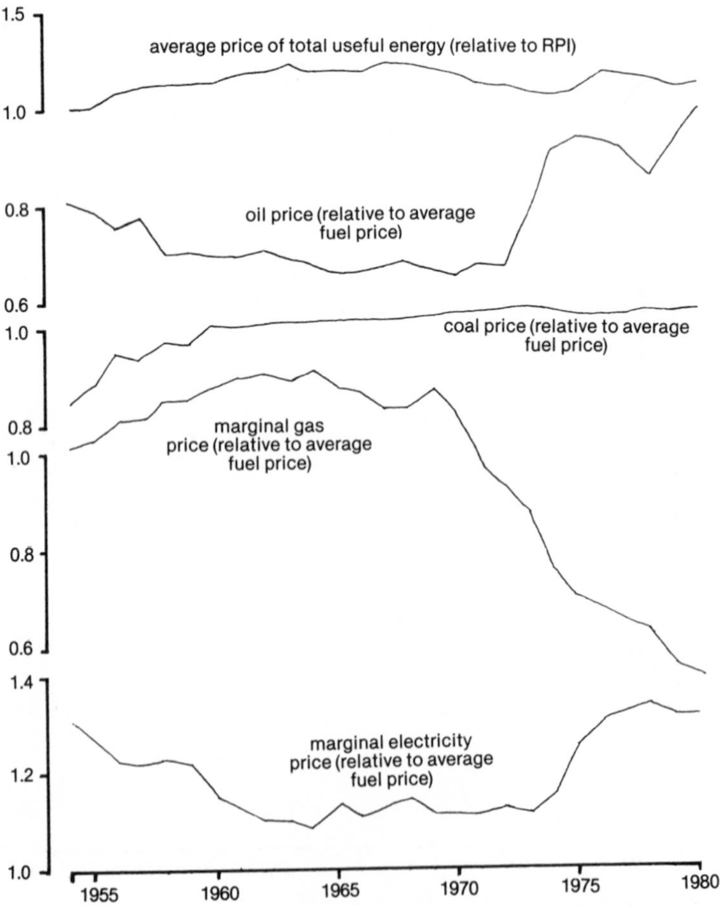

Fig. 11.3: Domestic Sector Relative Fuel Prices (useful heat terms)

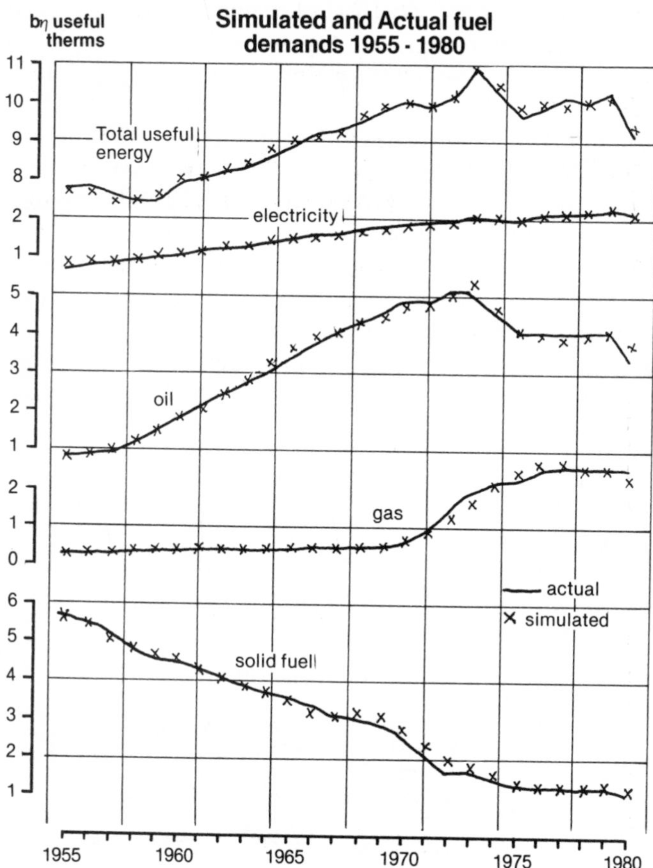

Fig. 11.4: Other Industry Sector

and industrial structure within countries rather than from any major changes in the underlying relationships, for individual sectors within an economy, between energy demand, fuel prices and economic activity.

41. It is clearly important when searching for long-run relationships, to investigate whether any change in structure or coefficient values have occurred over the data period.

42. The total useful energy equation for other industry has been estimated over an early period 1955–1973 and a later period 1961–1979 within the overall data period 1955–1979. Both sub-periods cover nineteen data points compared with the twenty five data points available overall. The upper panel in Table 3 provides estimates of the coefficients in equation (1) of the Appendix estimated

over the three periods. The fitted equation for the earlier period 1955–1973 has a non-significant price coefficient and a coefficient for the lagged term greater than unity which would imply dynamic instability.

43. Figures 2 and 3 illustrate the movements in the real price of energy and in relative fuel prices for the two sectors over the data period. The period up to 1973 contains relatively little movement in the price variable for either sector, the greater part coming after 1973. It is not surprising therefore that the equation fitted over the period 1955–1973 for other industry is unable to capture any significant price response in either level or lag structure.

44. The lower panel in Table 3 provides re-estimates of the equation in the three periods with the lagged coefficient constrainted to

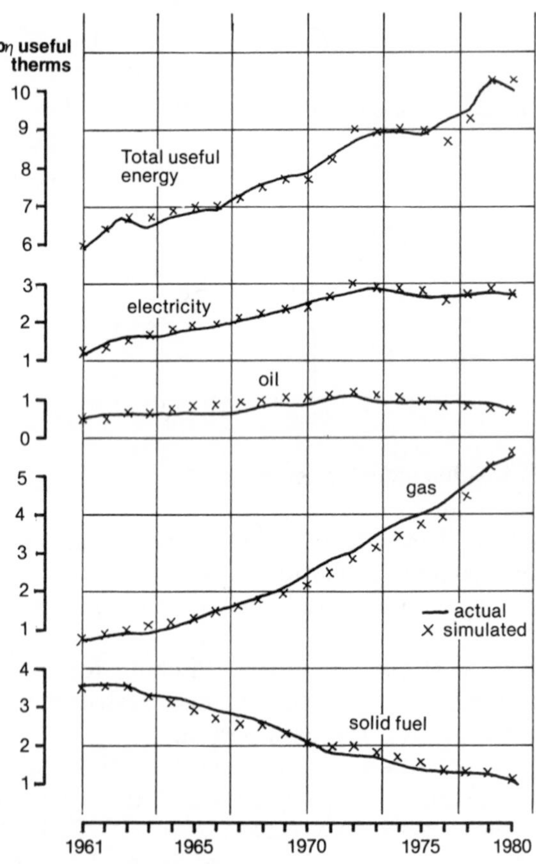

Fig. 11.5: Domestic Sector

Simulated and Actual fuel demands 1961 - 1980

be the value 0.619 estimated over the whole data period. There are no significant differences between the estimates of the output elasticities (coefficient of YE). In particular there is no evidence for a decline in output elasticity. Suggestions that this elasticity for total industrial energy demand might fall as the estimation period is extended to include additional years after 1973 may be due to the inclusion of the Iron and Steel sector which has a high energy intensity and which declined in both output and energy consumption relatively quickly after 1973.

45. There is limited information available in the data on the effects of price changes on energy demand which may be used to test stability in estimated coefficients. At best the statistical estimates in Table 3 provide no evidence supporting variation in output elasticity but are inconclusive on variation in price elasticity and lag structure. However the simulation fits illustrated in Figures 4 and 5 give no indication of a breakdown of the model after 1973.

6. FURTHER DEVELOPMENT

46. Further work is planned in the Department on energy use in the domestic sector taking into account the introduction of energy conservation measures which may throw light on possible saturation levels in domestic energy demand. Additional econometric studies for energy demand in both domestic and industrial sectors are also planned.

REFERENCES

1. *Energy Forecasting Methodology*, Energy Paper Number 19, Department of Energy, HMSO, March 1978.
2. *Energy Projections 1979*, Department of Energy, 1979.
3. *Traffic Appraisal Manual*, Department of Transport, May 1981.
4. *Technology, Prices and the Derived Demand for Energy*, E.R. Berndt and D.O. Wood, Department of Economics, University of British Columbia, Discussion Paper 74-09, May 1974.
5. 'Models and Projections of Demand in Post-War Britain', A.S. Deaton, *Cambridge Studies in Applied Econometrics: 1*, Chapman and Hall, 1975.
6. *Energy Demand Models in the USA and UK*, D. Hawdon, M. Tomlinson, Surrey University, Energy Economics Discussion paper Number 8, January 1982.
7. *Energy Digest*, Department of Energy HMSO, Annually.
8. *Structure of World Energy Demand*, MIT Press, Cambridge, Mass, 1979.

APPENDIX

Energy Demand Models for the Other Industry and Domestic Sectors

Other Industry

1. The form of the model selected for the other industry sector, estimated on annual data over the period 1954–1979 is set out in the following five equations:

Equation for total useful energy:

$$\begin{aligned}\log E_t = \underset{(6.3)}{2.32} &+ \underset{(8.5)}{0.622}\,[\log YE_t - 0.619 \log YE_{t-1}] \\ &- \underset{(3.3)}{0.0871}\,[\log T_t - 0.619 \log T_{t-1}] \\ &- \underset{(3.1)}{0.0854} \log RPE_t + \underset{(2.4)}{0.619} \log E_{t-1} + e_t \\ &\bar{R}^2 = 0.987 \qquad DW = 1.82 \end{aligned} \qquad (1)$$

Equation for share of useful electricity demand in total useful energy;

$$\begin{aligned}\log (EL/E)_t = &- \underset{(3.1)}{1.63} - \underset{(4.6)}{0.247} \log (PEL/PAV)_t \\ &+ \underset{(2.9)}{0.244} \log YEL_t + \underset{(4.1)}{0.496} \log (EL/E)_{t-1} \\ &- \underset{(2.6)}{0.0509}\, DUM + e_t \\ &\bar{R}^2 = 0.989 \qquad DW = 1.72 \end{aligned} \qquad (2)$$

Two-equation set (plus identity) allocating non-electricity, useful energy demand over the three fuels coal, gas and oil. This form of model is termed a multi-nomial logit model as described in Ref. 8.

$$\log (SO/SC)_t = \underset{(1.3)}{0.144} - \underset{(2.8)}{0.223} \log (PIO/PAM)_t$$

$$+ \underset{(4.5)}{0.585} \log (PIC/PAM)_t + \underset{(23)}{0.870} \log SO_{t-1}$$

$$- \underset{(15)}{0.940} \log SC_{t-1} + e_t \qquad (3)$$

$$\log (SG/SC)_t = - \underset{(1.3)}{0.213} - \underset{(4.7)}{0.432} \log (PIG/PAM)_t$$

$$+ \underset{(4.5)}{0.585} \log (PIC/PAM)_t + \underset{(4.9)}{0.724} \log SG_{t-1}$$

$$- \underset{(15)}{0.940} \log SC_{t-1} + e_t \qquad (4)$$

$$SO_t + SG_t + SC_t = 1 \qquad (5)$$

List of variables:

$t, t\text{-}1$ Suffices denoting year t and previous year t-1;

E total annual useful energy demand (m.u. therms) in other industry using efficiency factors: coal 0.5, coke/breeze 0.55, coke-oven gas 0.6, town gas 0.6, natural gas 0.65, electricity 0.9, petroleum 0.55 and creosote pitch mixtures 0.35 (estimates of non-energy uses of gas are excluded);

YE energy weighted output index using 1975 = 100 as base and 1975 useful energy weights of food, drink and tobacco 0.122, chemicals and allied 0.172, engineering and allied 0.260, textiles, leather and clothing 0.075, bricks and cement 0.091, pottery and glass 0.041, paper, printing and publishing 0.076 and other manufacturing 0.163;

T	average temperature for January - April and October - December in °C;
PAV	average price of useful energy obtained by weighting together the average prices of coal, gas, fuel oil and electricity delivered to large industrial users[7] in p/th converted to p/uth using the above efficiency factors;
RPE	real price of energy, PAV, deflated by wholesale (output) price index for manufactured goods (1975 = 100);
e	residual error term;
EL	electricity demand in useful therms including electricity consumption from own generation;
PEL	average price of electricity delivered to large industrial customers in p/uth;
YEL	weighted production index using electricity weights;
DUM	a dummy variable for the 3-day week which takes the value 1 in 1974 and 0 otherwise;
SO, SC, SG	shares of oil, coal and gas in non-electricity, useful energy (i.e. $E - EL$);
PIO, PIC, PIG	average prices of fuel oil, coal and gas to industrial consumers in p/uth;
PAM	arithmetic mean of PIO, PIC and PIG

Estimation

2. Equation (1) may be rewritten as

$$\log E_t = a + b\,[\log YE_t - k^* \log YE_{t-1}] + c\,[\log T_t - k^* \log T_{t-1}] + d \log RPE_t + k \log E_{t-1} + e_t \qquad (6)$$

This equation was estimated using OLS regression by choosing a value for k^* and estimating a, b, c, d and k, replacing k^* by the estimated value k and repeating until no difference appeared between k and k^*. Equation (2) was estimated using OLS regression and the pair of equations (3) and (4) estimated using a 'seemingly unrelated' regression technique which allows restraints to be imposed across equations, e.g. equality constraints on the coefficients of log $(PIC/PAM)_t$ and log SC_{t-1}.

3. Statistical measures of goodness of fit are provided as 't' statistics in brackets below coefficient estimates, values of $\overline{R}^2$ and Durbin Watson statistics (although the presence of a lagged dependent variable renders this last statistic inapplicable in its customary form).

Dynamic Properties of the Model

4. Using the lag operator L such that

$$L \log E_t = \log E_{t-1} \tag{7}$$

equation (6) may be rewritten (assuming $k^* = k$ and the expected value of the residual error is zero) as

$$(1-kL) \log E_t = a + b\,(1-kL) \log YE_t + c\,(1-kL) \log T_t + d \log RPE_t \tag{8}$$

Dividing through by $(1-kL)$ and recalling that $La = a$, equation (8) becomes

$$\log E_t = \frac{a}{1-k} + b \log YE_t + c \log T_t + \frac{d}{1-kL} \log RPE_t \tag{9}$$

The coefficient of log RPE_t may be expanded as a power series so that equation (9) becomes

$$\log E_t = \frac{a}{1-k} + b \log Y_t + c \log T_t$$
$$+ d\,(1 + kL + k^2 L^2 + k^3 L^3 + \ldots) \log RPE_t \qquad (10)$$

$$\log E_t = \frac{a}{1-k} + b \log Y_t + c \log T_t$$
$$+ d\,(\log RPE_t + k \log RPE_{t-1} + k^2 \log RPE_{t-2} + \ldots) \qquad (11)$$

5. Thus the form of equation (1), as re-expressed in equation (11), implies that changes in output YE_t and temperature T_t affect total useful energy demand E_t only in the year in question. However E_t depends on current and all past values of real energy prices RPE_t, RPE_{t-1}, REP_{t-2}... etc. Correspondingly any change in REP_t will affect all later values of E, i.e. E_t, E_{t+1}, E_{t+2}... etc, but with decreasing weights as K^n decreases with n ($o \leqslant k < 1$), specifically the elasticity of E_{t+kn} with respect to RPE_t is $d\,k^n$. For $k = 0.619$, the weights in the power series indicate the contribution to log E_{t+n} from a step change in log RPE_t of unit height. These coefficients build up in the manner shown in Table 4.

Thus 38% of the effect of a change in the real price of energy on total useful energy demand will occur in the current year, 62% by

Table 11.4.

Time period	Weight	Cumulative weight	%
t	d = 0.0854	0.0854	38%
$t+1$	dk = 0.0529	0.1383	62%
$t+2$	dk^2 = 0.0327	0.1710	
$t+3$	dk^3 = 0.0203	0.1913	85%
$t+4$	dk^4 = 0.0125	0.2038	
$t+5$	dk^5 = 0.0078	0.2116	
$t+6$	dk^6 = 0.0048	0.2164	97%
$t+7$	dk^7 = 0.0030	0.2194	
$t+8$	dk^8 = 0.0018	0.2212	
$t+9$	dk^9 = 0.0011	0.2223	99%
$t+10$	dk^{10} = 0.0007	0.2230	
.	.	.	
.	.	.	
.	.	.	
$t+\infty$	dk^{∞} = 0	0.2241	100%

the first year after, 85% by the third year, 95% by the sixth year and so on.

6. Lags are also present in the electricity equation (2) and may be illustrated using a similar mathematical procedure. Lagged values of both price and output variables were found to affect the share of electricity demand in total energy (both in useful energy terms).

7. The lag structure in the equation set (3), (4) and (5), providing the fuel allocation system for non-electricity useful energy demand, is complex and long lived. Furthermore these equations provide shares which must be multiplied in each year by $(E_t - EL_t)$ whose terms are themselves subject to lagged effects. More complex lag structures are used in the Department for narrowly focussed energy demand analysis.

A numerical illustration of the dynamic properties of this model is illustrated in Fig. 6. The equation system has been calculated out over the period 1980 to 2010, holding energy prices and industrial

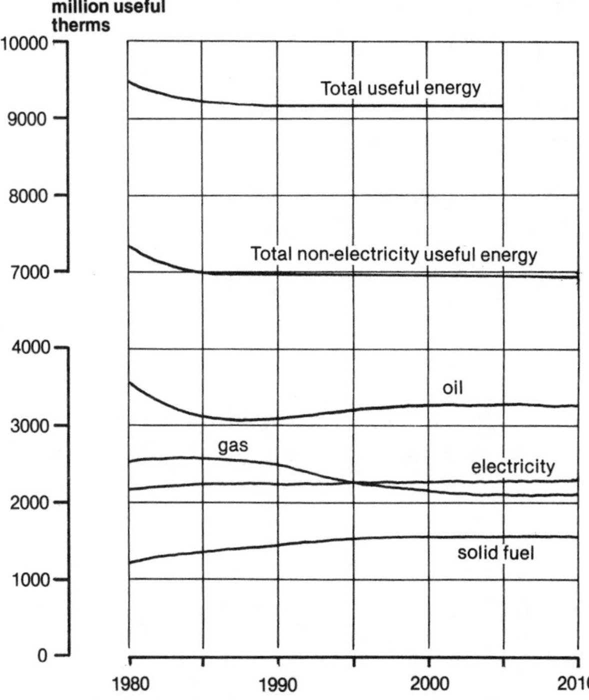

Fig. 11.6: Dynamic Response of Energy Demand Model for Other Industry
at constant 1980 values of output level and energy prices.

output levels constant at their 1980 levels. The disequilibrium existing in 1980 arising from past changes in outputs and prices is gradually removed as the dynamic system settles down to equilibrium values. Most of the effects are worked through by 1990 but some small effects are visible after 1995. The implication is that some effects of the sharp movements in energy prices in the early 1970s on choice of fuel as the stock of plant and equipment in manufacturing industry is replaced are still occurring (possible supply constraints have been excluded from this analysis).

Domestic Sector

9. The equations for the domestic sector are set out below:

Equation for total useful energy for space and water heating, estimated over annual data over 1954-1979;

$$\begin{aligned}\log EPC_t = {} & \underset{(20)}{2.57} + \underset{(21)}{0.534} \log RDI_t \\ & - \underset{(5.9)}{0.276} [\log T_t - 0.4 \log T_{t-1}] \\ & - \underset{(2.7)}{0.255} \log (PH/RPI)_t + \underset{(3.2)}{0.4} \log EPC_{t-1} + e_t \end{aligned} \tag{12}$$

$$\overline{R}^2 = 0.98 \qquad DW = 2.2$$

Three equation set (plus identity) allocating shares of useful energy demand for space and water heating, estimated over the period 1961-1979;

$$\begin{aligned}\log (SC/SE) = {} & \underset{(3.7)}{-0.0637} - \underset{(2.9)}{0.220} \log (HPC/AMH)_t \\ & + \underset{(2.9)}{0.220} \log (HPE/AMH)_t + \underset{(5.4)}{0.928} \log SC_{t-1} \\ & - \underset{(5.4)}{0.928} \log SE_{t-1} + e_t \end{aligned} \tag{13}$$

$$\log (SO/SE)_t = \underset{(3.7)}{-0.137} - \underset{(2.9)}{0.220} \log (HPO/AMH)_t + \underset{(2.9)}{0.220} \log (HPE/AMH)_t + \underset{(5.4)}{0.928} \log SO_{t-1} - \underset{(5.4)}{0.928} \log SE_{t-1} + e_t \qquad (14)$$

$$\log (SG/SE)_t = \underset{(2.1)}{0.064} - \underset{(2.9)}{0.220} \log (HPG/AMH)_t + \underset{(2.9)}{0.220} \log (HPE/AMH)_t + \underset{(5.4)}{0.928} \log SG_{t-1} - \underset{(5.4)}{0.928} \log SE_{t-1} + e_t \qquad (15)$$

$$SC_t + SE_t + SO_t + SG_t = 1 \qquad (16)$$

Equation for electricity specific demands

$$\log NCE_t = \underset{(69)}{5.10} - \underset{(38)}{3.92} \frac{1}{RDI_t} + e_t$$

$$\overline{R}^2 = 0.98 \qquad DW = 0.84 \qquad (17)$$

Equation for total useful energy demand for cooking, estimated over the period 1963-1976 for England and Wales only;

$$\log Cook_t = \underset{(345)}{2.53} + \underset{(7.2)}{0.116} \log (RDI)_t + e_t$$

$$\overline{R}^2 = 0.80 \qquad DW = 1.76 \qquad (18)$$

Equation for splitting gas and electricity demands for cooking, estimated over the period 1963–1976 for England and Wales only;

$$\log (SGC/SEC)_t = \underset{(2.6)}{0.238} - \underset{(1.0)}{0.177} \log (PGC/PEC)_t$$

$$+ \underset{(6.5)}{0.707} \log (SGC/SEC)_{t-1} + e_t$$

$\overline{R}^2 = 0.859$ $\qquad$ $DW = 1.68$ $\qquad$ (19)

$$SGC_t + SEC_t = 1 \qquad (20)$$

List of Variables:

EPC Useful energy demand for space and water heating per head of population, using fuel efficiencies of coal 0.3, coke and breeze 0.5, other solid fuel 0.45, town gas 0.6, natural gas 0.65, electricity 0.9 and petroleum 0.65;

RDI real personal disposable income per head of population;

PH Unit value of useful energy to domestic consumers, p/uth;

RPI retail price index;

NCE m. useful therms of electricity per head for use in other electrical appliances;

COOK energy use for cooking (m.uth per head);

SGC,SEC shares of gas and electricity in COOK:

PGC,PEC costs of gas and electricity for cooking calculated as prices of gas and electricity plus estimates of annuitised capital (cooker) costs per useful therm.

Estimation

10. The estimation procedures for the equations in the domestic sector are similar to those used for other industry. Additional cross-equation constraints were required in the fuel allocation system for space and water heating to provide meaningful coefficients. Price terms were not found to be significant in the equations for electricity specific demands or for total energy use in cooking.

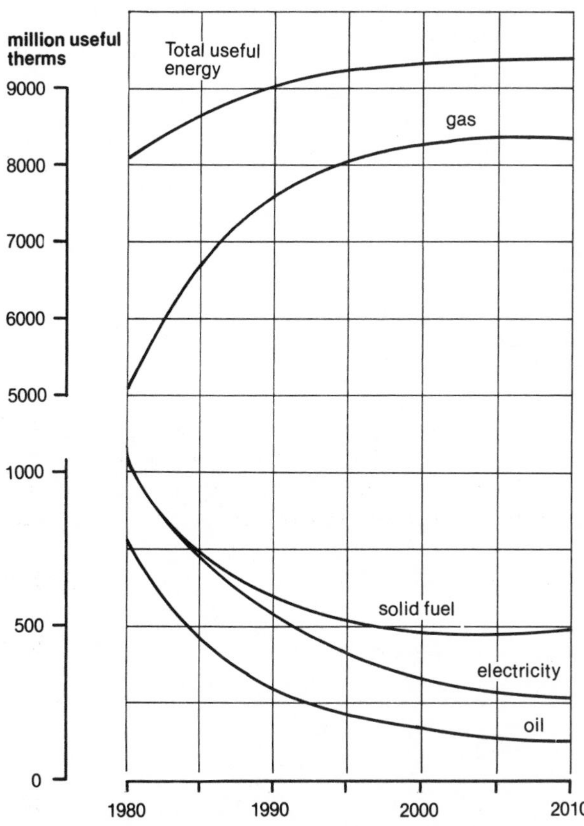

Fig. 11.7: Dynamic Response of Energy Demand Model for Domestic Space and Water Heating at constant 1980 values of real income and energy prices.

Dynamic Properties

11. Lagged terms are included in equations (12), (13), (14), (15) and (19). The response in total energy demand for space and water heating is rather slower than for other industry. A lagged effect through income is included to capture 'permanent income' effects. Again the

interaction of lagged effects between the equations is complex. A numerical illustration is provided in Figure 7 of how the disequilibrium in both prices and income effects in 1980 settle down over time.

Chapter 12

Forecasts in Decision Making: Help or Hindrance?

*P.W. Beck**

Any enterprise is built by wise planning, becomes strong through common sense and profits wonderfully by keeping abreast of the facts.

Solomon, Proverbs 24 v. 3 and 4.

For a number of years now I have been more and more concerned about the widening gap between the accepted principle of reaching policy decisions and its actual practice. In theory, the approach to policy decisions is cool, analytical, scientific, objective. In practice, it more often than not turns out to be confused, messy, subjective and expedient . . . in short, human. The more sophisticated the available tools and methods, the more confused the decision process appears to become. Yet we persist in paying lip service to the theory, and the question I would like to put before you is whether the activity of making the decision process more 'scientific' is a triumph of expectation over experience (as someone said about a third marriage). And if we turn away from the 'scientific approach', does this destroy the need for statistics, forecasts and planning?

***Planning Director, Shell UK Ltd. This chapter is based on an address first given by Mr Beck to an Institute of Energy Conference on Energy Statistics in 1981.**

1. PAST FORECASTS EXAMINED

I would like to concentrate on the type of forecasts which are generally thought to be needed for decisions on energy policy, strategy or projects. Bearing in mind the lead times between decision and effects, this implies forecasts stretching at least five years ahead, and possibly as much as 20 years.

For the purpose of this paper, I would like to define a forecast as an estimate about some aspect of the future. There can be any number of forecasts on any particular aspect of the future, but if there is only one such forecast, it becomes a prediction of the future or a single point/line forecast.

Firstly let us look at past experiences — four examples taken at random:[1]

(a) UK oil demand and production for 1980, published in mid 1974:

Million T	*Estimate*	*Actual*
Demand	113-123	80
Production	150–170	81

(b) World energy demand (outside CPEs*) for 1980, published mid-1972:

	Total	*Oil*	*Nat.Gas*	*Solids*	*Nuclear*	*Other*
10^6 b/doe	115	63	20	17	8	7
Actual	94	49	17	17	3	8

(c) Figure 1 provides a comparison between forecasts and actual for electricity demand in England and Wales[2] and Fig. 2 shows a comparison of estimates provided by my own organisation in Shell UK of oil demand in UK for 1980 as estimated during various years of the 1970s.

There can be only one conclusion from these examples, especially when one remembers that many were developed either at the request of, or to influence, decision makers, and that major policy or investment decisions could well have been based on them: they are not just misleading, they are dangerous. With such evidence of our own failcians for not providing us with stable and logical energy policies?

The decision takers are far from blameless themselves. The fact that most forecasts are wrong has been known for a long time and is

*CPEs: Centrally Planned Economies.

well documented. Again, a random example: Sir Paul Chambers[3] — then Chairman of ICI — provided a full review of the problems with forecasting in the chemical industry in 1966 and comments: 'perhaps one of the major tasks of management in a large chemical company is to recognise the inevitable imperfections of its forecasting and to make allowances'.

The experience of the petrochemical industry since then has not shown that this advice has been heeded. Forecasts continued to be demanded and were used for decisions on capacity needs — and what forecasts they were: in 1972 estimates of European ethylene production for 1976 were 16 mt, against an outturn of 10 mt!

In 1968, Anthony Harris (Financial Times 17th May) quotes Professor Solomons of Wharton School, Pennsylvania: '. . . far more ink is spilt on the details of how to turn forecasts into planning decisions . . . argument over DCF versus net present value which would have been enjoyed by the scholastics of the dark ages . . . than on the quality of the forecasts. . . .'

So by then the problems of forecasting were well known, but rescue appeared to be at hand. The ability of fast data processing which became available from the more powerful computers developed in the 1960s seemed to offer substantial possibilities for improving forecasts.

2. MODELS

Instead of using past statistics and 'judgement' to provide forecasts, these tools appeared to make it possible to analyse the past, determine relations between independent variables, and use the results for predicting future trends. Here then we are back to the scientific method — collect data, analyse, determine relationships, develop theory and project the results.

The method appears to work well in science and engineering. Voyager 2 was only 3.1 seconds out in its approach to Saturn after a four-year journey of 1.22 billion miles. Bridges are designed, built and usually behave as predicted, but that cannot be said for the estimate of either the time the bridge will take to build or its cost. Prediction of these latter elements has to encompass economic factors — inflation, exchange rate, energy price; and human factors — how hard people work, their efficiency, their bargaining power, their expectations, fears.

All these are phenomena which are not accounted for in the natural sciences, and they are difficult to cram into algebraic equations.

The future of energy demand and supply depends largely on economic, social, political and technological developments. Can these be modelled individually, their inter-relationships defined so as to make prediction possible? Surely not.

The truth is that most model makers would not attempt such a task. They would simplify and examine the effect of specific relationships on the factors under study. They know that their model is not a reality, but might be related to it as a model aeroplane to Concorde. Unfortunately, should the results of such modelling work be interesting and topical, a metamorphosis often takes place: the analogous model comes to be seen as a portrait of reality — perhaps not by the model maker, but by the user. Colleagues have labelled this the 'Baal' syndrome.[4] The symbol of god comes to be seen as god in itself.

Perhaps the most complex modelling effort yet attempted in the energy field was the Energy System Programme at the International Institute of Applied Systems Analysis (IIASA). Paul S. Basile,[5] summarising the results of these studies, comments:

> 'No one knows the future. This cannot be said too often or too strongly — particularly after eight chapters of detailed thinking about the world and its energy systems in the year 2030. Yet after (and during) these analyses, some facts of the energy puzzle seem to be better known than the others. There are perhaps (subject, of course, to different interpretations) a finite number of truly important uncertainties — a few large imponderables.'

No pretence at forecast here — and yet Prof. Meadows[60] providing a critique of the IIASA work, gives a timely warning:

> 'Basile provides a painfully honest assessment of the modelling process and its relationship to the remainder of the report. He points out often and explicitly that energy scenarios in 2000 and 2030 "are of course simply constructs for the future; they are neither forecasts nor prescriptions. They are intended as 'what if' possibilities." Yet scenarios are almost inescapably taken as forecasts. Even the press kit for the two books blurs the distinction: "IIASA's high and low scenario projects for the next 50 years indicate that . . . coal production, after growing slowly to the end of this century, must expand rapidly thereafter." And when only a few scenarios are presented, the one that appears "best" in terms of the performance indices generated by the model will automatically be taken by most readers as a prediction or a recommended goal.'

Although the model builder is at times more sinned against than sinning, and fights to stop the meaning of the model being misunderstood, there are others who succumb to the temptation of 'playing god', or to the belief that 'notwithstanding all the uncertainties' a view has to be taken — which results in a 'best estimate'. A 'best estimate' has a tendency to become accepted as a single line forecast, or prediction, and it is in the nature of the system of such predictions that more often than not the forecaster will be proved wrong if believed. Human choice and activity is affected by such belief and will tend to act to nullify the prediction. The ancient Greeks knew all about this: Cassandra could foretell the future only because Apollo put a curse on her that no one should believe her. In the story of Oedipus the gods' intervention was needed before the prediction could be fulfilled. Perhaps we forget the classics at our peril.

From examples shown in Section 1, there must be strong doubt whether forecasts have improved since the mid 1960s. We have replaced 'overt judgement' by pseudo science. My feeling is that as a result the situation has got worse.

An examination of this assertion could be interesting and might make a good subject for research.

3. THE ROLE OF THE DECISION TAKER

My argument so far has concentrated on the forecaster and the modeller, the danger of misleading, and of being misunderstood — and perhaps not doing all that much about it. But as already mentioned earlier, many decision takers have an even greater guilt to bear.

How many times have we heard of managements or cabinet ministers who consider themselves too busy to read voluminous briefs and require one or two page summaries of all the salient factors of a policy or project: When complex and inter-related issues (a description which applies to most major energy matters) are involved, such a short brief is only feasible if it is a summary of previous debate, and if the level of understanding by the user and the provider of the brief are roughly equal.

If that is not the case — in other words, if the user is not intimately familiar with the scheme, if he has not the key factors determining the success of the project at his fingertips — a short brief is worse than nothing. No brief at all means that the decision-taker has to ask questions and possibly start a debate which might provide him with information. The dangers of the short brief go beyond the mere fact that it does not fully inform the decision-taker. It may not even give sufficient grounding or incentive for the decision-taker to ask the right questions. There is a natural tendency for people to be reluctant to ask questions which expose their ignorance. Two common responses in this situation are silence and acceptance (the line of least resistance) or, alternatively, instant rejection without reasoning or guidance.

Alas, Parkinson's Law about the atomic reactor and the bicycle shed is as true today as when formulated in the late 1950s. When the decision-taker is not interested in the complexities and uncertainties of the scheme presented to him, he is in essence opting out; he lets others take the decisions for him, giving them the power, but keeping responsibility for the result. This may be relatively acceptable and harmless if done consciously on the basis of justified trust in his advisers, but extremely dangerous if neither the decision-taker nor his adviser realize that this is happening.

Perhaps the most important task of the decision taker is to ensure that the right staff is given the right incentive to produce the right kind of information, so that neither uncertainties nor options are suppressed, and that in the end his decision is taken with a full knowledge of the alternatives rejected and the potential risks and rewards of the chosen course.

4. INFORMATION FOR DECISIONS

Nothing said hitherto has implied that statistics, forecasts or models have no place in the information package for decisions; they have — and very vital ones too — but they must be chosen to be relevant, to inform, not to obscure, to enhance understanding of the future and its uncertainty, and to avoid single line forecasts of an intrinsically unpredictable future. Since much of the future will be moulded by human agencies, the information package must include soft as well as hard data, descriptions as well as statistics.

The aim of the package must be to enhance understanding, to improve the quality of the debate, not to point to single answers. Each decision requires a certain amount of information. If this is exceeded, the result will be less, not more understanding.

Some of the elements often omitted, but vital in such an information package, include the following.

(a) *Key Issues and Their Effect:* First, and possibly most important, one has to identify the key uncertainties and develop a list of key issues which would have a major effect on the outcome of the decision. Such issues can be technical (e.g. will the process work?), economic (e.g. the competitive environment), and socio-political (e.g. can we get planning permission?). Only when such a list is available can one determine what type of data and analysis about the past, the present, and the future, has to be assembled for an adequate debate of the subject under review.

(b) *Long Term Consequences:* When it comes to major policies or projects, especially for countries, one has to bear in mind that an analysis of their potential effect has to include not just the primary one but also the secondary and tertiary effects on the socio-economic system; these are often more important than the primary.

As an example, one can trace the effect of a decision by a country to subsidise energy prices for industry:

The *primary* effect is simple. Energy costs for industry will go down and so, in the short run, will total industry costs.

The *secondary* effect, usually a medium term one, is more uncertain and complex: industry could become more competitive, sell more, become more profitable, expand and increase the wealth of the country. However, it might instead reduce pressure on conservation, dissipate the advantages of lower energy prices, and so waste the subsidy.

The *tertiary* effect is long term and can be even more complex. Lower energy prices could shelter inefficient industry and attract energy intensive industry from other areas. Energy demand would grow and eventually reach the point where the cost of providing marginal energy would outstrip the benefit of having high energy-using industry in the country. If there were a possibility that such a point would be reached soon, the policy would obviously be very dangerous. On the other hand, if there were security of low cost energy for many decades, then that policy could have many advantages. Clearly Saudi Arabia can afford to take this route. But most other oil producing countries would have to think very hard before committing themselves to such a policy.

(c) *Understanding of the Past and Present:* Whether one uses models, debate or just hunch, it does help to consider past experience and know from what position and under what circumstances one is starting out. For this, statistics are essential. However, while collection of statistics is easy, their interpretation is not. Not for nothing has it been said that the past is nearly as uncertain as the future.

It has also been noted on many occasions that the same set of statistics can be interpreted in different ways to prove diametrically opposed theses. Thus statistics on their own — however scrupulously collected and collated — do not necessarily lend an objective light to one's consideration of the phenomena they are attempting to quantify.

Before one begins to interpret statistics, one has of course to be sure that these statistics have indeed been adequately collected and collated. But this can only be checked by someone with some knowledge of the subject and, just as important, some appreciation of the conditions under which the statistics are collected. Unless these conditions are met, the statistics are generally not safe to use.

Unfortunately, the greater the demand by companies, public authorities and international bodies for different data, the less likely is it that such a check can, in practice, be made.

(d) *Predetermined Elements:* Not all factors are uncertain. The analytical work must also include a study of those aspects which are predetermined — developments which are 'in the pipeline' and which, in the time span under consideration, have measurable effects and limits. An example could be an estimate of the number of fields likely to be in operation in the North Sea within 5 years. Indeed, one could even make a stab at the maximum number of fields that could be developed during the 1980s. Alas, the 'likely' number cannot usefully be estimated as a single number. It depends too much on government policies and indeed on the international energy picture. Here, therefore, a range of figures can be the only useful forecast.

(e) *Alternative Solutions:* However qualified a forecast may be — however much it is hedged in 'ifs' and 'buts' — as soon as it is accepted as the 'best estimate' and used as a planning line, technologists or economists will attempt to determine an 'optimum solution' against that forecast. Hence there could be a tendency to propose one solution only. If, however, wide uncertainties are accepted and there is no 'best estimate', people have to search for different solutions; more in the direction of flexibility, keeping options open, looking at decisions which neither cause delays, nor involve crippling penalties if these decisions turn out to fall short or overrun actual future demand. Alternative solutions have therefore to be put forward and considered by the decision takers. Of course, decisions based on a 'best estimate' will be the most rewarding if such an estimate actually materialises. But 'best estimates' seldom do.

5. CONCLUSIONS

Arguments and evidence in this paper point to the conclusion that statistics, models and forecasts tend — at least in the way they are currently used — to hinder debate, increase confusion and generally undermine and obstruct the decision-making process.

Computers have made collection, storage and analysis of statistical data so easy that there is inevitably temptation to collect more information, whether or not it can properly be checked and interpreted. As a result, we may, in many areas, be creating a statistical fog which obscures the landmarks of the real world. When the decision taker, frustrated by this phenomenon, asks for greater clarity, the temptation is to provide him with yet more statistics and larger and more sophisticated models, making the fog even more dense.

Acceptance of uncertainty by decision takers and their advisers — involving an overt admission that it is impossible to foretell the future — should lead to a different use of models and forecasting tools, and to a more qualitative approach to decision making. Statistics have a vital role to play in this — as a means of checking assumptions and thus helping to improve understanding — but this is quite different from the role in which they are predominantly cast at present.

I have heard it suggested that decision takers might be better off if they threw out all planning techniques and relied exclusively on hunches — or 'gut feel'. But if there is inadequate understanding of the key determinants, this is unlikely to result in better decisions. Techniques are tools, and it is the bad workman who blames them.

REFERENCES

1. It would be invidious to single out one or two wrong forecasts out of the many. The reference can however be obtained by application to the author.
2. *Medium Term Development Plan 1980–87*, Electricity Council, May 1980.
3. Sir Paul Chambers, Alfred Watson Memorial Lecture 'Problems of Forecasting in the Chemical Industry', *Journal of Actuaries*, (September 1966).
4. B.J. Taylor, 'The Baal Syndrome: When 'Spectacles' become 'blinkers'', *Training News* (published by the Group Training division of Shell International Petroleum Company, Shell Centre London), Number 14, (1978).
5. Paul S. Basile, 'Balancing Energy Supply and Demand: A Fifty-Years Global Perspective', *The Energy Journal*, (July 1981).
6. Dennis Meadows, 'A Critique of the IIASA Energy Model' *The Energy Journal*, (July 1981).

Chapter 13

The Future of Crude Oil Prices

*Colin Robinson**

It never is a good time to try to assess the future trend of crude oil prices, but the present can be regarded as particularly difficult. It is nine months since the official price of light Arabian 'marker' crude was fixed at $34 per barrel fob. Since then, although the official 'marker' price has been maintained, differentials in favour of the higher-priced crudes have been reduced and in the spot market light Arabian dropped as low as $28 in the early months of 1982 before recovering to just below the official price by mid-June and then varying in the $31 to $33 range. There is considerable uncertainty not only about what crude oil prices may be in the future but even about what they are now.

In such circumstances, a discussion of possible crude price trends in the 1980s and 1990s might seem a foolish venture. One should also be mindful of how unsuccessful some past efforts at oil price prediction have been. Nevertheless, energy forecasts and plans have to use assumptions about oil prices so it is clearly important to reduce the region of uncertainty as much as one can. Obviously

*Professor of Economics, University of Surrey. This paper was delivered at the Annual BIEE/IAEE Conference held in Churchill College, Cambridge on 28/30 June 1982.

attempts at single line 'forecasts' are of no interest in such an uncertain market, and indeed are likely to be more misleading than helpful, but we need to try to define a reasonable plausible range within which crude prices can be expected to lie. Plans to exploit indigenous coal reserves, to construct nuclear power stations and to invest in renewable energy forms are very sensitive to what one assumes about the price of the fuel which still supplies over 40 per cent of the world's energy. Real GNP growth rates may also vary according to the rate of change of real oil prices.

There are two things this paper will not do. It will not set out the results of yet another model of the world oil market; anyone who wishes to read what results can be obtained from existing models can find them, for example, in a recent Energy Modelling Forum[1] report. The paper will try to use economic analysis to identify key relationships, to indulge in some simple quantification and to demonstrate the uncertainties which abound. Second, the paper will not attempt to deal with oil prices to the consumer. In the 1970s and early 1980s, the export price of crude oil rose much faster than consumer prices: the crude price rise was very considerably damped by depressed tanker freight rates, by comparatively small increases in refining, marketing and distribution costs and by tax increases on oil products which were also small relative to the crude price increase. It may well be that, in future, consumer prices will continue to move differently from crude prices. Perhaps for a time we shall see product prices to the consumer rising *faster* than crude prices (as they have been doing in Western Europe recently): the oil companies now seem to have little alternative but to try to make downstream operations profitable in their own right to the extent that competition allows, and governments may increase product taxes in real terms for revenue reasons and to sustain conservation incentives. So crude oil export prices, though clearly very important, are only one of the determinants of the price paid by the oil consumer.

1. PAST TRENDS

Since understanding of the past is a necessary (though not sufficient) condition for successful forecasting, we can best begin by examining the history of price changes in the world crude oil market. For this purpose 1950 is a convenient starting point so as to cover the relatively long period of comparatively steady world economic growth from 1950 to 1973 — during which real GNP was rising at

Table 13.1. Crude Oil Prices Annual Average F.O.B. (Export Price of Light (34° API) Arabian Crude Oil, Persian Gulf ($ per barrel).

	*Posted or Official Price**	*Posted or Official Price in 1981 Dollars†*
1950	1.71	6.9
1955	1.93	6.9
1960	1.86	6.1
1965	1.80	5.5
1970	1.80	5.0
1971	2.20	5.8
1972	2.48	6.0
1973	3.29	6.8
1974	11.58	19.5
1975	10.72	16.1
1976	11.51	17.3
1977	12.40	17.1
1978	12.70	15.2
1979	17.26	18.1
1980	28.67	27.2
1981	32.50	32.5

*Posted price from 1950 to 1974; Official Selling Price from 1975 onwards.
†Deflated by UN Dollar Index of Unit Values of World Exports of Manufacturers.
Sources: M.A. Adelman, *The World Petroleum Market*, Johns Hopkins University Press, 1972, Colin Robinson and Jon Morgan, *North Sea Oil in the Future*, Macmillan 1978. *The Petroleum Economist* (Monthly), various issues. *UN Statistical Yearbook* (Annual) and *UN Monthly Bulletin of Statistics.*

an average annual compound rate of some 5 per cent — as well as the more turbulent recent past.

Table 1 gives some estimates of world crude oil price trends from 1950 onwards, using the light Arabian 'marker' as an example. The first column shows the 'posted' (tax reference) price of light Arabian up to 1974 and the official sales price from 1975 onwards. Column two converts the prices into real terms, using as a deflator the United Nations index of unit values of world exports of manufactures. There were changes in the UN index during the period considered but successive indices have been linked, ignoring the changes, since the intention is merely to give a broad idea of how much a barrel of oil would buy in terms of manufactured imports in any given year. The trend of real oil prices is downwards both in the 1950s and, more strongly, in the 1960s. Then in the 1970s there is the massive jump which raised the 1981 annual average real crude price to over six times the 1970 annual average. Examining the table more closely, we can see that two step increases in real prices occurred, from 1973 to

1974 and from 1979 to 1981. Between the two steps there was little net change in the real price of crude.

Table 1 does not reveal the full story for two reasons. First, in the 1950s and more especially in the 1960s discounts on posted prices tended to increase; thus the true real price trend was more firmly downwards than Table 1 suggests. Second, because in some crucial years the price trend altered, the annual averages given in the table can be a little misleading. In a very imperfect attempt to correct both these failings, Table 2 illustrates some calculated rates of change over what seem to be the relevant periods at which we should look. Estimates of crude discounts in Adelman's 'The World Petroleum Market'[2] have been used to arrive at the figures.

Table 13.2. Estimated Annual Rates of Change of Market Price of Light Arabian Crude Oil.

	% per Annum, Compound	
	In Nominal Terms	*In Real Terms*
1950–1960	−0.2	−2.4
1960–First Half 1970	−3.0	−4;5
First Half 1970–Second Half 1981	+33.3	+21.9
1950–Second Half 1981	10.0	5.2

Source: As Table 1.

Assumed market prices (including discounts) in nominal terms are as follows ($ barrel)

	1950	1.71
	1960	1.67
First Half	1970	1.25
Second Half	1981	34.00

What Table 2 shows is that real crude prices were falling at about 2½ per cent per annum in the 1950s. Then in the 1960s as discounting increased, the rate of decline became steeper at about 4½ per cent per annum. By early 1970, the real price of crude oil was about half what it had been in 1950. However, from the second half of 1970 onwards (after the Libyans had enforced production cutbacks for most of the companies operating there), real prices began to increase. Over the following eleven years they rose at the remarkable annual average compound rate of about 22 per cent. By late 1981 the real price was nearly ten times what it had been early in 1970. Taking the whole period, 1950 to second half 1981, the annual average compound rate of rise of real crude prices was about 5 per cent so that the real price late in 1981 was about five times its 1950 value.

How can one explain the dramatic change in oil prices? In the 1950s and more especially in the 1960s real oil prices were on a clearly declining trend; from 1970 onwards they rose massively, mainly in two big steps. The popular simple explanation, which regards OPEC as the villain of the piece, is entirely unconvincing since the Organisation was present in both periods. Nor is the view that oil price shocks have resulted simply from political events (such as the Yom Kippur War and the Iranian Revolution) convincing. But if we cannot explain the very different price movements of the 1950s and 1970s we have little hope of being able to discern what may happen in the future. We then need to see if our explanation of the period up to late 1981 can also explain the fall in prices from Autumn 1981 to Spring 1982.

At the risk of over-simplifying some complex issues, it seems that the principal elements of the explanation can be found within the standard economist's theory of resource depletion. This says, in essence, that oil producers will make decisions about producing marginal barrels or holding them back for the future according to whether they think oil in the ground is likely to be more or less valuable than money invested.[3] In more technical terms, producers will compare expected rates of price appreciation (net of costs) with their discount rates. Oil companies producing in the Middle East in the 1960s probably had rather limited time horizons, because it is likely they anticipated partial or complete takeover of their producing operations and thus their discount rates were higher than they would normally have been; they also subscribed to the general expectation of the time that real oil prices would remain approximately constant or decline for many years. The resulting coincidence of high discount rates and low price expectations seems to have resulted in a strong tendency to produce oil sooner rather than later, thus holding prices down. World oil output more than doubled between 1960 and 1970. However, as oil output grew rapidly, fears of future scarcity eventually emerged and price expectations changed from the late 1960s onwards. At the same time 'host' countries with relatively long time horizons took over producing decisions and to them money in the bank began to look a poor proposition compared with the apparently excellent prospects of price appreciation if oil was left in the ground. There can have been few better investments than a barrel of oil left in the ground early in 1970, extracted late in 1981 and sold at a price ten times as high in real terms (with only a small increase in production costs). Though *ex ante* no one anticipated such huge increases, there is no doubt that in the early 1970s expectations of big price increases were formed — a common view was that crude prices would double or treble by the 1980s.[4] These altered expectations were important determinants of the change from rapidly rising world production to constant or modestly increasing output. Enhanced price expectations coupled with lower discount rates gave a strong incentive to hold marginal barrels of oil in the ground. Thus supply behaviour altered. Producers' supply curves shifted to the left along demand curves which in the short-run, were very inelastic with respect to price and prices therefore rose sharply. Demand curves shifted too, because of reduced real income, but not by enough to avoid price increases induced from the supply side.

OPEC's role in the price increases of the 1970s seems generally to be exaggerated. Clearly, by the early 1970s its members had gained in confidence, were anxious to lead a Third World crusade against 'exploitation' and were both more willing and more able to exploit monopoly power than they had been in the 1960s. The 1973 Arab-Israeli war also provided an occasion for the Arab members of OPEC to take supply-restricting action. But in the 1970s OPEC had no formal output-sharing scheme, as a true cartel would have done. Perceptions of OPEC's power may well have been a significant factor in generating fears of scarcity in the early 1970s but the huge price increases which occurred would hardly have been possible had background economic forces (especially the change in price expectations) not been propitious. To put the matter another way, even with no OPEC, individual oil-producing countries would have had an incentive to cut output in the 1970s, thus raising prices sharply.

In the more recent past, OPEC as such seems to have had little price-increasing influence. Prices increased in 1979–80 mainly because of anticipated shortages and uncertainty — which revived expectations of higher prices in the future — resulting first from the Iranian revolution and subsequently from the Iran–Iraq war. As prices rose, OPEC appears to have done little more than meet *ex post*, to try to reach agreement on what the crude price actually was and what differentials should be from the light Arabian 'marker crude', in somewhat confused market circumstances. Then, in late 1981 and early 1982, OPEC had the novel experience of trying to cope with a falling market which it did first by agreeing to reductions for some of the over-priced crudes and then by output adjustments by some of its members in an effort to stop prices from declining. There is little evidence from the last few years to support the popular view of OPEC as the price-maker in the world oil market.

The behaviour of OPEC's dominant producer, Saudi Arabia, has in recent times been more influential than anything done by the Organisation itself. The Saudis clearly decided that, following the 1979-80 price explosion, further big oil price increases in the next few years would not be in their interests. Political and economic ties with the United States and other industrial countries mean that Saudi Arabia has some interest in avoiding economic instability in the West, and the country's very large crude oil reserves induce caution in raising prices sufficiently to cause accelerated development of substitutes for oil. That is not to say that the Saudis wanted prices to drop quite as much as they did in the early part of 1982. Indeed in the second quarter of 1982 they had to cut output substantially to around 6 million B/D in an effort to maintain the price of their 'marker' crude.

2. THE FUTURE OF PRICES

Discount rates and price expectations

It seems that a change in property rights which altered suppliers' discount rates and a change in price expectations because of anticipated scarcity were two fundamental factors which altered supply behaviour and subsequently demand behaviour and which help to account for the remarkable change in oil price trends between the 1960s and 1970s. If we assume that property rights will not revert to what they were in the 1960s, so that there is unlikely to be a substantial alteration in suppliers' real rates of discount, then we ought, in contemplating future oil prices, to begin by examining what has happened to price expectations. An important message from the experiences of the postwar period seems to be that the oil market is dominated by producer and consumer perceptions of events, rather than necessarily by what is actually happening. Particularly important at any given time is whether perceptions are of future surplus or scarcity since on that basis price expectations will be formed, and the behaviour of producers and of consumers will differ very significantly depending on their expectations of oil price movements. For example, belief in future scarcity with associated price expectations will *ceteris paribus*, cause producers to reduce planned output. Consumers will, in the short run, try to increase stocks because they expect prices to keep increasing and so they will add to the pressure of demand, though in the longer term, they will switch away from oil, thus tending to depress prices.

It is plainly hazardous to generalise about price expectations, but there is surely no doubt that they have been very considerably damped in the last two years or so, which is as one would predict given the second step change in prices from 1979 to 1981 and the subsequent accelerated move away from oil (of which more later). In a 1975 paper[5] I suggested that the oil market would begin to change as price expectations altered and that the change might come sooner than anticipated by those people who thought large amounts of non-OPEC energy had to be available before the market changed. I argued that 'Expectations could alter long before new supplies come to market. . . ', that ' . . . the most likely change to expectations in the near future concerns the producers' view of the future rate of price appreciation . . . ' and that 'It seems inevitable that the price elasticity of demand for OPEC oil will increase as energy-saving measures and the drive to develop non-OPEC energy forms take hold'.

In retrospect we can see that price expectations were beginning to change in the mid 1970s when there was a period (1976–78) of declining real crude oil prices but that two political events — the Iranian Revolution and to a much lesser extent the Gulf War — upset those expectations and revived fears of supply insecurity and future scarcity. As it has become clear that consumers are moving away from oil, as recession has deepened and as the supply reduction has been absorbed, expectations have again altered however. Indeed, they apparently changed very sharply in the early months of 1982 when a number of people argued that oil prices might remain depressed or continue to fall throughout 1982–83 and possibly for longer. Those views may or may not turn out to be correct but they contained elements both of wishful thinking and of attempts to talk the price down so as to institute a change in price expectations. Moreover, they revealed a very common feature of comment on oil market trends — the undue weight placed on very recent experience which sometimes expresses itself in projections for years ahead based on a few weeks' experience. Because prices had been falling it was assumed they would fall further, just as in the 1970s there were incautious statements about prices rising for ever. However, not all statements about oil prices are translated into general price expectations and the rather exaggerated views expressed early in 1982 seemed to have moderated by the middle of the year: to the extent that they were based on projections of recent experience that was bound to happen as prices moved up off their floor in Spring 1982.

Unlikely change in prices

In contemplating future prices and price expectations there are some kinds of changes we can probably rule out. It is as well to go through this elimination process because it should help to reduce the area of uncertainty about future oil prices. First, a repetition in the 1980s and 1990s of the huge real price increases of the 1970s seems very unlikely. Those increases should probably be regarded as a sharp once-for-all upward movement which the world economy is still attempting to digest by reducing its oil intensity. After the big upward steps in prices in the 1970s and given the development of substitutes for oil, we can probably assume that oil consumption is more elastic with respect to price than it was at the price levels of the early 1970s. Not only has the demand curve shifted leftwards because of income and other changes, it has also flattened. To that extent, consumers are more resistant to price increases than they were. Moreover, as suggested above we no longer have the well-formed expectations of future scarcity and sharply rising oil prices which existed in the 1970s and were themselves extremely important elements in the large price increases which occurred.

We can also probably rule out *any* kind of smooth change (upwards or downwards) in crude oil prices. The oil market has in recent times swung from surplus (1977–78) to scarcity (1979–80) and back again (1981–82) and it is probably realistic to anticipate further such swings. Fluctuations in the oil market are reminiscent of the inventory cycle which economists believe helps to magnify changes in real GNP. Let us postulate as a starting point some event in the oil market which causes expectations of scarcity and thus of rising prices. Given the experiences of the 1970s such an event — which might be a revolution in an oil-producing country, a spurt in economic growth, or possibly just a very cold winter — will probably cause a scramble for supplies. Added to the demand from consumers will therefore be a demand for oil for inventory, so that demand on the oil producers increases sharply for a period as storage tanks are filled and tankers steam more slowly. Supply may also be restricted as producers see some advantage from holding off the market to take advantage of higher expected prices. The rate of addition to inventory must, however, decline as physical limits of stock holding come near. Demand on the producers will then fall and price expectations will also tend to come down. At some stage stock holders will then compare the poor prospects for price appreciation with the interest and other costs of holding inventories and decide to reduce those inventories, thus depressing demand on the producers below the level

Table 13.3. World Energy Consumption.

	1965		*1973*		*1981*		*Average Annual Compound Rates of Increase %*	
	MTOE	*% of Total*	*MTOE*	*% of Total*	*MTOE*	*% of Total*	*1965–73*	*1973–81*
Oil	1529	38.7	2798	47.3	2902	42.4	7.8	0.5
Solid Fuels	1525*	38.6	1668	28.2	2007	29.3	1.1	2.3
Natural Gas	647	16.4	1076	18.2	1332	19.4	6.6	2.7
Nuclear	6*	0.2	49	0.8	191	2.8	30.0	18.5
Hydro	242*	6.1	329	5.5	417	6.1	3.9	3.0
TOTAL	3949	100.0	5920	100.0	6849	100.0	5.2	1.8

Source: BP Statistical Reviews of the World Oil Industry (Annual) and BP Statistical Review of World Energy 1981.
*Partly estimated.

of final consumption. By this time the producers will be concerned about their falling revenues as prices drop, and will start fighting for market share thus depressing prices still more. The price fall will, however, induce those consumers who can at the margin substitute oil for other fuels (such as large electrical utilities) to do so, oil demand will begin to increase, inventories will be re-built and the inventory cycle will eventually go into reverse, producing rising prices once more.

The above description is stylised but nevertheless appears to be consistent with recent experience. After the upswing in 1979–80 came the downswing in 1981–82. Presumably another upswing is somewhere around the corner — indeed it may be under way in the second half of 1982 — but unfortunately we do not see round corners very well so it is hard to anticipate the timing and the extent of the rise. Whether it will cause a relatively small increase in prices, or whether there will be larger rises because a 'natural' increase is augmented by faster economic growth and/or supply restrictions in the producing countries one cannot at present be sure.

Abstracting from the immediate issues, however, and contemplating the 1980s and early 1990s, it does seem likely that there will continue to be considerable fluctuations in oil prices, output and consumption rather than the smooth trends which analysts sometimes build into their investment appraisals of energy projects. What trends we shall see are more difficult to determine but we can try to comment on some of the determinants of oil prices and oil price expectations.

Future oil consumption

The world energy market is now in the midst of the process of adjusting to greatly increased oil prices. Table 3 compares trends in world commercial energy consumption in the eight years before 1973 with corresponding trends in the last eight years. The rate of growth of world energy consumption has fallen from over 5 per cent per annum to less than 2 per cent per annum; oil consumption, which pre-1973 was rising at nearly 8 per cent a year, has hardly increased since 1973; gas consumption has also increased more slowly. Coal consumption, on the other hand, has been growing faster than previously and use of nuclear electricity (though still small on a world scale) has continued to increase rapidly in percentage terms.

These market changes are all consistent with what one would predict from knowledge of the sharp change in oil price trends and the rather less dramatic change in price trends for other fields which occurred in the early 1970s. There are, of course, significant time lags inherent on the demand side and the supply side of the energy market[6] which slow the adjustment process and probably result in price elasticities which are considerably greater in the long run than in the short run. It is, therefore, not at all surprising that energy market changes have been greater in the last two or three years than in the mid 1970s. Table 4 concentrates attention on the 1979–81 period to illustrate that world energy consumption fell slightly both in 1980 and 1981 and that in each of those years world oil consumption declined by 3–4 per cent.

Table 13.4. World Energy Consumption (MTOE).

	1979	*1980*	*1981*
Oil	3124	3001	2902
Solid Fuels	1991	2021	2007
Natural Gas	1255	1278	1332
Nuclear	155	167	191
Hydro	408	415	417
TOTAL	6933	6882	6849

Source: BP Statistical Reviews of the World Oil Industry (Annual) and BP Statistical Review of World Energy 1981.

In looking to the future we need to form some views on the likely direction of change of world oil consumption and the approximate magnitude of change. Unfortunately, no one can be sure of the relative strengths of the four main determinants of the fall in oil consumption since 1979:

- economic recession;
- the structural shift in industrial countries away from energy-intensive activities (such as steel-making), so that the changing mix of activities makes for a less energy-intensive economy;
- the reduction in energy-intensity of any given activity which has reduced the potential market for oil;
- within the energy used in any activity the fall in oil's share.

Each of these changes is, to a greater or lesser extent, a consequence of the big increase in oil prices and the smaller increases in prices of other fuels. However, the second, third and fourth are likely to have caused some longer-lasting depression of oil consumption (by reducing the energy intensity and especially the oil-intensity of economic activity) than the presumably more transient effects of recession. Though we do not yet have sufficient experience to do more than guess at the relative sizes of the effects, we can be fairly sure that though oil intensity has been reduced, oil consumption will, *ceteris paribus*, still be positively correlated with real GNP changes. That is, if one imagines a situation in which oil prices are expected to remain constant relative to prices in general and to other fuel prices, in which the effects of past oil price changes have worked through the system (which could take several years yet), and in which other non-income determinants of oil consumption also remain constant, then a change in real GNP in a given country would probably yield a change of the same sign in oil consumption.

Over the 1980s and 1990s as a whole, if real GNP increases in the industrialised world there may therefore be some tendency for oil consumption to rise, though that tendency will most likely be more than offset for a time by the lagged effects on consumption of past price increases even if real oil prices stay constant. Assuming that economic growth is only modest in the 1980s and 1990s the chances seem to be that we shall see some further fall in oil consumption in the industrial world though there are circumstances in which the scale of any decline might be quite limited. In a recent analysis of future European energy trends[7] George Ray and I suggested that oil consumption in Western Europe might fall by 12 to 14 per cent between 1980 and 1990. It was assumed that real oil prices would rise moderately (up to 30 per cent by 1990) though in erratic fashion. We did, however, qualify that assessment by pointing out that there may be even greater difficulties and delays than we had assumed with new fuel supply plans such as nuclear power plants, gas import schemes and coal mining projects; we said that, as a consequence, the fall in oil consumption might be constrained below our most probable estimate.

There is plenty of evidence that oil substitution projects are not going according to plan. Postponements or cancellations of coal liquefaction, coal gasification, oil from shale and oil from tar sands schemes have recently been announced because of escalating costs, uncertainty about prices and doubts about government policies. A few years ago it seemed that such fuel sources might set an upper limit on oil prices, but the 'upper limit' seems to be continually rising. Most of these oil substitution projects are suffering from technical difficulties. Moreover, they are themselves energy-intensive so that oil price rises are a mixed blessing, causing cost increases as

Table 13.5. Primary Energy Consumption

	1973 (MTOE)	*1981 (MTOE)*	*% Change 1981/1973*
North America	2014	2028	+ 0.7
Western Europe	1241	1241	0
Japan	348	354	+1.7
Australasia	67	89	+32.8
USSR, Eastern Europe and China	1590	2138	+34.5
Latin America, Africa, Middle East, South and South East Asia	660	999	+51.4
TOTAL	5920	6849	+15.7

Source: BP Statistical Review of World Energy 1981.

Table 13.6. World Oil Consumption.

	1973		*1981*	
	Million tonnes	*% of Total*	*Million tonnes*	*% of Total*
North America	902	32.2	825	28.4
Western Europe	749	26.8	630	21.8
Japan	269	9.6	224	7.7
Australasia	35	1.3	36	1.2
USSR, Eastern Europe and China	455	16.3	631	21.7
Latin America, Africa Middle East, South and South East Asia	389	13.8	556	19.2
TOTAL	2799	100.0	2902	100.0

Source: BP Statistical Review of World Energy, 1981.

well as rising prospective realisations. Nor is nuclear power a very effective competitor for oil in most countries because it has failed to win public acceptability; once plants under construction are (belatedly) completed there may be a period in which little new nuclear capacity is commissioned. Only strip-mined coal from low-cost regions (such as Australia, the United States and South Africa) and to a lesser extent natural gas seem capable of displacing substantial amounts of oil from the market. For all these reasons one needs to be cautious about predicting a further big decline in oil consumption even in an industrialised world where total energy consumption will probably increase only very slowly.

It is also important in considering future oil consumption not to become too obsessed with the Western industrial world. As Table 5 shows, energy consumption in North America, Western Europe and Japan was very little higher in 1981 than in 1973, whereas in the Communist world and especially the developing countries energy demand has continued to rise since 1973. Similarly, Table 6 illustrates that the near-constancy of world oil consumption from 1973 to 1981 is compounded of sharp falls in North America, Western Europe and Japan with continuing growth in the Communist bloc and the developing world. The share of the last two groups in world oil consumption is now over 40 per cent compared with about 30 per cent in 1973. Although one can see reasons why oil demand may rise less rapidly in both groups in the future - for instance, the debt problems which may restrict growth in some developing countries and the increases in domestic oil prices which a number of oil-producing countries have imposed recently - a continued rise in oil consumption outside the Western industrial world does seem probable.

Estimating the net effect on world oil consumption of these contrary trends is very much guesswork. My own guess would be that some slight rise in world oil consumption is quite probable up to the end of the century, most likely occurring just as erratically as the oil price changes discussed earlier. One might perhaps suggest an area of uncertainty for the late 1990s ranging from a little below present annual world consumption of about 3 billion tonnes up to 3½ or 3¾ billion tonnes — a growth rate of 1½ per cent per annum at maximum from the present. Such figures are of course vastly different from the end-century oil consumption levels of about 9 billion tonnes which were being forecast in the early 1970s. The expected life of world oil reserves thus now looks very much longer than the trend-projectors of a few years ago imagined.

The supply side

On the supply side of the oil market there are some daunting uncertainties; experience in recent years should make us show a due humility in any comments about how oil suppliers may behave.

One factor which might be expected to increase the real price of crude oil in the long run is the rising cost of extraction from the more remote regions (such as the Canadian Arctic) into which exploration has moved. In a sense, such cost increases are 'artificial' since there is probable a good deal of lower cost oil still to be found in the Middle East. Nevertheless, political events have moved the oil companies into high-cost areas of production and, unless one foresees a significant revival of exploration and development in the OPEC countries, the consequence is likely to be long run upward cost pressure on prices. Eventually rising costs may price oil out of all but the uses where close substitutes are lacking (particularly transport) but that day is probably very distant — most likely well into next century.

The strength and cohesion of OPEC are popularly regarded as important supply-side influences on oil prices. For reasons already given (see above), the power of OPEC seems to me to have been exaggerated. There are more fundamental variables we should be concerned about than whether the OPEC members will maintain their present imperfect union of whether the organisation will fall apart. Nevertheless, in looking to the future one might reasonably argue that OPEC, guided by Saudi Arabia, will probably have some supply-restricting influence in the sense that it may well succeed in setting a floor to oil prices when the market is tending to decline because some of its members will agree to cut production. We have seen recently that, when there is an oil surplus at existing prices, even though some members of the Organisation opt out of the cuts, provided Saudi Arabia and the others are willing to reduce output substantially it does seem possible to limit a price decline. Thus Saudi Arabia and some other OPEC members may be able to insert a ratchet effect into the market place: some time after a price increase a consequential surplus may start prices falling but the drop will then be constrained by reduced output. As a result the oil market cycle discussed earlier may continue to be one with a rising floor.

Perhaps the biggest imponderable on the supply side is the extent to which there will be supply interruptions and sharp changes in output in major producing countries. It is quite possible to sketch a scenario which is optimistic (viewed from the oil consuming countries) of a world in which the major supply upsets are behind us. The Iran - Iraq War ends without serious spill over effects in the Gulf. Iran and Iraq both increase oil output, Saudi output rises from its present depressed level and in the longer term the Saudis decide to vary output to keep real oil prices constant or even slightly falling because they are concerned to avoid too quick a development of substitutes for oil. Such an outcome is certainly possible but I would place only a low probability on it. It is much too close to an accident-free scenario for it to have much plausibility. The difficulty seems to me to be that we can see existing problems in the Middle East and the optimists among us even believe they can see solutions to some of these problems (such as the Gulf War). What we cannot so easily see are those problems which have not yet fully emerged but which may be very important influences on future oil supplies, especially from the Middle East. My own view is that, though we are not sufficiently far-sighted to perceive what the political future of the Middle East will be, there are sufficient sources of unresolved conflict in the area that our most probable expectation for the next ten to fifteen years should be that there will be further wars and revolutions, which are more likely to restrict oil supplies than to increase them. Apart from the continuing Arab–Israeli problem we have to consider what may be the long-run effects of an Iranian victory in the Gulf War. Indeed, there are various possibilities of internal revolutions and takeovers which could significantly reduce output in major producing countries. The oil market seems to me likely to remain sensitive, finely-balanced and very prone to supply uncertainties which in general will tend to promote expectations of rising prices. In other words, for some years yet we may never be far from what Shell have aptly termed 'the region of vulnerability'.[8]

CONCLUSIONS

Oil price predictions in the past have not been so strikingly successful that we can say anything with great cofidence about how prices may move in the future. The opinion I would venture, however, is that if we try to form a judgement by looking at likely demand and supply influences the most reasonable conclusion we can reach is that expectations will in general be for real oil price increases and that real prices will probably rise in the 1980s and the early 1990s. The plausible scenarios seem to be to be those in which real oil prices fluctuate a good deal, but about a moderately rising trend. It appears likely that occasional supply shortages (actual or perceived) and spurts of demand about a slightly increasing world demand for oil are likely periodically to drive up real prices in steps; though there will no doubt subsequently be some downward drift caused by inflation and discounting by producers, it would be surprising if the price floor and the price ceiling were not rising. In other words we may in the 1980s and early 1990s see several small-scale repetitions of the events of recent years. The average rate of increase of crude prices in the rest of the 1980s and in the 1990s is a matter about which, in all honesty, we can only speculate: I would take, as a working assumption, real annual average increases in the range 1 to 5 per cent per annum, though the upper end of the range does not at present seem very probable.

Therefore, although I have since 1973 argued that big oil price rises in the 1970s would turn out to be a temporary phenomenon (since the market would adjust and damp down the increases), I do not think we have yet reached the stage when we can reasonably anticipate falling or even constant real prices. In the long run we cannot expect oil prices to continue rising relative to the price level in general — if they were doing so the supply and demand shifts would be so large and the behavioural changes so great that the real price rise would cease. But the time lags in the system are sufficiently lengthy that the long run in this context may mean the late 1990s and early next century rather than the next ten years.

REFERENCES

1. Energy Modelling Forum, *World Oil: Summary Report*, EMF Report 6, Stanford, California, February 1982.
2. M.A. Adelman, *The World Petroleum Market*, Johns Hopkins University Press, 1972.
3. For further explanation see R.M. Solow, The Economics of Resources or the Resources of Economics, *American Economic Review* May 1974, and Colin Robinson and Jon Morgan, *North Sea Oil in the Future: Economic Analysis and Government Policy*, Macmillan for the Trade Policy Research Centre, 1978, Chapter 2.
4. See, for example, James Akins, *The Oil Crisis — this time the wolf is here*, Foreign Affairs, April 1973.
5. Colin Robinson, *Energy Depletion and the Economics of OPEC*, Henley Centre for Forecasting, 1975.
6. More details are in Colin Robinson, Ahmed El Mokadem and Paul Stevens, The *Future of OPEC* Surrey Energy Economics Discussion Paper no. 7, August 1981, pp. 6-10.

7. George Ray and Colin Robinson, *European Energy Prospects to 1990*, Staniland Hall, 1982.
8. J.M. Raisman, *Oil-World Supplies and North Sea Development*, address to "ANSWER" Conference, Brussels, March 1982.

PART VI

Contingency Planning

Chapter 14

Oil Crisis Management

*Robert Belgrave**

The author of this paper has recently been engaged in an analysis of the events of the two oil crises, following the Iranian Revolution in 1978/79 and the outbreak of the Iraq/Iran war in 1980. This work was done in collaboration with Mr Daniel Badger, to whom the relevant statistics and records of the International Energy Agency were made available. It was published in May 1982 under the title *What went right in 1980?* by PSI for the British Institutes' Joint Energy Policy Programme.

The purpose of this paper is to consider the need for preparations to deal with any future oil supply crisis of similar magnitude, and the best way to avoid rapid escalation of prices, such as took place in 1979.

What went right in 1980? investigates the reasons why a net supply cut of roughly the same size, on each occasion, under 2.5 mbd (5 per cent of requirements), led to a price increase of 150 per cent on the first occasion but had no long-term price effect on the second. It is argued that the price increase of 1979 was a 'self-inflicted wound' on the part of the industrialised countries, caused by faulty perception of events, panic by consumers, and poor response by

*Director, British Institutes' Joint Energy Policy Programme

governments. In 1979, the effects of a relatively small cut in crude oil supply, at a time of rising demand, were exacerbated by fears on the part of refiners and consumers that supplies would not be available and by collective inaction on the part of consumer governments, which each sought to improve its own position. OPEC members, even those who took a relatively long view, were not reluctant to take advantage of the situation to increase their export prices. The organisation of OPEC was sufficiently effective to defend these higher prices, once established. The part played by political considerations in OPEC decisions varied from time to time and from country to country, but by and large their action stemmed from a very accurate perception of their own economic self-interest, at least in the short term. In 1980, by contrast, stocks were high, demand was falling in response to the 1979 price increases, and government action, both individually and through the EEC and IEA, reinforced the downward market pressure on prices, by encouraging use of commercial stocks and by restraining themselves from competitive bidding.

The statistics shown in the charts in this previous paper show that in 1979, 'official government selling prices' followed the steep rise in spot prices steadily upward, but that this scarcely happened at all in 1980. They also show two other less expected features, firstly that deliveries into consumption, as measured by deliveries from the refinery gate, increased sharply after the onset of each crisis. Much of this increase must have represented increased stock holding by traders and final consumers. Secondly, the statistics show that, although official and industry stocks were drawn down at the onset of the 1978/79 crisis, as the crisis went on and prices continued to increase, these stocks also were greatly increased. They were higher at the end of 1979 than they had ever been before. The conclusion is drawn that it is the phenomenon of hoarding and indeed increasing stocks, in the hands of government, industry and final consumers, that multiplies the effect on demand of even a minor shortfall, and therefore its effect on price. Conversely (as happened in 1980 for reasons that were largely fortuitous), the existence and timely release of stocks, at the onset of a crisis, can do much to damp down price increases.

The popular view in mid-1982, is that the pressure on oil supplies has gone away, that the analysis of past events is at best of academic interest, and that it is no longer desirable or necessary for governments, or companies, to concern themselves with contingency planning for some hypothetical future event, that is now unlikely in the foreseeable future. Not desirable, because such matters should, as a matter of principle, be left to the market. Not necessary, because world oil demand has fallen and is unlikely to rise again, at least in the industrialised countries, as a result of investment in efficiency and in alternative fuels. It is said that non-OPEC oil production has increased and this increase is likely to be maintained, while demand for OPEC oil has fallen to 17 million barrels a day, from the level of 30 mbd at which it stood in 1979 — and is never likely to reach that level again. Finally, it is argued that this so-called glut will ensure that the type of price escalation experienced in 1979 cannot be repeated.

These predictions may turn out to be more accurate than those made about 1982 by most forecasters as recently as 1980. They may not. Increases in demand for imports in the Third World, and in the Soviet Bloc, could offset any decreases in the West. Increases in non-OPEC supply could be offset by decline in North America. Demand in the industrialised countries could pick up with economic recovery, as sharply as it fell with the recession. Much of the apparent spare productive capacity in OPEC might not be available when wanted. Some two and a half million barrels a day of it is in each of Iran and Iraq. It is likely that, even if an end is declared to their undeclared war, one or both of these countries will suffer from an extended period of internal anarchy and neighbourly hostility. The conservationist attitude of producer governments and their populations in countries such as Kuwait will not quickly change. The only substantial amount of readily available spare capacity in the physical sense, is in Saudi Arabia. It would be imprudent indeed to assume that that country will be willing, on demand, to increase production to pre-1981 levels, even if they enjoy continued internal stability, and an absence of overriding discontent with the West over Palestine.

The market remains fragile. It could quickly return to equilibrium. At that point, an extraneous event could easily provoke a supply cut of the same order of magnitude as in 1979 — or greater. Recent events in Lebanon and the South Atlantic have provided more reminders, if more were needed, of the unpredictability of events in the Middle East and in Latin America, and it is rather luck than good management that has so far prevented either of these having a direct effect on oil supplies.

So what should Western governments do, and what should gatherings like this demand of them? A distinguished British financier and politician, speaking last week — on the record — at Chatham House, said that the trouble with politicians was that they always deal with the things that press in on them. They prefer crisis management to strategic thinking — which ensures that they never run out of crises.

I am arguing that a little advance preparation for crisis management may not be a bad thing — that it may even avert a crisis.

Fortunately, in the event of a major emergency, the International Energy Programme, with its obligatory allocation procedures, exists. If it did not, we ought to invent it. And I have no reason to suppose that the twenty-one governments which signed the agreement to set it up in 1974 would not honour their obligations, including the US and the UK whose circumstances have both changed in important ways since then. My concern is with smaller shortfalls, which cause widespread disruption, rocketing prices, and all the economic dislocation that follows.

I do not believe that it is sufficient in such a case to 'leave it to the market'. There is no such thing as an international market in crude oil in the textbook sense. Decisions on oil exports are in the hands of governments. Commercial entities in importing countries have no countervailing power to offset arbitrary exporter government action or acts of god or of war. Nor do I believe that even the most *laissez-faire* government Washington has seen for many years would sit on its hands if the Senators from New England came one day and said that their utilities will be out of fuel in a week.

Nor is it sufficient to wait till a crisis breaks and then trot out the same old set of cosmetic measures that failed to stop the rot in 1979 — exhortation to consume less (which simply causes consumers to build up stocks), speed limits, thermostat limits, alternate day driving, price controls, import limits and so on. These measures may all be necessary, and rationing too, as adjuncts to the full emergency allocation procedures of the IEP. By themselves they are useless.

The one measure which could damp down the quick rise of the spot market in the event of a relatively minor crisis, and thus head off the subsequent chain of nasty events, would be to have stocks of crude oil available for rapid release to those refiners whose supplies have been cut by an outside event constituting *force majeure*. The volume need not be great — say the equivalent of 5 days of the 90 days of imports which the IEA agreements already require members to hold. The cost would be trivial compared with the cost of maintaining a Rapid Development Force, to say nothing of the cost of another price explosion. It does not matter whether these stocks are held by governments or by industry; it does not matter whether they are part of the '90 days' or on top of them; or whether or not they are part of governmental strategic reserves — so long as they are earmarked and available for instant release — and known to be available.

I fear that the US government may be reluctant to discuss contingency planning of this kind, partly for reasons of economic theory, partly because the US has succeeded in greatly reducing vulnerability to oil imports. But continental Europe and Japan cannot afford to do nothing. They are still dependent on oil imports for half their energy. With or without the US, they will be obliged to make some plans. If they are forced into a position of trying to take action without the US, their chances of success are obviously much less. This would provide yet one more instance of a divergence of view on a matter of vital national and international interest, and one more source of strain on the Western alliance. If the United States takes the alliance seriously, they cannot afford to let this happen.

At the entrance to the exhibition of Islamic pottery in the Metropolitan Museum in New York there stands a beautiful dish made in Samarkand in the year 1600. The Arabic inscription around it reads 'Planning in advance avoids regret. May you have peace and prosperity'.

Chapter 15

Petroleum Futures Markets

*Walter Greaves**

Quotation from Platt's Oilgram Price Report of 6th April, 1982.

'*Atlantic Coast*
The General feeling was the cash-market again being led by the Merc., which was led by the I.P.E.

The International Petroleum Exchange in London commenced trading gas oil futures on 6th April 1981, by which time No. 2 Heating Oil had been traded on the New York Mercantile Exchange for thirty months — since 14th October, 1978.

There would have been very few participants at the previous international conference of the IAEE in Cambridge in June 1980 who could have foreseen the Platt's quotation but it is appropriate to recall the comment by Sir David Steel in his opening address that:

> 'The recent proposal by the London Commodity Exchange for a properly organised futures market in Europe in some oil products certainly deserves study and my company is co-operating with that study'.

***Adviser to Czarnikov Schroder on Petroleum Futures**

The clear success of the New York Mercantile contract in No. 2 Heating Oil and the increasing volumes of trade in the London contract for gas oil have stimulated consideration of other contracts. The Chicago Board of Trade, which is the world's largest futures exchange, has been given approval to trade in gasoline and No. 2 Heating Oil; the Chicago Mercantile Exchange is proposing two motor gasoline contracts and the International Petroleum Exchange is considering motor gasoline and fuel oil contracts with European deliveries.

The main purpose of this paper is to review the potential for further development of futures trading in the oil industry and to consider the potential impact of futures markets on the way in which the oil industry conducts its business.

It is useful in this context to look at experience so far.

THE EXPERIENCE OF 1974

The crude oil price increases of October 1973 stimulated consideration of futures markets by four separate groups in Amsterdam, Rotterdam and New York. As a result three separate markets commenced trading in September/October 1974.[1]

The 'Forward Contract Exchange Company' in Amsterdam commenced trading contracts for EEC gas oil and premium grade gasoline with barge delivery fob Rotterdam. Most of the initial trading was by floor traders for their own accounts and the exchange failed.

The New York Mercantile Exchange traded contracts in gas oil and heavy fuel oil futures (of 100 tonne lots) with Rotterdam delivery. The total volume of trading in late 1974 and early 1975 was 104 lots of heavy fuel oil and 19 lots of gas oil before trading was terminated.

The New York Cotton Exchange had been trading contracts in propane futures (lots of 100,000 US gallons) since 1971. The volumes traded in 1973 and 1974 were 7013 and 8293 lots but peaks of 400 lots a day were reached in December 1973–January 1974 following the introduction of rationing to distributors of propane and distillate fuel oils. This encouraged interest in the possibility of crude oil futures.

The contract was for 5000 barrels of crude oil of 34° API delivered in tankage in Rotterdam. Trading volumes were 14,446 lots in the last four months of 1974, 34,326 lots in 1975, and 7346 lots in 1976 when trading ceased.

This short burst of activity in petroleum futures was led by futures traders in existing exchanges whose interest had been stimulated by the sharp rise in prices for crude oils in the last quarter of 1973, when the posted price for Arab Light was increased from US $3.01 to US $11.65 per barrel.

By mid-1974 the crisis was over, demand for crude oil fell away and spot prices dropped sharply. The maximum variation in spot price assessments for Arab Light crude oil during the year September 1974-August 1975 was from US $10.15 to US $10.40 a barrel. Spot product prices in the Rotterdam barge market drifted over a range of about US $8 per tonne over the last four months of 1974 which was the critical period for the two product futures markets.

The price environment did not favour the promoters and this was probably the major reason for failure. They were not helped by the indifference or antagonism of most sectors of the oil industry, which was at an early stage of the process of fragmentation, with most crude oil supplies still being controlled by the major oil companies.

The comparative success of the New York Cotton Exchange's crude oil contract may provide some encouragement for the current promoters of crude oil futures markets. A total volume of 14,446 lots of 5000 barrels (i.e. 72,230,000 barrels) was traded between 10 September and 31 December 1974. Comparison with the growth in volume of trading in the New York Mercantile's successful No. 2 Heating Oil contract (see Table 1) shows that a similar volumetric measure of trade was not reached until June to September 1980, twenty months after starting trading, when contracts equivalent to 51 million barrels of No. 2 Heating Oil were traded.

It is perhaps not surprising that a crude oil contract based on Rotterdam delivery should have a wider interest for both world wide oil traders and speculators than contracts in individual products, the prices of which would have appeared to be specific to the North-West European marketing area. Previous US users of the New York Cotton Exchange's propane futures market would have been attracted by the greater relevance to them of the crude oil contract by comparison with the New York Mercantile's product contracts.

The Cotton Exchange also had the advantage of its reputation of already operating a viable propane futures market.

These advantages and its early success in achieving volume were not sufficient and the crude oil contract collapsed.

RECENT NEW YORK MERCANTILE EXCHANGE CONTRACTS

The next step was the decision by the New York Mercantile Exchange to start trading contracts for delivery in New York Harbour on 14 November 1978. Many will be surprised to learn that trading started in No. 6 Industrial Fuel Oil as well as No. 2 Heating Oil.

Interest was low with the total number of contracts of 1000 barrels by 31 December 1978 being only 116 for No. 2 Heating Oil and 28 for the No. 6 Fuel Oil. Trading in No. 2 Heating Oil gradually increased in volume (see Table 1) but the No. 6 Fuel Oil contract had ceased trading by May 1979 when the total volume traded since the start was only 61 lots.

The Iranian crisis forced No. 2 Heating Oil features up from 45 cents/US gallon in January 1979 to 105 cents in early June and it appears clear in retrospect that this was fundamental to continued trading in this contract. Even so the average daily volume of trade in June, after seven months trading, was only 66 lots per day. The oil trade did not appreciate the potential benefits of a futures market and it was not until November 1979, after a year's trading, that the market's existence was made secure by the achievement of an average daily volume of 446 lots.

The pattern of trading has shown increases in each succeeding winter (see Table 1) reaching a peak monthly volume in March 1982 with a record volume for any single day of 13,806 lots on 1 April 1982.

The success of the No. 2 Heating Oil contract in New York Harbour delivery led the exchange to start trading a contract with Gulf Coast delivery on 17 August 1981.

This contract traded 1856 lots in 1981 and 72 in early 1982 but at no time was sufficient interest generated to suggest that continuation could be viable and trading lapsed.

Gulf Coast delivery meant delivery at any shore facility having access to the Colonial Pipeline between Pasadena in Texas and Collins, Covington County, Mississippi, including Beaumont, Port Arthur, Lake Charles and Baton Rouge. It has been suggested that potential offtakers will have been deterred from considering taking delivery by the possibility of being forced to pick up separate parcels from locations some distance apart and the New York Mercantile Exchange is now proposing changes in the contract to limit delivery to a more restricted range in the Houston area of Texas.

While a valid criticism of the contract, it is more likely that the basic problem was one more fundamentally related to the viability of separate futures markets.

It is always difficult to attract both trade hedgers and speculators into a new market in the presence of an existing market trading a similar contract which already has an adequate or high volume of trade.

Many of the professional non-trade participants in futures markets need a high volume if price changes are small to justify their participation in a market. The trade hedger also needs the liquidity provided by high volume if futures contracts equivalent for example to a tanker cargo are to be bought and sold without adverse price movements. The trade hedger will prefer the definable inefficiency of an existing market in a related contract to the uncertainty of price movement in a thin market in a contract which might otherwise more closely match his hedging requirements.

The history of commodity markets provides many examples of failures for this basic reason and the Gulf contract is probably a valid addition to this list.

The next innovation by the New York Mercantile Exchange was the start on 5 October 1981 of a leaded regular gasoline contract with delivery in New York Harbour. This had the most successful beginning of any of the New York Mercantile's contracts. By May 1982 after seven months trading the Leaded Gasoline contract was trading an average of 658 lots a day a level not reached by the No. 2 Heating Oil contract until September 1980 after twenty-two months trading.

This comparative success clearly results from the increasing understanding by oil traders of the relevance of futures trading to their physical activities. It is not surprising that physical traders should find more use for the market in May than in earlier months.

Speculators and jobbers who had been concentrating their activity on the busy No. 2 Heating Oil market in earlier months will also have been encouraged by the seasonal reduction in volume in No. 2 Heating Oil futures and the increase in gasoline volume to divert some of their activity to the second market. There has also been some evidence of arbitrage between futures contracts in the two markets.

At this stage it appears likely that the gasoline futures market could have a growth rate similar to that already achieved by the No. 2 Heating Oil market.

Encouraged by their two successful contracts the New York Mercantile Exchange decided to try a Gulf Coast delivery contract for Leaded Regular Gasoline on 14 December 1981. Only two contracts were traded and the market failed for the same reasons as applied to the Gulf Coast No. 2 Heating Oil contract.

Of five petroleum contracts, which started trading on the New

York Mercantile Exchange since 1978, three have failed and two are successes.

THE INTERNATIONAL PETROLEUM EXCHANGE

The International Petroleum Exchange in London started trading its Rotterdam delivery contract for gas oil on 6 April 1981. At this time the New York contract in No. 2 Heating Oil had been trading for 29 months and had achieved an average daily volume of 3,369 lots (approximately 448,000 tonnes).

The average level of trading in the first two months was 782 lots (of 100 tonnes) a day. Volumes increased in the winter months reaching an average of 3099 lots per day in April 1982 and a peak of 5154 lotts on 22 April. Current trading levels are below this peak but experience with No. 2 Heating Oil on the New York Mercantile shows that a reduction in volumes in the spring, for seasonal demand reasons, can be consistent with continuing annual growth (see Table 1).

There is no doubt that the London market benefitted considerably from the favourable publicity about the New York Mercantile Exchange in the 1980/1981 winter immediately preceding its opening. There is a significant volume of US based trade from US commission houses and there is some arbitrage between the two markets when relative prices are favourable.

PROPANE

The live petroleum contracts also include the liquid propane contract on the New York Cotton Exchange. This had been trading since 1971 but had gradually faded into insignificance. The contract was modified in December 1981 and now provides for delivery of 1000 barrel lots in either Mont Belvieu, Texas, (near Houston) or Conway, Kansas.

The modifications to the contract and increased publicity about both the propane and other petroleum futures contracts have resulted in an increased volume of trading with an average of 53 lots (53,000 barrels) per day being achieved for a two week period at the end of April and early May. This is however trivial compared with the average daily sales of 870,000 barrels per day in the related physical market areas. The market is clearly of only limited use to a small number of the potential users.

ANALYSIS OF MARKET USAGE

A similar comparison for the No. 2 Heating Oil contract during the busy first quarter of 1982 shows a total volume of 490,246 futures contracts compared with a total US physical demand for Distillate Fuel Oils of 283 million barrels i.e. a ratio of futures to physical volumes of 1.7 to 1.

Actual physical deliveries in New York Harbour against futures contracts during January and February, 1982 were 9,5 million barrels which was 10%of all Distillate Fuel Oil supplies into PAD District 1, (which includes all the East Coast states from Florida to Maine plus Pennsylvania and West Virginia).

The arrangements for physical delivery against futures contracts in New York Harbour are relatively simple and inexpensive. As a result a small number of traders have used the market to make or take delivery against futures contracts in the difficult peak winter demand period so that the volume of deliveries via the medium of the futures market has varied markedly between the summer and winter months:

The seasonal pattern of demand, and the price variability associated with it, have a major impact on monthly volumes of trading (see Table 1) and also influence the ways in which traders use the exchange.

This is illustrated by comparison of the data on trader commitments in Tables 2 and 3 showing the open interest of speculative and hedging traders at 30 June and 30 September 1981.[2]

Between these two dates those traders describing their activities as hedging moved from being net long by 3700 contracts to being net short by approximately the same amount. The increase in open interest held by hedgers from 20,660 contracts to 45,410 contracts consisted of 16,110 short contracts and 8639 long contracts.

We would expect most trade hedging to be short hedging to cover the risks of carrying inventories and of commitments to suppliers of crude oil and products. (A review of 25 US futures markets from 1947 to 1965 gave the percentages of the value of open interest held by long hedgers as 18%and short hedgers 38%).[3]

The large increase in short hedging was associated with an increase in the volume of short contracts held by the four largest traders from 24.2%of the total at the end of June to 60.8%at the end of September. Analysis leads to the conclusion that the four largest traders held a percentage of somewhere between 77%and 91%of the total short position shown for hedgers at 30 September and between 85% and 99%of the 1982 short hedging contracts.

The analysis also suggests that the volume of short hedging by non-reporting traders is probably small and that non-reporting traders are likely to be mainly speculative.[4]

The high level of short contracts held by the four largest traders must mean that other short hedgers held relatively small positions. By inference we arrive at the following conclusions:

1 The 66%proportion of short contracts described as hedging at 30 September is probably a good estimate of the total proportion inclusive of non-reporting traders which appears unlikely to exceed 70%
2. A significant proportion of the short hedging contracts — perhaps up to one third were held by oil traders who eventually delivered No. 2 Heating Oil against these contracts.
3. The four largest traders held 80 to 90%of the short hedging contracts and it is probable that most of these, apart from those committed to delivery, were valid hedges in the sense that they were intended to protect inventories, or forward physical oil sales, or purchase commitments.
4. It is probable that a high proportion (perhaps half) of the long hedging contracts at 30 September and both the long and short hedging contracts at 30 June are of a speculative rather than hedging nature.
5 There is a seasonal change in the use of the market by the oil trade with the main emphasis being on short hedging and delivery in the winter months (albeit by a small number of large traders) and with the emphasis, at a lower volume, changing to speculation, or taking a view about prices, in the summer months.

It is the general concensus that the use of the market by the major oil companies is small and that most majors have not used the market at all. The relatively large number of short contracts held by the four largest oil traders could well mean that one or two mini-majors may be amongst the four.

The main trade users would appear to be independent oil companies and oil traders. We know that Apex Oil Company has been a major contributor to deliveries on the market in the last winter and the suit they have filed in the US District Court mentions Coastal Corp., Belcher Oil Co., and Northeast Petroleum Corp., as being involved, according to Apex, in attempting to squeeze the New York Heating Oil market in February 1982.

There have been some examples of fixed price contracts to end-consumers based on the purchase and sale of futures contracts. The best known was the award of a one year contract by the Washington Metropolitan Area Transit Authority which included pre-determined monthly prices for automotive diesel based on the supplier hedging the cost of physical oil supplies by the purchase of futures.

It would appear however that the volume of price fixing in this way by suppliers, and of hedging by end-consumers is relatively small by comparison with potential use. (There is of course no statistical evidence on the subject.)

There is no statistical data available for the International Petroleum Exchange of the type published by the US Commodity Futures Trading Commission, but there appears to be a general consensus that trade interest is of the order of 60-70% of turnover.

Most of the trade participation is by international product traders and Rhine barge traders. There appears to have been no significant use by major oil companies although some product trading subsidiaries have 'tasted' the market.

Despite the virtual absence of the majors the volume of futures trading in the 3 months March-May 1982 was the equivalent of 16,840,000 tonnes. Demand for gas oils and diesel oils in the countries bordering the Rhine and the North Sea is estimated at 129 million tonnes a year, giving a ratio of futures trading to actual demand of approximately 0.5 to 1.

The contract specification is based on the German domestic heating oil, 'Heizol EL', which provides the major gas oil movement out of Rotterdam up the Rhine and many of the German distributors initially envisaged the market as a potential alternative source of physical gas oil performing a function similar to that provided by the New York Mercantile Exchange in the winter.

The delivery procedure is both more complicated and expensive than is the case in New York Harbour and delivery into the exchange approved tankage installations appears to have been used by product traders as a disposal outlet for gas oil in the summer months rather more than a mechanism for meeting peak winter demand as in New York Harbour. Comparative deliveries in the summer and winter periods have been:

There has been some hedging of inventories and of purchase and sales commitments by Rhine barge traders but routine hedging of the shorter term price risks involved in barge trading has been discouraged by the price volatility which can occur in the low trading volumes of delivery month contracts in the second half of the delivery month.

It is probable that most of the trade volume has been provided by

Table 15.1. New York Mercantile Exchange. Volume of Trading in No. 2 Heating Oil Contract (Lots of 1000 Barrels).

	1978	*1979*	*1980*	*1981*	*1982*
January		365	8,512	67,368	165,071
February		515	8,427	58,514	148,794
March		182	5,146	55,299	176,373
April		369	4,798	61,826	146,821
May		502	3,421	58,933	98,440
June		1,377	5,923	76,580	
July		2,156	6,074	86,394	
August		2,205	11,564	100,102	
September		2,847	27,430	99,790	
October		5,895	40,525	121,455	
November	37	9,371	53,098	78,972	
December	79	8,010	63,366	126,749	
TOTAL	116	33,804	238,284	991,460	

	Monthly Average Price		*Month to Month Mean Price Change*
	Mean	*Standard Deviation $ per tonne*	
Premium Gasoline	356.10	30.49	17.15
Gas Oil	297.11	20.06	13.35
3.5% S Fuel Oil	167.28	3.97	3.84
		$ per barrel	
Crude Oil	32.17	1.75	1.20

	Volume of Transactions Reported '000 Tonnes	*Number of Transactions*
Motor Gasolines	2,554	710
Naphtha	5,595	402
Gas Oil	12,439	5,050
Fuel Oils	10,333	1,264

	Total Deliveries Tonnes	Average Monthly Delivery Tonnes	Deliveries as percentage of volume traded
July to October 1981 & May 1982	272,600	54,520	2.12
November 1982 to April 1982	123,900	20,650	0.73

	Total Volume Delivered '000 Barrels	Average Monthly Volume Delivered '000 Barrels
December 1979–February 1980	850	283
May 1980–August 1980	416	104
December 1980–February 1981	4,729	1,576
May 1981–August 1981	2.302	576
December 1981–February 1982	12,187	4,062

the international product traders. They have been accustomed in recent years to taking a view about prices, are used to selling short, and have found it relatively easy to combine trading in futures with their physical operations because the basic requirements of market information and willingness to take decisions quickly are common to both activities. In most cases there is no bureaucracy to convince before entering futures trading.

It is the common assessment that a high proportion of the futures market activities of the product traders was speculative, in the sense of taking a view about price trends, rather than hedging until early 1982.

The backwardation in futures prices in January 1982 and the price collapse during February, have convinced many traders of the merits of hedging their physical activities. The downward price movements in February and the subsequent rapid recovery in April (see Fig. 1) had a significant impact on the volume of trade, attracted new participants to the market and increased awareness of the usefulness of the market as a hedging mechanism.

It would still appear that speculation is a more important contributor than hedging to total oil trade usage of futures.

Fig. 15.1: London Gas Oil Futures Prices for June Delivery

Use by end-consumers to fix forward the cost of their supplies has been small as is also the use of the market by suppliers to provide fixed price contracts. Some of the smaller marketers (the mini-majors) are showing interest in such contracts but only appear to be prepared to respond to pressure from the largest consumers. The purchasing managements of most large end-consumers are attracted by the prospect of choice of price offered by the futures market but are still at a learning stage in considering the implications. Companies which already use other futures markets are likely to be amongst the first to use gas oil futures but the number of such companies which are also large consumers of gas oil is small.

There is some arbitrage between the London and New York markets and better than the promoters had expected but the volumes in London can still be too low in quiet trading for efficient and rapid placing and lifting of cargo size hedges, of say 30,000 tonnes. Neither market is being used by most integrated oil companies and end-consumers and it is relevant to their potential growth to understand why this should be so.

PARTICIPATION BY THE MAJOR OIL COMPANIES

It is clear that most integrated oil companies cannot see the gas oil futures markets having any significant relevance to their current major problems. The senior managements most likely to be interested will have been concentrating over the last year on such major problems as (a) modifying their crude oil purchasing programmes to get out of higher priced commitments (b) rationalising refining and supply operations and costs and shutting down refinery plant (c) reviewing and reducing oil inventories (d) rationalising and cost cutting all activities to correspond to lower demand expectations etc.

It is perhaps not surprising that most companies have been prepared to be observers only of the futures markets at this stage.

The 'chicken and egg' problem is also relevant for the larger companies. Most feel, justifiably, that the markets are too small to accept their major hedging decisions without the risk of adverse price movements and the larger of the majors are afraid of the adverse publicity which might follow such price movements. But even minor participation by some majors would increase volumes to levels at which such problems would be reduced.

The most fundamental problems however are those of the intellectual acceptability of futures trading as a business management tool. The issue of acceptability has several facets.

To many oil company managements price changes are seen as presenting opportunities as well as risk and there is a confident feeling, sometimes publicly articulated, that major oil companies are accustomed to dealing with risk and are good at it. It is also true that price changes on individual products which might cause serious problems to smaller refining or marketing companies operating in a single market do not pose the same risks to the multinational majors with their vertical and horizontal integration.

It is perhaps a pity that the public relations literature published by the futures markets. and some of the simpler discussions on hedging by the commodity houses concentrate on the use of hedging to eliminate the risks associated with price fluctuations and neglect the scope provided by hedging in giving greater freedom for business action which is so well discussed in the academic literature on the subject.[5]

It is this lack of understanding of the ways in which futures trading is integrated with the basic business activities of industries which have long had futures markets, which may yet be the most important limitation on the growth in use of the market. The number of senior executives in the oil industry who have any practical experience of the use of other futures markets must be very low.

It would appear that in most oil companies approval to trade in futures must be sought at the highest management levels, and that in addition to the problems of understanding, there is often concern at the apparently speculative nature of the way in which the futures markets have been used by some trade participants. There have been rumours of large speculative losses.

These various inhibitions may require time to resolve. The successful introduction of contracts for other products, and perhaps particularly motor gasoline and crude oil, would significantly widen the potential usefulness of futures trading to the integrated oil companies and ease the problems of acceptability. Oil companies could well study the ways in which the soyabean industry manages its operations with the 'complex' of futures markets in soyabeans, soyabean meal and soyabean oil.[6]

PARTICIPATION BY CONSUMERS

The other area of potential growth which is still at a very low level of use is that of fixing the costs of supply to end users. The problems are again of various types.

With a few exceptions most large consumers of gas oil and automotive diesel oil have no previous experience of the use of futures markets and managements will tend to have similar inhibitions about the use of the market to those of their opposite numbers in the major oil marketers.

In Europe there are several national markets in which price ceilings for oil products are determined by government controls. In both France and Italy the formulation of prices has been a political affair and domestic prices for sensitive 'social' products such as domestic heating oil and automotive diesel oil have been insulated from the major changes taking place in international product markets.[7]

Belgium and the Netherlands have designed explicit formulae in which changes in various costs automatically lead to changes in petroleum price ceilings. In both cases Rotterdam spot prices are a major element in the determination of price ceilings. The product price formulae have been designed to allow consumers to enjoy low product prices when spot market prices are below the costs of domestic refiners and to protect consumers when spot prices are higher than domestic refiners' costs. When spot prices are high the formulae effectively restrict domestic prices from following spot prices.

The French control system has recently been changed to a formula of similar type[8] and it would appear that Italy is also likely to follow this approach.

The restriction on upward alignment of domestic prices with Rotterdam spot prices is a complication in the use of the futures market to fix forward prices and it reduces the efficiency of hedging. Hedging of the Rotterdam related element in the price formulae could still be possible and useful in appropriate circumstances but would require more sophistication and interest on the part of both consumers and suppliers than now appears to exist.

Even in markets where there are no government controls, price movements can be partially insulated in the short term from the movements in spot Rotterdam prices. An example is the United Kingdom where large consumers typically buy gas oil and automotive diesel oil on contracts of one to three years duration, with pricing clauses related to the supplying company's published schedule prices.[9] Changes in schedule prices are normally led by Esso and Shell with BP and Mobil occasionally taking the initiative. Between June 1980 and June 1982, schedule prices were changed nine times, but the system of rebates to individual consumers resulted in rebate changes of about the same number. Rebated prices tend to follow Rotterdam prices, but changes are 'sticky' and depend on the relative competitive status of the price leaders. As a result, margins on sales to large consumers over the last twelve months have varied from a minimum of about 0.25 pence per litre in September 1981 to a maximum of 2.35 pence per litre in March 1981, although it is clear that the price leaders are aiming at a long term average margin above Rotterdam prices near the middle of this range.

Hedging on contractual price terms by end consumers makes little sense in such circumstances, and the major marketers have given little indication so far of any significant initiative in either offering fixed price contracts or in offering larger consumers the type of contract which could facilitate hedging by the consumer himself.

In the longer term, as (or if) oil futures markets grow, we would expect such contracts to consist of two components of price - one equivalent to the Rotterdam spot price or the future prices for the delivery month, and a second component which includes premia for quality, supply costs, credit terms, etc., and a margin for profit and overhead costs.

With contracts of this form, which are typical of products traded in other futures markets, it would be possible for both supplier and consumer to hedge their commitments as they wished.

Germany is probably the freest and most competitive market in Europe and it can be shown that the prices of domestic heating oil (Heizol EL) and automotive diesel oil, which are reported widely in publications such as Europe Oil Telegram, are closely related to spot prices in Rotterdam. Prices in long term contracts with major consumers are reviewed on a monthly basis against published prices.

Existing price relationships are appropriate to hedging by both suppliers and consumers, but there is little evidence of the use of the futures market by either group.

It has been suggested that contractual relationships are so weak in this highly competitive market that consumers can withdraw from contracts if prices do not match those known to be on offer from other suppliers, and that it might not be possible to hold customers to contracts with fixed prices which turned out to be higher than those applying in contracts of the conventional type.

In general in all countries the major marketers appear to be prepared to react to pressure for changes in contractual forms, including hedging facilities, from the larger consumers, but do not appear prepared to take initiatives themselves. There has so far been little pressure from major consumers, although there is now some evidence of active interest.

Reasons for the slow development of interest in those markets such as Germany and the UK which appear to be the most appropriate for use of futures appear to be:

(a) Many major consumers of gas oil do not understand how to use futures markets to fix forward costs, and education and explanation are necessary;

(b) for most industrial companies which may be regarded as large consumers by their suppliers, the cost of gas oil is only a minor element in the final cost of their products, so that fixing the gas oil price provides no real competitive advantage in helping to fix the price of their final products;

(c) most transport organisations, for whom the cost of fuel may be a major element in total costs, are either owned by governments or local authorities. Managements have inhibitions about the use of future markets, because of the public concept of them as speculative. (This is also true of most private enterprise companies which have not previously used futures markets.)

Purchasing by public authorities may be subject to guidelines on competitive bidding, and audit of contract awards, which appear to inhibit the use of hedging to fix prices.

(d) in most markets, the current system of contracts and price review has led to management appraisal systems for purchasing departments being based on comparison of prices from several suppliers and evidence of prices paid by similar size buyers. The major objective has been to ensure that prices are at least comparable and if possible better than those of other known purchasers. Fixing prices forward, by taking a view about the levels currently on offer, poses the risk that the view might be wrong and that prices will be higher than those paid by other known buyers.

The evidence from other commodity markets is that these inhibitions and codes of conduct gradually change over time, with a high proportion of the larger consumers eventually becoming users of futures markets.

The rapid price changes which occurred between February and April provided an example of the opportunities which can be made available by the use of futures, and there is evidence of greater interest by some large consumers.

It is to be expected that change will result from pressure by large consumers for modification of contracts to permit hedging and from the use of fixed price offers by smaller marketers in order to increase market share. Problems arising from the reluctance of some consumers to become directly involved in futures markets operations will be resolved by suppliers offering contracts based on futures prices which are covered by the suppliers' own futures market operations.

PROPOSALS FOR NEW CONTRACTS

The clear success of the New York No. 2 Heating Oil contract, and the encouraging start of the Rotterdam gas oil contract, have stimulated consideration of other contracts.

The Chicago Board of Trade intends to start trading in a gasoline conract with Gulf Coast delivery early in July, and has approval from the Commodity Futures Trading Commission to trade in contracts for both leaded and unleaded gasolines and No. 2 Heating Oil, again with Gulf Coast delivery. It is to be assumed that trading in the No. 2 Heating Oil contract will be started some time in the third quarter of 1982, to take advantage of the seasonal trade interest in No. 2 Heating Oil for winter delivery.

The delivery procedures adopted by the Chicago Board of Trade avoid the delivery problems associated with the New York Mercantile contracts. The main problem for these new contracts is likely to be that of generating rapidly a sufficient volume of trade to make the Chicago markets more attractive to both hedgers and speculators than the existing markets with New York Harbour delivery. There must be considerable doubt that this is feasible in the case of No. 2 Heating Oil because of the relatively high volume already traded on on the New York Mercantile Exchange. The much lower volume New York Leaded Regular Gasoline contract could, however, come under considerable pressure from the Chicago gasoline contracts.

The Chicago Board of Trade is the world's busiest futures exchange. Its trading volume in 1981 was 49 million contracts, which was 50% of all US futures contracts. By comparison the Chicago Mercantile Exchange traded 24.5 million contracts, the New York Mercantile 1.8 million contracts, and the London Commodity Exchange 3.8 million.

A major strength of the Chicago markets is the volume of turnover and liquidity generated by their locals — the traders who operate on the floor for their own account, but it remains to be seen whether the Board of Trade can generate sufficient liquidity to meet the requirements of hedgers.

The Chicago Mercantile Exchange is also seeking authority from the CFTC for approval to trade in Leaded and Unleaded Gasoline with Gulf Coast delivery.

It is probable in the longer term that there will be one major contract in US motor gasoline futures. The price differentials between Gulf Coast and New York Harbour delivery, and between Leaded Regular and Unleaded Gasolines do not show enough variability to generate the levels of speculative activity to support two major gasoline markets and it is probable that most trade hedging and speculative use of the market will be attracted to the exchange having the largest turnover and liquidity. This could well remain a Leaded Gasoline contract until such time as decreasing volumes and trade pressures eventually resulted in its conversion into an unleaded specification contract.

Both the Chicago Board of Trade and the New York Mercantile Exchange are seeking approval to trade in crude oil contracts. The Chicago Board of Trade contract is based on delivery of a wide range of light low sulphur crude oils at the Louisiana Offshore Oil Port storage and pipeline terminals, while the New York Mercantile

Exchange is proposing contracts for light low sulphur and heavy high sulphur contracts at pipeline terminals in Cushing, Oklahoma.

A successful crude oil contract could be of fundamental importance for the world oil industry and raises many possibilities which will be touched on later.

The early experience with the New York Cotton Exchange contract based on Rotterdam delivery, suggested that a market could be successful given both an appropriate contract and the right environment.

A summary of the criteria used by the New York Mercantile Exchange to evaluate new contracts is attached (Appendix 1).[10] Missing from it is perhaps the single most important factor in the failure of earlier petroleum futures markets; the presence of a body of potential users who understand how to use futures in their business activities and who are prepared to do so.

The oil industry's understanding of futures markets has certainly increased since the start of the New York Mercantile's contracts in November 1978, but the earlier discussion showed that usage was still mainly restricted to the product traders and independent oil companies.

It is to be expected that major oil companies will abstrain from early use of crude oil futures until such time as turnover increases to a level appropriate to the volume of their hedging requirements. The market for a viable crude oil contract, as distinct from most product markets would, however, be virtually world-wide and the number of potential participants many.

Some of the international product traders now using the gas oil markets are also engaged in crude oil trading. The gradual development of the crude oil surplus during 1981 and 1982 has led to a weakening of the rigid contractual relationships it had been possible for OPEC countries to impose — such as restrictions on spot sales and the rights of refiners to resell oil. Major oil companies are prepared to shut down refining capacity and buy products from traders, who have a wide choice of processing possibilities if they can obtain crude oil. Some producing countries are willing to move crude oil by barter deals and processing arrangements they would not previously have considered. The result is a greater flexibility in the spot crude oil market and a greater number of potential participants in crude oil futures trading. In this sense, the timing for a new crude oil contract is probably appropriate.

If we now turn to the criteria used by the New York Mercantile Exchange, the most important would appear to be that of price uncertainty on which it is said that 'Variations up or down of at least

20%within 12 month periods are assumed to be the minimum necessary to sustain futures trading'.

Spot crude oil prices have had this sort of variability since early 1979, but the success of the market will depend upon the industry's expectations of price changes in the future.

In current conditions of crude oil surplus, with OPEC having succeeded in holding the $34 per barrel marker price, there might well be the sort of price stability which existed between February 1974 and December 1978.

It is, however, the expectations of the oil industry which will be important for the early viability of a crude oil futures contract. Those expectations will be influenced by the difficulties of 'fine tuning' around the defined marker price, the problems of reconciling the production ambitions of individual producers, the behaviour of Iran in expanding production, and the continuing political instability of the Middle East.

If all these problems looked as if they were solved, the crude oil contracts would fail. It appears more likely that the oil industry will not be so satisfied.

The Chicago Board of Trade contract with delivery at the Louisiana Offshore Oil Port would appear to have the better prospects of success because (i) it is likely to be the first to trade; (ii) it will be the more directly linked to the international crude oil market, and (iii) it is more likely to provide liquidity with its 'local' floor traders.

Success could be determined by the comparative ease of making and taking delivery, since it is the delivery process which maintains close relationships between prices in the futures market and in the spot physical market. The delivery by crude oil traders of large cargoes in otherwise low volumes of trading around the LOOP terminal could distort the price relationships between those in the futures market for LOOP delivery and prices for the same crude oil at other locations. Trade hedgers will prefer that market which maintains the best defined relationship between futures prices in the delivery month and spot physical prices and the value of a well defined relationship will be higher if the basic price variability in the physical market is low.

There is a case for a contract based on Arabian Light and similar crude oils, with Rotterdam delivery, but it now appears probable that the viability of a contract of this type, or any other international crude oil contract, could be pre-empted by the Chicago and New York proposals.

The International Petroleum Exchange in London is preparing contracts for premium grade motor gasoline based on delivery in

North-West Europe, and for fuel oil with a wider delivery range, and it has been reported that the gasoline contract will be introduced early in 1983.

The volume of the North-West European spot market in motor gasoline is significantly lower than that for gas oil. Data reported by Joe Roeber Associates in their report on the market to the EEC Commission[11] were:

Motor gasoline tends to be more closely controlled by the major marketers because there is less variability in demand, retail outlets are company owned or controlled, and its profitability can be directly related to optimum utilisation of refinery conversion and upgrading capacity, and retail outlets. There is, however, a high level of imports into both Germany and Switzerland.

The futures market will be of use to product traders, independent marketers, barge traders, and small distributors, but to a lesser extent than is the case with gas oil. There are few major end consumers.

Price variability is relatively high (although only about 15% as compared with the New York Mercantile criterion of a minimum of 20%).

The relative disadvantages of a motor gasoline contract as compared with the gas oil contract will be offset to some extent by the more favourable response to be expected of potential users following the success of the gas oil contracts and the New York Mercantile's gasoline contract. There should also be some attraction to independent refiners and traders processing crude oil who wish to cover part or most of the risk of refining incremental crude oil with no firm outlets.

The fuel oil contract being considered by the International Petroleum Exchange would be a high sulphur fuel oil of marine bunker quality. The possibility of delivery points outside of North-West Europe is being considered. The number of potential oil trade users of such a contract is higher than is the case for motor gasoline and there is a large end user market which could be interested.

A potential problem of a heavy fuel oil contract would be the relative price stability which can exist for some time. The most marked price change over the last three years in the Rotterdam price quotations for 3.5% Sulphur fuel oil was an increase from US $153 per tonne in August 1980 to US $232 per tonne in November, from which prices dropped again to US $165 per tonne in June 1981. Price changes of this type would make hedging attractive to a wide variety of users and would attract the speculative interest necessary to provide the counterpart to the hedging requirements.

During the twelve months immediately following prices have been

Table 15.2. Heating Oil – New York Mercantile Exchange Commitments of Traders June 30, 1981.

	Total	Reporting (Large) Traders								Non-Reporting	
		Speculative								Non-Reporting	
	Open Interest	Long or Short Only		Long and Short (Spreading)		Hedging		Total		(Small and/or Foreign) Traders Speculative and Hedging	
		Long	Short	Long	Short	Long	Short	Long	Short	Long	Short
					(Contracts of 42,000 U.S. Gallons)						
All	16,822	741	2,181	1,264	1,264	12,205	8,456	14,210	11,901	2,612	4,921
1981	14,723	754	2,222	892	892	11,601	7,492	13,247	10,606	1,476	4,117
1982	2,099	190	162	169	169	604	964	963	1,295	1,136	804
					Percent of Open Interest held by each Group of Traders						
All	100.0%	4.4	13.0	7.5	7.5	72.6	50.3	84.5	70.7	15.5	29.3
1981	100.0%	5.1	15.1	6.1	6.1	78.8	50.9	90.0	72.0	10.0	28.0
1982	100.0%	9.1	7.7	8.1	8.1	28.8	45.9	45.9	61.7	54.1	38.3
	Reporting Traders				Number of Traders in each Group						
All	99	13	25	23	23	46	34	73	72		
1981	98	12	28	21	21	46	34	71	71		
1982	23	7	5	6	6	8	4	16	14		

Concentration Ratios

Percent of Open Interest Held by the Indicated Number of Largest Reporting Traders

	By Gross Position			
	4 or Less Traders		*8 or Less Traders*	
	Long	*Short*	*Long*	*Short*
All	32.9	24.1	45.9	34.4
1981	36.7	23.1	50.1	34.7
1982	25.8	51.0	37.2	59.4

Table 15.3. Heating Oil — New York Mercantile Exchange Commitments of Traders September 30, 1981.

	Total	Reporting (Large) Traders								Non-Reporting	
		Speculative								(Small and/or Foreign) Traders Speculative and Hedging	
	Open Interest	Long or Short Only		Long and Short (Spreading)		Hedging		Total			
		Long	Short	Long	Short	Long	Short	Long	Short	Long	Short
		(Contracts of 42,000 U.S. Gallons)									
All	36,996	2,235	1,273	3,416	3,443	20,844	24,566	26,495	29,282	10,501	7,714
1981	19,528	1,576	2,077	653	653	13,711	12,281	15,940	15,011	3,588	4,517
1982	17,468	2,151	668	1,271	1,318	7,133	12,285	10,555	14,271	6,913	3,197
		Percent of Open Interest held by each Group of Traders									
All	100.0%	6.0	3.4	9.2	9.3	56.3	66.4	71.6	79.1	28.4	20.9
1981	100.0%	8.1	10.6	3.3	3.3	70.2	62.9	81.6	76.9	18.4	23.1
1982	100.0%	12.3	3.8	7.3	7.3	40.8	70.3	60.4	81.7	39.6	18.3
	Reporting Traders	Number of Traders in each Group									
All	108	20	18	32	32	54	24	92	63		
1981	100	21	24	16	16	46	22	75	53		
1982	78	20	11	22	23	42	14	69	40		

Concentration Ratios
Percent of Open Interest Held by the Indicated Number of Largest Reporting Traders

	By Gross Position			
	4 or Less Traders		*8 or Less Traders*	
	Long	*Short*	*Long*	*Short*
All	21.0	60.8	33.4	65.6
1981	27.6	52.9	44.9	60.2
1982	17.4	69.6	27.5	73.9

remarkably stable, within a total price range of US $160 to US $177 per tonne, although this period includes the major weakening of spot crude oil prices to US $28 per tonne for Arab Light in March 1982. The price variability as a percentage of the mean price has been about 35% of that for gas oil and 27% of that for motor gasoline:

Some of the factors which resulted in the price rise of late 1980 could recur as European catalytic cracking and visbreaking capacities are increased, but their impact is likely to be reduced by the product exports from the USA which are now possible since the relaxation on US product exports in October 1981.

The success of a heavy fuel oil contract cannot be taken to be certain. Perhaps the most realistic assumption is that in its early existence it might trade at low volumes in parallel with the gas oil and motor gasoline markets, to flare into activity whenever significant price changes were taking place in the spot physical fuel or crude oil markets.

THE LONGER TERM PROSPECT

We might then expect in about two years time to have viable futures markets in Europe for gas oil, premium grade motor gasoline and heavy fuel oil, to have markets in the United States in No. 2 Heating Oil and gasoline, and to have a market, possibly that of the Chicago Board of Trade with Louisiana delivery, trading in international crude oils. We would expect there to be active interest in a contract with Singapore delivery.

We would expect the New York Mercantile Exchange to attempt to revive its No. 6 Fuel Oil contract with New York Harbour delivery, and to have started trading a contract in tanker freight. The prospects of a viable market in both cases within this time appear doubtful.

The availability of an international crude oil contract and a West European fuel oil contract would open up new possibilities of hedging of considerable significance for the growth of the futures markets and for the commercial decision making of the supply and refining sectors of the oil industry.

It will become possible to hedge the processing of incremental crude oil by the simultaneous purchase of crude oil futures and the sale of futures for the three main products. The processing of incremental fuel oil to catalytic cracking and other conversion processes will similarly become capable of being hedged.

It is useful to make comparisons with the ways in which the soyabean industry uses the Chicago Board of Trades' 'soyabean complex' of futures markets, consisting of contracts in soyabeans, soyabean meal and soyabean oil. The industry's management philosophies are well discussed in the literature.[6] While these vary to some extent between the major firms there is a common emphasis by the major crushers and refiners that their basic skills consist of their abilities to manage the technical, organisational, and marketing functions of the industry and that their ability to do this profitably should not be put at risk from avoidable price fluctuations in their feedstock and products. The managements of some of the larger companies insist that all activities should be hedged at all times, while others make the major decisions on hedging policy a top management function.

The complete integration of futures trading into the basic business decisions in this way has resulted in the 'soyabean complex' being the most heavily traded of the world's futures markets.

The total volume traded in 'soyabean complex' futures contracts in 1981 was 16.6 million lots, one sixth of all US futures. This total was equivalent to approximately 14 times the world production of soyabeans (or 24 times the US production), about 14 times the US supply of soyabean oil and 12 times the US supply of soyabean meal.

In a busy day's trading (but not a record) on 25 February the market traded 53,000 lots of soyabeans, 30,000 lots of soyabean oil and 15,000 lots of soyabean meal with a total paper value of US $2.29 billion. Markets of this size provide adequate scope for major hedging decisions by the largest companies in the business.

The way in which the industry uses the 'soyabean complex' provides some measure of the potential scope for petroleum futures markets.

At this stage of development the major oil companies probably regard the futures markets as irrelevant to their major problems for the reasons already discussed. Current volumes of turnover are too low for major hedging requirements and they are not convinced of the merits of hedging their activities in single products.

The markets are growing as the industry's understanding of them increases and this process can be expected to continue.

While this process goes on the refining and marketing sectors of the oil industry are being forced to react to the heavy costs and highly competitive pricing which result from massive surplus capacity and decreasing demand. In the process of structural change now taking place each activity is judged on the basis of its performance against external criteria. Companies are choosing to cut refining capacity and buy products, to move from long term to short term purchase commitments for crude oil supplies, to purchase fuel oil to feed to catalytic cracking rather than increase crude oil throughputs, to sell processing capacity, and so on.

The previous emphasis on the integration of crude oil supply, refining and marketing is being replaced by a process of radical examination of alternative external choices at every stage.

Amongst these choices from now on will be the use of futures contracts. Decisions to process additional crude oil can be protected by the sale of futures contracts until such time as physical sales are made. In the longer term, as the new contracts come into being, refinery margins will be protected by the purchase of crude oil futures and the sales of futures contracts for products, and management philosphies similar to those of the soyabean crushers will begin to emerge.

Futures prices will be used as the basis for medium term supply planning and programming and will determine the decisions on incremental crude oil purchases or sales. These decisions will be hedged at the time by the purchase or sale of futures contracts at those prices which resulted in the optimum decision. Transfer prices between associated companies or activities will be based on futures prices and will be 'locked in' by hedging when appropriate.

All of this will take time but the process of acceptance will accelerate as different sectors of the industry begin to appreciate that *the integrated use of futures in business decision making should give greater freedom for business action.*

REFERENCES

1. *The Petroleum Economist*, October 1974.
2. Commodity Futures Trading Commission. Commitments of Traders. As of June 30, 1981 and September 30, 1981.
3. Charles Rockwell, 'Normal Backwardation, Forecasting and the Returns to Commodity Futures Traders', Proceedings of a Symposium on Price Effects of Speculation in Organised Commodity Markets, Food Research Institute Studies. Supplement 7 (1967), 117.
4. Analysis available from author.
5. See (a) *The Economics of Futures Trading* edited by B.A. Goss and B.S. Yamey, The MacMillan Press, 1978.
   (b) Gerald Gold. *Modern Commodity Futures Trading*, Commodity Research Bureau Inc., 1975.
   (c) R.J. Teweles, C.V. Harlow and H.L. Stone, *The Commodity Futures Game*, McGraw Hill, 1977.
6. Henry B. Arthur, 'Commodity Futures as a Business Management Tool', Division of Research;Graduate School of Business Administration, Harvard University, Boston. 1971.

7. Edward N. Krapels, 'Pricing Petroleum Products', McGraw Hill, 1982.
8. *Bulletin Officiel de la Concurrence et de la Consommation*, No. 11, 30 April 1982.
9. Price Commission, Report 37 *B.P. Oil Ltd., — Oil and Petroleum Products, HC87* (1979). Report 38 *Esso Petroleum Company Ltd., — Oil and Petroleum Products, HC88* (1979), Her Majesty's Stationery Office.
10. J.B. Ball and K.M. Forstik, 'The Feasibility of Coal Futures', New York Mercantile Exchange, presented at the Financial Times World Coal Conference, London, 20/21 January 1982.
11. Joe Roeber Associates, *The EEC Registry of Spot Transactions*, The Directorate General of Energy, Commission of the EEC, 15 September, 1980.
12. *Petroleum Intelligence Weekly*, 14 June 1982, pp. 6 and 12.

APPENDIX I

Abstract from New Commodities Evaluation System used by New York Mercantile Exchange

Commodities will be analyzed by the NYMEX Research Staff in the context of the following criteria to determine a commodity's suitability for futures trading. The criteria are listed in descending order of importance. No one criterion should be viewed with undue emphasis; failure to meet any single requirement does not necessarily mandate dismissal of a commodity under consideration for futures trading. In many instances, a successful commodity will not qualify in all categories. Rather, the criteria must be viewed collectively, and a commodity evaluated on an integrated basis.

Criteria

1. Price volatility or uncertainty This criterion should be considered as one of the most important, for it provides the economic justification for futures trading. The purpose of the futures market is to provide protection to the hedger against adverse price fluctuations. If a commodity was characterized by a relatively stable price base, there would be little associated risk; hedging futures against the spot market would be unnecessary. Price uncertainty therefore, allows for the existence for futures markets. Furthermore, price volatility is necessary to attract speculative interest. Profit potential is realized through price fluctuations.

Quantitative Indicators: Variations up or down of at least 20%

within 12 month periods are assumed to be the minimum necessary to sustain futures trading.

2. Uncertain Supply and demand The production of price volatility arises from the condition of an uncertain supply and demand. If both were to be certain and predictable, the market would establish a firm price. Furthermore, if supply and demand do not vary, market participants would need not be concerned over fluctuating inventory values, future marketing strategies, etc. However, when a situation exists where supply and demand are constantly changing, the interplay of these uncertain economic forces produces price volatility, and hedging in the futures market becomes a valuable management tool.

Quantitative Indicators: Variations of at least 10% over a two year period in either supply or demand are assumed to be the minimum necessary to sustain futures trading.

3. Sufficient Deliverable Supplies Supplies of a commodity must be deliverable in sufficient quantities to support anticipated delivery requirements in futures markets. This requires the absence of government controls over price or allocation, and sufficient transportation and storage facilities to support the anticipated volume of trading.

4. Product Homogeneity and Perishability Futures contracts are traded on the premise that the product taken (or made) on a delivery call meets certain specifications. This requires that the commodity is capable of being standardized or graded. There must be certain characteristics which are quantifiable, thus allowing for the differentiation of the product from similar, but not identical lots. The product then becomes describable and therefore suitable for trading. When the commodity is able to be so described, then different lots could be interchanged. This is essential for futures trading, where trading is impersonal; contracts are not negotiable but, rather call for delivery of a specific product. Therefore, the very design and arrangements of futures contracts mandate that the commodity exists in homogeneous, exchangeable lots. This differs from spot market transactions, where buyers and sellers are able to negotiate contracts on a personal basis, and are able to arrange for particular quality specifications, delivery arrangements, payments terms, etc.

Since a futures contract may call for the delivery of a commodity in a distant month, the commodity must be capable of being stores, so as to meet these requirements. Additionally, futures are used as a hedge against any inventory. Therefore, if a commodity is subject to rapid deterioration and is not capable of being stockpiled, then no futures contracts can be written to accommodate it.

5. **Market Concentration** A successful futures market is a competitive market, marked by broad spot market activity. If there is a large number of buyers and sellers; there exists amply supply and demand. No one market participant is large enough or able to control the flow of supply or direction of demand, i.e. not able to exert price effecting influence by causing an artificial shortage or glut in the market place. In a competitive market, each participant produces (demands) such a small fraction of total output that increasing its output (demand) will have no perceptible influence upon total supply (demand), or therefore, product price. Rather, there should be a sufficient number of buyers and sellers, who through their collective actions form a competitive market. With this large number there is more of a guarantee of market liquidity; a buyer is more apt to find a seller at an agreeable price. When there is a large number of participants, each individual becomes a price taker, not a price effector. He must adjust to the market price (the price established through the collective actions of all market participants) rather than have the price adjust to his actions.

6. **Available Price Information** In order to insure competitiveness, information must be readily available to all market participants. This dissemination will enable the convergence of futures and spot prices. The absence of competitiveness in price determination results in a futures price that does not accurately reflect the underlying supply-demand condition. The use of futures as a hedging mechanism becomes impracticable.

Quantitative Indicators: Daily cash market prices should be available from at least two independent sources.

7. **Unique Trading Opportunity** In general, a successful commodity futures contract should offer a unique trading opportunity and not duplicate similar contracts on other exchanges.

PART VII

Interfuel Substitution

Chapter 16

Towards Three 'Laws' of Energy Substitution*

Professor R.J. Deam and Carlos Giescke†

THE FIRST 'LAW'

At equilibrium the *international* prices of all forms of energy at all locations are uniquely related to the *one* price, that of the marker crude. These unique prices are those found in the market place after time lags. A two or multiple tier price structure is unstable and, in time, reverts to a single tier price structure.[1–4,6])

THE SECOND 'LAW'

In the short term it is reasonable to assume that the production of alternative energy is fixed and independent of the price of the marker crude P_M (new investment has long lead times). Thus, in the short term, the only supply variable we need consider is oil production.

*Copy of Working Paper read to the meeting of the British Institute of Energy Economics, Chatham House, 9 St. James' Square, London SW1 4LE, on 27 January, 1982.

†Queen Mary College, University of London.

The second 'law' is as follows:

To maximise the present net worth of an oil producer's resource, its ratio of production to that of world production is equal to the modulus of the price elasticity with respect to world oil production, suitably corrected for present net worth, i.e.

$$\frac{q_i}{q_o+q_i} = |\Sigma| \frac{P_M-P_N}{P_M}$$

where

q_i = production of the ith producer
q_o = sum of production of all other producers
$|\Sigma|$ = the modulus of the price elasticity with respect to q_o and q_i
P_N = present net worth of oil i
P_M = price of marker crude

It is convenient for the moment to assume $P_N = 0$ and using $|\Sigma| = 0.23$ and $q_o + q_i = 50$ mbd, (approximately the current values) and then determine q_i, giving $q_i = 11.5$ mbd.

Since all producers save one, Saudi Arabia, have physical production limits well below 11.5 mbd, only Saudi can be marker crude. Saudi is the price leader and all other producers are price takers.

OPEC is *not* a monopoly; our second law would be as follows:

$$\frac{q_{OPEC}}{q_{non\text{-}OPEC}+q_{OPEC}} = |\Sigma| \frac{P_M-P_N}{P_M}$$

Neglecting P_N as before and noting $q_{non\text{-}OPEC}$ is roughly 25 mbd, we find

$$q_{OPEC} = 7.47 \text{ mbd}$$

which is to be compared with 24 mbd or so actual.

Our solution for q_S (Saudi production) was 11.5 mbd, which is in excess of the 10 mbd actual. Relating this back to the formula, this gives P_N = \$4.29/bbl (present net worth of Saudi oil in the ground). If we define

$$p_N = \frac{\text{real cost of 'syn-crude'}}{(1+r)^n}$$

and solve for r the discount rate.

With the real cost of 'syn-crude' at \$60/bbl, and n the life of the reserve at 80 years. Our estimate for r is about 2.6%; this figure is in line with the interest paid in government index-linked bonds (2.7 to 2.9%).

This second law, assuming the current price leader - price taker relationship remains in being, has immediate applications, for example:

Conservation

Conservation shifts the price elasticity curve to the left. This will cause very little change in

$$|\Sigma| \frac{P_M - P_N}{P_M}$$

and hence in q_S.

Conservation does not change consumption, it alters price. Indeed 1 mbd of conservation lowers P_M by \$2.61/bb1.

Change in Production of any Other Producer than Saudi

Since

$$\frac{q_S}{q_0 + q_S} = |\Sigma| \frac{P_M - P_N}{P_M} = \text{a constant over reasonable ranges.}$$

1 mbd increases in q_0 will increase q_S by 0.30 mbd, a total increase of 1.3 mbd, or a price reduction of the marker crude of \$3.39/bbl.

Crude Run Tax

If we assume all consumers or all importers put a tax of t \$/bbl on crude, we amend our formula to

$$\frac{q_S}{q_0 + q_S} = |\Sigma| \frac{P_M - P_N - t}{P_M}$$

$|\Sigma|$ is the consumers elasticity for crude oil; the producers elasticity is less than $|\Sigma|$ by

$$\frac{P_M - P_N - t}{P_M}$$

Thus, if t was, say \$15/bbl, the producers elasticity is roughly half what it was before and hence q_S is roughly half. Producers price is sensibly unchanged, and little, if any, of this tax is paid by the producer.

This conclusion makes nonsense of such a scheme as previously advocated by myself and others.

THE THIRD 'LAW'

Whilst in the short term it was reasonable to assume the production of alternative energy was independent of price, we need to be more careful in the longer term.

In the longer term the supply of alternative energy will increase if and when the price of the marker crude is greater than the cost of producing alternative energy.

In the previous section we defined

$$P_N = \frac{\text{real cost of 'syn-crude'}}{(1+r)^n}$$

If there was only one form of alternative energy and it was 'syn-crude' and its real cost was \$60/bbl, then no production of 'syn-crude' would start until P_M was \$60/bbl. Nothing would stop the inevitable rise in crude prices until a ceiling of \$60/bbl (real) is reached.

Current wisdom in the UK government Department of Energy, alternative planners and so on, seems to be a real increase of 2 to

3% per annum in the price of marker crude.

This can be no more than a guess.

I believe the consumer outlook is not that pessimistic for three reasons.

1. Alternative energy substitutes oil products as follows:
   - coal and uranium for fuel oil
   - natural gas (LNG + methanol) for gas oil, kerosine and fuel oil
   - alcohols, synthetic gasoline for gasoline, kerosine and gas oil

   which in turn substitute for crude.
2. Whilst distillation is cheap, the capital cost of producing 1 tonne per annum of gasoline and white products from fuel oil is about $500 and is significant. Coal and uranium have to bear the cost; synthetic gasoline production saves it.
3. The second 'law' of energy substitution.

$$\frac{q_S}{q_0 + q_S} = |\Sigma| \frac{P_M - P_N}{P_M}$$

Consider Coal

If we produce coal and burn it instead of heavy fuel oil, considerable effects take place.

If we substitute 1.5 tonnes of coal per annum for 1 tonne of fuel oil, then at first we will lift less crude to make exactly the same products in a refinery less one tonne of heavy fuel.

Crude can be approximated as 50% white products and 50% fuel oil on distillation. It takes about 1.2 tonnes of fuel oil to make 1 tonne of white products.

Thus 1.5 tonnes of coal/annum will mean 0.9 tonnes of crude/annum less, and about $225 capital in refinery crackers.

If we assume operating and capital charges for a cracker to be 25% of capital it follows:

1.5 tonne of coal ≡ 0.9 tonnes of crude − $56
For crude at $30/bbl and 7.4 bbls/tonne
1.5 tonne of coal = 200 − 56 = $144
or 1 tonne of coal = $95 (its current equilibrium price)

This price of $95 is to be compared with current cost of coal. The price (cost) of US coal at Rotterdam is $75/tonne and if we add $10/tonne for coal handling and stack cleaning we see coal as a potential rent of about $10/tonne. Crude could drop by $2.50/bbl before coal was uneconomic against heavy fuel oil. Now taking into account our second 'law' of energy substitution.

$$\frac{q_S}{q_A + q_0 + q_S} = \overset{x}{|\Sigma|} \frac{P_M - P_N}{P_M}$$

Here we have added q_A production of alternative energy.

$\overset{x}{|\Sigma|}$ is the modulus of the price elasticity of the marker crude against total world energy, not just total crude.

$$\overset{x}{|\Sigma|} = |\Sigma| \frac{q_S}{q_A + q_0 + q_S}$$

If we let $q_A = q_0 + q_S$ (roughly correct), then

$$\overset{x}{|\Sigma|} = \tfrac{1}{2}|\Sigma|$$

We can calculate how much coal we can produce before the price of the marker crude falls by $2.50/bbl, i.e. about 55 mt/annum.

Of course, US coal does not have to go to Rotterdam, and my figures for coal costs are far from accurate.

However, we see that a fairly limited increase in coal production can bring down the price of crude to some $27.50/bbl, and can hold it there for a very long period if production and increased energy demand are balanced.

World coal production will be limited by price, therefore, rather than the physical limits outlined in the World Coal report. Since uranium attacks the heavy fuel oil end of the barrel, similar arguments and limits apply.

Methanol/Synthetic Gasoline from Natural Gas

Unlike coal and uranium, methanol/synthetic gasoline attacks the premium end of the barrel and decreases refinery investment. Indeed coal/uranium is synergetic with synthetic gasoline production.

Now the capital and operating costs of converting natural gas and methanol to synthetic gasoline are about the same as converting heavy fuel oil to white products.

It takes about 1.2 tonnes of heavy fuel to make a tonne of white products and about 1.6 tonnes of natural gas to make a tonne of synthetic gasoline. Thus, natural gas at the plant fence has an equilibrium value of about 1.2/1.6 price of heavy fuel oil, i.e. about $120/tonne or $3.00/mm BTUs.

Many exportable natural gas producers (non-pipeline gas) currently make LNG with net backs of 50 to 75 cents/mm BTUs. Thus the excess rent is, say, $2.00/mm BTUs, which roughly translated means the marker crude would fall some $14/bbl before the gas-to-methanoll route became uneconomic. Some 200 mta would bring about this price reduction. (The second law indicates a production of 4.13 mbd of synthetic gasoline.)

Natural gas is very wide-spread and the proven reserves of exportable natural gas are roughly equal to those of Middle East oil reserves.

Again, my figures are very first order, but they indicate the price of the marker crude and could be held at some $16/bbl real over a long period (30 years or more).

The physical lead in erecting and commissioning methanol plants is relatively short. New Zealand expects its plant on stream within 3 years.

With such a drop in crude prices, as alternative energy increases the second law needs modification.

This is indicated in Ref. 5 'The Long Range Pricing of Crude Oil'.

From this paper the third law of energy substitution can be stated as follows:

'There is an optimum price for Saudi crude which maximises its asset value in the long term and which minimises the long term cost of all energy to consumers'.

Reference 5 shows how the profile of energy prices can be calculated as well as the optimum investment and production schedule of alternative energy.

REFERENCES

1. Deam, R.J. and Leather, J., 'World Energy Modelling', *Energy: Demand, Conservation and Institutional Problems*, MIT Press, 1974, pp. 71–77.
2. Deam, R.J. *et al.*, 'World Energy Modelling Part 1: Concepts and Methods', *Journal of Energy Policy* (special publication) on 'Energy Modelling', pp. 70–90, (October 1973).

3. Deam, R.J. *et al.*, 'World Energy Modelling Part 2: Preliminary Results from the Petroleum/Natural Gas Model', *ibid*, pp. 91-117.
4. Deam, R.J., Laughton, M.A., Hale, J.G., Isaac, J.R., Leather, J., O'Carroll, F.M., Ward, P., 'World Energy Modelling: The Development of Western European Oil Prices', *Journal of Energy Policy*, pp. 21-34 (June 1973).
5. Deam, R.J., 'Long Range Pricing of Crude Oil', in *Mathematical Modelling of Energy Systems*, I Kavrakoglu (editor), Sijthoff and Noordhoff, 1981, pp. 229-246.
6. Deam, R.J., 'Understanding Energy', *ibid.*

Chapter 17

A North Sea Electricity Ring Main: The Benefits of Interconnection

C.H. Gosling

1. INTRODUCTION

The simplified title of a 'Ring Main' conjures up the concept of a domestic 13 amp system with its numerous outlets to accommodate our familiar square-pin plugs. We all know the great flexibility of this system and the great convenience of being able to tap off power wherever we need it. I shall show that on a much larger scale we could develop the same basic concept for Europe, with the added advantage that each point of connection can provide either an input or an output at any moment in time.

The United Kingdom is an island and if we are to interconnect with the rest of Europe we must pass beneath the sea. France, Belgium, Holland, Germany, Denmark, Sweden and Norway are our closest neighbours to the south and east, with Northern Ireland and the Republic of Ireland to the west. There is one low power 160 MW link from the UK to France existing and a new 2000 MW link proposed. Denmark is already connected by substantial electrical links to Norway and Sweden and these will be reinforced by additional links in the near future.

What are the benefits of interconnection between large electrical power systems?

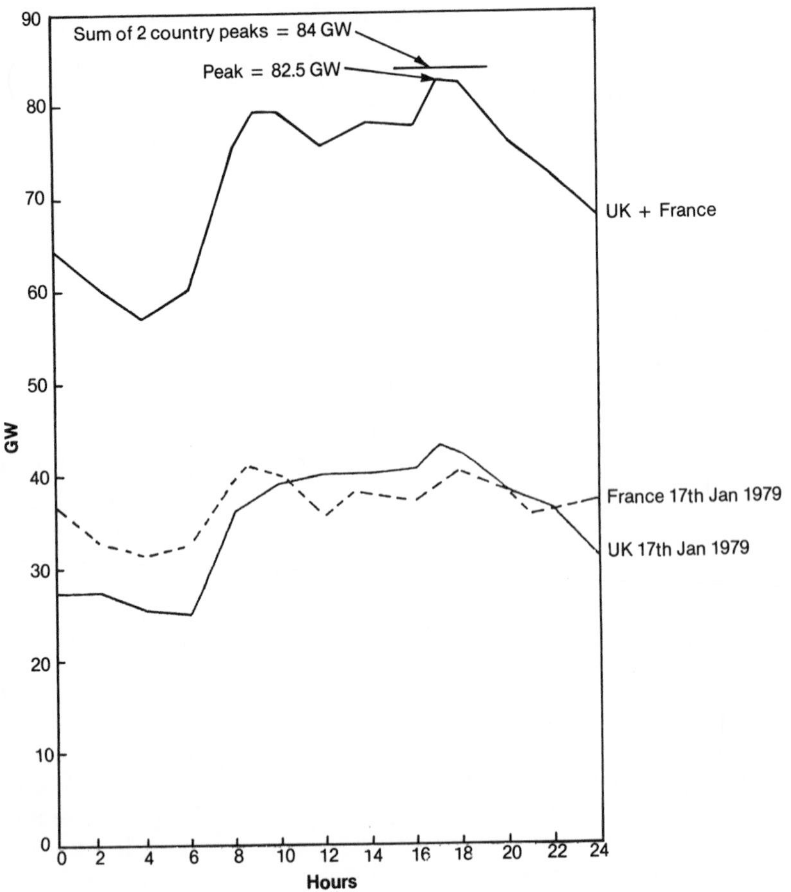

Fig. 17.1: Daily winter load cycle for France & UK

2. THE ADVANTAGES OF INTERCONNECTION IN REDUCING CAPITAL COSTS

In 1979 the United Nations[1] indicated the Capital benefits of interconnection to be:

(i) Capacity needs relative to peak loads can be reduced.
(ii) Lower reserve requirements are needed.
(iii) The possibility of incorporating larger scale units to gain benefits of scale.

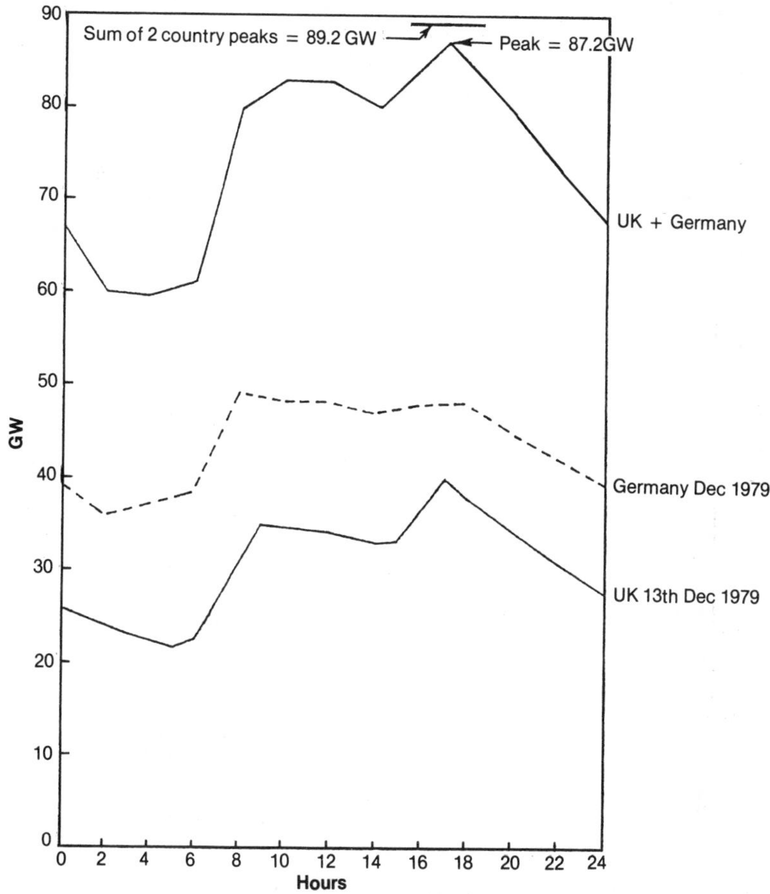

Fig. 17.2: Daily winter load cycle for Germany & UK

(iv) A large but ill-defined gain due to the expanded pool in service and scope to use plant diversity.

To illustrate the possibility of reduction in Capital requirements, reference should be made initially to Fig. 1, which shows the different daily load cycles for France and the CEGB (UK). Without interconnection, the sum of the individual peak loads is of the order of 84 GW, but the maximum load requirement with interconnection for the combined loads of France and the UK is 82.5 GW. There is an

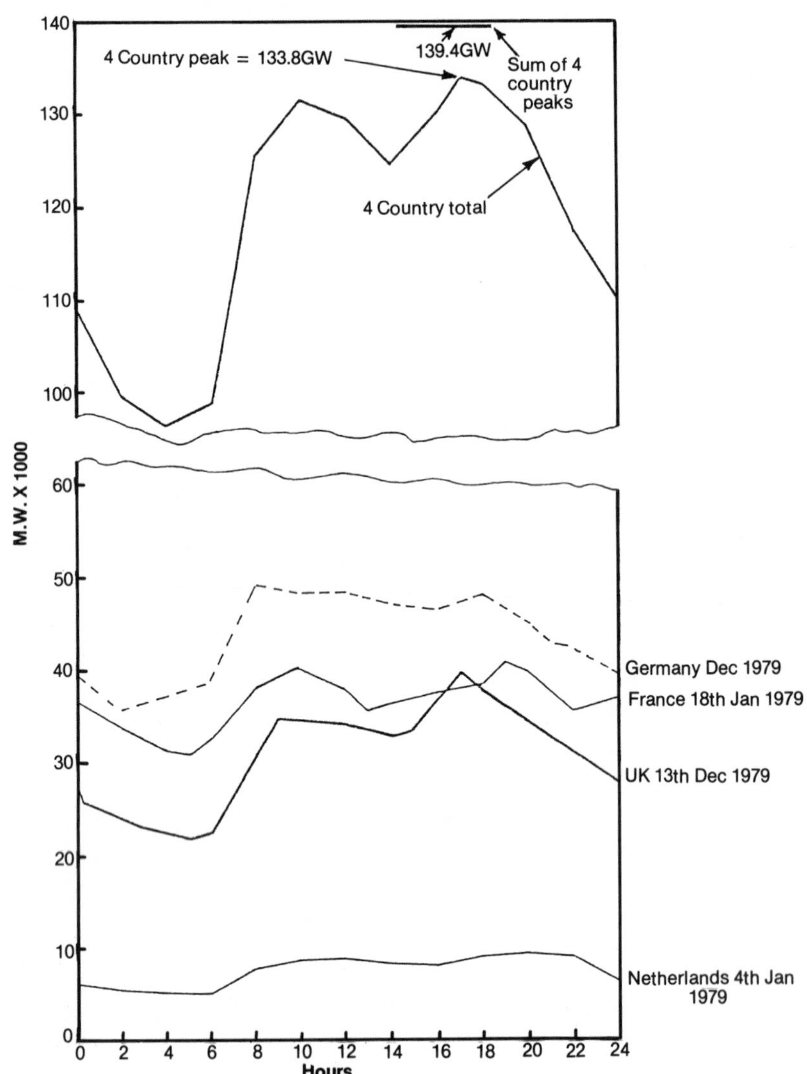

Fig. 17.3: Daily winter load cycle for 4 countries. (UK, Germany, France & Netherlands)

overall saving of some 1500 MW of generating capacity.

Figure 2 indicates that a saving of 2000 MW of generating capacity would be possible if there was an interconnection between the UK and Germany.

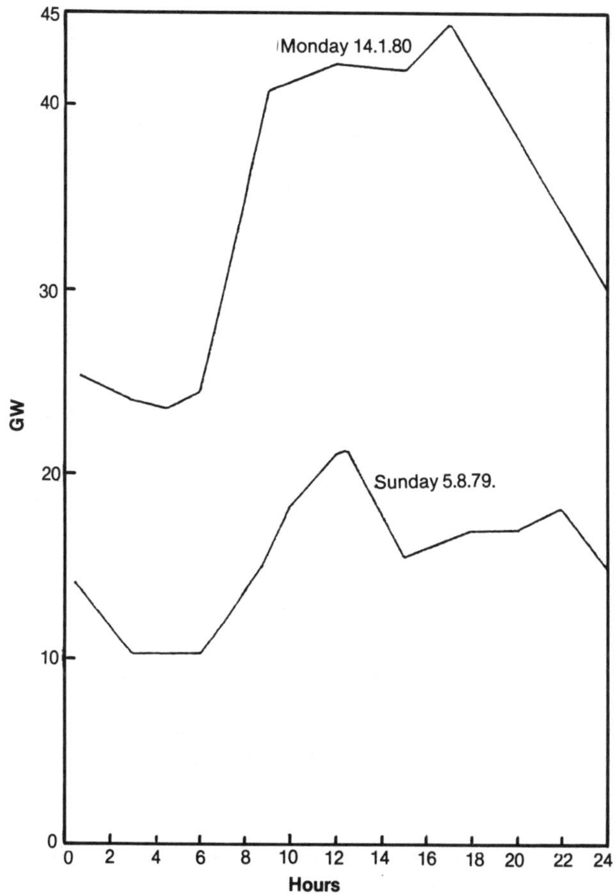

Source: C.E.G.B. Annual report

Fig. 17.4: C.E.G.B. Maximum & Minimum Demands

Figure 3 shows the combined effects of a four-country interconnection, with a saving of some 5600 MW of generating plant. These figures are not considered to be precise but these overall savings are broadly true for the daily load patterns of the countries concerned.

In addition to the daily variations in load, there are large variations in demand from working days to week-ends. Superimposed upon both the daily and weekly patterns will be the monthly variations throughout the year. The various load patterns will normally fall within the envelope contained within the maximum and minimum

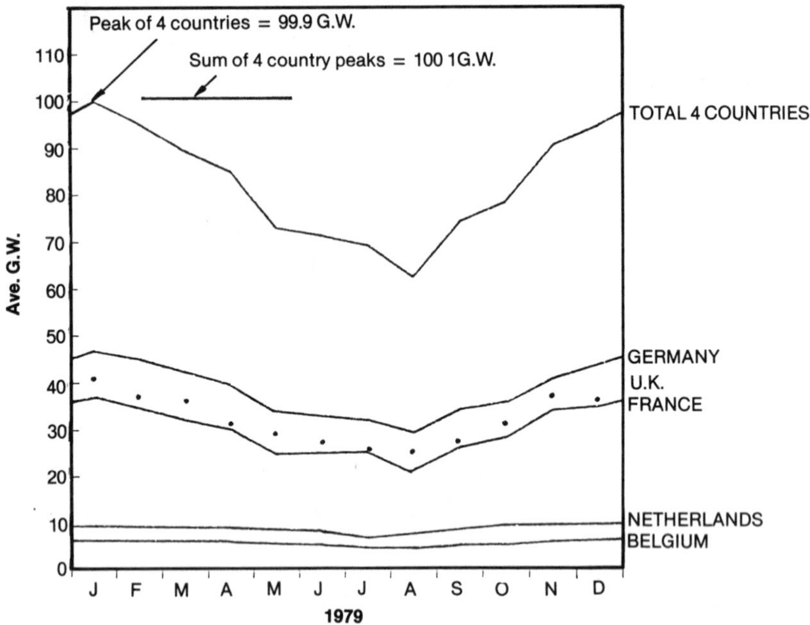

Sources:- Annual reports & other sources

Fig. 17.5: Monthly Variations in Load in 4 Countries. (Germany, France, Netherlands & Belgium.)

demands, such as is shown in Fig. 4. The load pattern is both different in magnitude and shape and would give an opportunity to reduce the necessity to construct new generating stations. The monthly variations in Northern Europe closely follow the climatic conditions and are all very similar (Fig. 5) and from this consideration alone there is not a great gain in Capital reduction. Consideration should be given, however, to future interconnections to countries bordering the Mediterranean, where greater use of air conditioning in the summer months could fill the summer troughs of demand from Northern Europe.

Reserve capacity is a most important aspect of an electricity supply system for there is no convenient method of storing electricity as such, although pumped storage of water for hydro-electricity is growing. Figure 6 shows the forecasts made by OECD in 1978 for Germany, France, Netherlands and the UK, indicating both the reserve capacities required and the forecast surplus or deficit. Particular note should be made of the large surplus in the UK, with very small surpluses or even deficits in the other three countries. We have an opportunity here to make greater use of Capital already expended and available in the UK.

Overall Capital savings need to be very carefully considered and

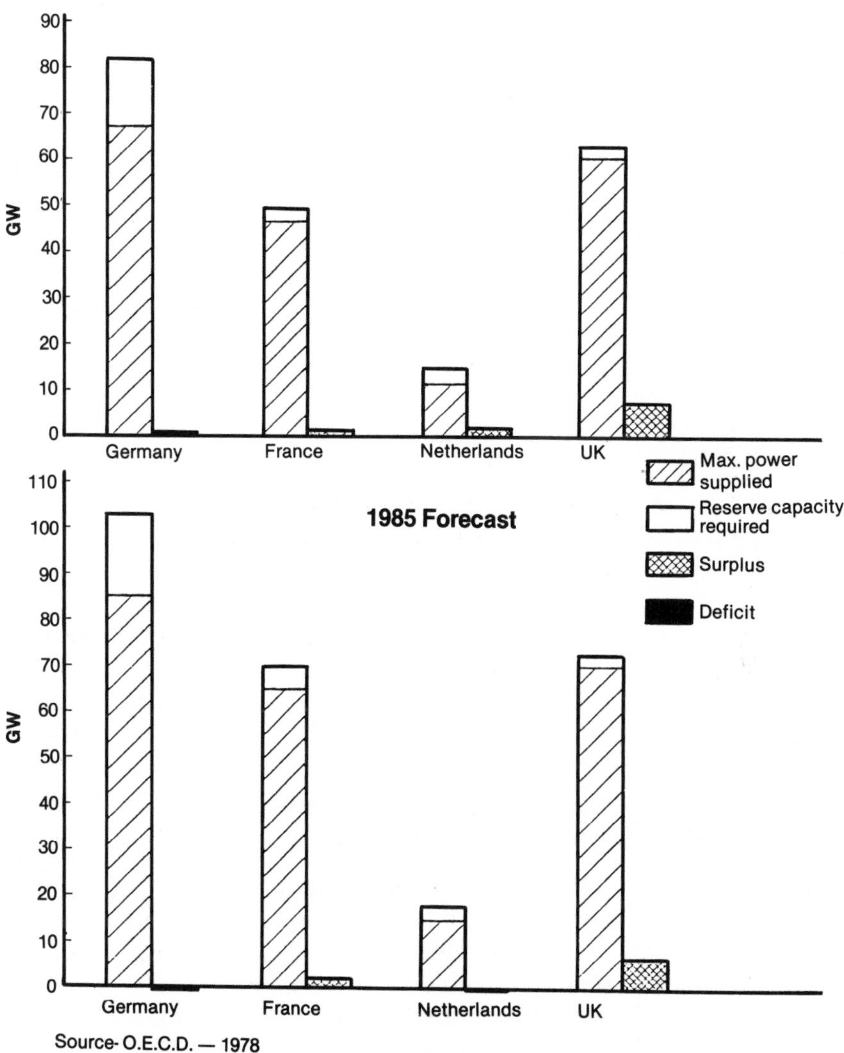

Fig. 17.6: Available Capacity at Time of Maximum Demand 1980 Forecast

detailed studies are essential. But very broadly, the UK/France interconnection should avoid the necessity to construct some 2000 MW generating plant. A UK/Germany interconnection could well save the Capital for a 3000 MW station. These alone represent huge savings of the order of £1200m for UK/France and £1800m for UK/Germany.

The corresponding costs of the 2000 MW interconnection between UK and France is broadly given in Fig. 7 as of the order of £500m.

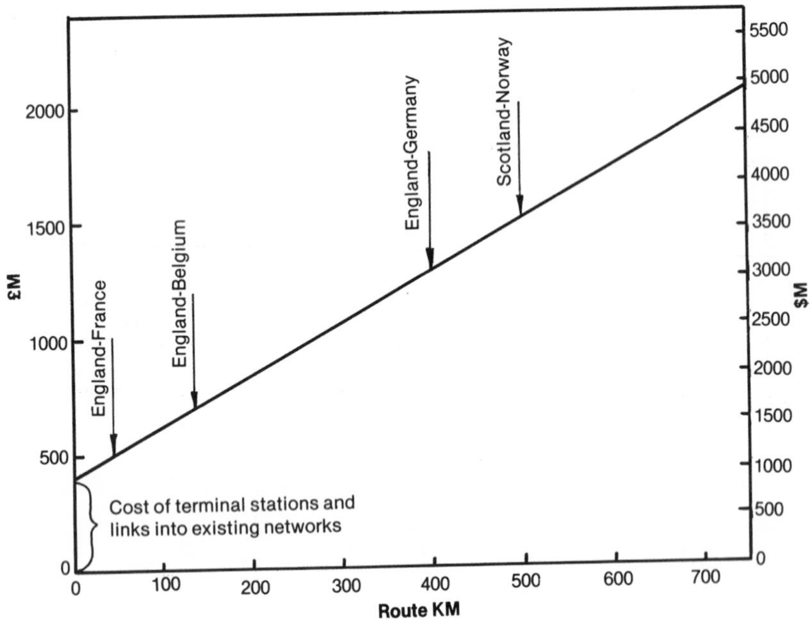

Fig. 17.7: Cost of 2000MW D.C. Lines with 4 Pairs Submarine Cables (including 1 spare pair) Buried in Sea-Bed

The cost of a 2000 MW link to Germany on the same very conservative design of the Cross Channel link would be £1280m. With development of lower cost techniques and as further links to Europe provide greater security, it will be possible to carry 2000 MW on 3 pairs of cables, with a corresponding reduction in cost to £880m (Fig. 8). This represents a cost of about £1320m for a 3000 MW capability. If an earth return system was acceptable, then the total cost of a 3000 MW link would be below £1000m compared to generation costs of £1800m.

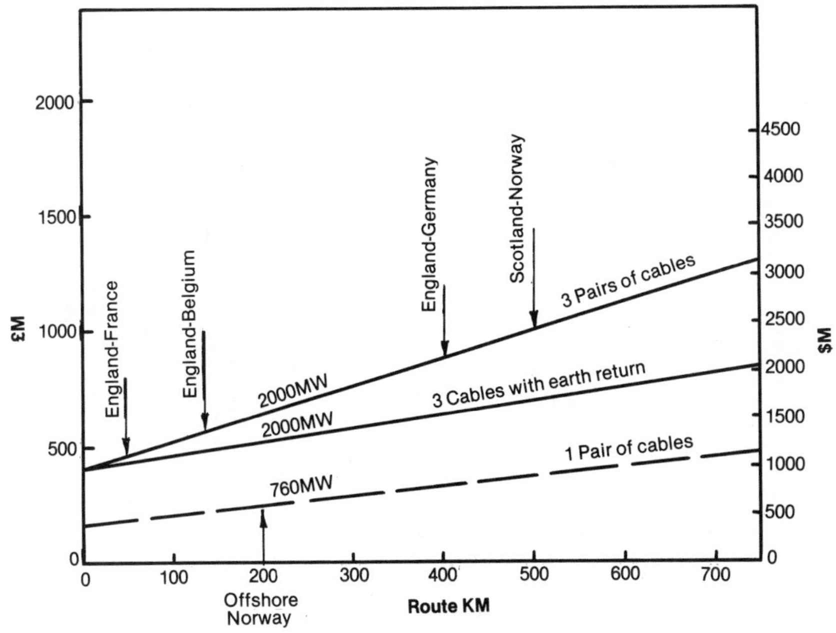

Fig. 17.8: Alternative Costs of 2000MW & 760MW D.C. Links Cables Buried in Sea-Bed

3. THE ADVANTAGES OF INTERCONNECTION IN REDUCING REVENUE COSTS

The reduction in Capital costs of generating plant can by themselves justify the interconnection of major electricity power systems. There are considerable additional benefits in the day-to-day running of the electricity supply business.

Each country has generating stations deriving energy from different sources (coal, oil, hydro, nuclear, etc.) and with units of different ages and efficiencies. Figure 9 shows the different thermal efficiencies. Figure 9 shows the different thermal efficiencies of plant within the CEGB in the UK. As the load grows, the most efficient plant (depending also on type and cost of fuel and distance from load demand) is operated first, but eventually less efficient plant needs to be brought into service to meet the demand. The greatest use is made of the most efficient plant (Fig. 10) but it will be seen that there still

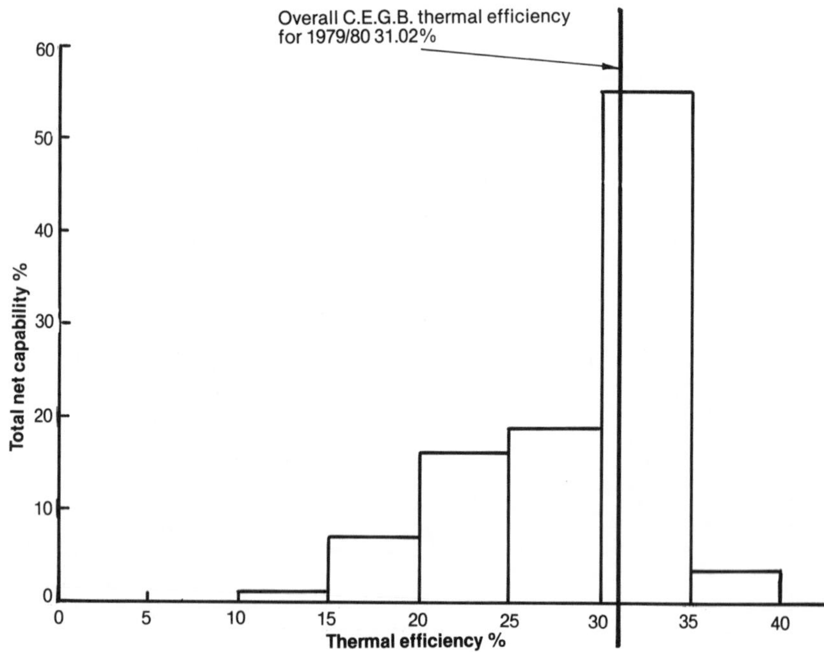

Source:- C.E.G.B. Annual report 1979/80

Fig. 17.9: 1979/80 C.E.G.B. Plant Capability at Different Thermal Efficiencies

remains spare capacity during periods of low demand, even for the most efficient plant.

Other countries will have a similar spread of efficiencies in their systems although the overall average figures do vary (Fig. 11). The opportunity to use spare, high-efficiency, low-cost electricity available from another country becomes self-evident. This could be made available at close to marginal costs as fixed costs of generation would normally be covered by the existing tariffs. Exchange of power in both directions could be mutually advantageous in avoiding the use of low efficiency, high cost plant.

The losses incurred in the interconnecting links are shown in Fig. 12. This shows a figure of about 3% for the England–France link and less than 8% for a link to Germany. Both of these figures would be acceptable with the spread of thermal efficiencies shown in Fig. 10. Larger conductor size cables could reduce these losses if this was worthwhile after capitalisation of the losses.

The savings in avoiding a spinning reserve and using more high

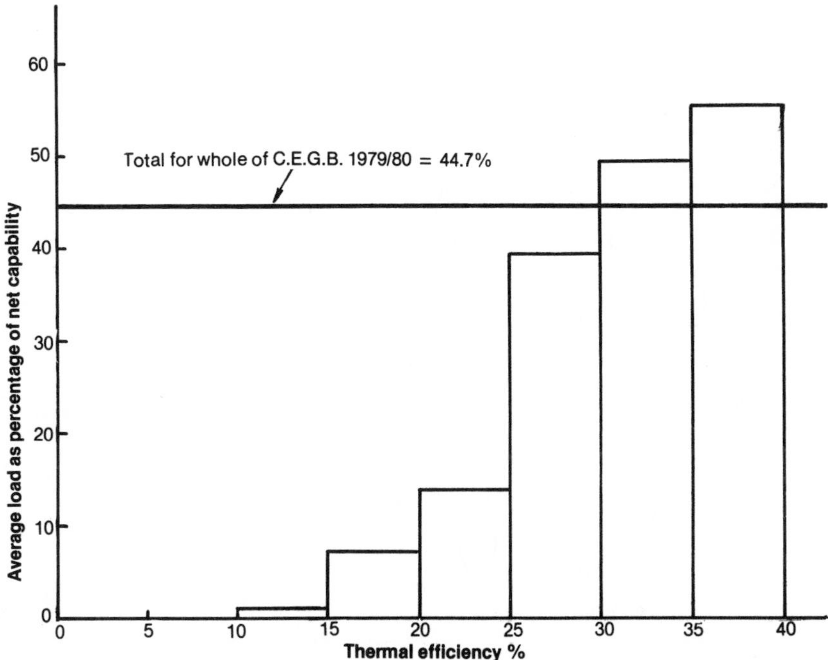

Fig. 17.10: The C.E.G.B. Uses the Most Efficient Plant Most but the Most Efficient Plant Could be Used More to Supply Other Countries.

efficiency plant will provide additional savings over the Capital savings given.

It is believed that the new 2000 MW England/France link will be a very sound economic proposition. The same 2000 MW of power will be available for half the cost, with the opportunity for lower cost electricity in addition. It is likely that further benefits will ensue as the system becomes fully operational and experience is gained.

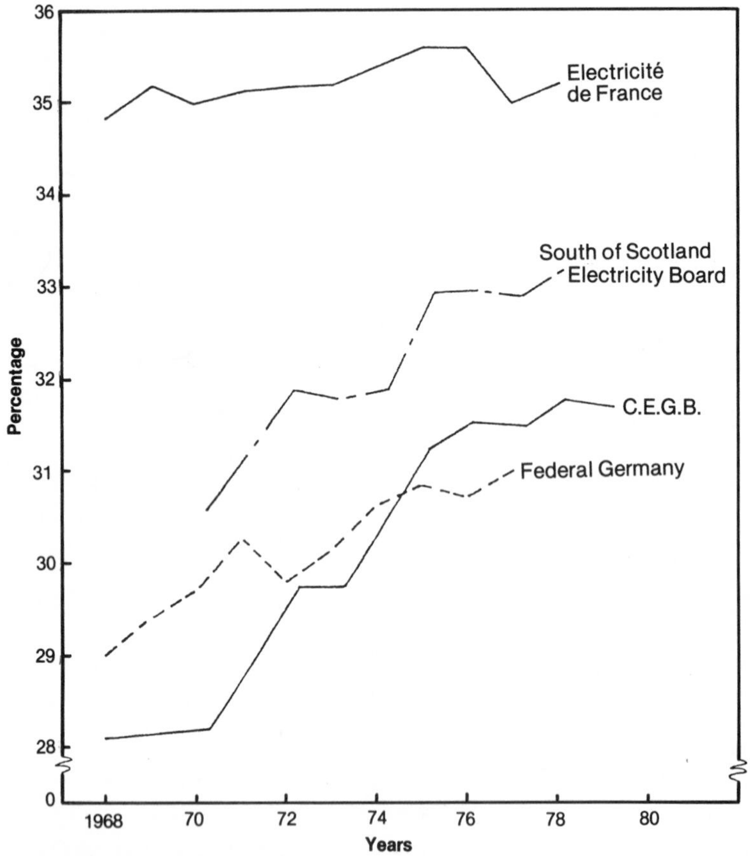

Fig. 17.11: Trends in Conventional System Thermal Efficiency

4. THE PROVISION OF A LONG TERM ASSET

In the broadest terms it has been shown that interconnection has many advantages. This could be developed in many ways. Figures 13 and 14 show possible interconnection systems — a North Sea Ring Main — or, more correctly, a number of European rings.

It would not be constructed completely as a total entity but developed gradually. The Cross Channel link first, perhaps UK/ Germany or Belgium next. Each individual link will be self-supporting

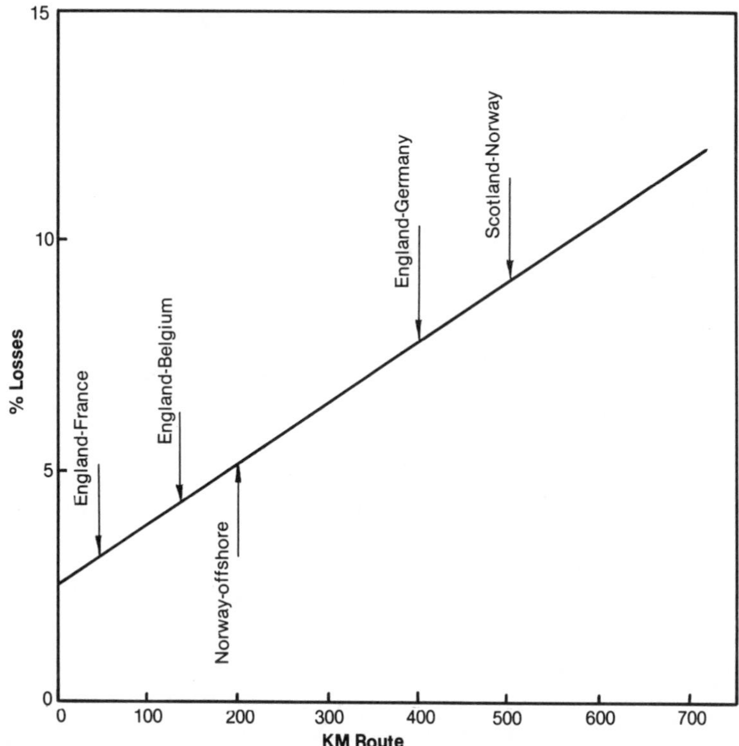

Fig. 17.12 Losses as Percentage of Load for D.C. Interconnection by Cables Operating at Normal Loadings. (Not optimised for capitalisation of losses)

financially to provide an economically worthwhile solution but each link will be compatible with others so as to be fed the energy developed from wind power, wave power, tidal, solar power and, of course, offshore generation. Trading of electricity offered at competitive prices could be fed into the system and extracted by the purchaser. This would have the net effect of reducing electricity costs, conserving energy and reducing oil imports, with an overall greater security of electricity supply.

5. WHY AN ELECTRICITY SYSTEM?

Consideration is being given to many ways of transporting energy throughout the world, oil by tankers or pipes, gas by pipe-

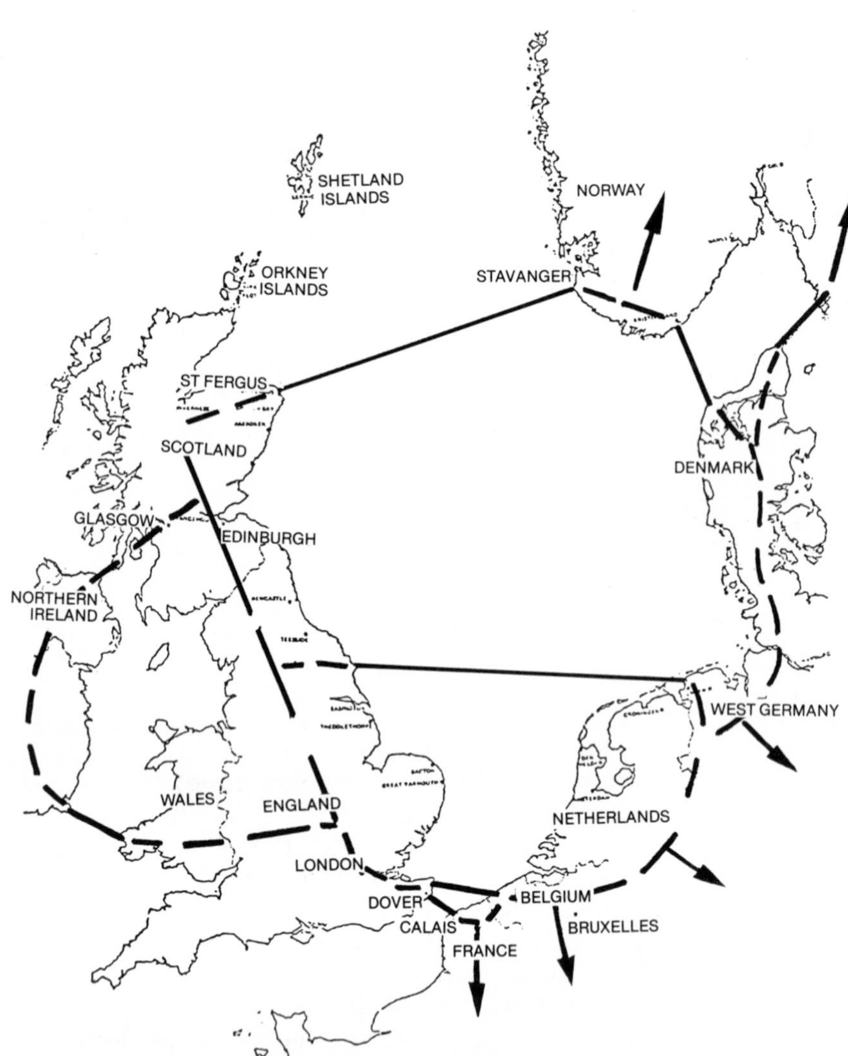

Fig. 17.13: Possible European links to the U.K.

lines, liquefied gas or methanol by tanker, coal by pipe or collier. Consideration of all the alternatives of processing our hydrocarbon reserves, transportation and use should be considered as a whole to optimise our developments to meet our overall objectives.

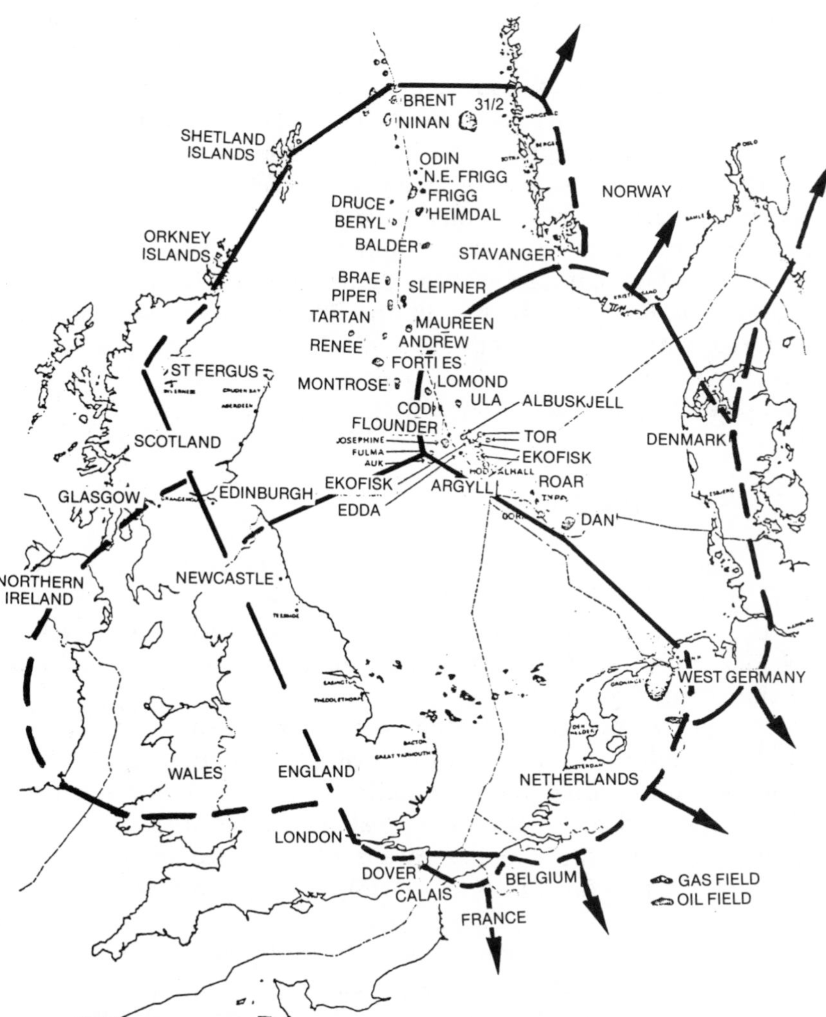

Fig. 17.14: Modifications and additions to a European Ring to Accept Offshore Generation

The growth of electricity demand is predicted to be about the same as for natural gas from 1973-1990[2] ans has to be met. We should reduce the use of imported oil for electricity generation in Europe. Rapid development of nuclear power and further exploration of the European hydro reserves are projected but there are already signs that environmental considerations may delay the anticipated progress. We believe that an electricity ring system linked with offshore generation has an important role to play in addition to oil and gas pipelines in the North Sea. We need gas, oil and electricity from the North Sea. There is no doubt that natural gas has a prime role in space and process heating. Oil and petrol are unique in providing high energy in a convenient, safe and transportable form for vehicles on our roads but electricity has strong and expanding markets in providing power for our factories, long distance traction, supplying our computers, lighting our roads and homes. Development of the heat pump and combined heat/power systems will conserve energy in the future. All aspects must be compared with an open mind, weighed carefully on an economic basis blended with the political policies of the UK and Europe. We believe electricity has an important role to play.

6. FEASIBILITY

Engineering feasibility has not been mentioned earlier as this has already been established. Important submarine links have been in successful commercial use for 15 years and longer. A system has been developed for the burying of submarine power cables to give additional security.

There are likely to be further developments in the solid state converter equipment to improve reliability and reduce costs. Offshore generation could be on a platform, tanker or in other forms. The European Ring could be looped into these offshore units or possibly fed into the ring by means of a subsea unit. There are many options but flexibility is certainly assured from an engineering standpoint.

Commercial considerations need to be ironed out at an early stage of any project and the commercial basis of inter-country trading, together with pricing of inputs from offshore generation needs clear understandings and firm agreements.

The provision of the necessary finance should be established and commitments cleared early in any negotiations.

Finally, it is important to appreciate that the development, design, manufacture, construction and maintenance can all be carried out from within Europe with the UK playing a major role. Alternatives may require expensive imports into Europe and may not provide such a stimulus to manufacturing and construction industries as the construction of a North Sea Electricity Ring Main.

REFERENCES

1. *Energy Reserves and Supplies in the ECE Region: Present Situation and Perspectives*, UN 1979.
2. *Energy Policies and Programmes of IEA Countries 1979 Review*, OECD Paris 1980.

APPENDIX 1

Load capacity of a 2000 MW link

A 2000 MW electrical link has the capacity to carry the equivalent energy of the following:

Per Day	48	GWh of Electricity
	3984	Tonnes of Oil
	28070	Barrels of Oil
	6000	Tonnes of Coal
	164.6	Millions SCF of Natural Gas
	165	Billion BTU
	1.65	Million Therms
Per Annum	17.52	TWh of Electricity
	1.45	Million Tonnes of Oil
	2.2	Million Tonnes of Coal
	60.0	Billion SCF of Natural Gas
	10.3	Million Barrels of Oil
	60.2	Trillion BTU
	602	Million Therms

Note: Assuming a 33 1/3% Thermal Efficiency, the above figures should be multiplied by three for energy consumed for generation of 2000 MW.

e.g. 164.6 × 3 = 493.8 MMSCF/Day of Natural Gas for 2000 MW
= 296.3 MMSCF/Day for 1200 MW

Chapter 18

'Is There a Future for UK Power Generation Without Fossil Fuels?'

*I.C. Price and M.R. Starr**

The need to balance long and short term goals is often mentioned but long-term needs are not readily defined. However, energy evangelists provide us with two pointers. These are that demand for electrical power will increase steadily with time and the cost of generating electricity by non-conventional methods — including small-scale installations — will fall dramatically. If this is so, the dream of disaggregated power generation using new technologies — albeit within a grid framework — could become a reality within the foreseeable future.

Figure 1 gives details of recent cost projections for photovoltaic power generation against other methods.[4]

It has been said that the world's only truly inexhaustible energy sources are solar and nuclear. This simple proposition is a key factor directing attention towards the day when fossil fuels will have been eliminated for all practical purposes from the electrical generation scene. Increases in the value of petrochemicals will determine just when this will be.

Such a statement raises many issues but, in the end, a balance has to be struck so that environmental, social and commercial factors are

***Sir William Halcrow & Partners Consulting Engineers.**

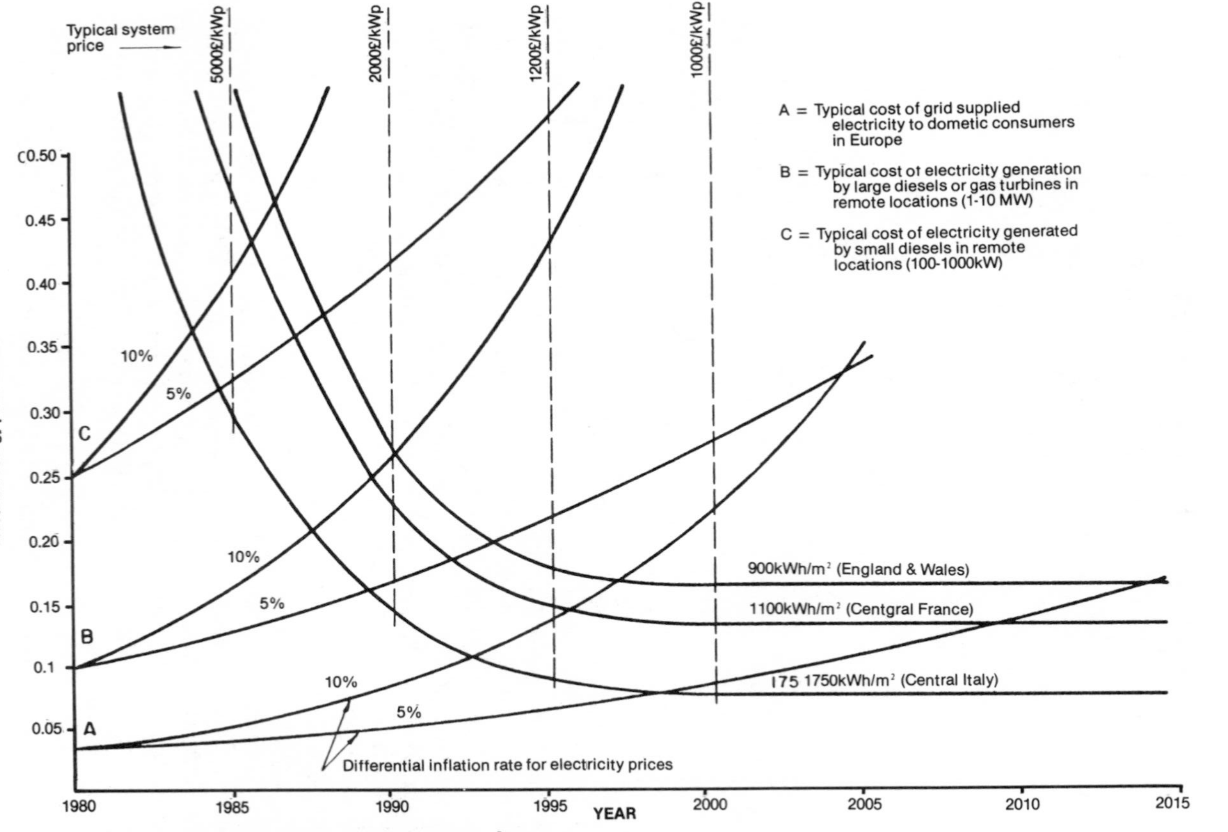

Fig. 18.1: Photovoltaic generation break-even curves

Table 18.1. Present Day View of Various Choices of Primary Energy Source for Electrical Power Generation Neglecting Storage and Ocean Thermal Energy Conversion.

	Fossil		*Nuclear*		*Direct Solar*		*Indirect Solar*			*Planetary*	
Feature	*Coal/Oil*	*Diesel/Gas Turbines*	*AGR/PWR*	*FBR*	*Thermal*	*Photo-voltaic*	*Wind*	*Wave*	*Hydro*	*Tidal*	*Geothermal*
Size range	MW–GW	kW–MW	GW	GW	kW-MW	W–MW	kW–MW	kW–MW	kW–GW(1)	kW–GW	MW
Firmness	●●	●●	●●	●●	–	–	–	–	●	●(2)	●●
Load matching	●●	●●	●	●	–	–	–	–	●●	●(2)	●
Predictability	●●	●●	●●	●●	●(3)	●(3)	●	●	●	●●	●●
Dominant periodicity	–	–	–	–	a,d,h,	a,d,h,m	a,d,h,	a,d,h,	a,d,	a,d,	–
Capital cost 1982 £/kW(e) (4)	400–600	200–300	1000–1500	1500–2000	15000—— 8000	15000—— 2000	3000—— 1500(5)	5000—— 1500	700–1000	1000	1500
Generation cost 1982 p/kWh(e) (6)	2–3	5–10	1.0–1.3	1.5 (7)	1.0	0.2	0.5 (5)	1.5	0.5	0.5	1.0

Notes

1. Run-of-current for kW size.
2. For two basin scheme, otherwise –
3. – for m 8 h, ● for d, ●● for a
4. Present day —— possible mature technology.
5. Offshore.
6. Excluding capital servicing costs
7. Expected in time to become competitive with fossil and other nuclear, with future real fuel price increases.

Key

●● Good
● Partial
– Very low or nil
a Seasonal or longer
d (semi) diurnal
h Hour
m Minute

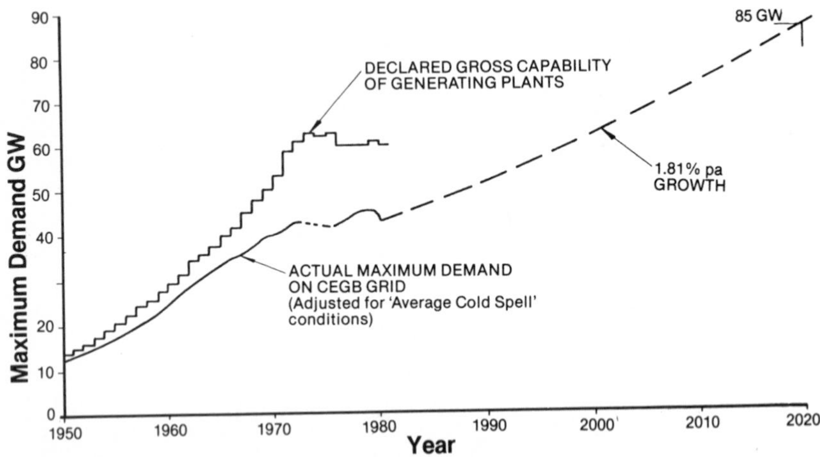

Fig. 18.2: Projected Maximum Demand on CEGB System

optimised in an acceptable manner. The nuclear debate will doubtless continue until technological advances permit effective decoupling of power generation and weapons manufacture. However, one thing is virtually certain and that is that world and UK electrical demands will increase at the expense of other energy forms.

Figure 2 shows the maximum demand for electrical power according to published CEGB statistics. The projection is to 2020 and based on an annual short-term growth rate of 1.81%.[1,2]

This presentation was prompted by a recent study carried out for the CEC on prospects for photovoltaic power for Europe.[4] Having concluded that production costs of PV cells will have fallen dramatically by the year 2000, the consequential effect on electrical generation is of considerable interest. The more so as other renewable energy based technologies have limited potential.

Whilst it is true that solar and nuclear sources are virtually inexhaustible there are practical difficulties. An important characteristic

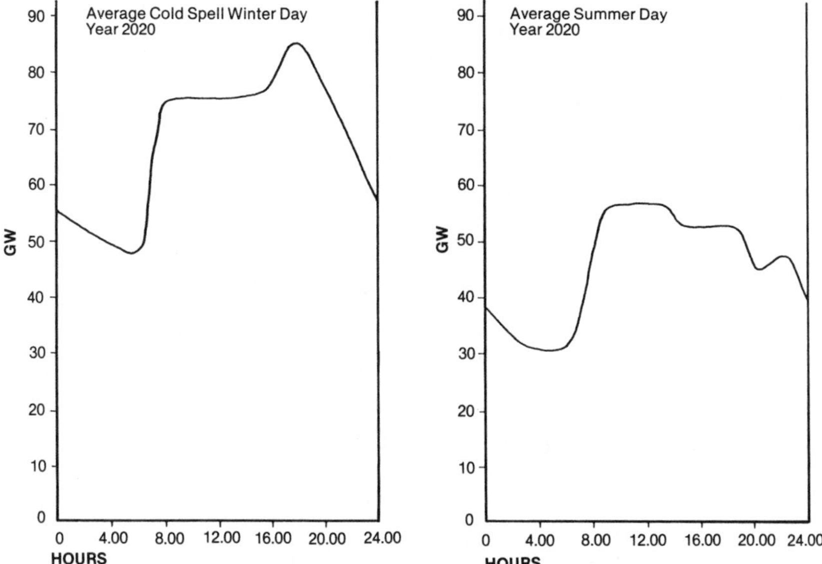

Fig. 18.3: Average Cold Spell Winter Day — Year 2020

Fig. 18.4: Average Summer Day — Year 2020

of electrical generation using solar or nuclear energy is the inflexibility of these methods from a load-matching point of view as compared with fossil fuel alternatives. This has important consequences if unnecessary and large-scale waste is to be avoided.

Table 1 gives a present day view of the various choices of primary energy source for electrical power generation neglecting storage and Ocean Thermal Energy Conversion.[5]

Essentially the problem is one of providing generating capacity to meet maximum demand where wide daily and seasonal variations can be expected. There exists a serious mismatch between peaks of human activity (in energy demand terms) and the availability of solar energy in its various forms so a buffer must be found.

Figures 3 and 4 indicate daily load variations for typical winter and summer days based on the maximum demand projection for the year 2020 given in Fig. 2.

The inflexibility of the solar and nuclear alternatives has been mentioned. Whilst output from a solar generator fluctuates, the chief characteristic of a nuclear reactor is its steady release of energy

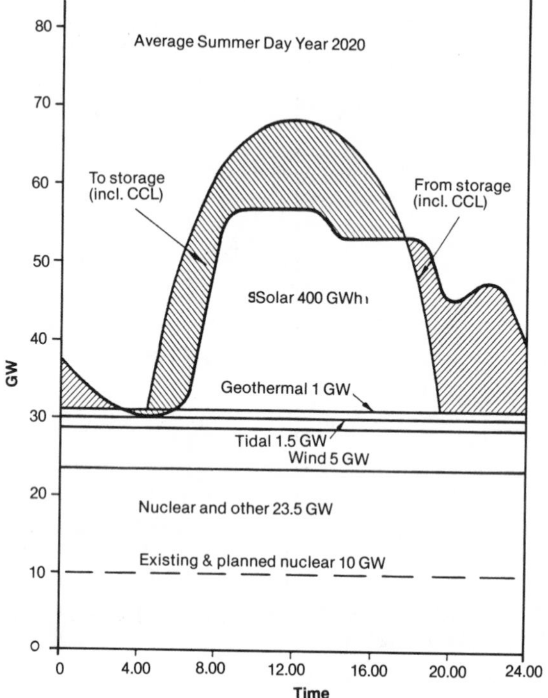

Fig. 18.5: Generation Mix, Average Summer Day

which is not conserved when demand for electrical power drops. Also, nuclear generating systems have a poor response to sudden load fluctuations though it is understood that the most recent designs are much improved in this respect.

Though clean by conventional environmental standards, nuclear power generation remains for many the choice of last resort. Doubts about safety are slowly disappearing but proliferation, disposal of active wastes and eventual station decommissioning remain as live issues. It therefore seems probable that renewable energy sources — e.g. solar — will take whatever market share is commercially justified plus a margin to compensate for social and environmental preferences. An attempt is made here to show what is feasible.

Solar power may be divided into several components — notably wind, tide, biomass, wave and direct radiation. It is the latter which offers a major prospect for a new style of electrical power generation though tidal power and wind are also important for Britain. There is the question of supply/demand mismatch to be faced but deficiencies of this kind can be offset against the potential for medium/small-scale applications and the security provided by such a disaggregated approach.

Demand smoothing by daily and seasonal storage becomes a critical issue if relatively inflexible electrical generation systems such as solar and nuclear dominate the generation scene. With the notable exceptions of Dinorwic (pumped storage) and the proposed Severn Barrage (tidal,[3] work done so far has not anticipated any significant shift in the pattern of electrical generation. Research into storage options is therefore seen as an important feature of any development involving diminished use of fossil fuels. Avoidance of demand coincidence by means of ripple switching and small-scale devices including

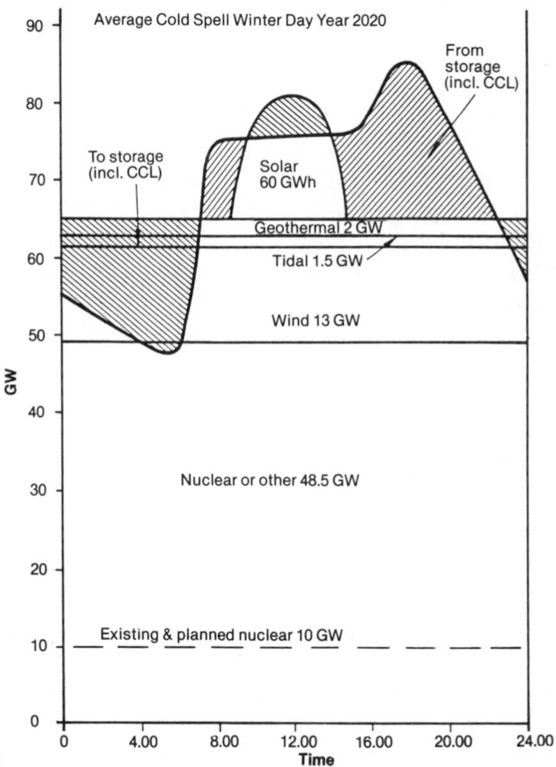

Fig. 18.6: Generation Mix, Winter Day (ACS Conditions)

heat storage can also make a useful contribution as present CEGB studies have shown.

For analytical purposes a definition of long-term is required. a figure between five and ten years is perceived to be the 'short term' and some convenient multiplier is therefore needed. One approach is to take the notional working life of an individual or the working life of a conventional power station which are both around thirty to thirty five years. Inevitably the choice is arbitrary but this figure also represents about twice the popularly accepted lead time (15 years) for a major engineering project. The point here is that near and long-terms are actually quite close together in the context of planning and decision making. The year 2020 is just beyond this limit.

Taking the assumptions of potential for renewable energy resources given at Appendixes 2 and 3, possible electrical generation mixes for summer and winter days (year 2020) are shown in Figs 5 and 6. Even allowing a good margin of error in these projections some of the conclusions are inescapable.

CONCLUSIONS

(i) The relative inflexibility of solar and nuclear generation characteristics emphasises the importance of storage including the Cross Channel Link. Daily balancing storage of around 1000GWh is needed (120 GWh — winter, 90GWh — summer) with a peak capacity of 20 GW.

(ii) Renewable energy resources can make an important contribution but their role will be limited. Given the projected maximum use of direct and indirect solar energy, there will be a need for new generating capacity over and above that now planned. About 50GW will be required to meet the projected winter demand and about 25GW for summer.

(iii) If over-season storage can be provided as distinct from daily storage then an additional installed base-load generating capacity of about 38GW can meet all-season needs. Further peak-load capacity, say 20–25GW might be hydrogen fuelled perhaps.

(iv) If fossil fuels are phased out during the next 30–35 years and the problem of over-season storage remains, then up to 25GW of nuclear capacity will be under-utilised. In other words, UK nuclear power stations will have an overall load factor of around 70–75% which has important implications for the design and operation of such stations and their economics.

(v) Summarising, there is a future for electricity generation in the

UK without fossil fuels but many problems will have to be overcome. These are mainly associated with the management and control of a generation mix to which the suppliers of commercial electricity are, at present, unaccustomed. Storage on a greatly increased scale will be required if renewable energy resources are to be fully exploited and nuclear power plants may have to be operated at lower load factors than is currently assumed.

Whatever energy source is chosen, the bulk of electricity generated will remain centrally controlled. Nevertheless, solar energy offers the prospect of limited disaggregation with the enhanced security that this will bring.

REFERENCES

1. Central Electricity Generating Board, *Annual Report & Accounts 1980–81.*
2. Electricity Council, *Handbook of Electricity Supply Statistics* (1981 Edition).
3. Working Party on Tidal Power, *Severn Tidal Power Prefeasibility Study Interim Report to the Severn Barrage Committee.*
4. M.R. Starr, 'The Potential for Photovoltaics in Europe', *Proc. of 4th European Photovoltaic Solar Energy Conference*, Stresa, Italy, May 1982.
5. A.M. Muir Wood. 'Energy Research — whence & whitherwards', Unwin Lecture 1982.

APPENDIX 1

Electricity production in 2020

1. If total production increases at average rate of 1.81% pa from 1980-81 value (as CEGB current estimate).
   Production in 1980-81 was 215,600 GWh
   Hence production in 2020 will be about 435,000 GWh (Fig. 2).
2. Summer and Winter demand patterns for 2020 assumed similar to 1980-81 (Figs 3 and 4).
3. If fossil fuels are excluded, summer and winter demands in 2020 will be met by combination of:
   - nuclear (or other)
   - wind
   - tidal
   - geothermal
   - solar
   - storage
4. Assumptions used for wind, tidal, geothermal and solar capacities are given in Appendix 2.
5. Possible generation mixes are illustrated in Figs 5 and 6.

APPENDIX 2

Solar photovoltaic capacity in 2020

1. Households in England and Wales: say 20 million
   Assume 50% equipped with PV system of average size 5 kWp ($50m^2$ of array?).
   Total = $0.5 \times 20 \times 10^6 \times 5$ kWp = 50 GWp
2. Industrial, commercial, institutional systems
   Assume 100,000 installations of average size 100 kWp ($1000m^2$ of array?).
   Total = 100000×100 kWp = 10 GWp
3. Central generation
   Assume 200 solar farms of average size 200 MWP ($2km^2$ of array¾).
   Total = 200×200 MWp = 40 GWp

Total PV installed = 100 GWp

4. 100 GWp of PV provides about 100,000 GWh/year (i.e., about 20–25% of total electricity consumption 2020).

   100 GWp of PV provides about 60 GWh on a typical cold winter day.

   100 GWp of PV provides about 400 GWh on a typical summer day.

   GWp - Giga Watt Peak.

APPENDIX 3

Wind capacity in 2020

Assume total installed capacity	20 GW
average output in winter	13 GW
average output in summer	5 GW
Total production over year about	70000 GW

Tidal capacity in 2020

Assume largest Severn Barrage scheme installed (Ref. 3)

Peak output 7.2 GW Average output	1.5 GW
Total annual production	12800 GWh

N.B. periodic nature of tidal power output, whether one basin or two basin schemes is ignored as influence small on total situation.

Geothermal capacity in 2020

Assume geothermal heat used either to generate electricity or for district heating/industrial/agricultural purposes.

Effective capacity say 2 GW in winter, 1 GW in summer.

Cross-channel link (CCL)

The cross-channel link is treated as storage equivalent: i.e. no net supply or demand.

(Note: If arrangements were to be made for solar capacity to be installed on behalf of UK in Southern Europe, power fed north across France and across the channel via CCL the latter would, in effect, become a large solar power station, as well as storage.)

PART VIII

The Impact of Energy on the Economy

Chapter 19

The Long Term Macroeconomic Role for Energy*

L.G. Brookes†

THE ECONOMICS OF ENERGY PRICE

Arguments about the role of energy in economic systems are incomplete without analysis of the effects of changes in the price of energy. It may be true (because energy can substitute for so many other things) that we can continue to increase energy output per capita as long as we are prepared to increase energy consumption per unit of output, but if the price of energy is higher than consumers are prepared to pay the process will come to a stop. It follows that the output at any point in time is the result of an equilibrium between a great many factors in the economy one of which is the price of energy. The question that I now pose is whether the price of energy is an especially important factor.

Conventional (rather superficial) studies suggest that it is not. Simple log linear regression analysis produces an income elasticity of energy consumption (more familiarly known as the 'energy co-

*The analysis in this paper is not uniquely relevant to nuclear energy. Any large low cost or potentially low cost addition to World energy supplies would meet the requirement identified in this paper.

†Consultant Bournemouth UK and former Chief Economist of the United Kingdom Atomic Energy Authority

efficient') of about 1.0 and a short-term price elasticity* (the percentage change in demand for energy that goes with a 1% change in price) of about 0.3 or less. The trouble with this type of analysis (and indeed with most more sophisticated models of economic and energy systems) is that it takes GDP growth as autonomous and then sees energy demand as one of the things that flows from that growth, though modified by responses to changes in energy prices. Modellers tend not to consider the feedback upon the original assumption of GDP growth that might follow from a reduction in energy demand following a price increase.* At best they may simply deduct from the economy an amount equal to the value of the lost energy consumption. They make no allowance for the effect on the general level of economic activity of a smaller energy input into the economic machine.

George Kouris, when with the Economics Department at Surrey, noted that for long term trends national income alone was sufficient to explain changes in the demand for energy (Kouris 1978). It was only in the short term that the statistical explanation was improved by including a term for the price of energy. This phenomenon is partly explained by the familiar pattern of consumers responding immediately to a change in energy price but fairly quickly back-sliding and resuming their old consumption patterns. The fact that the long term trend can be wholly explained by national income changes, without the intervention of energy price, may lead some people to conclude that energy price is not an important factor in determining the level of energy consumption. It leads me to the opposite conclusion. Or rather it leads me to the thought that it may be the level of energy consumption that is greatly influencing the level of output per capita (hence national income) with energy price influencing the long term level of energy consumption. This means putting the causality the opposite way round from the familiar assumption, and it means that — at one remove — energy price may very well be a major influence upon the equilibrium level of economic activity. (Sam Schurr of Resources for the Future Inc. and the US Electrical Power Research Institute has discussed this question in published papers and reached the tentative conclusion that it may be energy that drives modern economic systems rather than such systems creating a demand for energy.) It is important to think in terms of long term equilibria because a substantial change in the

*An increase in price in the absence of an increase in demand constitutes a reduction in the availability of energy to the economic system and it would be surprising if this did not adversely affect output.

price of energy in current money terms may very well lead to quite lengthy disequilibrium whilst the economy adapts to the new situation — with inflation in the prices of other goods and services bringing about a new real relationship (after inflation has been deducted) which substantially modifies the original price change. This is what has happened since the 1973 oil price hike. We are still in disequilibrium. There are three main reasons for this — not all of which are relevant to the main theme in this paper. They are:

1. *The OPEC monetary surpluses.* By the mid-1970s these were widely reported to be much lower than they were in the first year after the big price increase; and most observers have been surprised at the speed with which the imbalance between OPEC countries and the rest of the world was eroded. This erosion has been only partly due to OPEC countries increasing their imports from the oil consuming countries. Much of the imbalance has been taken up by price inflation of goods imported by OPEC (which might be seen as part of the equilibrium-seeking process). The OPEC surpluses nevertheless remain important because they are subject to economic multiplier effects that make their effect upon the world financial system more damaging than would at first sight appear. The cumulative surpluses, with the obligation to pay interest, will also hang over the oil consuming countries for a long time. The effect of the surpluses is, however, a temporary one that should be solved in time. The problem has, however, re-established itself with the 1979 Iran crisis with a further major oil price rise occurring at a time when Saudi Arabia at least was showing some concern to keep inflation in check and avoid damage to Western economies and was acting as a moderating influence within OPEC.*
2. *Income Effect.* This is simply the effect of having purchasing power mopped up by essential spending on more expensive energy. Other things being equal it will have a deflationary effect upon economies in the consuming countries. It is one of the ways in which the transfer of real income from consuming countries to the OPEC countries takes place. This effect too has been mitigated by inflation and by governmental measures to deal with unemployment (which also tend to be inflationary — see 'The Nuclear Power Implications of OPEC prices', *Energy Policy*, June 1975.
3. *Price and Substitution Effects.* These result in producers opting

*1982 has seen something of a collapse of the oil price. This was predictable according to the thesis given later in this chapter.

for somewhat less energy intensive methods than hitherto; for prices of goods in general to move somewhat in favour of the less energy intensive goods; and for final consumers of fuel to make marginal shifts in spending patterns between fuel and other things (see 'The Energy Price Fallacy and the Role of Nuclear Power', *Energy Policy* for June 1978, Brookes 1978; and 'Energy, Inflation and Economic Prospects', Brookes 1979).

Most commentators see the damage from the OPEC price rise in terms of 1. above; some also recognize 2.; very few of them have paid much attention to the third effect. The reason is that the first effect swamps the other two and has been seen by governments as the big problems to be tackled. The second effect was seen more as an internal problem and has led to recognition of the phenomenon of inflation and deflation existing side by side — with steep price inflation mopping up spending power and having a deflationary effect upon demand and hence bringing about unemployment.

The third effect is the most difficult to detect because its influence tends to be long term. Producers cannot quickly change their technology and spending habits die hard. Nevertheless, the papers quoted above suggest that a substantial sustained real increase in energy prices would have catastrophic effects upon national income in the long term. However, as the papers themselves indicate, such catastrophes are unlikely to occur because sustained large real price increases in energy are themselves very unlikely to occur. What happens in practice is that attempts to make substantial changes do a good deal of short term economic damage but the change is not sustained because of the very strong economic counterforces that are set up. The penalties of bad energy planning may therefore show themselves in halting and uncertain economic progress rather than economic catastrophe. The lesson to be drawn is that energy consuming countries should see to it that they do not allow situations to develop in which they are subject to arbitrary price changes — but this would be to defend themselves mainly against impermanent damage to their financial systems and bouts of inflation rather than against the permanent effect of a sustained large real price rise (because, as I have said, I do not believe that such price rises can be sustained — the point is developed in the next section).

It follows that the importance of studying the economics of energy prices lies in recognizing the limitations on the range of movement of energy prices in the long term and planning in the light of that recognition. Any new energy system that looks as if its prices can never be brought down to the levels of today should, on this thesis, be abandoned — because real average energy prices are never likely to rise to the point that makes it economic. The new source should only be pursued if further development, large scale production, and the learning process generally seem likely to bring its costs down where it can be offered on the market at prices currently ruling for established sources. This view of the situation needs to be qualified of course by some regard for energy quality and the possibility of a higher degree of specialization in energy use in future.

Series and graphs published in the UK Digest of Energy Statistics show that real average energy prices have not changed very much since 1970. On one measure the average price of industrial fuels has fallen over this period.

A FIRST ATTEMPT TO MODEL LONG TERM EFFECTS

A detailed discussion of the possible approaches and the derivation of the approach used here is given in *Energy conservation response to price increase — is it sufficient to resolve a problem of energy shortage?* by the author of this paper (Brookes 1981). The discussion and analysis in that paper will be summarized here.

The effects of changes in energy price upon productivity and hence upon the level of economic activity and its rate of growth were the subject of a special workshop held by the United States Electric Power Research Institute at Palo Alto, California, in January 1981. Widely differing views were expressed at that gathering — reflecting a wide range of opinions and judgements about how energy price changes influence the productivity of the economy. At one extreme, Professor Leonard Waverman argued that energy represents such a small part of total expenditure (less than 10%) that the relatively small changes in the real price of oil (and other fuels as they followed suit) could hardly account for the very large changes in the economic fortunes of the developed countries since 1973 (Waverman 1981). In complete contrast, Professor Dale Jorgenson reported an econometric study that showed that the increase in energy prices more than accounted for the fall in productivity of the United States economy since 1973 (there were some offsetting factors that were overwhelmed by the effect of the energy price increases).

More generally, some economists see no special role for energy in economic systems (Christopher Allsopp of Oxford, speaking at a meeting of the British Institute of Energy Economics on 28th

October 1981 said that an increase in the price of oil was no different from an increase in the price of copper) whilst others see an increase in energy price as having similar effects to an increase in the price of other commodities but, in addition, having the effect of damaging the economic productive process itself (see, for example, Professor Robert Pindyck writing in *The Structure of World Energy Demand*, Pindyck 1979).

It follows that the analysis in this paper is one among many that could have been made. It is up to readers to form their own conclusions about its soundness.

First, it is a highly simplified analysis. One of the speakers* at the EPRI. Workshop mentioned earlier suggested that the complexity of some models of the economic and energy systems was not justified. Models Models were, at best, very imperfect forecasting tools. There was a placefor simpler models that helped to provide insights rather than actual detailed figures and forecasts. The model described here is a simple model of this type. It treats the world economy as a single entity and — to avoid complications of fuel substitution and differences in fuel quality — the assumption is adopted of a single homogeneous source of energy. In addition, a distinction is drawn between improvements in the efficiency of energy use that are part of general technical progress (they do not need the stimulus of raised energy price or special governmental action) and those that take place as a direct response to an increase in energy price. The first category is subsumed in this analysis in a general concept of useful energy — in other words an improvement in the efficiency of energy use that takes place as part of an underlying trend is treated as an addition to useful energy inputs. The second category of improvement is assumed to take place as a direct response to raised energy price and it is modelled by the use of a price elasticity of energy conservation response — with the elasticity being defined as the percentage improvement in the efficiency of energy use that takes place as a direct response to a 1% increase in the price of useful energy.

Next, it is assumed that the process of industrialization is one of energy-and-capital-dependent activity penetrating a more primitive system with no energy inputs other than sunshine and human and animal muscle power. The arguments in support of such a model of industrial and economic development are given in Brookes (1972). They lead to the conclusion that the useful energy coefficient (percentage rate of growth of useful energy consumption divided by

*Professor Zvi Grilliches of Harvard.

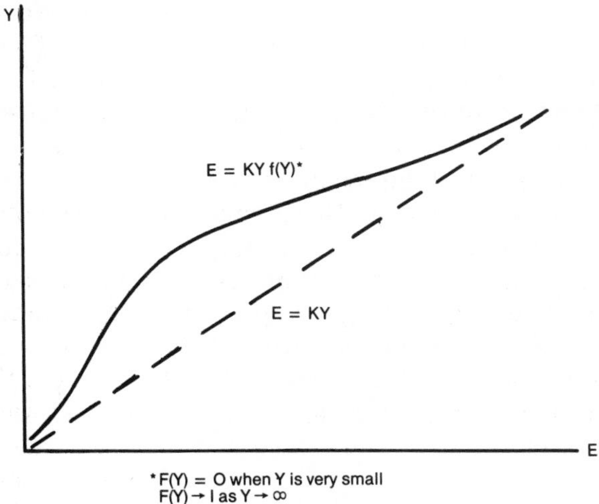

Fig. 19.1a: A penetration Model of Energy Consumption and Economic Activity

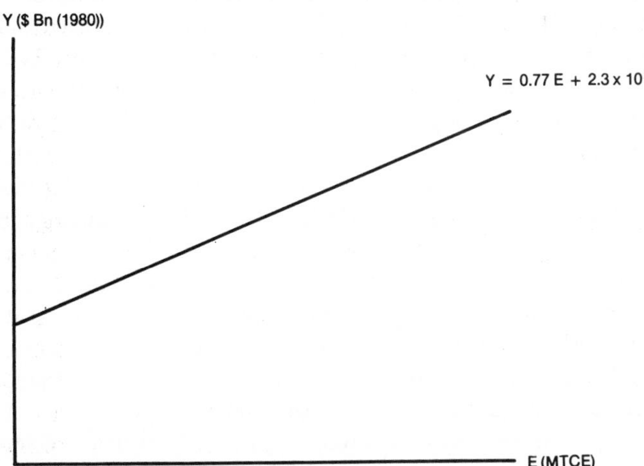

Fig. 19.1b: A Model of World Energy Consumption and Economic Activity

percentage rate of growth of economic output) tends to 1.0 from above. Strong statistical support for this hypothesis was found in work described in Brookes (1972). It leads to the model of energy consumption and economic activity shown at Fig. 1a. Figure 1b is a linear approximation to this model.* It shares with the more complicated model the property that the energy coefficient tends to 1.0 from above but is open to the objection that it effectively divides the economy into only two components — a relatively fixed non-energy dependent component and a growing energy dependent component with additional units of output requiring, on average, uniform increments of useful energy consumption. Despite its great simplicity, this more simplified model is a good approximation to actual experience in the real world (see Smil and Kuz 1976).

If we add provision for the price elasticity of energy conservation response mentioned earlier this simple model may be expressed in the following form.

$$Y = AE \left(\frac{P}{P_o}\right) + B$$

where Y = economic output; E = useful energy consumption; c = the price elasticity of energy conservation response; A and B are constants.

Few economists would object to the use of an inversion of this model to estimate the useful energy likely to be demanded when economic activity is at the level of Y. But most of them would object to its use as a 'production function', with the level of economic output shown as depending upon a single variable — namely the level of energy consumption. They would point out that the conventions of macroeconomics call for a production function in which economic output is shown as a function of capital and labour inputs. Other inputs like energy can be included, subject to suitable safeguards. They would argue, however, that, at the end of the day, aggregate incomes paid to labour plus aggregate incomes paid to capital must equate to the value of aggregate output and that a production function that excludes labour and capital is basically unsound.

Those who argue in addition that there is nothing special about energy and that it is simply one of many commodities that are consumed in economic systems would have an additional reason for rejecting the model.

*Figure 1b incorporates parameters that are a very rough approximation to real World values.

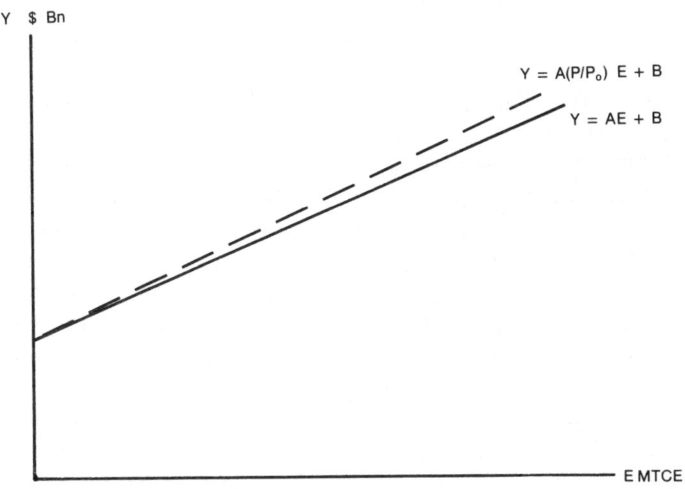

Fig. 19.2: A Model of Energy Consumption and Economic Activity with provision for Capital and Labour Substitution for Energy

The author would argue in reply that his *a priori* hypothesis about industrial development given in Brookes (1972) constituted a reasonable argument and that his own statistical validation and the statistical work of others — of which Smil and Kuz (1977) was a good example — were impressive. He would further argue that capital and labour inputs are implicit in the model: the initial slope of the line reflects capital and labour inputs at year t_0; the changed position of the line (shown as dotted in Fig. 2) reflects the capital and labour substitutions for energy that take place in response to raised energy price and whose magnitude is modelled by the value of the price elasticity of conservation response. In other words, the model is treated as bi-directional: an increase (or decrease) in the availability of energy will lead to an increase (or decrease) in the level of economic activity just as an increase (or decrease) in the level of economic activity will lead to an increase (or decrease) in the demand for energy. The extent of the increase or decrease may be modified by the responses to changes in the price of energy.

The demand for energy is affected by its price as well as by the level of economic activity. We therefore need an additional model of the way in which energy consumption responds to price even when the level of economic activity remains constant. The model usually adopted is the following:

$$\frac{t}{Y} = K(\frac{P}{P_o})^{-a}$$

where a = the price elasticity of demand for energy subject to income remaining constant; K = a constant.

This model should *not* be seen as modelling the improvement in the efficiency of energy use that takes place when energy price rises. Y is in the denominator simply to meet the stipulation that 'a' is an indicator of response to price change only, with income remaining constant. The ratio E/Y can fall even when there is no increase in the efficiency of energy use — it might fall, for example, simply because the economy has shed some energy-dependent activity or gained some non-energy dependent activity.

Finally, we need a model of energy supply. The one usually adopted is:

$$E = C(\frac{P}{P_o})^{b}$$

where b = the price elasticity of energy supply; C = a constant.

These three equations taken together constitute a simple world model of the way in which world economic activity, world energy supply and the energy price interact.

WHAT IS A PRICE HIKE

The large oil price hikes have been widely regarded as simply large step increases in the price of oil. (They have, of course, led to sharp increases — though not by so much — in the prices of other fuels.) Most studies of the effect of price hikes have taken the increase in price as exogenous (imposed from outside the system) and have then attempted to assess the effects of such exogenous increases. It follows that these studies do not distinguish between an increase in price that arises because of a change in demand and one that results from a change in supply.

In this chapter we shall take a different concept of a price hike — one which the author believes is much nearer the truth. We shall define a price hike as a shift in the demand curve as a whole (see Fig. 3) resulting in a higher price being demanded at all levels of output. This concept of a price hike reflects the author's belief that energy producers are not able to decree that 'from tomorrow the

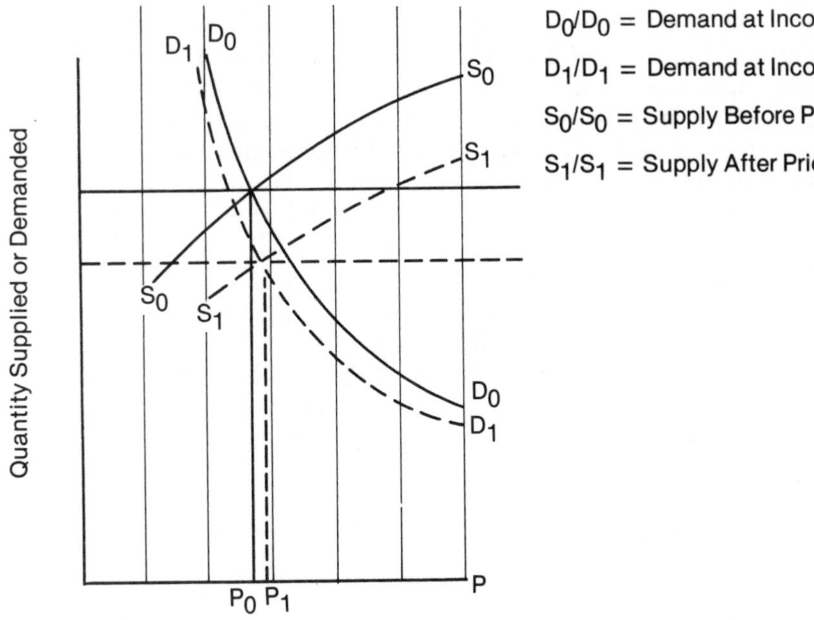

Fig. 19.3: Energy Supply and Demand Functions

price of energy shall be twice what it is today'. They can only say 'if you want as much as you have been getting you will have to pay more for it. If you are not prepared to pay more you will have to make do with less.' It follows that the result of a price hike is for energy consumption to fall and for the real energy price to settle down eventually at a level somewhere between the original price and the new nominal price announced by energy suppliers.

If this concept of a price hike is allied to the model of energy consumption and economic activity derived in the previous section we have the result (observed in practice) that an increase in energy price results in a fall in the level of economic activity (unless there is a most improbable conservation response to raised price), a fall in the level of energy consumption and a real price for energy that is somewhere between the initial price and the one that the energy producers attempted to impose.

This result is, of course, completely at variance with the projections of those forecasters who combine assumptions about economic growth with assumptions about future energy supply to produce forecasts that energy prices will rise in real terms by factors of between 2 and 3 in the next twenty years. These forecasts associate high levels of economic activity with high energy price. The explanation is that, in this case, the forecasters are making no allowance for the effect of restricted energy supply (as evidenced by high price) upon the level of economic activity and are assuming that the increase in energy price is due to increased demand, not an exogenous shift in the supply curve.

Events since 1973 support the hypothesis that the problem is one of a reduction in the availability of energy to the world economic system — in the form of a shift in the energy supply curve in a direction unfavourable to consumers. These events also support the hypothesis that a reduction in the availability of energy greatly damages the level of economic activity. (Begg, Cripps and Ward writing in the *Financial Times* for 6 January 1982, summarizing a paper of their, Begg *et al.* 1981, support this view, but offer a solution — the maintenance of a high oil price — that the author would reject.)

MODELLING ENERGY PRICE HIKES

The demand model mentioned earlier can be shown diagrammatically as a series of curves logarithmically in parallel to each other (that is to say they would be parallel if plotted on logarithmic graph paper), with each curve representing a different level of economic activity. We might now consider how an energy price hike might work its way through the economic system:

1. Energy producers impose a 100% price hike — doubling the unit price at each level of supply. This change is shown in the shift of the supply curve in Fig. 4.
2. This restriction upon the availability of energy — manifesting itself in the supply and demand curves intersecting at a lower level of output and consumption — leads to a reduction in the level of economic activity. This can be seen in the shift to a different point on the energy consumption/economic activity sub-model.
3. The existence of a non-zero price elasticity of conservation response produces a change in the slope of the energy consumption/economic activity sub-model that recovers some of the lost output.

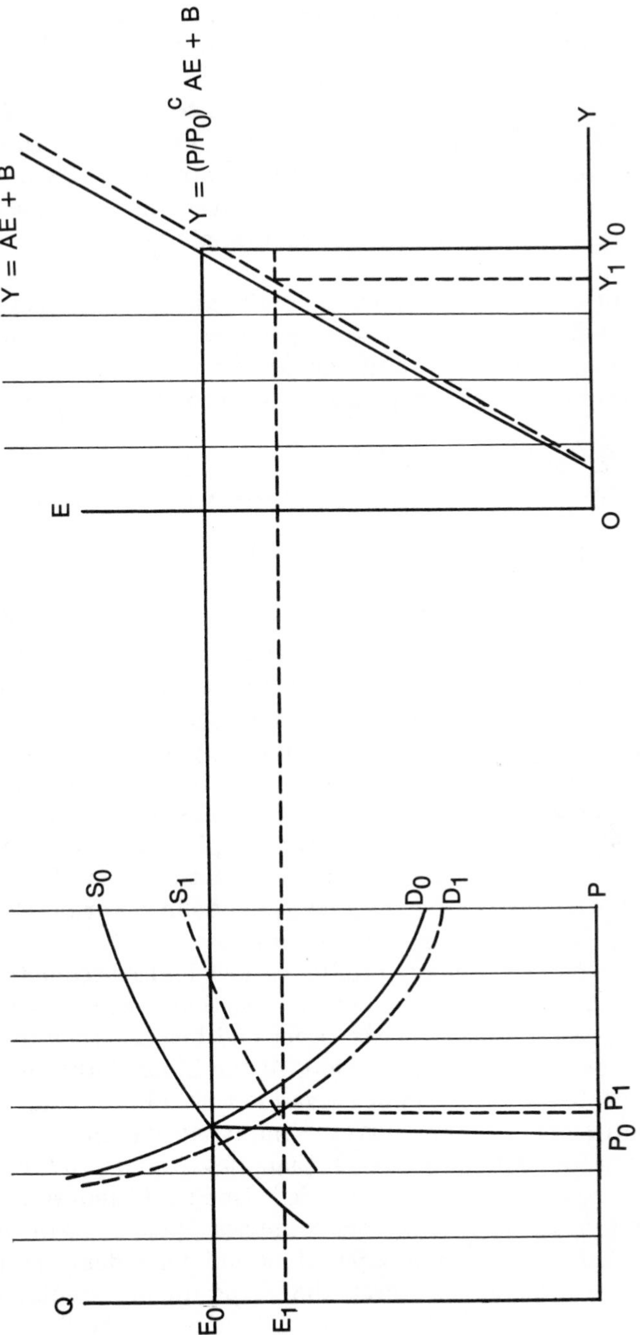

Fig. 19.4: An Interactive Model of Energy Consumption, Economic Activity and the Conditions of Energy Supply.

4. The net reduction in economic activity (taking the highly probable case of the conservation response being insufficient to recover all of the initial loss) produces a shift to a lower member of the family of demand curves.
5. Eventually, the system settles down to a new equilibrium with lower levels of economic activity and energy consumption, the price settles at a level which is, perhaps, only 10% or 15% above its original level, and some improvement in the efficiency of energy use results from this somewhat higher price for energy.

The results depend very much upon the assumptions made about the initial position and slope of the energy consumption/economic activity sub-model and the values chosen for the elasticities. The following values were taken representing a very rough approximation to the real world:

Y is expressed in \$ billion (1980)

E is expressed in millions of tons of coal equivalent (MTCE)

$A = 0.77$

$B = 2.3 \times 10^3$

a lies between 0.6 and 1.0

b lies between 0.2 and 0.4

c lies between 0.2 and the value chosen for 'a' (choosing a value for 'c' greater than 'a' produces nonsensical results: it implies that consumers over-compensate by improved energy efficiency for the reductions they make in energy purchases; the resulting increase in economic activity pushes up the energy price, producing yet another over compensatory response and so on and so on with economic activity spiralling to an infinite level.)

The high long run demand elasticities (0.6 to 1.0) are fully supported by studies conducted by the Energy Modelling Forum (EMF 1980). The fairly low (less than 0.5) values chosen for the supply elasticity reflect the fact that energy producers have limited scope for changing the level of output — at one end because they are limited by currently exploited resources and at the other end because they depend upon the revenue from their production. At the EPRI Workshop mentioned earlier, Professor Alan Manne suggested that oil producers might have backward sloping supply curves — implying that their concern for a given level of revenue was such that they would produce less when the price rose and more when it fell. One might indeed expect some such pattern of behaviour from countries — like some of those in the Middle East — with small populations and dependent upon depleting resource. In practice, however, the oil producing countries have sold oil at prices that reflect movements in prices on the Rotterdam Spot

Market — offering discounts on contract prices when spot prices fall and charging premia when spot prices rise. This implies low prices at low levels of output and high prices at high levels — a normal supply curve, in other words.

It is very hard to identify a true price elasticity of conservation response. For a very long time — at least 30 years — the economy-wide efficiency of energy usage in the UK has been improving at the rate of about 1% per annum. This pattern continued during periods of falling energy prices. The reasons for it are no doubt complex: the onward march of technical progress and the substitution of inherently more efficient fuels for older less efficient ones no doubt each played a part. There has been some slow down of technical progress since 1973 because investment in new plant has slowed down. The substitution of liquid for solid fuels — which no doubt accounted for much of the improvement in energy productivity in the last few decades — has gone into reverse. The substitution of natural gas for other home heating fuels has co-incided with greater use of central heating — which usually results in higher energy use per capita. Electricity usage has stayed level in the UK but has increased its share of total final energy consumption in some other industrial countries — the USA and France, for example. Some apparent improvement in the economy-wide efficiency of energy usage takes place as energy intensive activity is shed in a recession that is associated with raised energy prices. With all these confusing factors it would be a bold man who claimed to have identified a response in the shape of improvements in the efficiency of energy usage that was due solely to the raised price. A success story reported by the brewing industry in the UK in the autumn of 1980 could be translated into a price elasticity of conservation response of 0.6. Reports from the same industry in 1982 record disappointment that the early success has not been maintained.

Government officials responsible for encouraging energy conservation tend, for the most part, to report disappointing responses to the various inducements offered.

For all these reasons a wide range for the price elasticity of energy conservation response was chosen. Remembering that this parameter applies strictly to the response to raised price (excluding the long term trend of technical progress and the effect of reductions in the energy-intensive component of the economy) it seems likely that, in practice, the price elasticity of conservation response is less than 0.5 — perhaps significantly below this level.

Experiments with this model produce challenging results* —

***Shown graphically in Appendix 1.**

although it must be remembered that it has a purely hypothetical basis. Starting with an exogenous doubling of the energy price (shifting the demand curve so as to double the price at all levels of output) results — when equilibrium was regained — were typically as follows:

1. A fall in economic activity of between 6% and 16%
2. A fall in energy consumption of between 11% and 22%
3. A rise in the real equilibrium energy price of between 4% and 17%

These results were obtained with a price elasticity of conservation response of less than 0.5. If this elasticity is assumed to be higher

Table 19.1. UK Energy Expenditure as a Percentage of GDP with and without taxation.

	Total energy expenditure without taxation (£ million)	*Total energy expenditure with taxation (£ million)*	*GDP at factor cost (4 million)*	*Energy from GDP without taxation (%)*	*Energy from GDP with taxation (%)*
1955	1429.2	1742.3	16894	8.46	10.31
1960	1893.3	2302.1	22615	8.37	10.18
1961	2064.7	2575.0	24198	8.37	10.64
1962	2126.2	2670.6	25252	8.42	10.58
1963	2241.9	2833.6	26863	8.35	10.55
1964	2252.6	2926.8	29182	7.72	10.03
1965	2476.6	3261.1	31212	7.93	10.45
1966	2648.6	3536.1	33083	8.01	10.69
1967	2793.3	3762.7	34877	8.01	10.79
1968	3162.2	4289.1	37390	8.46	11.47
1969	3359.9	4669.4	39338	8.54	11.87
1970	3459.2	4855.0	43368	7.98	11.19
1971	4210.4	5653.5	49151	8.57	11.50
1972	4548.8	6104.3	54958	8.33	11.11
1973	4722.0	6297.0	63492	7.44	9.92
1974	7502.2	9307.2	73652	10.19	12.64
1975	9226.9	11141.9	93078	9.91	11.97
1976	11239.5	13424.5	109080	10.30	12.31

[a] UK Department of Energy statistics for this parameter date only from 1967. A method was developed for figures going back to 1955 which, for consistency, was carried through to 1976. Discrepancies between figures for the overlapping period were not great. Means and standard deviations for 1955 to 1972 were respectively 10.8% and 0.54 with tax, and 8.26% and 0.27 without tax.

than this the loss of economic activity is mitigated (it is wholly recovered when the elasticity of conservation response equals the demand elasticity but the economy must then find room for energy conservation investment that it did not previously need — an example of an increase in what welfare economists call 'regrettables'). Paradoxically, a higher energy conservation response *increases* energy consumption and produces a higher level for the real equilibrium energy price. This is not hard to understand if one recognizes that responding to high price by using energy more efficiently is a way of accommodating the raised price. For any given position of the supply curve this means striking a balance between supply and demand at a higher level of consumption and production — in other words using energy more efficiently in conditions of restricted availability of energy does not save energy or force its price down — it simply mitigates the loss of employment resulting from the imposed restriction upon energy supplies that a price hike constitutes.

By manipulation of terms it is easy to show that the proportion of national product expended upon energy is proportional to $(P/P_0)^{1-a}$. If the long term value of 'a' is 0.6 or above and the equilibrium real energy price increase following an attempt at a large price hike is less than 20%, this formula has the effect of keeping the proportion of national income spent upon energy within a very narrow band.

It would provide some support for the thesis advanced here if this proportion were in fact to stay within a fairly narrow band. Table 1 shows that it has in fact done so for a good many years in the UK. Oddly enough, the proportion fell in 1973 despite sharp increases in energy prices, but this was the year of the miners' strike and the three day week, which was introduced to meet restrictions on electricity supply caused by coal shortage. In the immediately following years there was an increase in the proportion by one or two percentage points — but these would be non-equilibrium values. There are signs now of a resumption of the old proportion. Dr Joy Dunkerley — speaking at the 1979 annual conference of the International Association of Energy Economists — reported similar stability in the USA.

IMPLICATIONS AND LESSONS FOR NUCLEAR ENERGY

Remembering once again that this is an excercise designed to producing insights rather than predictions, the implications are:

1. An energy conservation response to price rise can have only a mitigating effect at best;
2. The idea that raised oil price, in itself, brings a host of previously over-costly energy sources into the market is probably false: in practice a price hike that takes the form of a shift in the supply curve works itself out in the form of inflation (blunting the energy price rise), a reduction in the levels of energy consumption and economic activity and only a relatively small increase in the real equilibrium price of energy.

The further implications are:

1. A reduction in the rate of replacement of plant of all types — including electrical plant — because of the depressed state of national economies;
2. Very low or negative energy and electricity growth rates.

Paradoxically, the effect of an increase in the price of conventional fuels is to slow down the rate of introduction of new forms of energy like nuclear energy.* Table 2 shows what actually happened to nuclear power plans in the developed countries after 1973.

Thus, nuclear energy presents a dilemma as a source of relief to the restrictions upon energy availability that the world has suffered since 1973:

Table 19.2. Forecast nuclear capacity in 1985 (GWe).

	1973 forecast	*1975 forecast*	*1977 forecast*
Belgium	5.5	9.5	4.9–5.6
France	32.5	56.0	31–35
Germany	38.0	44.6	32.38
Italy	18.0	26.4	6.4–7.4
UK	35.0	15.4	11–13
Spain	12.0	23.7	14–20
Switzerland	8.0	8.0	3.3–3.8
Sweden	16.0	11.3	7.8–9.0
Japan	60.0	49.0	35.1
Finland	4.6	3.9	?
USA	280.0	205.0	152

*The author predicted this result in a paper presented to an expert meeting held in Milan in February 1974 (Brookes 1974).

1. The only real solution to the problem is the exploitation of new additional energy sources at costs and prices that will have the effect of forcing the world all-energy supply curve back towards its original position. Of all the feasible new sources of energy, nuclear energy is outstandingly suitable for this role — it is relatively cheap and abundant, and offers the opportunity to continue the march of technical progress towards the more modern forms of energy that Mr Sam Schurr draws attention to (Schurr 1978);

Table 19.3. France Electricity Production 1980, 1981 (TWh).

	Nuclear	*Coal and Oil Fired*	*Hydro*
1980	57.9	118.9	69.8
1981	99.5	92.1	72.4

European Community
Production in the First Nine Months – all Plant

Country	*1980*	*1981*	*% Change*
FRG	252.5	251.2	−0.5
France	176.6	189.7	+7.4
Italy	130-9	127.4	−2.7
Netherlands	45.4	44.6	−1.8
Belgium	37.4	34.8	−7.1
Luxembourg	0.8	0.89	+12.0
UK	194.4	187.3	−3.7
Ireland	7.6	7.5	−0.4
Denmark	17.6	11.3	−35.9

Electricity Prices to Large Industrial Consumers (Source – NUS Survey of International Electricity Tariffs.)

	cents/kWh
France	4.72
Netherlands	4.92
Italy	6.05
FRG	6.16
Ireland	6.41
UK	7.09
Belgium	7.38

2. But quite apart from the political problems caused by a vociferous anti-nuclear movement combined with institutional arrangements that favour dissent in important countries, the economic conditions that favour rapid introduction of nuclear energy are lacking because of the very factor — restricted availability of world energy supply — that makes its introduction important.

The saving grace is that thermal nuclear power may be considered a mature technology and the fast reactor is at an advanced stage of development. All that is lacking in most countries is a readiness to take the remedial action that is called for — namely investment in the developed countries in the production of the commodity (fuel) that is giving cause for concern. In *Getting from here to there* Walt Rostow (Rostow 1978) reported that on each of the previous four occasions in the last 200 years when the more developed countries found themselves faced with sharp rises in the prices of primary products they responded by investing in home production of those commodities. He noted that there were few signs of a similar response on this occasion. The lessons are clear in the experience of the one country — France — that has responded. As Table 3 shows, France — with the largest nuclear power component in its electricity system and plans for further substantial increases in that component — has the highest rate of substitution of electricity for other forms of energy in Europe and the lowest electricity prices.

THE PRESENT REALITY

In early 1982 we have falling oil prices and some euphoria in consuming countries at what seems to be cracks in the OPEC cartel. According to the thesis in this paper, the softening of the energy market is only to be expected — it is part of the approach to the new equilibrium after the last price hike. No satisfaction can be drawn from the state of the world economy: growth rates are severely depressed and all countries are grappling with the problem of inflation — another manifestation of the approach to the new equilibrium, as new price relativities struggle to take shape.

There is no cause for complacency in the present state of the oil market. The price at time of writing — about $30 per barrel, with prices somewhat lower on the spot market — has to be associated with a level of OPEC output of less than 18 million barrels per day, against nearly 30 million barrels only two years ago. An output of

17 mbd linked to a price of $30 is a point on a distinctly less favourable supply curve than existed before the last price hike and very much less favourable than the one that ruled before 1973. Possession of North Sea oil does not allow the UK to escape the sombre reality of the fall in the availability of energy to the World economic system — our dependence on international trade and hence our vulnerability to setbacks in the level of world economic activity is too great for us to be able to draw more than modest comfort from the possession of that ephemeral piece of wealth.

The imperatives remain unchanged. No country can afford to neglect the exploitation of new modest cost energy sources. Unfortunately this important example of supply side economics is being subjected to demand side thinking in most countries — with France and the USSR as the outstanding exceptions. We are in great danger of chasing out tails downwards as the rate of exploitations of new energy sources is tempered by regard for energy demand projections that in turn follow from economic forecasts that are lower than they need be because of tardiness in exploiting new energy sources!

REFERENCES

1. C. Allsopp, speaking at a seminar held by the British Institute of Energy Economics in London October, 1981.
2. I. Begg., F. Cripps and T. Ward, 'Why Oil Prices Must Stay High', *Financial Times*, 6 January 1982.
3. L.G. Brookes, 'More on the Output of Energy Consumption', *Journal of Industrial Economics*, (November 1972).
4. L.G. Brookes, 'The Complementary Roles of Nuclear and Other Fuels', a paper to an expert meeting on Alternative Strategies to Meet the Oil Crisis, held at the International Institute for the Management of Technology. 1974.
5. L.G. Brookes, 'The Energy Price Fallacy and the Role of Nuclear Power in the U.K.', *Energy Policy*, (June 1978).
6. L.G. Brookes, 'Energy, Inflation and Economic Prospects', a paper to a conference 'Design, "79"' held at the University of Aston-in-Birmingham, September, 1979.
7. L.G. Brookes, *Energy Conservation Response to Price Increase — Is it Sufficient to Resolve a Problem of Energy Shortage?*, published by A.P.G., 8 Ruvigny Mansions, Embankment, Putney, London, SW15, 1981.
8. J. Dunkerley, speaking at the 1st annual conference of the International Association of Energy Economists, Washington, D.C., June 1979.
9. Z. Grilliches, speaking from the chair in a session 'Incorporating Technical Change in Energy-Economic Modelling' at the workshop on Energy, Productivity and Economic Growth, EPRI, Palo Alto, Ca., January 1981.

10. D.W. Jorgenson, 'Energy Prices and Productivity Growth', presented at the 2nd annual conference of the International Association of Energy Economists, Cambridge, UK, June 1980 and included in full in *International Energy Options: An Agenda for the 1980s*, edited by Paul Tempest, OGH, Cambridge, Mass and Graham and Trotman, London, 1981.
11. G. Kouris, speaking at a seminar held by the Economics Department of the University of Surrey, January, 1978.
12. R.S. Pindyck, *The Structure of World Energy Demand*, MIT Press, 1979.
13. W.W. Rostow, *Getting from Here to There*, Macmillan, 1978.
14. S.H. Schurr, 'Energy, Economic Growth and Human Welfare', in the *E.P.R.I. Journal*, (May 1978). (Also in *Ethics and Energy*, the Edison Electric Institute 1979.)
15. M. Slesser, *Energy and the Economy*, Macmillan, 1978.
16. V. Smil and T. Kuz, 'Energy and the Economy — a Global Analysis', *Long Range Planning* **9**, (No. 3), (June 1976).

APPENDIX 1

At zero conservation elasticity, the loss of output is dominated by the supply elasticity and is relatively insensitive to the demand elasticity. This is because the larger the supply elasticity the more nearly the supply curve approaches the vertical (on the axes used in the model) and the more nearly the equilibrium price increase approaches the imposed price increase. In an energy-driven world (such as is assumed here) the fall in output is due to the fall in energy consumption which in turn is due to the less favourable conditions of supply. The higher the demand elasticity the larger the fall in energy consumption. But the new equilibrium is at least as much affected by the shift in the demand curve (in response to a reduced level of economic activity) and, as explained in the text, this shift is insensitive to the value of the demand elasticity over the range given here.

When a constant conservation elasticity of 0.4 is adopted the picture is dramatically changed. This is because the definition of this elasticity is such that the potential loss of output is wholly recovered when it is equal to the demand elasticity. The curves therefore converge to zero at this point.

When the more realistic assumption of demand and conservation elasticities moving in step is adopted the original pattern is largely re-established — but with the falls in economic activity mitigated by the conservation response. But even with a response of as high as 0.5 the relief is no more than by about 25%.

The effect upon energy consumption is similar but the percentages are all larger. This is because the price hike acts directly upon the level of energy consumption. Percentagewise the fall in economic activity is mitigated by the existence of non-energy dependent activity in the economy — which is left untouched by the fall in energy consumption.

At zero conservation elasticity the equilibrium energy price rise lies between just over 3% and about 18%, the supply elasticity having a dominating influence. The influence of the demand elasticity is greater than it is upon energy consumption and economic activity. At 5% supply elasticity the equilibrium price rise falls from 18% to just over 8% as the demand elasticity moves from 0.4 to 1.0.

Once again a dramatic change is brought about by assuming a constant conservation elasticity of 0.4 regardless of the demand elasticity and again the original pattern is largely re-established by adopting the more realistic assumption that the two elasticities march in step. The changes in equilibrium price are, however, larger than when zero conservation response is assumed. An energy conservation response accommodates higher price — and results in a higher level of energy consumption because in any given conditions of supply equilibrium is struck at a higher price hence higher level of supply and demand.

Nuclear Power Economics edited by L.G. Brookes and H. Motamen will be published in 1983 by Chapman and Hall.

At zero conservation elasticity, the loss of output is dominated by the supply elasticity and is relatively insensitive to the demand elasticity. This is because the larger the supply elasticity the more nearly the supply curve approaches the vertical (on the axes used in the model) and the more nearly the equilibrium price increase approaches the imposed price increase. In an energy-driven world (such as is assumed here) the fall in output is due to the fall in energy consumption which in turn is due to the less favourable conditions of supply. The higher the demand elasticity the larger the fall in energy consumption. But the new equilibrium is at least as much affected by the shift in the demand curve (in response to a reduced level of economic activity) and, as explained in the text, this shift is insensitive to the value of the demand elasticity over the range given here.

When a constant conservation elasticity of 0.4 is adopted the picture is dramatically changed. This is because the definition of this elasticity is such that the potential loss of output is wholly recovered when it is equal to the demand elasticity. The curves therefore converge to zero at this point.

When the more realistic assumption of demand and conservation elasticities moving in step is adopted the original pattern is largely reestablished — but with the falls in economic activity mitigated by the conservation response. But even with a response of as high as 0.5 the relief is no more than by about 25%.

The effect upon energy consumption is similar but the percentages are all larger. This is because the price hike acts directly upon the level of energy consumption. Percentagewise the fall in economic activity is mitigated by the existence of non-energy dependent activity in the economy — which is left untouched by the fall in energy consumption.

At zero conservation elasticity the equilibrium energy price rise lies between just over 3% and about 18%, the supply elasticity having a dominating influence. The influence of the demand elasticity is greater than it is upon energy consumption and economic activity. At 5% supply elasticity the equilibrium price rise falls from 18% to just over 8% as the demand elasticity moves from 0.4 to 1.0.

Once again a dramatic change is brought about by assuming a constant conservation elasticity of 0.4 regardless of the demand elasticity and again the original pattern is largely re-established by adopting the more realistic assumption that the two elasticities march in step. The changes in equilibrium price are, however, larger than when zero conservation response is assumed. An energy conservation response accommodates higher price — and results in a higher level of energy consumption because in any given conditions of supply equilibrium is struck at a higher price hence higher level of supply and demand.

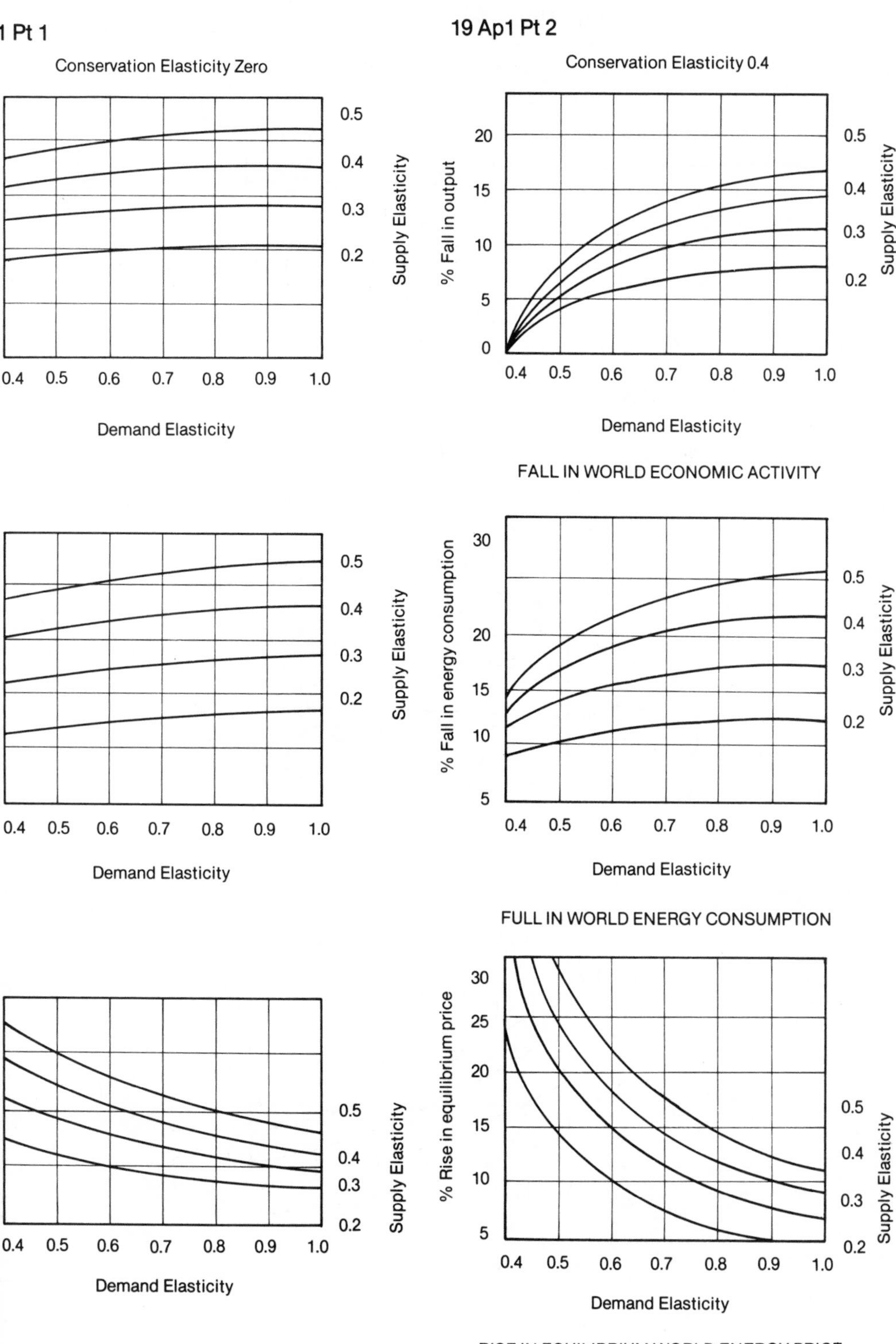
1 Pt 1
Conservation Elasticity Zero
0.5
0.4
0.3
0.2
Supply Elasticity
0.4 0.5 0.6 0.7 0.8 0.9 1.0
Demand Elasticity
19 Ap1 Pt 2
Conservation Elasticity 0.4
% Fall in output
0 5 10 15 20
0.4 0.5 0.6 0.7 0.8 0.9 1.0
Demand Elasticity
FALL IN WORLD ECONOMIC ACTIVITY
% Fall in energy consumption
5 10 15 20 30
FULL IN WORLD ENERGY CONSUMPTION
% Rise in equilibrium price
5 10 15 20 25 30
RISE IN EQUILIBRIUM WORLD ENERGY PRICE

19 Ap1 Pt 3

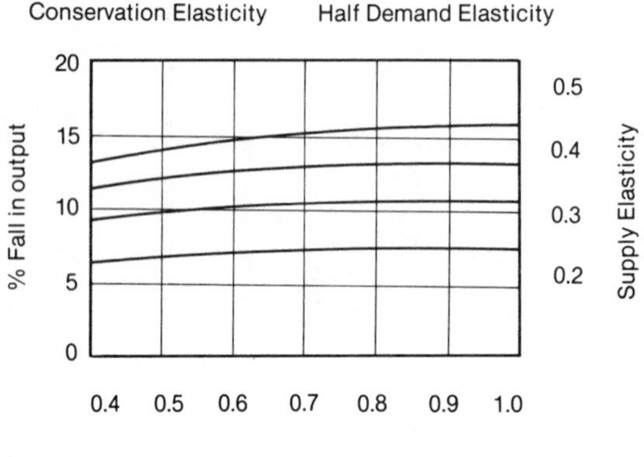
Conservation Elasticity
Half Demand Elasticity
% Fall in output
20
15
10
5
0
0.4
0.5
0.6
0.7
0.8
0.9
1.0
Demand Elasticity
0.5
0.4
0.3
0.2
Supply Elasticity

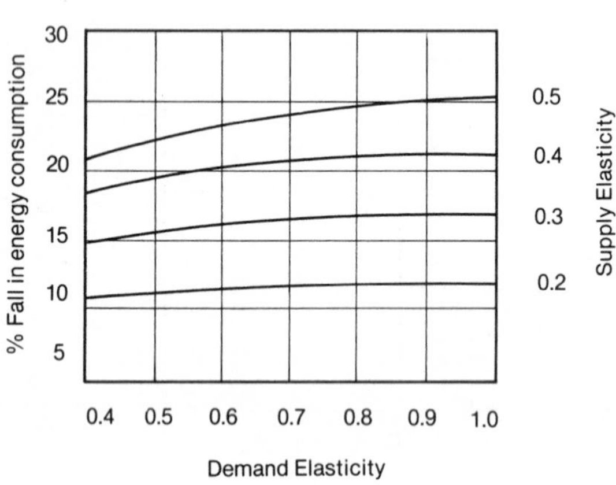
% Fall in energy consumption
30
25
20
15
10
5
0.4
0.5
0.6
0.7
0.8
0.9
1.0
Demand Elasticity
0.5
0.4
0.3
0.2
Supply Elasticity

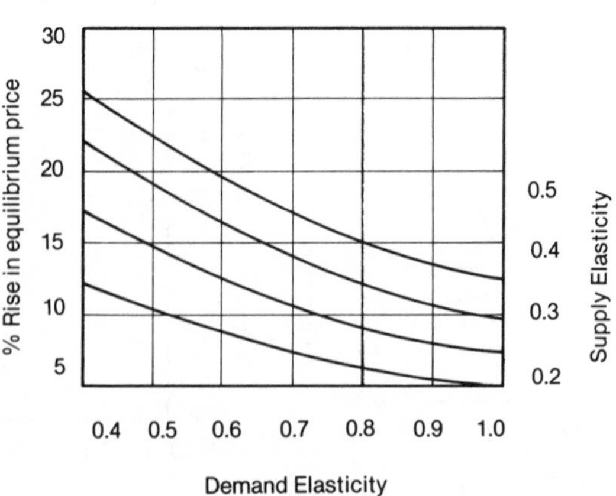
% Rise in equilibrium price
30
25
20
15
10
5
0.4
0.5
0.6
0.7
0.8
0.9
1.0
Demand Elasticity
0.5
0.4
0.3
0.2
Supply Elasticity

SECTION 3

A Historical Perspective

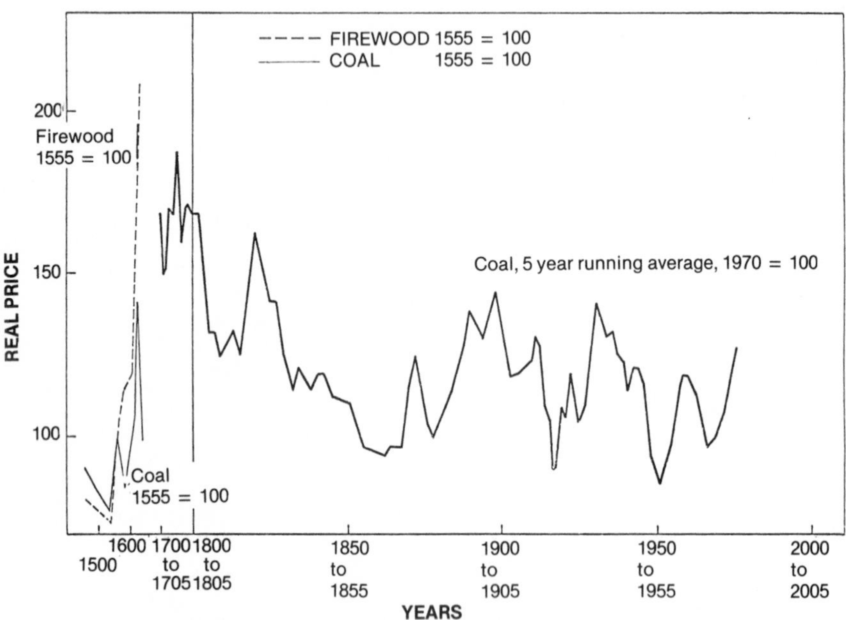

Illustration supplied by Sir William Hawthorne, Master of Churchill College, Cambridge

Between 1550 and 1600, the price of a cheap, convenient and clean fuel — firewood — went through the roof i.e. it actually increased about five fold. Fortunately, a less clean but plentiful fuel — sea coal — was available to rescue the UK economy. As you can see, apart from some flucuations, the last 300 years has seen a downward trend in the real price of coal.

'Real' Price of Coal and Firewood in Britain.

Chapter 20

Economic Issues in the History of UK Energy

*Eric Price**

The economic history of energy in the UK is essentially a record of individuals, and of groups of individuals being confronted by, and reacting to, changes in the economic environment — an environment over which they had little, if any, control or influence. People throughout history whether as buyers, sellers, producers, consumers, investors, employers or workers, have had to make adjustment decisions which are economic in character. It is, therefore, in no way remarkable that history abounds with evidence of inter-fuel substitution, technological innovation, technology transfer, distortions in demand and supply arising from tax imposts, changes in market hinterlands, the exploitation of monopoly and monopsonistic conditions, price and income elasticity effects and of substitution between factors of production. Further, most of the economic problems that face energy economists today are of a kind that have faced our predecessors throughout history: only the context and parameters are new. To illustrate this, it is chastening, and yet at the same time comforting, to reflect that the first energy crisis in

***Undersecretary and Head of Economics and Statistics Division in the UK Department of Energy and, since January 1983, Chairman of the British Institute of Energy Economics.**

England was not in 1972–73, nor 1956, nor even in the 1940s, but probably in the timber crisis of the second half of the 16th Century and first half of the 17th, if not before. Even the existence of external diseconomies of fuel use was recognised, if not quantified, at the start of the 14th Century.

Whilst little early evidence is available, the genesis of energy economics in Britain must surely go back into pre-history from the earliest exchange of energy forms for other resources. Some, albeit rudimentary, analyses of the opportunity costs of the various barter options must have been in the minds of those who traded. Obviously no records of their analyses exist today, but the very act of trading implied a view. It is known that the Romans exploited East Anglian peat from the Norfolk Broads and presumably its distribution and marketing in the larger settlements must have involved some assessment of the economic watershed beyond which the 'net-back' price after transport costs fell short of the perceived marginal costs of extraction.

In Roman times the main fuel source, as in many under-developed countries today, was timber from local forests. Much of the timber was used for charcoal production. Coal had a very minor role — indeed, it was a very localised technological innovation. Solinus,* for instance, refers in wonderment to the strange glowing coal at the altar of Minerva in Bath almost with the same awe and sense of novelty as a scientific correspondent might describe the fast breeder reactor today: 'The presiding deity of these springs is Minerva in whose temple a perpetual fire never turns into white wood ash, but when the flame dies down, into stone masses.' The stony masses were canal coal from the Somersetshire coalfield which supplies a limited number of sites in Somerset and Wiltshire, largely for domestic use. Coal provided a very minor percentage of energy requirements though it was known to have been used at Heronbridge near Chester at the end of the First Century serving both the legionary fortress of Chester and the military tile factory at Holt. Flintshire coal is also believed to have been distributed to the Anglesy Village of Din Lligwy, some 80 miles away, where it was used for iron smelting despite its sulphur content and the consequential risk of brittleness. It was also used for glass-making where this problem did not arise. All the coal came from surface working. Outcrops of coal were exploited in various parts of the country and often transported considerable distances with the economics of return loads being exploited wherever possible. For instance, corn and Castor pottery

*in Collectanea rer memor XX 11.10.

from the Fenlands was transported by sea to the North East coast and the ships returned with coal for the ovens which were used for drying unripe grain.*

Whilst economic decisions have been with us throughout history so have environmental constraints. In 1307, for instance, Edward I in the final year of his reign, forbade the use of sea-coal burning in Southwark because of the pollution it caused. In spite of this, the economics of cheap sea transport from Tyneside enabled London to consume coal as its normal fuel from the 14th Century onwards.

The earliest significant collection of economic analyses on energy issues is represented by the records of the early coal trade throughout England. Inspection of mediaeval records in London, Norwich, Bristol and the larger towns suggest that such trading was not always left to hunch. It would, of course, be comforting to conclude generally that those energy suppliers, who analysed their marketing and production costs rationally were those whose businesses grew — or at least survived longest, but valid evidence of this must await for some enlightening PhD thesis in the future. Certainly throughout English history, records abound of ex-post assessments of what went wrong. Typical of these are those of a former owner of Buckland House in Devon, who, when signing the contract for selling his mature trees at a very promising price for charcoal smelting purposes, failed, in so doing, to read the deed *in full* only to discover too late that he was committed to transporting them some 100 miles to a smelter at his own cost, with the result that he was forced to sell his stately home!

The experiences of England from the end of the Middle Ages until 1800 illustrates the problems of wood as fuel, and the transition of industrializing economies away from that energy source. By the end of the Middle Ages, England had a prosperous iron-making industry around the Weald and the Forest of Dean. Deforestation on a massive scale during the 14th and 15th Centuries resulted from uncontrolled consumption particularly for iron smelting. This caused financial failures among some smelters and led to a design of mobile furnaces. Further, competition for forests and environmental objections to the wood-based metals production caused England to change its law. By the 1600s however fuel shortages began to occur. Few woods larger than 20 acres remained, and in South East England there was very little fuel wood left. Hence the real price of timber increased.

Whether our predecessors carried out appropriate calculations of

***For those interested in the early use and trade in coal, G. Webster's 'A note on the use of coal in Britain' in the *Antequarians' Journal* (1955) presents a fascinating account.**

the economics of inter-fuel substitution is not known. What is certain is that such fuel switches occurred in response to relative price changes. In the century following 1530, the price of timber for burning increased eight-fold in money terms and three-fold in real terms, and coal took over the energy market as its own price began to fall.

It is doubtful whether any analytical economic studies were carried out during the period from Tudor times to the middle of the 18th Century when what may now be termed the 'timber depletion policy' was in force in an effort to prevent the destruction of forests by the 'extravagant' use of timber for the charcoal smelting of iron. (The iron ore typically being transported to the forests rather than vice versa as in the Buckland House instance.) In any case, the main consideration of that policy was not just the rising price of timber but also the defence argument, since the timber was to be conserved for naval construction purposes. The impact, however, was very clear: the 'timber depletion policy' led to the decline of iron smelting. By the beginning of the industrial revolution, the number of iron-producing smelters in England had declined from several hundred to 55. 26 of these were located between the Weald and the Forest of Dean. Trevelyan records that this fuel famine caused a decline of English iron production and an international movement of the iron industry to Scandinavia and America, where forests were plentiful. He also states that the scarcity of wood threatened England's ability to support its increasing population. What is certain is that by 1740 Britain was importing iron from Sweden, Russia and the American colonies. It is odd today to contemplate the operation of an energy depletion policy which, two-and-a-half centuries ago, directly caused deindustrialisation in a manufacturing sector rather than preventing it. The effects of policy action, in the event, all too often turn out to be contrary to the declared policy aim.

These fuel shortages forced England to search for new energy sources. Although coal had been mined since the twelfth century, it was the wood shortage that caused coal to win its market share. Abraham Darby developed the techniques for the production of coke, and in 1709, successfully substituted it for charcoal in the production of iron. This led to a massive change in the nation's fuel use. By 1788, coke-fired blast furnaces outnumbered charcoal-fired vessels by 59 to 26; and by 1809 the ratio was 162 to 11. This fuel change, of course, depended upon the development of a canal transportation network which connected the economy together and made coal transportation to inland areas economically feasible.

The economic rationale, which formed the basis of some of the policy-making led to some curious decisions. One of the monopolies, for instance, that Charles I sold to reduce his public sector borrowing requirement and meet increased defence spending was to grant the hostmen of Newcastle the control of the export of coal from that port. Not content with that, however, he then subsequently sold a 'sole right' monopoly to only *some* of them to sell colliers coal for the London market, thereby effectively getting paid *twice* by creating a monopoly within a monopoly.

The 'infant industry' argument for protection influenced the energy sector as early as 1689. Whilst James II was in Ireland, the Irish Parliament, in a 'UDI-type' initiative in declaring Poyning's Law invalid, forbade the importation of British coal into Ireland and imposed maximum price control on coal produced in Ireland. Also, at the time of the Act of Union, Scotland was exempted from the Coal Tax though whether on the grounds of political expediency or for regional industrial support is unclear.

Little is known about mining techniques in these periods let alone of production functions. One description at least survives, that by Celia Fiennes who, in William and Mary's reign, journeyed up and down England on horseback. In Celia's *Diaries* it is quite clear that it was a labour-intensive form of production! 'They make their Mines at ye Entrance Like a Well and so till they Come to ye Coale then they digg all the Ground about where there is Coale and set pillars to support it, and so bring it to ye Well where by a basket like a hand barrow by Cords they pull it up — so they let down and up the miners with a Cord.'

THE ORIGINS OF ENERGY ECONOMICS

With the advent of the industrial revolution, some academic discussion of the economics of energy issues started to take place. From then on many of the great names in economics — Adam Smith, David Ricardo, The Rev. Thomas R. Malthus, John Stuart Mill, Alfred Marshall — were, to a greater or lesser extent, concerned with the energy issues of their time, using examples in the energy field to illustrate the relevance of their respective theories to the real world. But, whilst they provided tools for the economic analysis of energy issues, none of these eminent economists specialised in energy.

COAL

It was not until W.S. Jevons published *The Coal Question* in 1866 that any book dealt with the economics of an energy form. In this book Jevons raised the coal depletion problem for the first time. Interestingly, in raising it, he claimed that at the rate Britain was using up its coal reserves they would very soon be exhausted. He went on to argue that since communications with the British Empire were entirely based on coal, depletion would lead to the end of the British Empire. Perhaps he may be considered to be the first energy economist to be right for the wrong reason, though not the last.

A great deal on the history of the coal industry exists in 19th Century official records. On the supply side, the Reports and Evidence of the 1842 Childrens' Employment Commission and the associated Parliamentary and other debates (as well as those associated with the Inspection of Coal Mines (1850) and subsequent Coal Mines Acts (1872, 1908 and 1912) give a graphic record of the working environment and also insights into the competitive conditions facing the industry. On the demand side, perhaps the first references to energy conservation were by Lyon Playfair and the Frenchman, Jordan, who in the 1860s accused Britain of inefficiency and of neglecting coal economy. Old processes, it was felt, were kept going too long and fuel economies known on the Continent were not practised in Britain. This was brought out subsequently and more starkly in the Royal Commission on The Depression of Industry and Trade 1886. Energy use per capita seems to have reached its peak about 1880 in Great Britain.

ELECTRICITY

About this time, and following the introduction of electric lighting in Britain in 1875, Lord Kelvin and Dr John Hopkinson published works which many feel secured their positions as co-founders of electrical engineering economics: in 1881 Lord Kelvin enunciated his law of cables which, not only established the principles for selecting the effective cross sections to employ for transmitting a known and steady current through bore conductors, but also those for choosing an economic balance between capital expenditures and operating costs for such plant. The cost of the Conductor was shown to be directly proportional to the cross-section area and the cost of the energy loss in the cable inversely proportional to this. He also in

1882 lit Peterhouse College, Cambridge with electricity. In the same year Dr John Hopkinson started his advocacy of the two-part tariff with one part to pay for the fixed costs of supply and the other for the running costs. Shortly after this Arthur Wright, working in close conjunction with Hopkinson, developed a simple maximum reading ammeter with an inverse time lag which, on a given voltage, provided an assessment of the effective power demand. By 1909 as a result of Lord Kelvin's work, A.D.M. Fleming and K.M. Faye-Hansen were able to establish the economies of scale for commercial transformers of the shell and core types. In 1916 J.R. Beard did further work on the economics of transmission losses and size of transformers.

Despite such developments, and the fact that Michael Faraday had been the first to propound the principle of the modern dynamo or electric generator, Britain, in the 1880's and the next few decades lagged in the introduction of electricity as a source of power, heat and light. In 1886–8, for instance, when according to G. Ziani di Feranti and R. Ince, there was "hardly a city or town of 20,000 inhabitants in the United States which had not a central (generating) station", electricty companies were rare in Britain, although in London some pioneer companies were conducting critical experiments. The delay was in wholesale production and distribution, and according to Col. R.E. Crompton, due to the state of the law and the apathy or hostility of local authorities. The necessary private Bills were costly and expensive especially as stipulations were inserted in them about laying the mains underground and supplying the peak at any time. There was also, not surprisingly, hostility from the entrenched gas companies, many of which were municipally owned. Moreover, in spite of a small pump in operation in a Trafalgar pit in 1882 (see Dep. Com on Electricity in Mines 1904 (XXIV) Q 5002 (p. vol II. 109), electricity was thought of as light. The first two electricity Acts of Parliament in 1882 and 1888 were entitled Electric Lighting Acts.

These Acts both envisaged that electricity would be municipalised. Indeed, the 1882 Act enabled the local authority to enforce the sale of an electric company after 2 years, at the then market value, though in 1888 this period was doubled. Both Acts gave the local authorities the chance to oppose any electric project and gave them full control over transmission in the public interest and over the breaking up of streets and laying of cables. In contrast, in the USA such institutional controls were less severe.

GAS

Insights into the economics of the gas industry in its early years are few in number and at best patchy. The various Parliamentary Private Acts setting up the undertakings, such as that of the first undertaking, the Gas Light and Coke Company in 1912, provide glimpses of the economic philosophy, and how this changed as the industry developed, but there is little of real interest to the economist. The same applies to the Gaswork Clauses Acts 1847 and 1871. The economic rationale of the time, however, emerges through the nature of the gas legislation and how this has changed over the years.

In the early days Parliament granted to gas undertakings the powers required for their operations with little provision for corresponding obligations. In this period of laissez-faire it was expected that the public interest would be safeguarded by competition between gas undertakings in the *same* locality. The Private Acts provided that powers given to one gas undertaking should also be given to any other undertaking commencing operations in that area. Faith in the power of competition to protect gas consumers soon weakened as the market economies of scale were realised and as competition in one area after another was replaced by local monopoly. From then on Gas Acts began to embody clauses to protect the consumer against abuses. After 1840, Private Acts usually limited Gas Companies' dividends. The Clauses Act of 1847 standardised the limit to dividends at 10% per annum. The limitation on dividends in the Clauses Acts of 1847 was as high as a risky business. As the industry became better established, the limit on dividends was reduced to 7% on new capital. After 1845 the maximum dividend provisions usually had a clause to prescribe a maximum price for gas. As a check on abuse of monopoly in a period of falling costs, however, this was of limited value. Moreover, as the technique of gas-making improved and the scale of operations increased the prices fixed in the Acts bore less and less relation to costs. Hence in 1875 the 'Sliding Scale System' of price and dividend control made its appearance. This was introduced to meet a major defect of the maximum price and dividend regulation — that a well-established gas company, paying its maximum dividend had no economic incentive to reduce its price and increase efficiency. In place of a maximum price and a minimum dividend, the system provided a 'standard price and a 'standard' dividend but the dividend payable could be increased if the price fell below the 'standard' price. The 'Sliding Scale' was soon regarded as a valuable means of harmonising shareholders' and consumers' interests in a monopoly, and was accepted by most of the larger gas companies. Nevertheless, to make effective the control of the price of gas whether by the maximum price coupled with maximum dividends, or by a sliding scale, it was necessary to restrict the amount of capital issued as well as the undertakings' reserves. The provision of depreciation was not permitted since Parliament ruled that public utility undertakings should be maintained out of the current year's revenue. In these circumstances, new capital works, i.e. works representing development and not merely renewal of existing plant, had to be financed by new issues of capital, and with the statutory restriction on the undertakings' capital, the companies had to apply for further capital powers, thereby making it possible for Parliament to review periodically the companies' operations.

The consumer in addition to the risk of having to pay an excessive price for his gas, was liable to the risk of getting a poor service: the early Acts did not attempt to prescribe a minimum quality and pressure of gas. After 1850, however, Private Acts prescribed a standard of illuminating quality. The 1871 Clauses Act went much further. It prescribed quality, purity and pressure standards, as well as the administrative machinery for testing and enforcement. Parliament was also concerned lest monopoly gas undertakings refused to supply any potential consumers where the provision of service might not be profitable. As a result the obligation to supply was standardised by the Gasworks Clauses Act of 1871.

Although the 'Sliding Scale' was *initially* regarded as a highly satisfactory means of regulating the price of gas, it had grave defects: in periods of changes in the value of money, it permitted, and even compelled, changes in the dividends payable, regardless of the efficiency of management. In periods of falling cost, such as the last quarter of the 19th Century, this meant increased dividends to shareholders without any *extra* effort. In periods of rising cost, such as the first World War, it meant penalising the shareholders for cost increases quite independently of the quality of the management; in fact, the dividends of some companies on the 'sliding scale' fell to vanishing point during that War, so that it became necessary in 1918 to suspend Sliding Scale provisions. The Gas Regulation Act 1920 authorised the Board of Trade to fix new standard prices (as well as new maximum prices) to cover cost increases since 1914, but by then the 'Sliding Scale' had fallen into disfavour.

On the oil industry in Great Britain there is little to say, but it is salutary to recall that, in 1882, a learned American Journal stated that, on the evidence of estimated costs, it was clear that liquid fuels would never replace solid fuels in general use.

THE INTER-WAR YEARS

Largely as a result of Alfred Marshall's comprehensive and unifying book on the 'Principles of Economics', economic theory by the inter-war years developed into a disciplined academic subject. Moreover, a nucleus of energy economics was in existence for each of the main fuels in use.

Thereafter a host of issues in the field of energy economics were opened up for discussion. These included the development of coal cartels, problems of exhausted pits and rationalisation schemes, impacts of technological change and of inter-fuel substitution of oil for coal in marine bunkers, development of the electricity transmission grid and the plight, over a century before, of the technologically-redundant charcoal producers of the Sussex Weald. These, and similar issues, deeply concerned a whole range of eminent men including Sir John Clapham, H.S. Jevons, Sargent G.D.H. Cole, Lord Sankey, Viscount Samuel, Prof. Cannan and Sir William Beveridge as well as others whose names may now be known only more narrowly in energy circles, such as R.A.S. Redmayne, D.J. Williams, R.C. Smart, J.W.F. Rowe, R.W. Dron, I. Lubin and H. Everett, D.H. Macgregor, J.U. Nef, J.H. Jones and J.R. Bellerby — names which reflect either the applied academic economist or operators in the coal and other energy industries with very evident interest in energy economics.

Even so, the amount of analysis was meagre: much of the work was either historical, partial, or at best descriptive. This was partly a reflection of the more limited staffing and other expenditures of universities in those days; partly a reflection of the newness of economics as an academic discipline, and partly a reflection of the very limited statistical data availability for economists to analyse. Generally, however, the fashionable thing to be in the academic world in this period was to be an economic historian, not an economist or, indeed, if one really had to be an economist, it was more acceptable to be a theoretician not an applied economist equipped with numerical techniques in the energy field. It was only slowly being recognised, to quote Lord Kelvin, that 'If you cannot measure something, and cannot express it in numbers, your knowledge is of a meagre and unsatisfactory kind'. This deficiency was progressively improved in the inter-war years.

COAL INDUSTRY

Statistics of the coal industry were better than for other industries. Apart from the Reports of, and Evidence, to the various Royal Commissions on the coal industry and particularly the 1871 Coal Commission, statistical data became available. Notably, Richard Price-Williams made original and interesting estimates in his 1889 paper to the Royal Statistical Society entitled *The Coal Question*. Certain other descriptive works such as R. Reade's *The Coal and Iron Industries of the United Kingdom* (1882) helped to fill statistical gaps as did Ashton & Sykes *The Coal Industry in the Eighteenth Century* (1929) and J.U. Nef's *The Rise of the British Coal Industry* (1932). Elizabeth Schumpeter's study of English prices (1938) gave estimates of the values of coal exports from 1660 to 1822. Rising above all these, however, was Sir John Clapham's monumental work *An Economic History of Modern Britain* which, published in 1932, contained *inter alia* estimates of the coal trade from the Battle of Waterloo onwards. The First Annual Report of the Secretary of Mines and the Annual Report of HM Chief Inspector of Mines in 1921 provided the basic statistical source material for coal and by then could be supplemented by data from such respected authorities as *Iron and Coal Trades Review*, the *Colliery Guardian*, *O'Connell's Coal and Iron News* and *The Colliery Year Book*. *The Monthly Statistical Review of the Coal Industry*, published by the Mining Association of Great Britain from January 1925 onwards, also provided a wealth of statistical data for the energy economist to analyse. There was, thereafter, therefore no shortage of statistical data on coal.

Essential official reading for those interested in those days also largely centred on coal: foremost among these were the two Royal Commissions on the Coal Industry by Sankey (1919) and by Samuel (1925), the Coal Mines Reorganisation Commission Reports, League of Nations Memoranda on Coal, the Report of the Committee on Co-operative Selling in the Coal Industry (1926) and the Report of the British Coal Delegation to Sweden, Norway and Denmark (1929) — with the latter two both published by the Mines Department. The International Labour Office's *Hours of Work in Coal Mines* 1930, the PEP report on *The British Coal Industry* (1936) and a publication by J.H. Jones, G.G. Cartwright and P.H. Guenault in 1939 entitled *The Coal Industry, an International Study in Planning* were all interesting reading. Indeed, the economic history of the coal industry between 1919 and 1939 surely represents one of the most fascinating studies of economic/political relationships of any sector of the UK economy in any period of time. To the extent that history reveals lessons, this period provided a complete education course.

In contrast, very little was known about the economics of coal distribution in this period. In *The Distribution of Consumer Goods* by James Jeffries (NIESR), however, the gross margins for coal were estimated for 1938 to be 3.5% for wholesalers and 27% for retailers. The wholesalers' gross margin was the lowest of the 25 trades analysed, though that of the retailers was close to the average of all trades.

ELECTRICITY

Outside the coal industry, the bookshelf was in the main very bare. The Annual Reports of the Electricity Commissioners started in 1921 but, in themselves, provided little of interest to the economist. By 1933, however, the Electricity Commission on Electricity Supply published the *Return of Engineering and Financial Statistics relating to Authorised Undertakings and for Company Undertakings* and a wealth of interesting material became available for economic analysis for the first time. The only official publications of note to energy economists were the Weir Report 1925, and the (McGowan) Report to the Committee on Electricity Distribution (1936) issued, it should be noted, by the Ministry of Transport. There was also the PEP Report on *The Supply of Electricity in Great Britain* 1936. These reports led to the formation of the British Electricity Authority and the construction of a national electricity transmission system.

There was one area of energy economics, however, in which debate abounded: this was the field of electricity tariffs. The quest for the 'ideal' commercial electricity tariff was pursued with almost the same vigour as that for the Holy Grail eight centuries earlier. Everyone with a pretension of being someone in the electricity industry (and there were some 600 electricity undertakings each with senior executives) sooner or later proudly presented his concept of the ideal electricity tariff. As a result, the journals and proceedings of the (British) Electrical Research Association, of the Electrical Development Association and of the Institution of Electrical Engineers in this period were full of debate on this subject, though in most of the debate economic principles of resource allocation received scant attention. Indeed, many of the tariffs were designed uninhibitedly to recoup what the traffic would bear. The merits and demerits of all-in-tariffs, block tariffs, loadrate tariffs, off-peak tariffs, step tariffs, time-of-day two-rate tariffs, and variable-rate tariffs were hotly debated with each enterprise entering the fray to expound *how* they fixed tariffs, rather than discussing in any depth the underlying economic principles. So it was that the protagonists of the Glasgow, Oxford, Derby, Halifax tariffs did battle on such issues to prove their municipal virility.

D.J. Bolton requires special mention for his contribution. In 1928 he published *Electrical Engineering Economics* which dealt with the supply side of the industry and subsequently in 1938 *Costs and Tariffs in Electricity Supply*. These two books were subsequently revised and re-edited in 1951 and entitled *Electrical Engineering Economics* Volumes I and II (1950). They pulled together all the economic analyses that had taken place in the industry up to the dates of his original publications. The former dealt with production functions for the generation and the transmission parts of the electricity supply industry and with investment choice. It extended the analysis of the economics of transformer and transmission selection with special attention to those of the under-capacity running of electrical plant. Unfortunately, in places some irrelevant accounting considerations (e.g. concerning the choise of depreciation policy) obscured the economic analysis. It also considered the economics of voltage-dropping as explained by F.S. Naylor in 1936. The latter volume dealt with tariff theory, costs, bulk tariffs, consumer load patterns, power factors and retail tariffs. Whilst much of it was very detailed, it represented a most convenient bringing together and assessment of the considerable body of papers on electricity which had been written throughout the inter-war period in the technical journals. The contributions of such practical electrical supply economists as E.V. Woodward, W.A. Carne, Prof. Miles Walker, J.A. Sumner, P. Schiller, E.V. Clark, Punga, Lauriol and Green were all considered and, whilst much of their analysis would now be regarded as faulty in that it was, in the main, aimed at pricing geared to 'what the traffic would bear', we have to remember that they were employed as electrical engineers or commercial officers in privately owned public utilities with very different objective functions from their counterparts today. Moreover, they did not have the inestimable benefit of having read Prof. W. Arthur Lewis's *Overhead Costs* (1919) let alone Ralph Turvey!

GAS

The most marked information deficiency, however, was in

the field of gas for, apart from the PEP Report on *The Gas Industry in Great Britain* (1939), there was little of note. Nevertheless, there were some developments which reflected changed views on the 'desirable' economic performance of the industry. In 1920, the South Metropolitan Gas Company obtained an Act containing a new system of price control, known as 'the Basic Price System'. Broadly the differences from the 'Sliding Scale' were three-fold:

(i) it provided for a basic dividend which was also a minimum dividend, not *reducible* when prices to consumers were increased;
(ii) an incentive payment of extra dividend to shareholders was provided for and determined by the difference between the total revenue collected from consumers and what the consumers would have paid if they had all been charged for their gas at the basic price;
(iii) the Act required that as much money must be transferred to the employees through co-partnership schemes, bonuses, etc., as was paid in extra dividends to shareholders. (Under most 'Basic Price' Acts, one sixth of the difference between the actual and the hypothetical basic gas revenues could be transferred to each of the two interests — shareholders and employees.)

The 'Basic Price' system, however, was never embodied in *general* legislation, but it became increasingly popular. In 1938 more than half the gas in the United Kingdom was supplied under it. Its main merit was that it helped the sale of gas for heating, especially to industry, at the substantial economically-justified discounts necessary to allow gas to compete with other fuels. (Before 1920, in contrast, and in consequence of the effects of the Maximum Price and Sliding Scale Systems, it was the general practice for gas to be sold at the *flat* rate.) Thus the marked development of the industrial use of gas in the '20s and '30s was largely due to this more flexible basic price system. In 1945 155 statutory gas companies operated under the Maximum Price and Dividend system, 200 under the Sliding Scale system and 50, including most of the larger companies, under the Basic Price system.

The Gas Regulation Act, 1920, directly introduced the thermal basis of charge and adjusted maximum and standard prices, imposing obligations concerning calorific value, pressure and purity. It tried to ensure that consumers would not be overcharged through calorific value deficiency. Nevertheless between 1920 and 1929, it was becoming clear that if the development of the Industry was to continue, it should be given a substantially greater measure of freedom — hence the Gas Undertakings Acts of 1929, 1932 and 1934. The main provisions of the Act of 1929 enabled gas companies to obtain power by Departmental order of the Board of Trade (instead of by new authority of Parliament) to increase the authorised amount of their share or loan capital, and to borrow within certain limits without the necessity for any order. That Act also provided that all statutory undertakings with annual sales exceeding 20 million cubic feet should charge for gas on the thermal basis.

The provisions included:

(i) the compulsory imposition of statutory powers and obligations on non-statutory undertakings whose annual sales exceeded 30 million cubic feet;

(ii) the imposition of an obligation on non-statutory undertakings supplying more than 20 million cubic feet a year, and all statutory undertakings not selling gas on the thermal basis, to supply gas free from sulphuretted hydrogen, and the requirement that all undertakings should supply the gas at a pressure similar to that required in the case of statutory undertaking.

GENERAL ENERGY

Some important contributions to energy economics in these years were made which led to important developments many years later: firstly, H. Hotelling in 1931 published 'The Economics of Exhaustible Resources' in the *Journal of Political Economy*; secondly, R.G.D. Allen and A.L. Bowley in 1935 made the first assessments of the income elasticity of demand for fuel and light in *Family Expenditure*. This analysed the results of 23 budget surveys carried out between 1914 and 1929 in the UK, Europe and USA. Their study of family budgets, by the use of Engel curve cross-sectional analysis, provided the base for the subsequent development of many of the econometric techniques used in the analysis of consumer demand today. They were able to draw upon only three UK budget studies. The first was a study of clerks in English towns in 1926; the second, of Liverpool workers in 1929; and the third a London School of Economics study of all classes in 1932. The estimates of the income elasticity of demand for fuel and light which emerged from these studies were 0.5, 0.8 and 0.5.

There was one publication, however, which whilst not in the field of energy economics, had a profound effect on the economics of energy later after the Second World War. This was Mr Herbert Morrison's *Socialisation and Transport* published in 1933. It expounded the Morrisonian ideal of independent public corporations — 'a public corporation gives us the best of both worlds' for with it 'we can combine progressive business management with a proper degree of public accountability'. It became the model for later nationalisation.

Chapter 21

Energy Economics 1940–1960

Eric Price

During the Second World War energy economics was held at bay: the debate, to the extent that it existed at all, was concerned with the merits and demerits of energy rationing and of control systems (cf. *Fuel Rationing* by Sir William Beveridge, Report to the Board of Trade, HMSO 1942). Moreover, towards the end of that war, Planning for Peace became the fashionable issue. In the field of energy the Egerton Report on *The Heating and Ventilation of Dwellings*, HMSO 1945 was the key document. In neither of these reports were market mechanisms significant features; and, of course, the shadow price economics of Marxist economies were by then not sufficiently developed to be systematically used in the allocation systems. Indeed, one is tempted to conclude that the main constraint on the almost total rejection of the market mechanism was the shortage, because of *other* important events, of officials to administer the control allocation systems. Moreover the statistical techniques of queuing theory were only just being developed! One of the fascinating things about the 1945 Egerton Report (indeed perhaps its only claim to fame) is that it contained the first estimate in the UK of the external diseconomies of pollution. It estimated the resource costs of smoke, ash and sulphur dioxide discharged into the atmosphere by electricity generated from coal at £45 million per annum at prices then current.

The transition from war to peace was expected to be a difficult one. Could the demobilisation of the Services' personnel be achieved without unemployment? Would there be a return to the unemployment levels of the inter-war period? William Beveridge's study of *Full Employment in a Free Society* (1944) addressed this problem. Against the background of a dramatic fall in demand for coal in the inter-war years which had been 'accompanied by a catastrophic increase in unemployment' (the number in employment in the coal industry fell from 1.07 million in 1929 to 0.86 million in 1937), Beveridge paid special attention to coalmining industry because of its proneness to frictional unemployment viz. 'Coal mining stands apart from other industries and men do not leave it readily'. As an economist this appreciation of the problem, however, was hardly matched by his prescription of a remedy:

> 'It is clear, that the direct way of maintaining any desired level of employment in mining is by guaranteeing a demand up to that (production) level, that it to say, a market and price. For that purpose alone, nationalisation of production is unnecessary, as nationalisation is unnecessary for the purpose of guaranteeing a market and price for the fruits of agriculture. On the other hand, even with nationalisation, the problem of marketing the output remains. Socialisation of demand for staples like coal is wanted in any case, with or without socialisation of production. The executive departments should include accordingly, in any case, a Coal Marketing Corporation, which would place orders for coal for six months or a year ahead sufficient to employ the desired total of men in the industry. If the Corporation found difficulty in disposing of that quantity of coal, it would cut down its order for the future, while steps would be taken to reduce the supply of labour. If the Corporation found demand tending to outrun output, it might increase its orders. Management of demand for coal in this way presents practical problems. But they are problems which have to be solved on any assumption as to how the production of coal is organised.'

This heralded in a period in which the centre of the energy stage was occupied with debate concerning ownership and organisation — at least for those who were not actively involved in overcoming the physical shortages.

THE EARLY POST-WAR YEARS

Since the ownership and organisation of resources are valid subjects for economists, this historical perspective cannot entirely ignore the debate after the War concerning the public ownership of the energy industries. The relevance of that debate to this perspective rests partly in the role that economists played in it, partly in their opportunity cost in terms of the other important issues to which they could have contributed, and partly in the resulting institutional, and structural statutory framework of the nationalised industries, which was determined then, and which has influenced energy policy up to the present time.

In the early post-war years the field for debate on the form and organisation of public-ownership was very wide. Although Herbert Morrison had produced an outline for public corporations in 1931, there had been very little real discussion on their organisation, accountability, objectives, or relationships with ministers and almost no consideration of efficiency issues, investment criteria or pricing policy, let alone of performance monitoring. In fact, very little had really been written on the subject after Sydney Webb's 1918 pamphlet *Labour and the New Social Order.* Added to this some of the dialogue of the inter-war years was in retrospect rather curious: see Beatrice Webb's *Diaries* in which Arthur Henderson is stated to have asked 'Why should (only) the miners and the railway men have the privilege of being socialised'?

The problem of reconciling public ownership theory and practice fell on the post-war Ministers. They had to supervise Bills being drawn up not only to transfer the ownership to the State with compensation, but also laying down how the industry should be managed and by whom. See, for instance, Mr Emmanuel Shinwell, who, in his book *Conflict without Malice*, commented 'Now, as Minister of Fuel and Power, I found that nothing practical and tangible regarding the policy to be pursued existed. There were some pamphlets, some memoranda produced for private circulation, and nothing else. I had to start with a clear desk.'

That desk rapidly became burdened down with contributions from economists and others. Notable among these in the energy field were H.A. Clegg, T.E. Chester, G.D.H. Cole, G. Ardent, R.D. Best, F. Cassell, R.S. Edwards, Sir Charles Reid, B.C. and C.A. Roberts, A.H. Hanson, Sir Norman Chester, R. Kelf-Cohen and William Robson to name but a few. Many aspects were covered but analytical discussion on pricing policy, investment criteria, and performance monitoring was sparse and left a great deal to be desired. Subsequently, numerous official reports and contributions in learned journals over the next two decades made good this deficiency, but it is tempting to speculate how different the energy sector would have been today had such issues been resolved satisfactorily at the outset.

The early post-war years were also ones of damaging fuel supply and capacity shortages. This was particularly so for coal, and for generating capacity during seasonal peaks. In these conditions, operators and engineers were dominant. In contrast, those who propounded market solutions to the problems and advocated economic analysis were kept beyond the pale — at least until the '50s. For in those days the co-ordination of supply and demand in the energy sector was seen almost exclusively in physical terms, related to a layman's concept of 'needs' rather than to 'effective demand'. The overwhelming 'need' then was clear, namely to increase supply as fast as possible. Coal was still allocated, the gas industry was still coal-based, and all oil was imported. Under Lord Citrine a crash programme of constructing 30 MW and 60 MW generating sets was embarked upon with electricity demand regulated by the rate of new connections and by power cuts, particularly during the Energy Crisis of 1947 which restrained industrial output. That investment analysis, resource efficiency assessments, and optimal pricing policy could have played a part in solving these problems was recognised by very few, and economists who seriously proposed greater emphasis on such approaches to the problem, and there were some, were laughed out of court by technical experts who *knew* their industry. As a result a number of policies were pursued with vigour without proper consideration of the alternatives, e.g. rural electrification. So it was that, as a result of low energy price policies, income not spent on higher energy prices was diverted to other goods and services, though due to rationing and physical shortages and the narrow range of standardised 'Utility' consumer durable goods available, much of this disposable income spilled over into railway travel, speedway, football, greyhound racing and cinema attendance. Moreover, in this situation, energy demand forecasting was bedevilled by an extra factor, namely, the extent of unsatisfied or 'frustrated' demand in the historical consumption data.

Thus, apart from the very largely physically-based studies, such as E.C. Rhodes' paper in *Economica* in 1945, 'Output, Labour and Machines in the Coal Mining Industry in Great Britain', and those of the Anglo-American Productivity Teams (one of which considered the Electricity Supply Industry in almost exclusively physical terms, reaching the illuminating conclusion that the circumstances in both countries were different), economists concerned themselves either with nationalisation issues or, alternatively, with the organisation of energy industries. There were, of course, inevitably, a considerable number of technical efficiency studies and sample surveys but very little work covered what most of us today would regard as valid subject matter of energy economics. The HMSO publication *The Efficient Use of Steam* written by O. Lyle is an exception to this generalisation as is the 1947 PEP Report on *British Fuel and Power Industries.* The former was intended for the use of students and technical men in industry and covered 'both the fundamental principles and the essential operative features necessary to attain immediate results'. Its aim was to achieve 'the efficient use of our greatest mineral asset'.

Important published documents which held the centre of the stage in those early post-war days included the (Reid) *Report of the Technical Advisory Committee on Coal Mining* (1945), The (Heyworth) *Report of the Committee of Enquiry into the Gas Industry* (1945), the Simon *Report on Domestic Fuel Policy* (1946), the Clow *Report of the Committees to Study the Electricity Peak Problem in Relation to Non-Industrial Consumers* (1948), *Plan for Coal*, NCB (1950), the Ridley *Report of the Committee on National Policy for the Use of Fuel and Power Resources* (1952), the Fleck *Report on the Organisation of the Coal Industry* (1953) and the Herbert *Report of Committee of Inquiry into the Electricity Supply Industry* (1955). Many of these reports still make worthwhile reading. Many of the problems remain today, albeit in a different guise.

The post-war years were also ones in which labour relations took on a new and increasing importance; hence economists and other social scientsts sought to study issues of the relationships between morale and output rather more analytically or statistically than previously. The Action Society Trust, for instance, in its *Size and Morale: A Preliminary Study of Attendance in Large and Small Units* (1953), reported the results of a study of the relationship between absenteeism, accident rates and the size of pits in the British coal industry and concluded 'Not only was lost-time found to increase with size but it was also established that, when similar geological conditions were being worked, output per man-shift tended to be no higher, and was, in fact, often appreciably lower, in large pits than in small'. Interestingly, E.F. Schumacher the originator of the 'small is beautiful' concept was Chief Economist to the National Coal Board at that time.

Perhaps the most notable, indeed seminal, published work in the field of energy economics in this period was Paul Frankel's *Essentials of Petroleum: A Key to Oil Economics*, published in 1946. This represented the clearest exposition of the issues in the oil industry up to that date.

THE FIFTIES

The blend of the academics and of businessmen in energy economics, so evident in the inter-war period, was also present in the period after the Second World War and into the fifties. The names of H.S. Houthakker, Sir Ernest Simon, Sir Norman Chester, S.R. Dennison, Lord Citrine, Sir Charles Reid, Sir William Hawthorne, I.M.D. Little, E.F. Schumacher, Lord Fleck, Viscount Ridley, Lord Heyworth, H.A. Clegg, Sir Henry Self, R. Kelf-Cohen, Prof. Arthur Lewis, Sir Andrew Clow, Duncan Burn, Elwyn Jones, Sir Goronwy Daniel, Paul Frankel, William Robson, Clive Dalton and Ronald George stand out as predominant in the dialogue of this period. As time passed however, the range of energy issues discussed became wider: hence forecasting of energy demand and supplies, inflation of energy prices during the Korean War, economics of pit closures, price of coal imports, energy pricing policies, efficiency of the energy industries and, finally, both the economics of nuclear power and the disruption of oil supplies (post-Suez) entered into the centre of the energy debate. The predominant theme of the '50s, however, concerned the future 'Energy Gap'. This featured very prominently in the speeches of the late Sir Reginald Maudling, then Minister of Fuel and Power. Indeed, a key landmark in energy policy during this period was the paper given to the Royal Statistical Society by Sir Goronwy Daniel, Chief Statistician at the Ministry of Fuel and Power, on long-term energy forecasts. This led to a host of energy forecasts by other experts. Apart from this, the most authoritative economic work in the energy field was H.S. Houthakker's 'Some Calculations on Electricity Consumption in Great Britain' published in the *Journal of the Royal Statistical Society* in 1951.

Much of the debate, however, was set against a very different backcloth from today: the United Kingdom economy was growing fairly steadily if not rapidly. All the expectations were that it would continue to do so. There was almost an air of inevitability about it. Had not Keynes solved the unemployment problem and provided a new and continuing confidence in growth? The dark ages of the Depression of the inter-war period were gone — supposedly for ever. Such was progress. Coupled with this expectation of growth in national income, was the corollary of growth of energy demand. The debate largely centred on the size of the so-called 'energy co-efficient' (the relationship between growth in energy usage and that of the Gross Domestic Product) and on the economics of solutions for filling the 'Energy Gap'. Electricity consumption, along with that of oil, was the most buoyant sector, and electrical engineers were obviously the people who knew about such matters, forecast electricity growth, a subject they found very undemanding quite simply by projecting it logistically at 7 per cent cumulatively per annum. (Hadn't past experience amply shown that this was the trend?) At the opening of the '50s, the impact of price variables and of changes in the structure of the economy or of the manufacturing sector played little or no part in such forecasts. As will be appreciated since prices had increased smoothly with demand and incomes, the price effects in econometric studies tended to be swamped by income effects. Obviously, it was argued, price was unimportant. By contrast with electricity, gas (town gas as it was in those days) was seen as a relatively declining industry (even though it was still expanding at some ½ per cent per annum). It hardly interested the few energy economists in the UK, except perhaps in terms of how fast its relative market share would decline.

Much of the thinking in the '50s regarding the choice of fuel supplies was 'Energy Gap' orientated. It was not seen as a choice between the investment alternatives measured in terms of the economic or financial returns so much as where sufficient energy supplies to meet the projected levels of demand could come from. Thus, the decision to use nuclear power for generation of electricity in 1955 was taken at a time when coal was in short supply, and was thought likely to remain so for some considerable time. The intention, as set out in the White Paper *A Programme of Nuclear Power* (Cmnd 9389), was to provide 1500/2000 MW of installed nuclear power by 1965 but in early 1957, following the Suez War, the programme was trebled to a target of some 5000/6000 MW over the same period. At the time very little economic analysis took place concerning the choice. Few, if any, asked whether coal was appropriately priced, or considered analytically the probable values of the price elasticities of the demand and supply of energy forms. The scope for coal imports was dismissed as politically impracticable. The UK was within the Bretton Woods fixed exchange rate regime and energy deficits were reflected in the UK's Balance of Payments deficits on Current Account. Moreover the latter was seen at the time as the main constraint on the growth of GDP. Even so, some economists and others were already calling into question the basic decisions. It was, however, not until David Henderson produced his analysis in the following decade that a full economic appreciation of that nuclear policy was published.

The fifties, however, started with a renewed belief in the doctrine of economic liberalism. The practical expression of this was reflected after 1951 by a spectacular burst of decontrol, the scrapping of rationing and a conscious quest for optimal micro-policies in industrial sectors, and particularly in the nationalised energy sector. In this market-orientated context, it was natural that the other big issue in the early '50s should be how energy in its various forms should be priced. The Ridley Committee set up in 1951 by the Rt Hon. Geoffrey Lloyd MP as Minister of Fuel and Power had the following terms of reference:

> 'In view of the growing demands for all forms of fuel and power arising from full employment and the re-armament programme, to consider whether any further steps can be taken to promote the best use of our fuel and power resources, having regard to present and prospective requirements and in the light of technical developments.'

The Ridley Report was important because it represented the first significant post-war recognition of the role that *prices and costs* could play in the co-ordination of energy policy. Most interesting, from the energy economist point of view, however, was the technical debate it started as between those 'practical' men who supported *average* cost pricing of energy and those (mainly economists) who supported *marginal* cost pricing. In the Ridley Committee four members were for marginal cost pricing and four for average cost pricing. The Chairman, Viscount Ridley, however, gave his vote for the latter; and hence those who supported marginal cost pricing had to be content with having their case for marginal cost pricing set out in their Minority Report at the end. The Report was an important landmark in the history of energy pricing issues. Thereafter such issues became accepted as relevant to energy policy: see I.M.D. Little's *The Price of Fuel* (1953) and Stanley Dennison's attack on the NCB's average cost pricing, with zonal discriminations and its alleged inflexibility to changing prices as demand and supply conditions change ('The Price Policy of the NCB' in *Lloyds Bank Review* (1952)). Both ensured that the energy pricing debate was kept alive.

Questions concerning how one defined marginal cost pricing precisely in a practical situation (such as in the electricity supply industry), however, had to wait for another decade when notably Ralph Turvey and Michael Posner proved that it could be converted into prices and tariffs in the real world. Yet prior to Prof. Sir Ronald Edward's appointment as Chairman at the Electricity Council, the environment in which such energy economists operated could hardly have been less conducive to the economic viewpoint. Had the BIEE existed in those days the debates between the 'academic' members of the Institute and those of its members in energy industries trained in other professions and disciplines would have been fierce, interminable and complex with reverberations throughout the corridors of Chatham House. Indeed, it is just possible that the BIEE Chairman would have been taken to one side and the suggestion dropped that the BIEE was no longer to be welcomed! Yet as a result of this debate, some energy tariffs, notably those of electricity came to be approximately long-run marginal-cost based.

In retrospect, the fact that price elasticities of demand had hitherto played so small a part in the policy debate is not all that surprising: quite apart from an inbuilt resistance to the role of prices in the energy industries at that time, there was a very practical point: very little was known about the size of these elasticities.

Measurement in economics was still in its infancy and, indeed, it was not until the works of H.S. Houthakker and Richard Stone that any price and income elasticities for fuel and light and or any cross-elasticities were available. H.S. Houthakker in 1951 developed a model with the appliance stock as an exogenous variable, and lagged price variables. His aim was to establish the relationship between domestic electricity consumption per consumer, the number of electricity consumers, the average installed load, household post-tax income, the marginal price of electricity, and the marginal price of gas. He considered two-part tariffs only, on which the same marginal rate applied to all consumers in a given town irrespective of their consumption. Thus it was acceptable to use this marginal rate as the electricity price variable. A similar marginal rate was selected for the gas price. Since the marginal rate was independent of the quantity demanded in the short-run, it was not necessary to introduce a function defining the tariff to obtain consistent estimators. He did not include any long-run data, and supply was independent of the variables included in the equation. He estimated his equation from a cross-section of 42 towns in Great Britain in 1937-38. Houthakker went on to analyse a monthly series for total electricity generated 1927-44. The two main findings for domestic consumption were: the monthly pattern was almost entirely explained by two variables — hours of daylight and temperature; the sensitivity to temperature changes differed from month to month suggesting a curvilinear relationship with high sensitivity at winter temperatures but negligible sensitivity at summer temperatures.

Richard Stone (1954) in his *The Measurement of Consumers' Expenditure and Behaviour in the UK 1920-1938* developed simple static models of household demand for electricity from cross-section and time-series data based on the classical theory of consumers' behaviour with each consumer maximising his utility subject to a budget constraint. On conventional assumptions about consumers' preferences, the quantity the consumer demanded of each good (including fuel and light) was expressed as a function of prices and income. There were certain implied restrictions on the coefficients of these demand functions. Richard Stone, however, included certain natural and household needs variables. Subsequently, with D.A. Rowe, he extended his model in 1958 to allow for dynamic adjustment equilibria with discrete time periods and testing, in the process, a variable indicating the daily mean hours of sunshine. The result for fuel and light did not compare favourably either with those obtained for other goods, especially durable consumer goods or with his 1954 results for fuel and light from his static model.

After the mid-50s, economists in the energy field were allowed step by step to study a host of other issues. Within the nationalised public sector, in addition to pricing and forecasting studies, they carried out investment appraisals of new plant, cost minimisation transport studies, sourcing evaluations, optimal stocking policies, and appraisal studies of new technologies (such as nuclear choice); in the private sector, the scope of their studies was similar, but extended to areas more of a commercial nature, for instance, relating directly to companies' market shares in individual product markets.

This explosion of interest in the economics of energy stemmed from a number of factors; partly, it was a reflection of the general expansion in the number of academics reflecting university growth: partly it was a maturing of economics as a subject with establishment of theoretical tools and techniques: partly, it was the result of a greatly improved data-base on which to work in the energy field. Indeed, the Ministry of Fuel and Power's Survey of Steam and Power of 1953 provided a superior data base for the industrial sector than has existed since. The Reports of the various nationalised industries were making information available in the public domaine which had either not existed before or which had not hitherto been assembled in convenient forms. The statistical data base continued to improve: the scope and content of the statistical sources available on energy in the post-war period can be guaged from M G Kendall's *Sources and Nature of Statistics of the United Kingdom* Vols I and II published in 1952. This contains comprehensive statements of what was available by Ronald George, on 'Coal Mining Statistics' Goronwy Daniel on 'Electricity and Gas Statistics' and A.L. Kind on 'Petroleum Statistics'. (It was not until 1980, incidentally, that an update of these statistical sources was available in *Reviews of United Kingdom*

Statistical Sources Vol. XI with a Coal Statistics section by D.J. Harris, a Gas Statistics section by H. Nabb and an Electricity Statistics section by D. Nuttall.)

THE OIL INDUSTRY

As far as oil was concerned, the issues debated by energy economists in the '50s were rather different from those today: of course, the security of Middle East oil was in the forefront of people's minds with British military strategic involvement in the area being regarded primarily as a protection of the vital and valuable oil investments there. The economic issues, however, were largely focussed on the financial implications of the 'intrusion' of American oil companies into the Middle East, (as evidenced by the ARAMCO concessions in Saudi Arabia) and the disadvantageous position of UK oil companies *vis-à-vis* those supported by the world's strongest country. Energy economists were very concerned in preserving the UK's very substantial net foreign earnings from oil, and, to this end, in retaining the fifty-fifty profit sharing arrangement with sheiks in the area on the basis of 'posted prices'. The central question was how long the fifty/fifty profit sharing arrangements could last. There was a presumption that by yielding up the fifty/fifty basis reluctantly, eventually, and under pressure, expropriation could be avoided.

The other topic of economic debate in the oil sector concerned the magnitude of Britain's foreign earnings from oil. Although it represented the biggest single source from any foreign investment it was hidden away in the 'residual' item in official Balance of Payments statistics on the Current Account along with earnings from insurance, civil aviation, royalties, commissions and film rights. Indeed, when the oil earnings finally emerged to public gaze in the 1954 National Income Blue Book, they were seen to represent nearly two-thirds of net income from British overseas investment.

One of the first economists to be concerned with the economics of Middle East oil was Edith Penrose. In 1959 in a study of *Profit Sharing Between Producing Countries and Oil Companies in the Middle East* she analysed the underlying considerations determining the sharing of oil revenues between oil companies and producing countries and investigated the meaning of economic 'exploitation' in this context. She also examined the possibility of concerted action by all Middle East oil-producing countries to remove their bargaining weaknesses. Her conclusions are of more than academic interest today:

> 'Apart from the very real difficulties in obtaining such unity between countries whose national interests with respect to oil production differ substantially in many respects, this argument has substantial validity in the short-run; a single producing country is obviously more vulnerable than the group combined. But even for the group as a whole there is a considerable risk in relying on the effectiveness of joint action, for though Middle East oil is low cost, fear on the part of consuming countries of political instability or of extreme dependence on the whims of Middle East governments would intensify the development, not only of new sources of oil, but also of substitutes for oil . . . producing countries would do well to remember that world conditions can change rapidly in times of crisis.'

Tibor Barna in 1955 was the first person to establish the replacement cost of fixed capital assets in British manufacturing by means of examining five insurance declared values. One result of his study published in 1957 was that the massive capital-intensity of mineral oil refining came to be more generally appreciated by economists. At £13,350 per worker employed it was shown at that time to be over seven-fold that of manufacturing as a whole and even 2½ times that of chemicals. The debate that followed was centred on both the high concentration ratios in mineral oil refining and the high physical labour productivity increases in the post-war period in this industry.Tibor Barra's work, however, also led to the study by Philip Redfern which produced capital consumption estimates on a real replacement basis for UK industries including, of course, energy industries.

Within the oil industry, there was a great deal of economic analysis but, whilst the conclusions were widely publicised, the number of complete analytical studies published was remarkably few. J.S. Cramer in 'Private Motoring and the Demand for Petrol', *Royal Statistical Society* (1959), analysed private expenditure on petrol and oil in two household budget surveys in 1953–4. He produced a static model in his analysis of the demand for petrol and oil from private motorists, essentially based on the view that 'the structure of demand was determined by the fact that non-motorists cannot consume petrol, while motorists are to some extent compelled to do so'. Three assumptions had to be made to apply the model to the explanation of variations in fuel expenditure between income classes (using only information on the proportion of households in each class having the use of a motor vehicle and their fuel expenditure made). These were for each household — (a) its expenditure on motor fuel in terms of its income, (b) a 'tolerance' income and (c) a minimum consumption level for motor fuel. If their income was above the 'tolerance' level determined they had a car, if they had a car they had a minimum fuel consumption level and the extent of their actual purchase above this depended on the relationship between actual and 'tolerance' incomes. The model embodied the hypotheses (i) that a given variation in the proportion of households using motor vehicles was associated with different changes in fuel demand, depending on whether it was due to changes in tastes, as represented by tolerance incomes, or in income; and (ii) that marginal motorist households had below average demand. Cramer found support for these hypotheses in the slow growth of mean consumption per motorist household over the period 1950-57. He concluded that at that time the further rise of private petrol consumption depended on an increasing number of vehicles in the future rather than their more intensive use per car.

Robert S. Nielsen's *Oil Tanker Economics* Bremen: Weltschiff-fahrts Archia, 1959, together with Clive Dalton's work on the 'Economics of Oil Tankers', both led to a great debate in public on this topic. Discussions about economies of scale did not happen to the same extent in other energy sectors though some discussion took place.

THE GAS INDUSTRY

The Gas Council's assessment of the economies of scale of low pressure gas spirally-guided storage systems of different capacities carried out in the '50s indicated how the capital costs varied from 10 thousand cubic feet storage containers all the way up to 5000 thousand cubic feet containers. Yet they only came to light because some academics (in this case Ronald Edwards and Harry Townsend) happened to be interested in such economies of scale and wrote to the Gas Council. Similarly, a great amount of information exists in the pages of various learned societies specialising in the energy field. Typical of the latter was the paper given by T. Nicklin and M. Redman entitled 'The Economics of Gas Production' given to the Manchester and District Section of the Institution of Gas Engineers in December 1951. This led to a fascinating PhD thesis on 'Some Technological and Economic Problems of the Gas Industry' by Dr B.H. Wormsley, University of London, 1954, a thesis which, *inter alia*, showed the economies of scale for different rates of output which would arise from different types of plant, namely horizontal retorts, international vertical chambers and continuous vertical retorts. It provided a clear insight into the economics of the town gas industry as it then was. In the electricity field, R.N. Berry's *Economics of High-Voltage Transmission by Underground Cables* was an important study.

THE COAL INDUSTRY

In retrospect and considering its problems then as a declining industry, it is remarkable that so few economists in the '50s or '60s (at least outside the NCB) attempted any real economic analysis of the coal industry. One of the few attempts to analyse a supply function for the coal industry, and hence to measure the financial effect of a coal industry of different sizes, was in a Bow Group publication by Anthony Lines in 1961 (reporting the findings of a '50s discussion group) entitled *Concerns of State*. It used crude published NCB area data (and hence ignored differences in profitability *within* areas or within individual pits) and was very illuminating indicating, as it did, the tail of uneconomic coal output at that date. Little analysis emerged beyond this, e.g. to indicate how such production functions for coal would shift given further investment either in new pits or in greater mechanisation or how the Ricardo-Shove example of diminishing marginal productivity with increased output could apply to the coal industry.

Coal in the '50s also saw very starkly the conflict between micro- and macro-economic policy in the energy field, though the macro arguments then paraded were very different from the new monetary/supply side orthodoxy of today. The policy of doctrinal economic liberalism so evident in the '50s, may be thought to have reached its peak in the energy field with the spectacular increase of 10 per cent in the price of coal in July 1955. The micro-economic argument was that it was not possible to justify the sale of coal *below* world market price to British consumers who, as a group, were especially wasteful in its use. Yet Andrew Schonfield in *British Economic Policy Since the War* (1958) refers to this coal price increase as 'an act of bravado' coming as it did in the middle of an inflationary crisis when costs were rising and wage claims were growing dangerously. The arguments, though familiar, were ones which many would regard as 'cosmetic' today rather than of substance, namely that to control inflation, it was believed that the government had to use a combination of exhortation, moral pressure on interest groups, subsidies or a limited measure of temporary price control over some critical items since you could only make disinflation work if you first created the *feeling* of price stability. Similar macro arguments, of course, continued to be paraded with varying impact to constrain energy prices until the late '70s. During most of the period, and particularly in the early '70s, they prevailed against micro allocative resource efficiency arguments in the energy field disguising the real macro-problem, distorting the energy sector and storing up problems for the future.

Between the years 1950 and 1954, oil was replacing about half a million tons of coal a year according to G.F. Ray and F.T. Blackaby (see 'Energy and Expansion' National Institute Economic Review, Sept 1960): by 1955-6 this substitution had risen to 1¾ million tons a year. Thereafter, after a pause following the closure of the Suez Canal, it rose to a rate of over 6 million tons a year in 1958 and 1959. In 1960, however, the conversion of power stations to oil was checked though substitution of oil for coal continued at some 2 million tons a year.

This resulted from a combination of factors. First, between 1954 and 1958, coal prices rose at more than twice the rate of scheduled fuel oil prices, and after 1957 the price of oil products declined dramatically. Second, oil was a convenient fuel easy to handle and operate. Thirdly, there was the spread of smokeless zones, the disappearance of the steam engine, the switch from rail to road transport and the understanding of how inefficient domestic open fires were. Technological developments in several industries (e.g. iron and steel industry and coke consuming industries) also played an important part.

GENERAL ENERGY

On the supply side, some interesting work was done by econometricians on the coal, gas and electricity industries. In 1948 the Report of the Committee to study *The Electricity Peak Load Problem in Relation to the Non-Industrial Consumer* (Cmnd 7464) had given details of the economies of scale in relation to capital costs for electricity supply. K.S. Lomax produced production functions by cross section data (using linear logarithmic cost areas derived from simultaneous equations of the Cobb-Douglas form) for coal production (1950), for gas supply (1951), and for electricity generation (1952). An article by Donkin and Margen, published by the Institute of Electrical Engineers in 1952, made the case for larger generating units. At once this became a topic of considerable technical debate. They were followed by T.K. Gribben who, in the next year, also produced a production function for the gas industry by using the same approach. (None of these, however, considered the costs of distribution.) Subsequently, J. Johnston in 1960 developed statistical cost functions for electricity (both by cross-sectional and time series methods, and for coal (by sectional methods only). At a more practical level F.H.S. Brown and R.S. Edwards in 'Replacement of Obsolescent Plant,' *Economica* (1961) suggested that power stations faced an 80% increase in capital cost per kW for a 100% increase in output capacity.

The 1961 publication *Concerns of State*, referred to above, may also be worthy of note because it attempted to give a lead to energy policy. Its guiding principles were set out as: the consumer must have free choice, prices must reflect true costs, resources should be distributed between the public and private sectors according to their capacity to earn, consumer demand must determine the size of the nationalised industries, socially desirable services should be subsidised, to the extent that they are unremunerative out of *general* taxation, and NIs should be required to find an increasing proportion of their new capital by earning greater surpluses. At that time these statements were highly contentious and far removed from current practice. They raised issues that were to feature large in the 60's and beyond.

Chapter 22

Energy Economics Since 1960

Eric Price

The Sixties saw a major step forward in the expansion both of the technical tools of analysis in energy economics and in their field of application. It was a decade in which there was a conscious effort to improve and rationalise public decision-making. Informed people were becoming increasingly aware, as G.H. Peters stated, 'that a large part of public spending was voted on the basis of hunch, guessword, horse trading or barely-concealed electoral calculations' or as *The Times* put it:

> 'The truth is that many major public expenditure decisions have been taken since the war by old-fashioned "muddle through", "rule of thumb" methods. Investment has been pitifully neglected in some cases while in other spheres public money has been lavished often with a very hazy idea of the return to be expected.'

The Plowden Committee Report put special emphasis on efficiency in Public Expenditure.

In this situation it was no accident that improved methods of analysis and of decision-making were looked for; a variety of techniques came into wider acceptability. These included discounted cash flow, input-output, programme budgeting, cost effectiveness, linear programming, critical path analysis, and especially cost-benefit analysis. All were used by energy economists in the period but cost-benefit analysis made the biggest advance. Indeed, *The Guardian* described it in 1964 as 'currently the most fashionable branch of economics'. Even *The Times* admitted that it was 'catching on'.

The theoretical basis for cost-benefit analysis had existed since Alfred Marshall. It has been developed by A.C. Pigou early in the present century in *The Economics of Welfare*. In this book he distinguished between private and social costs both with respect to 'collective goods' but also to cases where there were externalities. The first application of a form of cost-benefit analysis was in the Tennessee Valley Authority Scheme which was part of F.D. Roosevelt's 'New Deal'. In the TVA Scheme water, electricity and employment were joint products (see Krutilla and Eckstein's *Multiple Purpose River Development* (1958)). Its initial application within the UK, however, was by Prof. G.P. Wibberley in the fields of agriculture and or urban growth and by Prof. C.D. Foster and Prof. M.E. Beesley in their evaluation of the Victoria Line and of the London-Birmingham (M1) Motorway.

Large energy projects, were prime targets for the technique and its use in Government grew steadily. In particular Prest and Turvey in their important 'Survey of Cost Benefit Analysis' *Energy Journal*, (December 1965) showed how the simple alternative of a single hydroelectric source versus a single private steam plant could be evaluated and how the evaluation would change if the implications of adding *another* source to a whole supply system were considered. They showed that, in general, a very complicated exercise involving the simulation of the operation of the whole system was essential if the right answer was to be forthcoming — a view Ralph Turvey had previously expressed two years earlier in 'On Investment Choices in Electricity Generation' (*Oxford Economic Papers*, November 1963).

THE NATIONALISED ENERGY INDUSTRIES

The '60s also, as part of the search for improved efficiency in decision-making, saw a number of attempts to set out the economic and financial framework of the nationalised industries more precisely. The White Paper on the *Financial and Economic Obligations of the Nationalised Industries*, 1961 (Cmnd 1337) interpreted the statutory provisions of their various Acts as meaning that these industries should aim to balance their accounts 'taking one year with another over a period of five years, after providing for interest and depreciation at historic cost plus a provision for replacement cost and after allocations to reserves sufficient to contribute some self-financing'. Also there were to be objectives or targets set for each undertaking, set in terms of rates of return on capital.

Subsequently, the 1967 White Paper *Nationalised Industries: A Review of Economic and Financial Objectives* (Cmnd 3437) sought to specify more precisely the role of the Nationalised Industries, on the one hand and the Government on the other. In particular, it was concerned with the allocation of 'resources upon an economically and socially rational basis'. To this end, it attempted to set investment criteria (involving discounted cash flow techniques, the concept of the test rate of discount and, where appropriate, cost-benefit evaluation techniques), rules for pricing policy (so as 'to contribute towards a more efficient distribution of resources') and it put forward certain proposals for controlling costs and increasing efficiency (including the strengthening of the National Board on Prices and Incomes to enable it to enquire into the efficiency of those industries whose price increases were referred to it). Paras 17-26 of that White Paper represented the first overt official recognition of the importance of appropriate price signals. The White Paper marked an important signpost in the development of energy economics:

> 'In addition to recovering accounting costs, prices need to be reasonably related to costs at the margin and to be designed to promote the efficient use of resources within industry.'

For prices in the energy field there was special mention:

> 'Where and when there is spare capacity, as there may be at some points in the business cycle, or excess demand, short run marginal costs (i.e. the additional costs of increasing output in the short run) are relevant; the object is to persuade customers to make use of spare capacity or to curtail excess demand. In the long run, the main consideration is the cost of supplying on a continuing basis those services and products whose separate costing is a practical proposition (i.e. long run marginal costs), though the problems of transition to a new technology or to a new source of supply may imply the need, in the medium term, for prices to diverge from long-run costs. These long-run marginal costs naturally include provision for the replacement of the fixed assets needed for the continued provision of services, together with a satisfactory rate of return on capital employed.

Moreover, in some industries — such as electricity and commuter services of the railways — the load at periods of peak demand rather than the growth of *total* sales determines the need for new capital investment. In such cases plant may be under-utilised for much of the time and, so far as is administratively possible, the price system recognises this characteristic of demand by providing adequate incentives to encourage users to shift from peak to off-peak. Provided off-peak charges do not fall below the levels needed to cover the variable costs incurred, differentiation can be increased with advantage until the balance between peak and off-peak is economically most efficient. The effect on revenue is neutral so long as lower receipts from off-peak users are offset by higher receipts resulting from higher charges made to peak-time users; indeed a net revenue gain is likely. Two-part and differential pricing systems are also used to improve financial results without distorting the allocation of resources when there are important elements in costs which cannot easily be allocated to specific services or products (e.g. costs incurred jointly by several services or costs which do not vary proportionately with output). In apportioning these costs among consumers, there is a wide choice of methods ranging from complex multi-part tariffs, designed to ensure that each customer pays for the costs he imposes, to simple quantity discounts which may be appropriate in cases where large quantities are more economical to supply than smaller amounts. The actual calculation of the different elements of such a price system is itself a complicated task: but the broad objective is clear enough.'

This was hardly a full treatment of the issues involved but still remarkable in historic terms.

Richard Pryke's *Public Enterprise in Practice* (1971) critically examined the economic performance of these industries and concluded that nationalised industries were tending to become more efficient and tended to have better performance than private industires — a view which was hotly contested amongst others, by George and Priscilla Polanyi in *The Moorgate and Wall Street Review* (Spring 1972).

What is also noticeable and, on reflection, rather surprising is that in those early sixties there were no professional economists in the then Ministry of Fuel and Power. Indeed, there were no professional micro-economists at all in Whitehall. Such economists as there were, and they were very few in number, were concentrated in the newly-formed Economic Branch of HM Treasury started by Sir Robert Hall and they were engaged almost exclusively in demand management of the macro-economy on Keynesian lines, then described, rather inappropriately, as fine-tuning. Outside, and particularly in the private business sector, energy economists had by the early sixties already proved their worth in a wide area of decision-making. With time the field of application of micro-economics and the variety of its applied techniques grew and eventually a Government Economic Service came into existence in which micro-economists specialising in energy — albeit a handful at first but modestly increasing in number over the years — became a distinct group. Their techniques, however, were in no way separate from micro-economists elsewhere and because of this, and the fact that the Service was centrally-managed, there was considerable mobility between Government Departments. Energy economists were not a special breed.

THE OIL INDUSTRY

In the oil sector, the overseas earnings of oil companies became a topic for increased interest with massive implications for the following decade: in a study carried out by Arthur D. Little Inc for the Organisation of Petroleum Exporting Countries, it was estimated that the average return on oil production was 66% on assets in certain Middle East countries in the period 1956-1960. This estimate was considered by Shell to be much too high (see *Current International Oil Pricing Problems*: Shell International Petroleum Co Ltd, London, 1963). Their estimate was a 20% average return on production assets for all Eastern Hemisphere oil company operations. A further estimate quoted by Shell was an average return of 5.6% for oil companies engaged mainly in refining and marketing operations in the (politically safe) Western European area in 1961. Following this, an estimate of a 10% minimum return for Middle East oil production was given by a study on *Taxation Economics in Crude Production* prepared by the OPEC Secretariat (Fifth Arab Petroleum Congress, Cairo, March 1965), where a return of 12% was quoted as approximately the level of return where the proposed progressive tax on oil production profits was expected to begin to have some impact.

The relations between oil companies and government were of major interest to energy economists and others in this period. F.E. Hartshorn's book on this subject, sub-titled *An Account of the International Oil Industry in its Political Environment* (1962), gave a well-informed picture of the economic and political issues and included a description of the economic characteristics, organisational and commercial activities of the industry. In particular, it stressed the vertical integration of the major firms in the industry and that prices (including crude oil prices and except for final products) were chiefly internal transfer prices for what, in essence, were barter deals between activities within these integrated companies and their accounting framework. George Polanyi, following the agreement on royalty payments and profit tax reached in December 1964 between the Middle East governments represented in OPEC and the leading oil companies, produced a useful analysis of the taxation for oil prices and taxation policy. He discussed whether the basis of taxation, then agreed, would tend to arrest the current downward trend of Middle East crude oil prices and, on the wider plane of taxation policy in general, examined how far the new oil-tax system, as agreed, conformed to the theoretically-ideal criteria for the taxation of producers. In the interests of optimum resource allocation, he noted 'the ideal standard would require that the tax should be imposed in a form which restricts its impact only to producers' rents and leaves the payments to factors of production unaffected'. The two questions were, of course, inter-related, since a tax which conformed to the theoretically-ideal standard could have no effect on the supply price at which oil was offered (i.e. the long-run marginal cost of oil). But he then noted that in the context of the conditions then current in the Middle East, the existence of a tax in this form would mean that prices would be free to fall from this prevailing level, far above marginal cost and down towards the long-run marginal cost of Middle East oil supply. The view he put forward was that neither the taxation system in the form established by the governments participating in the OPEC agreement, nor any other system that was consistent with their interests, would satisfy the theoretically ideal criterion of a tax falling *only* on producers' rents and therefore leaving supply price unaffected. This was because the governments' interest in maximising potential income from taxing producers' rents required the maintenance of a 'floor' price for oil at a level *above* long-run marginal cost; and the most practical and effective means of imposing such a floor price was through the system of taxation of oil production profits. The optimum level for this floor price, which would be in the interests of the governments to try to establish (i.e. the 'monopolist's optimum floor price') was at the point where the downward-sloping marginal revenue curve for Middle East oil intersected the long-run marginal-cost curve of Middle East oil supply. It was at this point that the sum of producers' rents from the outputs of all oil producers in the countries concerned, and therefore also the total potential income from taxation, was maximised. He pointed out that, in view of the interest of the governments of the oil-producing countries in maximising the potential revenue from the taxation of producers' rents, they would seek to maintain a taxation system incorporating a price floor at the point where the total of producers' rents was maximised. There was no prospect therefore of the introduction of a tax in the theoretically ideal form. Moreover he argued there was good reason for what the 'producer mentality' of the government of oil-producing countries (as expressed in their support for price maintenance and output restriction) — since this policy served the interests of maximising their potential income from the taxation of producers' profits. He then went on to argue, however, that from the point of view of the oil-consuming countries the 'ideal' character of the theoretically ideal form of tax was unaffected by security of supply considerations. The cheapest method of obtaining security of oil supplies was not achieved by switching over to politically-secure sources (e.g. North America) but rather by continuing to rely on low-cost sources within the OPEC countries (Middle East, Libya etc.) and providing protection against interruption of supply by increased strategic storage within the consuming country.

Hence, in his view, the increased dependence on oil from OPEC sources (which would result from the abolition of the floor-price element in crude-oil taxation) would not constitute a threat to security of supply.

Economic issues concerning domestic oil and gas exploration were of course new to the UK in the '60s as was the prospect of such reserves. K.W. Dam started the discussion of such issues in 'Oil and Gas Licensing and the North Sea', *Journal of Law and Economics* (1964). Subsequently the debate was continued by P. Hinde 'Fortune in the North Sea' (1966), Richard Bailey 'Natural Gas: How Big An Asset' (1967), R.L. Schantz 'Role of Petroleum and Gas from Outer Continental Shelf' 1970, and eventually 'The Pricing of North Sea Gas in Britain' (1970), again in the *Journal of Law and Economics.* The most interesting study of the spatial economics of oil and gas and their relationship with transport costs, was in Professor Peter Odell's inaugural lecture, 'Natural Gas in Western Europe' (1969).

It would, however, be reprehensible in this content not to mention the very useful and clear descriptive accounts of the economic aspects of oil and gas exploration and development contained in the high quality magazines of the leading oil companies in the UK. In particular, the *Esso Magazine* (Autumn 1966) provided a clear insight into their views of the potential of the United Kingdom Continental Shelf.

The Government was also becoming increasingly interested with the role of oil companies in their product markets. And (in 1965) the Monopolies Commission was asked to report on competition in petrol retailing. Their Report provides an interesting insight into the UK market at that time, especially when read in conjunction with the critiques by independent economists, such as Harry Townsend.

THE ELECTRICITY INDUSTRY

Even in the '60s, however, many of the really important economic papers in the energy field continued to be published in specialist journals rather than economic journals. Take, for instance, the very fine and complete analytical exposition by T.W. Berrie entitled 'The Economics of System Planning in Bulk Electricity Supply' published in the *Electrical Review* (1967). This essay by a practising electrical engineer provided insights into the structure and determinants of the costs in electricity supply with greater authority than any previously published works. It showed with great clarity both how the net effective cost and the incremental system's cost concepts could be applied in judging the relative merits of different types of power station investment. The significance of this article was not just in its informed content, but also in the pricing debate among energy economists that its publication caused to occur. R.L. Meek and P.E. Watts each wrote articles in the March 1968 *Economic Journal*, the former on 'The New Bulk Supply Tariff for Electricity' and the latter on 'CEGB's Bulk Supply Tariff and Long Run Marginal Costs'. Thereafter the battle was joined: first there was Ralph Turvey in 'Optimal Pricing and Investment in Electricity Supply' (1968), and then a discussion by all three (Meek, Watts and Turvey) in the December edition of the Journal and, subsequently, by Ray Rees in 1969 and Turvey again in *Economic Analysis and Public Enterprise* (1971) Chapter 6. Before long, a substantial body of theoretical literature had been built up on marginal cost pricing, much of it later to be reprinted in Ralph Turvey's Penguin book *Public Enterprise: Selected Readings* (1968). Additionally, G.S. Minto contributed an article on 'Economics of Scale and Technological Change in Thermal Power Generation' in *Economic Journal.*

Coupled with this interest in the structure of bulk and retail electricity tariffs was the development of greater sophistication in electricity forecasting. 1968 saw the publication of an important contribution to energy forecasting in the form of Baxter and Rees article on 'Analysis of the industrial demand for Electricity' in the *Economic Journal.* It examined the implications of the classical theory of demand model using the total demand for fuel as an exploratory variable (as then used by the Ministry of Power) and concluded that the fact that the coefficients of the fuel prices in all fuel equations had to sum to zero imposed a severe restriction on the cross-elasticities.

THE GAS INDUSTRY

In contrast, the gas tariff, as Michael Posner points out in *Fuel Policy: A Study in Applied Economics*, had 'received only scant attention, largely because public knowledge is small'. In this context it is worth recalling that at this very time E. Malinvaud was saying in *Statistical Methods in Economics* (1965):

> 'We must never forget that our progress in understanding economic laws depends strictly on the quality and abundance of statistical data. Nothing can take the place of the painstaking works of objective observation of the facts'.

Nevertheless, operational research came to be employed to resolve economic problems in the gas industry. Model-building in that industry had its origins in the statistical analysis of gas demand and the methods developed for forecasting that demand. Also in the mid-1950s, work had been done using linear programming techniques to find the pattern of transport routes from coalpits to gasworks which gave the minimum overall coal transport cost throughout an Area Board. In the early 1960s, network analysis models for calculating the flow of gas and pressures in a transmission or distribution network began to be developed and in 1964, the South Eastern Gas Board used consultants to set up a linear programming model to control the operation of its various plants. This was very successful and similar models were developed and used by many Boards whilst a significant number of works remained in operation. From 1966 onwards Stafford Beer, C.E. Faulkner and other consultants developed models which showed how operational research techniques could be applied to choose optimal economic strategies for the distribution of liquid methane and establish a planning model for the gas industry. The advent of natural gas from the North Sea in the mid-sixties gave an enormous impetus to operational research model-building both at the

Gas Council and the Boards because of the very large and complex problems that had to be tackled. The Operational Research Department of the Gas Council was set up at the beginning of 1967 to undertake model-building work and all Boards considerably increased the resources devoted to this activity. In 1968 the Gas Council established an Economic Planning Division with the aims of reviewing the industry's objectives, of determining the most efficient and economic way of achieving those objectives, of relating planning to what is actually being achieved, and of operating an efficient planning and control system. The various Operational Research Journals and the publications of the major professional institutions contain many articles of interest to the energy economist. These describe how modelling work was applied to the economic issues in the gas industry from the mid-sixties onwards.

THE COAL INDUSTRY

Very little existed in the public domain on the economics of the coal industry in the sixties. One of the better papers was the address by Lord Robens to the Coal Industry Society (6 March 1967). This illuminated the NCB current efforts to concentrate production at the most efficient long-life pits in an attempt to supply coal to power stations at an acceptable price. One of the few economic commentators to take a close interest in the UK coal industry in this period was Richard Bailey who, whilst at PEP and subsequently, contributed articles to the *Westminster Bank Review*, both on the coal industry and on fuel policy generally. This does not mean that little economic work was in hand. Indeed, in the '60s, the NCB developed an Area Board linear programming cost minimising model as an aid to detailed area planning. It considered in detail production, segregation, in pit transport, coal preparation, marketing and manpower alternatives at each pit, with several further sub-divisions in each category. It allowed for capacity to be varied within plants and for new capital investments to be considered. This was in addition to their national inear programming model which maximised the production and transport costs of meeting a *given* level of demand. It represented total production at each pit, divided into 5 coal types and the transport of each from 17 production *areas* to 7 sales regions. The coal types or market categories were: electricity, coke ovens, domestic bituminous, domestic naturally smokeless and others.

Moreover, the NCB used a three stage modelling and planning exercise involving national, area and colliery models. A consistent solution or plan was achieved by the iteration between these classes of model. (See National Board for Price and Incomes (1970) *Coal Prices* Second Report Appendices B and H.)

Very little economic analysis has been done on the specific subject of the labour issues in the energy field. *Pit Closure and the Community* by J.W. House and E.M. Knight (a report to the Ministry of Labour) (1967) and E.M. Knight's further report on *Men Leaving Mining* (1968) are more sociological studies than economic ones. However, in a little known, but impressive, PhD thesis by Peter Lehmann of Sussex University entitled 'Unemployment and the Opportunity Cost of Mining Labour' (1972) he produced an estimate of the marginal opportunity cost of displaced miners, though it tended to pay insufficient attention both to the displacement effect (of those who subsequently found work) on others and also ignored the macro-monetary effects on the economy.

GENERAL ENERGY

There was, however, one event of special note since it occurred in a hitherto barren world of econometrics: this was the development (as Vol. 8 of Richard Stone's *A Programme for Growth*) of a sub-model for the British Fuel Economy produced by Ken Wigley in 1968 at the Department of Applied Economics, Cambridge University under the title *The Demand for Fuel, 1948–1975*. Wigley related the value (in constant price terms) of the electricity consumed per head of population to (a) the ratio of the average temperature of the year in question to the long-run average temperature; (b) the total consumption of expenditure per head in real terms and (c) the average price of electricity in real terms. Equations of the same form were estimated for three other fuels — solid fuel, oil (other than motor spirit) and gas. In the study, he produced a rather high total expenditure elasticity of 3.65 which may have reflected the omission of changes in habits and the growth in the stock of appliances: but the elasticities of electricity demand with respect to the price were not unreasonable, being 0.2 to 0.4 for solid fuel, 0.02 to 0.05 for oil, 0.2 for gas and 0.6 to 0.5 for electricity. Its significance resides in the fact that it represented the first serious econometric attempt to develop fuel sector inter-industrial relationships within a model of the whole UK economy by means of a simple input-output technique. Its emphasis was on the demand side of the energy sector. It is particularly fascinating that the authors' foreword (whilst stating their indebtedness to the then Ministry of Power) stated that they hoped their results would contribute to the common task of improving industrial modelling in this country and that they understood that a similar development was envisaged by the Ministry of Power. Progress on this had in fact already started. In 1967 an Energy Model Group had been set up in the Ministry of Power with the prime function of forecasting energy supply and demand. The Department produced five separate models. These were the Coal, Electricity Investment, Coal Transport, Gas, Oil and Energy Demand Models. The intention was to integrate these models into a single energy model but they were never formally integrated. Instead they were partially integrated by making occasional *ad hoc* adjustments and iterations between them. Experiments were carried out with a view to formally integrating simplified versions of the models by (i) iterating systematically between them, hoping for convergence and by (ii) combining all five into a single large linear programme and solving them simultaneously. The forecasting techniques then developed formed the basis with some modifications for such work in the Department of Energy until 1979.

Economic forecasting is now rightly regarded with healthy scepticism: as the Secretary of State for Energy recently stated at the BIEE Cambridge Conference:

> 'In the last 20 years — the period in which forecasting has become a major industry — we have seen some startlingly wrong predictions. For example, the Electricity Council in the 1960s and early 1970s produced forecasts for maximum demand 7 years ahead which were never less than 20% too high and in one year were about 50% out. It is only fair to add that the Electricity Council were by no means unique in this — forecasting errors are the rule rather than the exception — and that their error was in no small measure due to highly optimistic forecasts of economic growth provided by the Government of the day.'

Francesco Guiccardini's comment in *Storia d'Italia* that 'Circumspection, carried to excess can be just as treacherous a guide as complacency because events rarely turn out as wisely as predicted and accidents will happen in the best-regulated families' is certainly relevant to this period of energy forecasting. Was this what previously inspired Sir Alec Cairncross in his address to the Royal Economic Society to quote:

> 'A trend is a trend is a trend,
> But the question is: will it bend?

Will it alter its course
Through some unforeseen force
Or come to a premature end?'

For these reasons, the latest set of long term energy projections which have now been published as an ANNEX to the Department's proof of Evidence for the Sizewell 'B' Public Inquiry (October 1982) are not *forecasts*, but *projections* based on a *range* of different economic assumptions chosen to point up the different ways UK demand might develop into the first decade of the next century. They have been prepared by new methods which are essentially econometric in character. It would serve little purpose to cover in this note the intervening years between the early 1970s and today. The *Energy Policy* Journal started in 1973 and the IAEE *Energy Journal* (started in 1980) contain most of the notable contributions to the subject and these and other articles will be well known to the reader. The last decade however, largely as a result of the oil price hikes has been one of both sizeable development in energy economics and growth in the number of economists in the field: but, even so, the number of energy economists here represents but a small fraction of those in the USA today.

It is, of course, easy to form the view that the analyses published on energy economics represent the sum total of the analyses carried out upto date. This is far from the mark: most of the analyses never get published. What is published represents the tip of the iceberg and may not be truly representative of the whole. There is a great wealth of economic analysis 'locked up' in commercial and other organisations. Some appreciation of this only comes to light when snippets, often for quite accidental reasons, become published.

In recent years, energy economics has flourished but it has also become very much more closely integrated with the main stream of macro-economic theory. Partly this is the result of the almost universal acceptance by academic economists (at least beyond these shores) of the validity of monetarist economics. The concern of monetarist economists with PSBR and with money supply impacts has concentrated attention in the energy sector both on the external financing limits of the energy nationalised industries and on the United Kingdom Continental Shelf tax-take from oil and gas production. But also this integration of energy economics with macro-economics has arisen following Gregory's article in the *Australian Journal of Economics* on 'Natural Resource Depletion and the Structure of the Economy' and reflected interest in the impact of UKCS oil and gas (in a floating exchange rate situation) on the industrial structure of the UK. These two factors have enabled the energy economist to get invited to 'the top table' of macro-economic debate. In this sense energy economics, energy economists and those interested in energy economics have 'come of age' and this has resulted in the creation of the BIEE. It has also been a factor in forging close and valued links with both Chatham House and the Policy Studies Institute.

SOME THOUGHTS ON THE FUTURE OF ENERGY ECONOMICS

So much for the past. What can we say of the possible future path of energy economics in Britain: Obviously one can only speculate, but at first sight, a variety of ways in which energy economics may develop to fill lacunae suggest themselves. Firstly, we may see a body of literature building up in this country that links energy projections to energy supply capacity requirements by Bayesian probability methods; secondly, we may see more work published seeking to reconcile the need for flexibility in energy supply with the cost of what (by adopting 'least regret' criteria for decision-making) will of necessity in the event imply a sub-optimal system in terms of the 'most probable' future outcome or even in terms of the 'average expected' outcome. Thirdly, we may see the conscious and overt development of decision-theory related to new supply and demand technologies with the explicit use of profit-lotteries, certain equivalents and risk tolerance levels in particular we may see more application of the techniques for 'rolling-forward' decision trees. The scope for agricultural and urban waste fuels, renewables, SNG, heat pumps, etc., will feature in the economic debate with each evaluated in terms of their marginal impacts on the other energy *systems*. No doubt the first economic assessments of producing hydrogen by splitting water electro-mechanically using solar energy and electrodes will be carried out in the next decade. We may see more work carried out using cost-benefit analysis and new techniques used as part of impact statements (on US lines?) for prospective developments. We may see debate developing on the economics of homeostatic control versus those of, say, pump storage or of cross channel electricity imports. And possible associated with homeostatic control, we may see assessments of the net benefits of the technical possibility of forward price electricity markets. At the more practical level, far more rational and quantitatively informed economic analysis will develop both in the architectural design of new buildings and in the economics of energy conservation retro-fit and energy-control options in existing buildings, particularly domestic ones. The economics of inter-fuel substitution may also see a new hey-day, possibly augmented by risk analysis. Indeed, one may even see energy evaluation 'kits' being sold to householders for use with their household computers so that everyone in one sense becomes his own energy economist. We will also see energy economists involving themselves far more in the estimation of capital costs — particularly for new technologies such as the fast-breeder reactor.

Whilst there are reasons for thinking that the impact of energy economics, and of related disciplines, will improve the process of decision-making in the future, it would be mistaken to conclude that by the end of the Century white elephants will be an extinct breed. As John Maynard Keynes wrote:

> 'Most major business decisions are taken as a result of animal spirits — of a spontaneous urge to action rather than inaction, and not as the outcome of a weighted average of quantitative benefits multiplied by quantitative probabilities.'

Thus it seems almost inevitable that many decisions in the future will continue to be made by *hunch*, and with the instinctive *feel* of the gifted amateur — so dear to British mythology — with delusions of his own omniscience and to whom Britain's relative decline owes so much. Nevertheless, energy economists have an important role to play firstly, in limiting the scope for *hunch*, secondly, in exposing the range of possible future outcomes and the sensitivities of venture to these, thirdly in stressing the key role of pricing policy, and finally in thinking the unthinkable.

This discursive, and necessarily partial, chronological account has I hope, put energy economics today into an appropriate historical setting, depicted the variety of subject matter covered by its practitioners in the past and the wide spectrum of individuals who have contributed to its development. It has exclusively confined itself to a discussion of the development of energy economics *within* the UK. There have been very few references to foreign economists or any mention of the debt which energy economists here owe to their opposite numbers in other countries. This is quite intentional. As a contribution to the BIEE in its nursery years the aim has been to consider energy problems in the UK and the growth of energy economics as a means of solving them. It has not sought to describe the contributions of economists overseas to this development. Thus Dupuis, Baumol, Boiteaux, Adelman, Balestra, Arrow, Masse, Odell, Nelson and even that most practical of all economists, Sheihk

Yamani, do not even receive a mention.

It will have been seen that statisticians, mathematicians, engineers, operational researchers, market researchers, natural scientists and accountants as well as economists and econometricians, have all played a part: it may also have served to show that energy economics is not a subject closely constrained within a water-tight box. To those then who ask what energy economics is, the answer is rather Delphic, namely that it is what it is, not what its name is called. So it has always been.

SECTION 4

Annexes

Annex I

Professional Institutions, University Centres and Specialist Journals in Britain Covering Energy Economics

PROFESSIONAL AND OTHER NON-UNIVERSITY INSTITUTIONS

The following list only includes institutions with a major programme in energy economics. However, as always in the past, major work on energy economics emerges regularly from institutions of a more general character: examples over the last two years include the work on the impact of North Sea oil and gas revenue on the UK economy undertaken in the Institute of Fiscal Studies and Policy Studies Institute.

Association for the Conservation of Energy, 39A, Gloucester Place, London W1H 3PD. Co-ordinates interest in energy conservation. Director: Andrew Warren.

British Institute of Energy Economics, 9 St James's Square, London SW1Y 4LE. Founded in London in 1978, the BIEE aims to further the understanding of all aspects of energy economics on both the national and international level. Full details are given in Annex 2.

British Nuclear Energy Society, 1-7 Great George Street, London

SW1P 3AA. Founded in 1962, this society provides a forum for discussion and presentation of papers on nuclear energy covering a wide range of engineering and scientific disciplines. Publishes *Nuclear Energy*. Academic membership welcome.

Energy Industries Club, c/o 5, Ridgelands, Penshurst Road, Bidborough, Tunbridge Wells, Kent (Hon. Sec: Dr R. Jackson). The Energy Industries Club is a private lunching club at which addresses are given by prominent members of the Energy and associated industries. Meetings are held monthly from October to April inclusive at the Connaught Rooms, Great Queen Street, London WC2.

Fifty Club, c/o BP International, 26th Floor, Britannic House, Moor Lane, London EC2 (Hon. Sec: Dr Graham Andrews). An informal policy-oriented meetings group founded in 1950 (hence the name). It runs some six or seven early-evening meetings a year, nearly always held in a private room of a public house in the vicinity of Victoria Station. It draws quite heavily on Whitehall and the nationalised sector. It is widening its membership to include other energy economists and planners. Membership is £7 per season.

Institute of Energy, 18 Devonshire Street, London W1N 2AU. The learned society and professional qualifying body for engineers, scientists and technologists in the energy field, founded in 1927. (There are associated membership grades for non-specialists.) Publishes *Energy World*, *Fuel and Energy Abstracts* and *The Journal of the Institute of Energy*. Organises some 80 meetings, symposia and conferences each year throughout Britain.

The Institution of Mining and Metallurgy, 44, Portland Place, London W1N 4BR. This institution, founded in 1892, has a very lively interest in energy economics, publishing articles and reviews in *IMM Abstracts* and *IMM Bulletin*. The Secretary is M.J. Jones.

Institute of Petroleum, 61 New Cavendish Street, London W1M 8AR. The professional institute most closely covering the petroleum industry. It publishes *Petroleum Review* and a number of technical books, and has specialist committees covering the whole range of the industry's activities including an Energy Committee. There is an annual Energy Seminar and an Energy Economics Group (Chairman: Mr P. Ellis Jones. Secretary: Miss C.H. Little), which meets 10–12 times a year usually at 4:00–6:00 p.m. on Mondays, in the Institute. The Institute also has 16 branches which provide technical and social meetings for individual members. The Institute started the World Petroleum Congress in 1933 and the 11th Congress will be held in London in 1983. The WPC permanent secretariat has its offices at 61 New Cavendish Street but the UK host body is The World Petroleum Jubilee Congress Ltd., (the British Organising Committee).

International Association of Energy Economists (UK). See Annex 2.

International Institute for Environment and Development, 10 Percy Street, London W1P 0DR. A non-profit making, policy-oriented research institution with branches in London and Washington. It has a strong interest in sustainable paths for Third World development. It has always had a strong energy input. Runs seminars to go with research projects, but has no general meetings or house journal. The President is William Clark and the two Co-Chairmen are Robert O. Anderson and Abdlatif Y Al-Hamad.

Joint British Institutes Energy Research Programme. See Annex 4.

London Oil Analysts Group, c/o P.H. McConnell, Rowe, Rudd & Co, 63 London Wall, London EC2M 5OQ. The group meets once a month over lunch in the Great Eastern Hotel to listen to a single invited oil company speaker. The 1981 subscription was £15 and the luncheon charge £7 (£10 for guests). About once a year LOAG run a 1-2 day conference. Members are almost all City-orientated and include many stockbrokers and bankers.

National Institute of Economic and Social Research, 2 Dean Trench Street, London SW1. Britain's leading non-governmental centre for policy-oriented economic analysis. At any one time, two or three staff members will be preparing energy imputs for the institute's model of the British economy and for its wider European forecast. This work can be followed in the *National Institute Economic Review*. The staff will often be engaged in one-off energy-related research projects such as a recent one on the conservation of energy in the United Kingdom.

Royal Institute of British Architects, 66 Portland Place, London W1. A professional institution with a particularly strong interest in energy matters. One subject being pursued by the RIBA Energy Group is the economics of investment in energy conservation within the building sector.

Royal Institute of International Affairs (also known as 'Chatham House'), 10 St James's Square, London SW1Y 4LE. This institute covers international energy developments in its active meetings, research and publications programmes (*International Affairs* and *World Today*).

Royal Institute of Public Administration, 3 Birdcage Walk, London SW1. The energy industries feature frequently in the research programme and seminars. A regular series of meetings is organised at Birkbeck College by David Steel of the University of Exeter and David Heal of the University of Glasgow.

Social Science Research Council, Hamilton House, Temple Avenue, London EC4. The Energy Panel of the SSRC has made considerable effort to stimulate the flow of public and private sector funds into energy research and to co-ordinate interest in energy economics.

Uranium Institute, New Zealand House, Haymarket, London SW1Y 4TE, promotes discussion of matters of common interest between uranium producers, electrical utilities, and other industrial, commercial or research organisations concerned with the development of nuclear power. Since its formation in 1975 its membership has grown from the original 16 to today's total ot 52, drawn from 15 countries. The members are divided roughly equally between mining companies, electrical utilities, and other organisations working in support of nuclear power. About one-third are publicly owned or governmental organisations.

Through its twice-yearly plenary meetings, and in the working committees on supply and demand, trade, and public affairs, the Institute provides frequent opportunities for its members to draw on the experience of their colleagues in the industry. Its publications document the industry's progress, and bring its point of view on important policy matters before decision-makers and the public. The constructive cooperation which exists within the Institute between the various sides of the industry is reflected in the constitution, and by the alternation of the senior appointments in the organisation between uranium producers and consumers.

Watt Committee on Energy, 75 Knightsbridge, London SW1X 7RB, was founded in 1976 and has the general objectives of promoting and assisting research and development and other scientific or technological work concerning all aspects of energy and disseminating knowledge generally concerning energy for the benefit of the public at large. Its membership comprises more than 60 British scientific, technical and professional institutions which have at least a tangential interest in energy issues. It increasingly serves as a channel for institutional comment on government position papers.

The Consultative Council of the Committee, held about twice per annum, discusses papers on selected energy-related themes and is attended by representatives of the member institutions and invited guests; the papers presented are often published, with other work, in the *Reports* of the Committee. Research contracts are undertaken. Publications include *Land for Energy Development*, a series of maps in loose-leaf volume form demonstrating potential land needs for energy developments in the United Kingdom; these are an extract from Report No: 4, *Energy Development and Land in the United Kingdom.* Other notable reports in the series are: No: 8 *Energy Education Requirements and Availability*, and (the latest available) No: 10, *Factors Determining Energy Costs and an Introduction to the Influence of Electronics.* Further details of all publications, with an order form, and information on future reports, are available on request. The Chairman is J.H. Chesters, OBE and the Secretary J.G. Mordue.

UNIVERSITY CENTRES

The following lists include only those universities and other academic centres where we know of a major sustained research interest in energy economics. The lists cover (1) global and UK energy modelling; (2) UK nationalised industries; (3) North Sea oil and gas development, finance and tax and (4) energy efficiency. We intend in the next edition of *Energy Economics in Britain* to expand this list giving a more detailed breakdown of projects (e.g. to include transportation economics and developing country energy economics, and allocating half a page to each university entry. We therefore invite all responsible to submit their texts for publication to the BIEE by latest end-September 1983. In particular we should like to list by name the various Directors and research staff.

For a more detailed review at present, see the Watt Committee's report *Energy Education Requirements and Availability* (£22.50 from 75 Knightsbridge, London SW1X 7RB). The register of projects maintained by the Social Science Research Council is probably the most comprehensive review. It is entitled *Energy: a Register of Research, Development and Demonstration in the United Kingdom*

(1980) Part 2 — Social Sciences (Parts 1 and 3 are published by the Energy Technology Support Unit at Harwell.)

1. General Modelling (Global/UK)

University of Aberdeen, Dept. of Political Economy (energy scenarios, energy demand forecasting, world coal markets).

Birmingham University, Dept. of Industrial Economics and Business Studies (UK energy models).

University of Cambridge, Dept. of Applied Economics (and Cambridge Econometrics) and Energy Research Unit, Cavendish Laboratory (global, regional and country studies).

University of London, Queen Mary College — Energy Research Unit (oil price and refinery economics).

University of Newcastle-upon-Tyne; The Energy Centre (regional modelling).

Open University; Energy Research Group (long-term).

University of Oxford; the Energy Centre and Seminar (global, particularly OPEC).

University of Sheffield, Division of Economic Studies (UK demand forecasts).

University of Southampton, Dept. of Economics (UK demand forecasts).

University of Stirling, Dept. of Economics.

University of Strathclyde, Energy Studies Unit (global supply).

University of Surrey, Dept. of Economics (coal and energy transportation).

University of Sussex, Science Policy Research Unit/Dept. of Economics, Energy Policy Programme (energy supply technologies, energy demand and conservation).

2 UK nationalised industries

University of Aberdeen, Dept. of Political Economy (nuclear power, gas).

University of Bath; School of Management (Corporate planning of energy).

Heriot Watt University, Dept. of Economics (coal).

University College, London, Departments of Geography and Political Economy (coal, nuclear).

University of Newcastle-upon-Tyne; The Energy Centre (risk assessment; gas demand).

University of Nottingham, Institute of Planning Studies (coal).

University of Sheffield, Division of Economic Studies (environmental risk assessment; electricity)
University of Strathclyde; Energy Studies Unit (coal, nuclear).
University of Surrey; Dept. of Economics (coal, gas).
University of Sussex; Science Policy Research Unit (nuclear; electricity).
Thames Polytechnic; School of Social Sciences (electricity).
University of York, Dept. of Social Administration and Social Work (electricity).

3. North Sea Oil and Gas Development, Finance and Tax

Aberdeen University, Dept. of Political Economy (development, policy and taxation).
University of Surrey, Dept. of Economics (development, policy and taxation).
University of Sussex, The SPRU Energy Programme (advanced technology and development).
University of London, Imperial College (taxation).

4. Energy Efficiency

University of Aberdeen, Dept. of Political Economy (low energy scenarios, conservation economics).
Bristol University, Dept. of Economics (low energy options).
University of Cambridge, Energy Research Group, Cavendish Laboratory (industrial fuel consumption, interfuel substitution).
Open University; Energy Research Group (transport).
University of Sheffield, Division of Economic Studies (interfuel substitution).
University of Southampton, Department of Economics.
University of Strathclyde, Energy Studies Unit (energy audits in industry and agriculture).
University of Sussex, Dept. of Operational Research (industrial boilers and turbines; conservation projects).

JOURNALS

Ambient Energy, Ambient Press Ltd, Hornby, Lancaster LA2 8LB.
Atom, 11 Charles II St, London SW1Y 4PQ (of UKAEA origin).
Atomic Energy News, 28 Southway, Carshalton Beeches, Surrey.

British Nuclear Forum Bulletin, 1 St Alban's Street, London SW1X 4SL.

BP Statistical Review of the World Oil Industry (Annual), BP, Britannic House, Moor Lane, London EC2Y 9BU.

Coal and Energy Quarterly, National Coal Board, Hobart House, Grosvenor Place, London SW1X 7AE.

Coal International, Queensway House, 2 Queensway, Redhill, Surrey RH1 1QS.

Coal News, National Coal Board, Hobart House, Grosvenor Place, London SW1X 7AE.

Colliery Guardian, Queensway House, 2 Queensway, Redhill, Surrey RH1 1QS.

Contents of Recent Economics Journals, HMSO PO Box 569, London SE1 9NH.

Digest of United Kingdom of Energy Statistics (Annual), Her Majesty's Stationery Office, PO Box 569, London SE1.

Electrical Review International, Quadrant House, The Quadrant, Sutton, Surrey SM2 5AS.

Electrical Times, Quadrant House, The Quadrant, Sutton, Surrey, SM2 5AS.

Energy Digest, PO Box 32, St Albans, Herts AL1 3QU.

Energy Economics, PO Box 63, Westbury House, Bury Street, Guildford, Surrey GU2 5BH.

Energy Economist, Financial Times, Bracken House, 10 Cannon Street, London EC4P 4BY.

Energy Exploration and Exploitation (Quarterly), Graham and Trotman Ltd, Sterling House, 66 Wilton Road, London SW1V 1DE.

Energy for Industry and Commerce, The School House, Haydon, Royston, Herts SG8 8PW.

The Energy Journal (Quarterly), The International Association of Energy Economists (see IAEE), available through the BIEE, 9 St James's Square, London SW1Y 4LE.

Energy Management, Department of Energy, Room 1395, Thames House South, Millbank, London SW1P 4QJ.

Energy Policy, PO Box 63, Westbury House, Bury Street, Guildford, Surrey GU2 5BH.

Energy Report, PO Box 3, Newman Lane, Alton, Hants GU34 2PG.

Energy Trends, Department of Energy, Millbank, London SW1.

Energy World, Institute of Energy, 18 Devonshire Street, London W1N 2AU (particularly strong in energy efficiency).

European Energy Report, Financial Times, Bracken House, 10 Cannon Street, London EC4P 4BY.

European Energy Profile, Financial Times, Bracken House, 10 Cannon Street, London EC4P 4BY.

European Offshore Petroleum News, Noroil Publishing, 50 Gresham Street, London EC2V 7AY.

Europ-Oil Prices (London), 104–108 Grafton Road, London NW5 4BD.

Fuel, PO Box 63, Westbury House, Bury Street, Guildford, Surrey GU2 5BH.

Fuel and Energy Abstracts, PO Box 63, Westbury House, Bury Street, Guildford, Surrey GU2 5BH.

Gas World, Benn Publications Ltd., 25 New St Square, London EC4A 3JA.

Hydrocarbon Processing, Gulf House, 30 Cambridge Road, Barking, Essex 1P11 8NW.

Industrial Energy, United Trade Press Ltd, UTP House, 33/35 Bowling Green Lane, London EC1R 0DA.

International Coal Report, Financial Times, Bracken House, 10 Cannon Street, London EC4P 4BY.

International Energy Agency/OECD - Quarterly Oil Statistics, IEA, Paris.

International Journal of Energy Research, John Wiley and Sons, Baffins Lane, Chichester, Sussex.

International Petroleum Times, Quadrant House, The Quadrant, Sutton, Surrey SM2 5AS.

Journal of the Institute of Energy, 18 Devonshire Street, London W1N 2AU.

London Oil Reports, 1 Kelso Place, London W8 5QD.

LP Gas Review, Benn Publications, 25 New St Square, London EC4A 3JA.

Natural Gas, Benn Publications, 25 New St Square, London EC4A 3JA.

Noroil, 31 Summer Street, Aberdeen AB1 1SB.

North Sea Letter, Financial Times, Bracken House, 10 Cannon Street, London EC4P 4BY.

North Sea Observer, Flat 2, 94 Cornwall Gardens, London SW7.

North Sea Service, Wood MacKenzie, Erskine House, 68/73 Queen Street, Edinburgh EH2 4NF.

Nuclear Energy, 1–7 Great George Street, London SW1P 3AA.

Nuclear Engineering International, Quadrant House, The Quadrant, Sutton, Surrey SM2 5AS.

Offshore, 6th Floor, Alliance House, 12 Caxton Street, London SW1H 0QS.

Offshore Engineer, Telford House, PO Box 101, 26–34 Old Street, London EC1P 1JH.

Offshore Intelligence Ltd, Marshallsea House, Merchants Quay, Dublin 8, Ireland.

Offshore Oil International (Weekly(, Unit 1, Deemouth Centre, S. Esplanade East, Aberdeen AB1 3PB.

Offshore Services and Technology, 55–59 Fife Road, Kingston-upon-Thames, Surrey KT1 1TA.

Oil and Petroleum Pollution (Quarterly), Graham and Trotman Ltd, Sterling House, 66 Wilton Road, London SW1V 7DX.

Oil City News, 46A Union Street, Aberdeen.

Oil Facts, Hoare Govett, Heron House, 319/325 High Holborn, London WC1V 7PB.

Oil Focus, North Esplanade East, Aberdeen.

Oil and Gas Journal, 6th Floor, 12 Caxton Street, London SW1H 0QS.

The Oilman, 30 Old Burlington Street, London W1X 2AE.

Petrodata, Garretts House, Cavendish Maltings, Cavendish, Sudbury CO10 8A.

Petroleum Economist, 107 Charterhouse Street, London EC1M 6AA.

Petroleum Intelligence Weekly, 8 Bouverie Street, London EC4Y 8BB.

Petroleum Review, 61 Cavendish Street, London W1M 8AR.

Platts Oilgram, 34 Dover Street, London W1X 3RA.

Power, McGraw Hill Publications, 34 Dover Street, London W1X 3RA.

Quarterly Energy Reviews (i Western Europe; ii USSR and Eastern Europe; iii Middle East; iv Africa; v Far East and Australia; vi North America; vii Latin America and the Caribbean), Economist Intelligence Unit, Spencer House, 27 St James' Place, London SW1A 1NT.

Shell Briefing Series, Shell International, (PA/012), Shell Centre, London SE1 7NA.

Solid Fuel, Harling House, 47/51 Great Suffolk Street, London SE1 0BS.

World Coal, Chaussée de Charleroi 123a, Boite 5, B–1060 Brussels, Belgium.

World Gas Report, Noroil Publishing, 50 Gresham Street, London EC2V 7AY.

World Oil, Gulf House, 30 Cambridge Road, Barking, Essex IG11 8NW.

World Solar Markets, Financial Times, Bracken House, 10 Cannon Street, London EC4P 4BY.

Annex II

The British Institute of Energy Economics 9 St James's Square, London SW1Y 4LE

The British Institute of Energy Economics is an independent self-governing body whose aim is to further the understanding of all aspects of energy economics on both the national and international level: particular attention is focused on the energy policies of enterprises, governments and international agencies.

ORIGINS

The Institute was established in 1978 as the UK Chapter of the International Association of Energy Economists. It attracted an initial membership of about 120–140, fairly evenly distributed between the Department of Energy (who supplied the Chairman for the first two years), the nationalised industries, the private sector, the universities and the City. In June 1980 the UK Chapter was host at Churchill College, Cambridge, UK to the three-day annual international conference of the IAEE which was attended by 248 registrants from 16 countries. In late 1980, the UK members decided, after full consultation and agreement with the Council of the IAEE, to establish an independent national institute, which would nevertheless maintain very close links with the International Association of Energy Economists.

The BIEE is therefore the national organisation representing all United Kingdom interests in the International Council of the IAEE. In June 1982 the BIEE was again host at Churchill College, Cambridge, to the three-day annual international conference of the IAEE which was attended by 253 registrants from 23 countries (see below).

MEMBERSHIP

Roughly a third of the current members of the BIEE completed university degrees in economics. Another large group have an engineering or technical background. Other distinct groupings are members of the UK Department of Energy; a group of City analysts and bankers specialising in North Sea development and a group of oil and gas industry experts interested in refining and petrochemical economics. All share a lively professional interest in energy policy and in the viewpoints of each other.

Applications for membership should list name, address, affiliation and telephone number and be accompanied by the appropriate membership fee. The membership fee will be £15 for the year 1983 (subject to ratification at the Annual General Meeting). Corporate membership fee. The membership fee will be £16 for the year 1983 (subject to ratification at the Annual General Meeting).

The BIEE has negotiated a reduced rate for those BIEE members wishing to join the IAEE as individual members and therefore to receive directly the IAEE quarterly, *The Energy Journal*. This additional subscription is set for 1983 at £12.50.

COMMITTEE

The Committee members at present are Eric Price (Chairman) - Department of Energy; Ian Smart (Secretary) - Ian Smart Ltd; Philip Warland (Treasurer) - Bank of England; Anthony Scanlan (meetings programme) - BP; Gerry Corti (long-term planning); John Barber (research and publications) - H.M. Treasury; Christopher Buckley (membership) - BRITOIL; Jane Carter; Paul Tempest - British Gas Corporation; Walter Greaves; Christopher Johnson - Lloyds Bank Ltd; Niall Trimble - British Gas Corporation; Norman White - N. White and Associates.

MEETINGS PROGRAMME

General BIEE meetings, covering major current energy topics, are held about ten to twelve times a year. A balance is sought between distinguished foreign speakers and the leading authorities on the subject in the UK. Every effort is made to present differing sides of the debate and to allow time for free discussion. The general meetings are now held in the John Power Hall, 9 St James's Square, London SW1 at 6.30–8.00 pm, usually on a Wednesday. It is intended that all these open meetings will again be free to members in 1983. A reception for members and speakers is generally held in the Astor Room before general meetings. A programme of study sessions round a table in the Astor Room at 9 St James's Square caters for special interests. The Committee welcomes hearing from members and prospective members about their interests and suggestions for future topics.

BIEE PLENARY MEETINGS IN 1982/3

THE OUTLOOK FOR PRICES OF CRUDE OIL AND PRODUCTS – David Howell, Secretary of State for Energy; Tom Stauffer; Joe Roeber; Walter Greaves

CANADIAN ENERGY POLICY – John Helliwell; Sir James Menter

A NORTH SEA ELECTRICITY RING MAIN – Michael Laughton; Cyril Gosling; Robert Deam

THE PRICE OF GAS – David Watt; Malcolm Peebles; Christopher Brierley

CAPITAL CONSTRAINTS AND OPPORTUNITIES IN ENERGY DEVELOPMENT – Maurice Lauré; Robert Belgrave; David Anderson; Gerry Corti

THE SECURITY OF ENERGY SUPPLY – Robert Mabro; Sir Archie Lamb; Paul Frankel; Eric Price

THE UK NUCLEAR RECORD AND FUTURE – Roger Williams; Lord Kearton; Lord Hinton; Sir Francis Tombs

UNITED STATES ENERGY POLICY – James B. Edwards; US Secretary for Energy; Sir David Steel

A TURNING POINT IN NORTH SEA TAXATION – John Mitchell; Tom Stauffer; Colin Robinson

THE MACRO-ECONOMIC IMPACT OF ENERGY – John Flemming; Terry Barker; Christopher Allsopp

COAL IN BRITAIN: UNCERTAINTIES AND OPPORTUNITIES – Lord Robens; Gerald Manners; Michael Parker

THREE BASIC PRINCIPLES OF ENERGY ECONOMICS - Michael Posner; Robert Deam; Gerry Corti; Robert Belgrave

ENERGY CONSERVATION IN INDUSTRY - THE ANGLO-SWEDISH EXPERIENCE - Eric Petterson; Robin Gardner; Göran Wohlfahrt; Jan Fors; Tomas Johansson; Michael Roberts; Börje Kjellen; Chris Jacobson; Philip Taylor

THE CONTROL OF THE NATIONALISED INDUSTRIES IN THE UK - John Fleming; David Heald; David Steel

FUTURE GAS SUPPLY IN THE U.K. - Michael Clegg; Oystein Noreng; Peter Lehmann; Jonathan Stern

CURRENT NUCLEAR ISSUES - Ian Smart; J.C.C. Stewart; P.D. Henderson

THE FUTURE OF OIL - Paul Tempest; John Raisman

THE IEA ENERGY OUTLOOK - Eric Price; Hermann Franssen (meeting held 11.1.83)

SIZEWELL - THE ISSUES - Sir Francis Tombs; Nigel Evans; Chris Hope

COMECON ENERGY TRENDS - Tony Scanlon; Jonathan Stern

WORLD CRUDE MARKET PROSPECTS - Fereidun Fesheraki; Adrian Hamilton

THE FUTURE OF OPEC - M.A. Adelman; Paul Tempest

1982 BIEE/IAEE CONFERENCE PROGRAMME

DETAILS OF MAIN SESSIONS

OPENING REMARKS

Sir William Hawthorne, Master of Churchill College

INTRODUCTORY ADDRESS

Sir Peter Baxendell, Chairman of Shell Transport and Trading

World Oil and Gas Markets: The Changing Structure

Chairman:	Alirio Parra, Director, Petroleos de Venezuela
Guest Speaker:	Dr Ulf Lantzke, Executive Director, International Energy Agency
Speakers:	M.A. Adelman, James Sweeney, Fereidun Fesheraki, Peter Odell
Rapporteur:	B. Andrews, *Financial Times*

The Response of Governments and the Business Sector

Chairman:	Jane Carter, Under-Secretary, UK Department of Energy
Guest Speaker:	Michel Carpentier, Director General of the Commission of the European Communities
Speakers:	John V. Mitchell, John H. Culhane
Rapporteur:	H. Stonefrost, Bank of England

The Energy Policy Perspective of the United States and the United Kingdom

Chairman:	Paul Tempest, British Gas Corporation
Guest Speakers:	The Hon. James B. Edwards, US Secretary for Energy The Rt Hon. Nigel Lawson, UK Secretary of State for Energy

Rapporteur: R.C. Bending, University of Cambridge

First Dinner

Chairman: Mrs Jane Carter, Under-Secretary, UK Department of Energy
Speaker: The Rt Hon. Aubrey Jones, President of the Oxford Energy Policy Club

Coal, Nuclear and Gas

Chairman: Ian Smart, Ian Smart Ltd.
Speakers: Ravendra Pachauri, Fritz Lücke, H. Franssen, C.D. Kolstad
Rapporteur: Ian Smart

Energy Price Modelling

Chairman: Eric Price, Head of Economics and Statistics Division, UK Department of Energy
Speakers: Campbell Watkins, Colin Robinson, J. Wilkinson, H.D. Saunders, Len Brookes
Rapporteur: R.W. Byatt, National Westminster Bank

Oil and Gas Taxation, Tariffs and Licensing

Chairman: R.O. Jackson, Group Oil Adviser, Midland Bank
Speakers: Alexander Kemp, J.T. Fraser, Walter Mead, Laurence Jacobson
Rapporteur: R. Dargie, Bank of England

Electricity, Alternative Energy, Technical Papers

Chairman: Keith Williams, Shell International
Speakers: S.A. Ravid, K.H. Rising, T.W. Berrie, N. Evans, I.C. Price
Rapporteur: R.R. Jennison, British Nuclear Fuels

New Market Mechanisms in Oil and Gas

Chairman: Dan Ion, Chairman of the World Petroleum Congress 1983
Speakers: R. Netschert, Robert Deam, T.R. Dealtry, Joe Roeber, Niall Trimble
Rapporteur: M.W. Clegg, BP

UK and US Department of Energy Presentation

Chairman: John Barber, HM Treasury
Speakers: K. Wigley, J. Stanley-Miller
Rapporteur: R.C. Bending, University of Cambridge

The Economic Impact of Energy

Chairman: Mariano Gurfinkel, Petroleos de Venezuela
Speakers: Martha Krebs, Oystein Noreng, Elizabeth Parr-Johnston, Ira Sohn, T. Greening
Rapporteur: H. Stonefrost, Bank of England

Australia and Canada

Chairman: Stuart Harris, Professor, RIIA and Australian National University, Canberra
Speakers: Russell S. Uhler, David Gallagher, G.D. McColl
Rapporteur: D; Russell, Consolidated Goldfields

The Role of a State oil and Gas Company

Chairman: G. Corti, British National Oil Corporation
Guest Speaker: Jens Christensen, Chairman, Dansk Olie & Naturgas A.S.
Rapporteur: C.M. Buckley, BNOC

Global Strategic Issues

Chairman: Loren Cox, MIT

Speakers: A.F.G. Scanlan, John F. O'Leary, F.E. Banks, Robert Weiner
Rapporteur: L. Turner, RIIA

Energy Modellers Forum

Energy Futures Markets

Chairman: Philip Warland, Bank of England
Speakers: John E. Treat, Shanta Devarajan, Glenn Hubbard, Walter Greaves, Thomas McKiernan
Rapporteur: A. Thorney, BP

Energy Economics in the Developing World

Speakers: Lee Schipper and others

Responses to Disruption and Crisis

Chairman: Sir Archie Lamb, Samuel Montagu & Co.
Speakers: Robert Belgrave, Charles Ebinger, Philip Verleger
Discussant: Milton Russell, Resources for the Future
Rapporteur: R.M. Witcomb, BP

The 1982 IAEE Prize Lecture

Chairman: William Hughes, Charles River Associates and President of the IAEE

Speaker: Sam Schurr, Electric Power Research Institute, Palo Alto
Topic: Energy Efficiency and Productive Efficiency: Some Thoughts Based on American Experience

Demand Responses

Chairman: Campbell Watkins, President Datametrics Ltd

Speakers: Frank E. Hopkins, Lee Schipper, Leonard Waverman, Patrick O'Sullivan, Robin Wensley
Rapporteur: J.P. Prince, Royal Bank of Canada

Second Dinner

Chairman: Sir William Hawthorne, Master of Churchill College
Speaker: Michael Posner, Chairman of the Social Science Research Council

Adaptation in the Developing World

Chairman: Helmut Frank, Professor, University of Arizona and Editor of the *Energy Journal*
Speakers: James Plummer, C.M. Siddayao, Lutz Hoffman, Peter M. Meier, Marcus Fritz, C. Hope
Rapporteur: L. Turner, RIAA

Interfuel Substitution - Policy Opportunities in Changing Energy Markets

Chairman: Joy Dunkerley, Resources for the Future and President-Elect of the IAEE
Guest Speakers: Henry Jacoby, Melvin Conant, William R. Hughes, Robert Mabro, Jack Hartshorn, Christopher Johnson, Ray Dafter
Rapporteur: Paul Tempest

THE INTERNATIONAL ASSOCIATION OF ENERGY ECONOMISTS

IAEE, 80 South Early Street, Alexandria, Virginia 22304 USA. Telephone: 703.823.6966. Membership Secretary: Ms Debbie Trocchi. 1983 Membership Fee: $48 [$25 for students; $43 for members from the academic world and government]. For members of the British Institute of Energy Economics, a special rate of £12.50 gives full membership of the IAEE and personal copies of the quarterly *Energy Journal*. Please send the fee to the BIEE (Membership

Secretary), 9, St James's Square, London SW1.

The Officers for 1983 are President: Joy Dunkerley (Resources for the Future). Presidents Emeritus: James Plummer, M.A. Adelman, William Hughes. President Elect: Paul Tempest. Executive Vice-President and Secretary: Joan Greenwood; Treasurer: Richard Itteilag; Vice-President for Publications: James Sweeney; Vice-President and Newsletter Editor: Ted Breton; Vice-President for International Affairs: Jane Carter; Vice-President for Chapter Liaison: Jack Wilkinson.

There are US branches in Atlanta, Chicago, Denver, Houston, Los Angeles, Washington DC, New England (Boston), New York, Northern California, Northwest (Portland), Ohio, Oklahoma and Philadelphia.

National representative branches outside the United States can be contacted as follows:

United Kingdom:	British Institute of Energy Economics, 9 St James's Square, London SW1.
Germany:	Gesellschaft für Energiewissenschaft und Energiepolitik e.V. Wissenschaftszentrum, Ahrstr. 45, 5300 Bonn 2. Telephone 221.615.3949
Canada	IAEE (Canada), c/o Mitchel P. Rothman, Chief Economist, Ontario Hydro, 700 University Avenue, Toronto, Canada M59 1X6. Tel: 416/592.6375
India:	IAEE (India), c/o N.K. Gopalkrishnan, TATA Energy Research Institute, 40 Homi Mody, Bombay, India 400023. Telephone 245.070
Japan	IAEE (Japan), c/o Dr Kenichi Matsui, Institute of Energy Economics, No. 10 Mori Bldg, 1801 Ioranomon, 1-Chome Minato-Ku, Tokyo, Japan. Telephone: 501.7681.-3
IEA, Paris	IAEE (IEA), c/o Hermann Franssen, IEA.
France:	IAEE (France), c/o Jean-Paul Cléron, OECD, Paris. Telephone: 331.524.8200.
Benelux	IAEE (Benelux), c/o Professor Peter Odell, Erasmus University, Rotterdam.

Chapters are also being formed in Venezuela, Norway, Mexico, Italy, Austria, Australia and Finland.

FUTURE IAEE CONFERENCES

North American Conference

9-10th June, 1983
Capital-Hilton, Washington DC

Contact: Richard Itteilag,
American Gas Association,
1515 Wilson Boulevard,
ARLINGTON, VA 22203,
U.S.A.

(703 841 8505)

International Conference

4-6th January, 1984
New Delhi, India

Contact: R.K. Pachauri,
Tata Energy Research Institute,
Jeevan Tara Building,
Parliament Street,
New Delhi,
India 110 001.

European Conference (with BIEE)

9-11th April, 1984
Churchill College, Cambridge

Contact: Mrs. M. Harrison,
European Study Conferences Ltd.,
Kirby House,
31 High Street,
Uppingham,
Rutland,
Leics. LE14 9PY,
United Kingdom.

Telephone: 057 282 2711
Telex: 341352

This conference will follow the format of the 1980 and 1982 Cambridge Conferences. The theme will be International Energy Policy –

A European and Middle East perspective. The conference will be opened by Mr. L.C. Van Wachem, Chairman of Royal Dutch Shell. Specialist sessions organised by the Benelux, German and OPEC affiliates of the IAEE will be a feature of the conference. Numbers will again be limited to 250. Enquiries and advance registration (£20) to the above address.

Annex III

BIEE Archive: Registered Texts

The Archive of the British Institute of Energy Economics was established at 9, St. James's Square, London SW1 in 1980 to provide a system whereby, subject to the authors' permission, papers delivered to the Institute's meetings, seminars and conferences could be made available for copying. The current fee for this is £4 per paper (including postage). The Institute can only undertake the copying and despatch of papers once the fee has been received.

The papers covering the 1982 BIEE/IAEE Cambridge conference are also available from the Archive on the same terms. They are listed separately in alphabetical order after the list of the main archive.

The registration code consists of four parts:

1. Topic

Energy General (EG); Oil and Gas (OG); Nuclear (NU); Alternative Energy (AL); Coal (CO); Electricity (EL).

2. Geographical Coverage

Global (GL); United Kingdom (UK); European Community (EC);

United States (US); Canada (CA); OPEC (OP); OECD Countries as a group (OE); Third World (LD); Communist Bloc (BL); Other (OT).

3. Year of Registration

1979 (70); 1980 (80); 1981 (81); 1982 (82).

4. Rotation Number

In order of Registration (01, 02 etc.).

The notation † indicates that the paper has been included in *International Energy Options: An Agenda for the 1980s* — selected papers from the 1980 Annual Conference of the International Association of Energy Economists, in Cambridge, UK — published by Graham and Trotman Ltd, London and Oelgeschlager, Gunn and Hain, Publishers, Inc., Cambridge, Mass., USA and available to members through the BIEE, price £10 - including postage.

ENERGY GENERAL

ADELMAN, M.A.†	An Agenda For the Eighties — Decisions and Research (EG-GL-80-01)
ATTIGA, ALI A.+	Governmental Responses to Energy Policies and Issues (EG-GL-80-02)
BASILE, PAUL S.	The IIASA Global Energy Study (EG-GL-80-03)
CONANT, MELVIN†	The Geopolitics of Energy (EG-GL-80-04)
CONDAP, ROBERT J.	Market Penetration of Energy Technologies (EG-GL-80-05)
FOSTER, JOHN	World Energy Prospects (EC-GL-80-06)
GREENMAN, J.V.	Housing Retrofit Policy: An Application of Hierarchical Control Theory (EG-GL-80-07)
HANSON, JAMES	Exxon World Energy Outlook (EG-GL-80-08)

JOHNSON, CHRISTOPHER†	The Imperative of Preserving Global Economic Growth (EG-GL-80-09)
LEMON, J. RODNEY	Governmental Subsidisation of Domestic Energy Supplies (EG-GL-80-10)
LIU, BEN-CHIEH	Industrialisation, Energy Requirements and the Quality of Life: An International Comparison (EG-GL-80-11)
MITCHELL, J.V.	Comparison of Energy Forecasts (EG-GL-80-12)
NEWBERY, DAVID	Chairman's Report on 1980 Cambridge Conference Parallel Session on Inter-Fuel Substitution (EG-GL-80-13)
PACKER, ARNOLD (WITH WILBUR STEGER)†	Energy/Employment Policy Analysis: International Impacts of Alternative Energy Technologies (EG-GL-80-14)
PLUMMER, JAMES L.	A Conceptual Framework for Examining Governmental Responses to Energy Vulnerability (EG-GL-80-15)
STARR, CHAUNCEY†	Energy at the Crossroads: Abundance or Shortage (EG-GL-80-16)
SWEENEY, JAMES L.	Aggregate Elasticity of Energy Demand (EG-GL-80-17)
MANNE, S.	A Three Region Model of Energy, International Trade and Economic Growth (EG-GL-80-18)
LAURÉ, MAURICE	Restoration of the World Economic and Financial Balance After the Oil Crises (EG-GL-81-19)
POSNER, MICHAEL	Energy Economics Research — What Should We Be Doing in the UK? (EG-UK-79-01)
LAMONT, NORMAN†	A UK View of Energy Trends (EG-UK-80-02)
HOWELL, DAVID	Department of Energy Speech Notes

	on Energy Economics and the BIEE (EG-UK-80-03)
O'SULLIVAN, PATRICK (WITH FREDERIC ROMIG)†	Interfuel Substitution in European Countries (EG-EC-80-01)
LÜCKE, FRITZ†	Institutions for Managing Energy Shortages: A German Viewpoint (EG-EG-80-02)
JORGENSON, DALE W.†	Energy Prices and Productivity Growth (EG-ES-80-01)
SAWHILL, JOHN C.†	United States Energy Policy (EG-US-80-02)
WATKINS, G.C. (WITH E.R. BERNDT)	Energy-Output Coefficients: Complex Realities Behind Simple Ratios (EG-CA-80-01)
DIENER, STEVEN G.	Comparative Resource Costs and the Economic Limits to Energy Conservation in Canada (EG-CA-80-02)
HELLIWELL, JOHN F.	The Canadian National Energy Conflict (EG-CA-81-03)
FINIZZA, ANTHONY J.	Forecasting the Business Environment in an OPEC World (EG-OP-80-01)
TEMPEST, PAUL†	Financing Energy Development in the Industrialised Countries (EG-OE-80-01)
WAVERMAN, LEONARD	Investments in Energy Supply Industries and the Economy of the OECD 1970-1990 (EG-OE-81-02)
PACHAURI, R.K.†	Financing Energy Development in the Third World (EG-LD-80-01)
DUNKERLEY, JOY	Estimation of Demand and Conservation: The Developing Countries (EG-LD-80-02)
KASER, M.C.†	East West Factors in International Energy Production and Trade (EG-BL-80-01)

OIL AND GAS

BEIJDORFF, A.F.†	The Impact of Crude Oil Price Rises on Oil Product Consumption (OG-GL-80-01)
NORENG, OYSTEIN†	State Oil Trading and the Perspective of Shortage (OG-GL-80-02)
STEEL, Sir DAVID†	Risks in the International Oil Trade (OG-GL-80-03)
THACKERAY, F.G.	The Potential Role of Natural Gas in an Economy (OG-GL-80-04)
STAUFFER, T.R.	The Dynamics of Interdependence: Synfuels versus Middle Eastern Oil (OG-GL-80-05)
MACREADY, Sir NEVILLE	Petroleum for Transport (OG-GL-80-06)
DEAM, R.J.	The Long Range Pricing of Crude Oil (OG-GL-81-07)
JONES, DAVID Le B.	UK Policy Responses to International Influences — North Sea Oil and Gas (OG-UK-79-01)
ODELL, PETER R.†	A Possible Extension of the (UK) Oil Resource (OG-OK-80-02)
SPRIGGS, DILLARD P.	Oil Tax Policy in the North Sea (UK) (and North America) (OG-UK-80-03) (OG-US-80)
MITCHELL, J.V.	Taxation of Energy (Oil/Gas) Revenues: UK Experience (OG-UK-81-04)
PEACOCK, C.G.	The Growing Role of LPG in Europe (OG-EC-80-01)
TELSON, MICHAEL L.†	Managing Oil Contingencies: The US Experience And Choices for the Future (OG-US-80-01)
KOSOBUD, RICHARD F.	Endogenous OPEC Behaviour (and Consumer Nation) Policies (OG-OP-80-01)
PARRA, ALIRIO†	The Orinoco Petroleum Belt (OG-OT-80-01)

LAJOUS-VARGAS ADRIAN†	The Mexian Oil and Gas Sector — Selected Statistics (OG-OT-80-02)
STAUFFER, T.R.	Fiscalisation of Petroleum In Norway (OG-OT-81-03)
WOLF, CHARLES J.	Oil and Energy Demand in Developing Countries in 1990 (OG-LD-80-01)

NUCLEAR

BROOKES, L.G.†	The Nuclear Route to Renewed Growth (NU-GL-80-01)
GREENWOOD, JOEN	International Developments and Trade in Uranium (NU-GL-80-02)
LEWINS, J.D.	Summary of 1980 Conference Session on International Nuclear Issues (NU-GL-80-03)
FERRARI, A.†	France's Nuclear Power Programme (NU-EC-80-01)
EBINGER, CHARLES K.	The Nuclear Nonproliferation Act as a Constraint on (US) Foreign Policy (NU-US-80-01)
ROTH, ELI B.	Nuclear Power for Developing Countries: Attainable within this century? (NU-LD-80-01)
FRITZ, MARCUS	The Role of Nuclear Power in the Third World (NU-LD-80-02)

ALTERNATIVE ENERGY

TYNER, WALLACE E.†	The Potential of Using Biomass for Energy in the United States (AL-US-80-01)
STAUFFER, T.R.	Gasohol: The Costly Road to Autarky (AL-US-80-02)

ELECTRICITY

BABU, VSS SURESH	Social Opportunity Cost of Electricity (EL-GL-80-01)
DAVIS, PATRICIA	Pricing Policies for Cogeneration and other Small Power Production (EL-EG-80-02)
GOSLING, C.H.	A North Sea Electricity Ring Main — The Benefits of Interconnection (EL-UK-81-01)
LAUGHTON, MICHAEL	Offshore Electricity Generation in the North Sea — An Enhancement to a West European Grid (EL-EC-81-01)
SCHRAMM, GUNTER	The Value of Time in Powerplant Licensing Procedures (EL-US-80-01)

IAEE/BIEE CAMBRIDGE CONFERENCE 1982 LIST OF PAPERS IN BIEE ARCHIVE

The notation † indicates that the paper has been included in *International Energy Markets — The Changing Structure* published by Graham and Trotman Ltd, Sterling House, 66 Wilton Road, London SW1V 1DE, United Kingdom and Oelgeschlager, Gunn and Hain, Publishers, Inc, 1278 Massachusetts Ave., Harvard Square, Cambridge, MA 02138, United States. The volume also includes abstracts of most other papers. The figure in brackets gives the number of pages in the full text.

M.A. ADELMAN†	(MIT) — The Changing Structure of the Oil and Gas Market (7)
F.E. BANKS†	(Uppsala) — Soviet Gas and the Western European Energy Shortage (22)
SIR P. BAXENDELL†	(Shell) — Forces and Forecasts in the Energy Business (8)
R. BELGRAVE	(BIJEPP) — Oil Crisis Management (5)
L.G. BROOKES	(Bournemouth) — A Model for Energy Price Hikes on the World Economy

	and the Long-Term Macro-economic Role of Nuclear Energy (26)
M. CARPENTIER†	(Director-General, E.C. Brussels) — The Energy Problem: The Response of the European Community (12)
M. CONANT†	(Conant Associates) — The Strategic and Economic Aspects of Gulf Gas (9)
J.H. CULHANE†	(Occidental) — The Changing Economic Climate of the Oil Industry (17)
S. DEVARAJAN	(Harvard) — Drawing Down the Strategic Petroleum Reserve: A Case for Selling Futures Contracts (35) (with G. HUBBARD)
C.K. EBINGER†	(Georgetown) — Energy Crises and the Third World — An Opportunity for the West (34)
J.B. EDWARDS†	(US Secretary for Energy) — US Energy Policy (8)
F. FESHARAKI†	(Honolulu) — Hydrocarbon Processing in OPEC Countries; Excess Capacities and Readjustment Pains in the World Refining Industry (62) (with D.T. ISAAK)
J.T. FRASER	(Tennessee Gas) — Prospects for US National Gas Imports Post Deregulation: A Supply-Demand Analysis (63)
M. FRITZ	(UNESCO) — Problems in Implementing Alternative Energies in the Developing World (24)
D. GALLAGHER	(University of New South Wales) — Natural Resource Scarcity: The Case of Australian Coal (36) (with G.D. McCOLL)
W. GREAVES	(NEDC) — Prospects for Petroleum Futures Markets (23)
T. GREENING	(1st National Bank of Chicago) — Finding and Financing the Next Trillion Barrels (22)
L. HOFFMAN	(Regensburg) — The Impact of Rising Oil Prices on Oil Importing Developing Countries and the Scope for Adjustment (51) (with L. JARASS)

C. HOPE	(Cavendish Laboratory, Cambridge) — Adaptation under Uncertainty: Energy Costs as a Constraint on Growth (8)
F.E. HOPKINS	(ORI) — The Interconnection Between Productivity, Energy Efficiency and the Location of Industry (64) (with P. BACK)
H. JACOBY†	(MIT) — The Influence of 'Policy' on Future Oil Prices (17) (with J.L. PADDOCK)
A.G. KEMP	(Aberdeen) — The Effects of Taxation on Petroleum Exploitation: A Comparative Study (64)
ULF LANTZKE†	(Executive Director, IEA) — Achieving Structural Change — The Policies Required (10)
The Rt Hon. N. LAWSON†	(Secretary of State for Energy, UK DEn) — UK Energy Policy (14)
W. LEONTIEF	(New York University) — Population, Food and Energy in the Prospects for Worldwide Economic Growth in the Year 2030 (75) (with I. SOHN)
F. LUCKE†	(Kiel) — Recent Developments in Nuclear Energy in the Federal Republic (9)
G.D. McCOLL†	(University of New South Wales) — The Energy Situation in Australia in the 80s (41) (with D. GALLAGHER)
T.F. McKIERNAN	(Dixel Burnham Lambert, New York) — Futures Markets as a Pricing Mechanism (28)
P.M. MEIER	(Brookhaven National Laboratory) — Energy Sector Investment and Pricing in Developing Economies: Case Studies of the Dominican Republic, Tunisia and Indonesia (23) (with V. MUBAYI and R. CHATTERJEE)
J.V. MITCHELL†	(BP) — The Response of the Business Sector (10)
R. NETSCHERT	(NERA) — Interfuel Competition and Energy Policy in the OPEC Area (24)

P.R. ODELL†	(Erasmuc University, Rotterdam) — Towards a System of World Oil Regions (11)
J.F. O'LEARY†	(J.F. O'Leary Associates) — Price-Reactive versus Price-Active Energy Policies (22)
P. O'SULLIVAN	(University of Wales) — Energy Conservation Policy in the Building Sector (13) (with R. WENSLEY of the London Business School)
R.K. PACHAURI†	(West Virginia University) — Changing Markets for Coal in the Developing Countries (28) (with W. LABYS)
E. PARR-JOHNSON	(Shell Canada) — Mega Project Energy Development as the Basis for Industrial Development: Some Potential Problems (21)
J. PLUMMER	(President, QED, Palo Alto) — The Current International Deadlock over Stimulating Oil Exploration in Less Developed Countries (7)
I.C. PRICE	(Sir William Halcrow) — A Scenario for UK Electricity Supply and Demand in the Year 2012 (12)
C ROBINSON	(University of Surrey) — The Future Oil Price (20)
A.F.G. SCANLAN†	(BP) — The Impact of Communist Bloc Energy Supply and Demand (17)
S.H. SCHURR†	(Electric Power Research Institute) — Energy Efficiency and Productive Efficiency: Some Thoughts Based on American Experience (20)
M. SIDDAYAO	(The East-West Resource Systems Institute) — Oil Importing Developing Countries: Capital Formation, Balance of Payments Constraints and Manufacturing Progress (29)
L.P. TEMPEST†	(British Gas Corporation/Bank of England) The International Energy Investment Dilemma (12)
J.E. TREAT	(New York Mercantile Exchange) —

	Energy Futures Markets (4)
N. TRIMBLE	(British Gas Corporation) — Gas Prices and Exploration (3)
R.S. UHLER	(The University of British Columbia) — Prices of Oil and Natural Gas Reserves in Canada (34)
P. VERLEGER†	(Booz Allen & Hamilton) — Rational Strategies for Meeting Oil Market Disruption (9)
R. WEINER	(University of Harvard) — The Sub-Trigger Crisis — An Economic Analysis of Flexible Stock Policies* (34) (with G. HUBBARD)
K. WIGLEY	(UK Department of Energy) — Methods for Projecting UK Energy Demand Used in the Department of Energy (24)
J. WILKINSON	(Sun Oil) — The World Oil Market: A Short-Term Perspective (11)

Annex IV

British Institutes' Joint Energy Policy Programme (BIJEPP) Programme 1983-1984

THE BRITISH INSTITUTES JOINT ENERGY POLICY PROGRAMME

The Royal Institute of International Affairs and the Policy Studies Institute in association with the British Institute of Energy Economics launched in 1980 a coordinated research programme on energy policy. The objective is to focus expertise from government, industry, the financial community and academics on major energy topics of current interest. A secretariat was established in Chasham House. Mr Robert Belgrave CBE, former Policy Adviser to BP has been appointed the Director of the programme.

The following six papers have been published so far and are available from Publications Department, Policy Studies Institute, 1/2 Castle Lane, London SW1E 6DR.

Short *Title*	*Author*	*Publication Target*
1. Energy Two Decades of Crisis	Foreword by Robert Belgrave to collected Energy Papers 1 to 6 (already published separately)	Book; Spring 1983 (Gower)
2. Institutions for International Energy Management	Professor Wilfrid Kohl	Energy Paper No. 7; March 1983 (BIJEPP) Also Spring 1983 (Gower)
3. Energy in Pacific Relations	Professor Stuart Harris	Book; Spring 1983 (Gower)
4. a) Geo-politics of the International Gas Market — Europe & its Suppliers	Jonathan Stern	Energy Paper; Winter 1983 (possible interim papers)
4. b) Ditto — U.S. & Japan	Jonathan Stern	Energy Paper or Book; Summer 1984
5. Energy Self-sufficiency in the UK?		
i) Oil	R. Belgrave/E. Marshall	Energy Paper; Autumn 1983
ii) Gas	Jonathan Stern	Energy Paper; Autumn 1983
iii) Coal	Louis Turner	Energy Paper; Autumn 1983
iv) Electricity	Nigel Evans	Energy Paper; Autumn 1983
v) Conservation	Mayer Hillman	Energy Paper; Autumn 1983
vi) The Economic Implications	Eileen Marshall)	
vii) The Policy and Defense Implications	) R. Belgrave)	? Book; Summer 1984
6. Energy Decisions in UK Industry 1979–81. A Pilot Survey	Michael White (PSI)	Autumn 1983 (SSRC Grant)
7. Models for Fuel Demand Fore-casting. A Pilot Survey	John Ermisch (PSI)	Winter 1983
8. Energy Conservation in Buildings	Mayer Hillman (PSI)	Spring 1984

ENERGY PAPER NO 1 EAST EUROPEAN ENERGY AND EAST-WEST TRADE IN ENERGY: JONATHAN P. STERN

Summary

This paper considers the consequences for East and West of two concurrent and interconnected developments:

i) The impending energy crisis in Eastern Europe;

ii) The consequences of increased Western, specifically West European, imports of, and therefore dependence upon, fuels from the Soviet Union and Eastern Europe, focusing in particular on natural gas from the USSR.

East European energy problems have become extremely serious and are likely to become more, rather than less, so in the coming decade. Stagnant or falling production, rising consumption and inability to pay for increasing expensive fuel imports make the most important tasks for these countries conservation and the substitution of imported oil by anything that can be domestically produced (low calorific coal and nuclear power) plus imported natural gas and electric power from the USSR.

Through the 1970s Eastern Europe was, to a great extent, cushioned against the energy crisis by the ability and willingness of the USSR to make increased quantities of oil and gas available at concessionary prices. In the 1980s, Soviet energy stringency and hard currency requirements have made it necessary for oil deliveries to Eastern Europe to be cut. One cannot yet be certain that these reductions signal the beginning of a long-term trend, or that they will not be more than offset by increased natural gas and electric power deliveries. The extent to which the USSR will be prepared to maintain energy deliveries, and the subsidy embodied in them, to its allies, will depend on how far this is seen to be penalising a faltering Soviet domestic economy. However, reduction of Soviet oil and gas supplies would have unthinkable economic and political consequences for East European countries and this is something that the USSR must worry about as it surveys its energy prospects over the next decade. *Eastern Europe is the Soviet Union's biggest energy problem and it is in this context that the eventual outcome of the great debate about Soviet oil production will be critical.*

A solution to the East European energy problem would be much larger imports of oil from the world market. Unconstrained, these requirements might rise to around 100 mt by the end of the decade; a minimum requirement for the maintenance of acceptable economic growth might be 50 mt. There is considerable uncertainty as to the means by and the terms on which even this lower volume can be obtained, given East European trade balances with OPEC countries and the hard currency debt problems of the region. Consequently, the acquisition of increased oil supplies for Eastern Europe may become a factor in Soviet foreign policy towards oil-producing countries. This must be a matter of considerable concern for OPEC countries themselves and for Western countries which depend on their oil.

Alongside these developments, East-West energy trade — concentrated on Soviet oil in the 1970s — will in the 1980s be increasingly dominated by Soviet natural gas deliveries. Western imports of Soviet gas — up to 35 per cent of total gas consumption in some countries — involve a considerable degree of interdependence between the partners. Despite the fact that more conservative elements in the US regard such interdependence as 'Finlandisation', it can be demonstrated that (in the true sense of the term 'interdependence') both sides stand to gain substantially should this trade take place and lose substantially if it does not. When one surveys the alternatives, Soviet gas appears favourable, both in terms of reliability and diversification of energy supplies. This is not to say that it presents no security of supply problems, merely that these are less acute than those of available alternatives.

The USSR is unlikely to cut off gas supplies to Western Europe, partly because it would stand to lose a great deal from such action, but primarily because the potential leverage would not be sufficiently great to guarantee a successful outcome. Furthermore, such action would bring Western Europe much closer to the US position on the economic, political and strategic threat posed by the USSR. In the last analysis, *it is their overall perception of the Soviet threat*, rather than the more specialised energy supply questions, that divides the Atlantic alliance on East-West energy trade and related issues.

ENERGY PAPER NO 2: OIL SUPPLY AND PRICE: WHAT WENT RIGHT IN 1980?

DANIEL BADGER AND
ROBERT BELGRAVE

Summary

This paper is about the oil supply crises following the Iranian revolution in 1978 and the war between Iraq and Iran in 1980. It investigates the reasons why a net supply cut of roughly the same size, on each occasion, under 2.5 mbd (5 per cent), led to a price increase of 150 per cent on the first occasion but had no long-term price effect on the second.

It is argued that the price increase of 1979 was a 'self-inflicted wound' on the part of the industrialised countries, caused by faulty perception of events, panic by consumers, and poor response by governments. In 1979, the effects of a relatively small cut in crude oil supply at a time of rising demand were exacerbated by fears on the part of refiners and consumers that supplies would not be available and by collective inaction on the part of consumer governmetns, which each sought to improve its own position.

The motives of OPEC are described mainly in economic terms. OPEC members, even those who took a relatively long view, were not reluctant to take advantage of the situation to increase their export prices. The organisation of OPEC was sufficiently effective to defend these higher prices once established. The part played by political considerations in OPEC decisions varied from time to time and from country to country. The key position of Saudi Arabia is discussed.

In 1980, stocks were high, the market was falling in response to the 1979 price increases, and government action both individually and through the EEC and IEA reinforced the downward market pressure on prices by encouraging use of stocks and by refraining from competitive bidding.

It would be imprudent to assume that because of the present so-called 'glut', it is not necessary to make preparations to ensure that a future crisis has a '1980' rather than a '1979' outcome, even if such a crisis is not of sufficient magnitude to trigger the automatic clauses of the International Energy Programme (7 per cent of requirements). A further paper is being prepared on future crisis management. This paper is based on statistical material provided by the International Energy Agency, which is published for the first time in the final section.

ENERGY PAPER NO 3: ENERGY CONSERVATION IN JAPANESE INDUSTRY: RONALD DORE

Summary

The Japanese Government deploys a wide range of administrative devices to promote the conservation of energy in industry. These are (modest) loan interest reductions and special depreciation tax allowances for specified energy saving equipment, and a variety of advisory services. All plants consuming more than certain quanta of heat or electricity are required to have energy managers trained and certificated to (quite rigorous) government standards (one certificate for heat; one for electricity). A very active Energy Conservation Centre derives from the courses it runs for these certificates, and the attendant publications, more than half of the £2.5m. budget with which it supports a wide variety of activities, including a large number of regional meetings and seminars at which working engineers read papers to each other describing the devices they have found for conserving energy.

The results, in a number of firms visited, were a great deal of activity to capture waste heat, improve insulation, reduce unnecessary pressures in process air and steam, etc., through re-equipment and retrofitted improvements. Some of this activity was the work of the shopfloor workers as well as of managers. The resultant saving of energy was considerable.

Britain lacks Japan's sense of urgency in energy matters, but has, in compensation, a stronger sense of the need for industrial efficiency in general. There is a good case for considering in Britain, too, the establishment of a conservation agency, licensing requirements for energy management, the rethinking of payback period criteria for investment and the mobilisation of shopfloor effort.

ENERGY PAPER NO 4: UK INTERESTS AND THE INTERNATIONAL ENERGY AGENCY LOUIS TURNER

Summary

The International Energy Agency is the industrialised world's answer to OPEC. The United Kingdom plays an active role in its operations — but membership involves some binding obligations. Chief among these is a commitment to the IEA's emergency oil allocation system, which is ready to come into play in the next oil crisis. Analysis shows that the formula at the heart of this system is remarkably favourable to the interests of a country such as the UK which has substantial indigenous oil production. The image of the UK diverting North Sea oil to foreign customers while the British consumer goes short is very wide of the mark.

The Agency is also very active in monitoring the energy policies of its member states. The annual IEA reviews of British policies complement the work of parliamentary committees and other special inquiries into major energy decisions. The UK also benefits from the IEA's energy research, development and demonstration programme.

This paper (which can be read in conjunction with Wilfrid Kohl's forthcoming paper in the same series) argues that the IEA is a responsive, flexible, international body which fully deserves continued British support.

ENERGY PAPER NO 5: ENERGY, THE UK AND THE EUROPEAN COMMUNITY: NIGEL LUCAS

Summary

The emphasis of effort in European energy policy should be placed on external relations rather than internal regulation. The divergence of the interests of the United States and Europe in energy policy will no longer allow Europe to depend on US initiative. The temporary relaxation of world oil markets has engendered unrealistic complacency. The European Community must develop its important role as a means whereby the member states can formulate common initiatives to press within international institutions.

Strong presentation of interests externally has to be complemented by internal adaptation. The Community has at the moment few means of influencing the form and nature of energy investment. This paper proposes a fund of the order of £1 bn per annum to be used for the promotion of projects whose intrinsic benefits are not fully translated into commercial advantage and which need political stimulus. Such a Fund might be, but need not necessarily be, financed by a small (around 1 per cent) levy on imported oil.

It has been frequently suggested that the UK could do more to adapt the development of the hydrocarbon resources of the UK continental shelf to the requirements of the Community. The scope for this is less than appears initially. The UK should, however, present more aggressively than she has so far done the considerable benefits which accrue already to the Community from UK resources. There is perhaps an opportunity to take a more extrovert view of the relationship between the UK and the continental gas transport systems. It is unlikely that the UK could make substantial net exports to the continent, but interconnection of systems could enhance security, reduce investment costs and eventually improve the access of the UK to the large resources of gas in northern Norwegian waters.

ENERGY PAPER NO 6: OIL SUPPLY AND PRICE: FUTURE CRISIS MANAGEMENT: ROBERT BELGRAVE

Summary

This paper follows the analysis of the oil crises of 1978/79 and of 1980 by Daniel Badger and Robert Belgrave, published jointly by the British Institutes' Joint Energy Policy Programme and the Atlantic Institute for International Affairs in May 1982.

It would be imprudent to assume that the present so-called glut of oil makes it unnecessary to plan for a supply cut within the next five years. The market could rapidly return to equilibrium and the spare productive capacity apparently available in some OPEC countries might not then be available. At that point, a relatively minor supply cut, on the scale of 1979 (2.5 million barrels a day), could again lead to steep price increases and severe economic effects, unless measures are taken in advance to avert this result. It makes no sense to maintain expensive military capability to protect Western oil supplies whilst neglecting the relatively simple measures available within the oil chain itself to avert or damp down a crisis.

Short of the mandatory allocation procedures of the International Energy Programme, which only come into operation in a major emergency, the measure which has most chance of having the desired effect is to maintain what need be only relatively modest levels of stocks of crude oil in government or private hands, in such a way that these can be released speedily to those refiners whose supplies have been interrupted by some extraneous event. This would make it unnecessary for those refiners to have recourse to the spot market and would thus avoid the one-way upward result of price escalation.

Belief in the efficiency of the market as a means of allocating supplied does not invalidate this recommendation, if only because the international oil market can never be free of political pressures. The European Community and Japan would be well advised to instal stock-holding and stock-release systems of their own, even if the US Government chooses not do to so. Those stocks could be part of, or in addition to, emergency stocks now held by governments and by industry, and need not amount to much more than, say, five days of consumption.

Index

U

V

W

Y